The Role of Advisory Opinions in International Law in the Context of the Climate Crisis

Nijhoff Law Specials

VOLUME 112

The titles published in this series are listed at *brill.com/nlsp*

The Role of Advisory Opinions in International Law in the Context of the Climate Crisis

Edited by

Maria Antonia Tigre
Armando Rocha

BRILL | NIJHOFF

LEIDEN | BOSTON

CATÓLICA FACULDADE DE DIREITO LISBOA · PORTO

CATÓLICA RESEARCH CENTRE FOR THE FUTURE OF LAW LISBOA · PORTO

This work was supported by Católica Research Centre for the Future of Law and Vieira de Almeida & Associados.

The Library of Congress Cataloging-in-Publication Data is available online at https://catalog.loc.gov
LC record available at https://lccn.loc.gov/2025010882

Typeface for the Latin, Greek, and Cyrillic scripts: "Brill". See and download: brill.com/brill-typeface.

ISSN 0924-4549
ISBN 978-90-04-73060-1 (paperback)
ISBN 978-90-04-73061-8 (e-book)
DOI 10.1163/9789004730618

This book is printed on acid-free paper and produced in a sustainable manner.

This work is dedicated to all the voices that have gone unheard and to the tireless efforts to bring them to light. It is also dedicated to the vulnerable communities that bear the heaviest burden of a changing climate and to those who continue to fight for justice, equity, and a livable future. This work is dedicated to the resilience and courage of those most affected yet too often overlooked. Their experiences and struggles drive the urgency for change and remind us of the power and necessity of collective action for a more just world.

Contents

SECTION 2
Voices and Participation in Advisory Opinion Proceedings

SECTION 3
The Lasting Impact of Advisory Opinions

FOREWORD

Advisory Opinions from ICJ, ITLOS, and IACtHR: Expectations and Risks

*Christina Voigt**

This book, edited by Maria Antonia Tigre and Armando Rocha, could not have been published at a more suitable point in time; a time which is marked by anticipation surrounding the advisory opinions on state obligations to address climate change being sought from three international courts. In an unprecedented scenario, advisory requests have been submitted to the International Court of Justice (ICJ) in The Hague,[1] the International Tribunal for the Law of the Sea (ITLOS) in Hamburg,[2] and the Inter-American Court of Human Rights (IACtHR) in San José.[3] These cases address at their core nearly identical questions of international law: what obligations do states have to protect the climate system, human rights, and the marine environment from the impacts of climate change?

Expectations of the Courts and First Findings

The advisory requests aim at authoritative clarifications of the law from these courts and ask them to provide their interpretation of international treaty and international customary law in the context of climate change.

* Professor of Law, University of Oslo, Department of Public and International Law, Co-Chair Paris Agreement Implementation and Compliance Committee, Chair of the IUCN World Commission on Environmental Law, and lead legal counsel for IUCN. IUCN participates in all three advisory processes described in this article.

1 ICJ, *Obligations of states in respect of climate change*, https://www.icj-cij.org/case/187.

2 ITLOS, *Request for an Advisory Opinion submitted by the Commission of Small Island States on Climate Change and International Law*, https://www.itlos.org/en/main/cases/list-of-cases/request-for-an-advisory-opinion-submitted-by-the-commission-of-small-island-states-on-climate-change-and-international-law-request-for-advisory-opinion-submitted-to-the-tribunal/.

3 IACtHR, *Request for an advisory opinion on the Climate Emergency and Human Rights submitted to the Inter-American Court of Human Rights by the Republic of Colombia and the Republic of Chile*, https://www.corteidh.or.cr/docs/comunicados/cp_27_2024_eng.pdf.

Ultimately, the focus will be on determining what actions states must take to limit global warming to 1.5°C in line with the Paris Agreement.[4] This raises, among other things, questions of intergenerational and intragenerational responsibility, global justice, and the role of precautionary measures to avoid greater risks.

An early example of such a clarification of state obligations came from the *KlimaSeniorinnen* decision by the ECtHR in April 2024.[5] That court stated that in order to fulfill their obligations under Article 8 of the ECHR, states must take adequate measures to mitigate the effects of climate change on living conditions and health. In a "Paris-compliant" interpretation of the ECHR, the ECtHR left member states no discretion regarding the objective of state actions: achieving carbon neutrality (i.e., net-zero CO2 emissions) by 2050 is a necessity to limit warming to 1.5°C. The specific measures to achieve this goal remain still within the discretion of states. However, the court significantly also narrowed this discretion.[6]

A New Step by ITLOS

In its advisory opinion of May 21, 2024, the ITLOS determined that all human-caused greenhouse gas emissions constitute pollution of the marine environment under UNCLOS.[7] Consequently, the States Parties are obligated under UNCLOS to take all necessary measures to prevent, reduce, and control marine pollution caused by such greenhouse gas emissions. In interpreting UNCLOS, the tribunal referred to the Paris Agreement, adopting the 1.5°C target and carbon neutrality by 2050 as benchmarks for state action. Given the high risk of severe harm to the marine environment, the standards are stringent, and due diligence is particularly demanding.

It is expected that the Paris Agreement will also play a central role as a legal source in the advisory opinion from the ICJ. However, it remains to be seen whether the ICJ will also derive obligations to protect the climate system from other international treaties and customary international law. Particularly relevant in this context are the UN human rights treaties, UNCLOS, but also the Convention on Biological Diversity, the Montreal Protocol and its Kigali

4 Paris Agreement, Art. 2.1(a).

5 ECtHR, 09.04.2024 – 53600/20 *Verein Klimaseniorinnen Schweiz u.a. v. Schweiz.*

6 Ibid, paras. 548–550.

7 ITLOS, Advisory Opinion, 21.5.2024, https://www.itlos.org/fileadmin/itlos/documents/cases/31/Advisory_Opinion/C31_Adv_Op_21.05.2024_orig.pdf.

Amendment, as well as, of course, the customary rule of prevention and prohibition of significant harm to the environment of other states and of areas beyond national jurisdiction. This so-called "no-harm" rule has been recognized by the ICJ as part of the general corpus of international law – but it has never been applied in the context of climate change.

In interpreting these treaties and customary norms, it is hoped that the Paris Agreement will serve as the interpretative standard. This could contribute to both the harmonization and consistency of international law. Additionally, it would provide greater clarity and predictability, which are crucial for states and private actors transitioning sustainably toward carbon neutrality (and later carbon negativity). A clarification of legal questions would also be significant for national legislation and, especially, jurisprudence, as climate lawsuits continue to be filed. A clearer international legal framework could assist national courts in interpreting climate-relevant laws or constitutional provisions.

Risks in Parallel Proceedings

However, the parallel proceedings at different international courts are not without risks.

First, there are no formal channels for coordination and communication among the courts. This raises the possibility that the advisory opinions may contain differing legal assessments, standards and interpretations. Such discrepancies could not only increase the fragmentation of international law but also hinder effective climate policy.

Another challenge lies in balancing diplomacy and international adjudication. Climate change is a global issue that can only be effectively addressed through multilateral solutions. International negotiations at the annual Conference of the Parties (COP) under the auspices of the United Nations have – albeit slowly – created a framework that member states generally view as legitimate, effective, and fair.[8] The Paris Agreement is front and central in this multilateral climate change framework, or, as the Executive Secretary of the UNFCCC Secretariat, Simon Stiell, said at the closing plenary at COP29 in Baku, November 2024:

> *the UN Paris Agreement is humanity's life-raft; there is nothing else* [...]

8 Dan Bodansky (2016) *The legal character of the Paris Agreement*, 25 RECIEL 2, 142–150.

The Agreement establishes fundamental goals and unites 195 states in coordinated, iterative processes aimed at progressively enhancing nationally determined contributions (NDCs). While the level of ambition in current NDCs is insufficient to meet the 1.5°C temperature threshold,[9] guiding states toward this goal is the very purpose of the agreement. It is also worth noting that the core processes enshrined in the agreement are just about to take effect at the time of publication of this book.

In 2025, for the first time since ratifying the agreement, all States Parties will be legally obligated to submit a new, successive nationally determined contribution (NDC).[10] This obligation recurs every five years, with the next upcoming deadline set for February 10, 2025.[11] "Successive" in this context means extending the implementation time frame beyond the one in the current NDC—likely to 2035.[12] States must also consider the outcomes of the Global Stocktake (Dubai, 2023) in preparing their contributions.[13] Furthermore, the new NDCs must demonstrate progression, i.e. increased ambition, relative to current plans, and reflecting each Party´s highest possible level.[14] This implies that states with greater responsibility for greenhouse gas emissions and greater capacity for action must achieve carbon neutrality before 2050, enabling developing countries, which need more time, to also meet the global net-zero target by 2050.[15]

The 2025 NDC will be pivotal in determining whether the international community can collectively limit global warming to the stated goal. The UNFCCC Executive Secretary, Simon Stiell, stated in this context that "[t]his next round of NDCs may be the most important documents to be produced in a multilateral context so far in this century."[16]

---

9 UNFCCC Secretariat, *Nationally determined contributions under the Paris Agreement, Synthesis report*, FCCC/PA/CMA/2024/10, 28 October 2024.

10 Paris Agreement, Arts. 4.2 and 4.9.

11 Decision 1/CP.21, *Adoption of the Paris Agreement*, para 25, und Decision 1/CMA.5 *Outcome of the First Global Stocktake*, para 166.

12 Decision 6/CMA.3 *Common time frames for nationally determined contributions referred to in Article 4*, paragraph 10.

13 Paris Agreement, Arts. 14.3 and 4.9. Decision 1/CMA.5 *Outcome oft he First Global Stocktake*, para 166.

14 Ibid, Art. 4.3.

15 Christina Voigt (2023) *The Power of the Paris Agreement in International Climate Litigation*, 32 RECIEL 2, 237–249.

16 UN Climate Change Secretariat, Message to Parties and Observer States, *From Vision to Reality: NDCs 3.0 – bending the curve*, 14. März 2024, https://unfccc.int/sites/default/files/resource/message_to_parties_ndcs_%203.0.pdf. Stiell continued stating "They will determine which direction the world will take over the coming decades. It can be a direction where economic growth is gradually cancelled out by the cost of disaster management, rebuilding, and loss and damage. Or it can be one where we manage to

Additionally, all States Parties must, for the first time, fulfill the legal obligation to submit a Biennial Transparency Report by December 31, 2024, outlining how and to what extent they are implementing their current NDCs.[17] These reports will be required every two years thereafter, producing a wealth of data and facts valuable for decision-makers, research, and education.

The periodicity of these processes, combined with clear objectives and legal obligations for States Parties, forms the core of the Paris Agreement and underscores its significance. Clarifying obligations within these processes through the advisory opinions of international courts could be beneficial and strengthen state actions, provided the opinions align with the Paris Agreement. If they do not, there is a risk that these essential multilateral processes could be undermined, which would be the worst possible outcome.

The expectation on the international court's advisory opinions are high – but so are the stakes.

This excellent book discusses many of these expectations and risks, functions and impacts of advisory proceedings and is a very welcome and up-to-date contribution to the global discourse on climate justice and the role of the judiciary.

---

set our economies and our societies on a sustainable, long-term pathway over the coming 5–10 years." UNFCCC Secretariat, Building Support for More Ambitious National Climate Action Plans, 14 March 2024, available at: https://unfccc.int/news/building-support-for-more-ambitious-national-climate-action-plans.

17 Paris Agreement, Art. 13.7(b).

Abbreviations

ACHR	American Convention on Human Rights
AfCtHPR	African Court of Human and Peoples' Rights
AfCHPR	African Committee of Human and Peoples' Rights
ACOPS	Advisory Committee on Protection of the Sea
AO	advisory opinion
AOSIS	Alliance of Small Island States
AR6	IPCC's Sixth Assessment Report
AU	African Union
CBDR-RC	common but differentiated responsibilities and respective capabilities
CEO	Chief Executive Officer
CIEL	Center for International Environmental Law
CJEU	Court of Justice of the European Union
COSIS	Commission of Small Island States on Climate Change and International Law
COP	Conference of the Parties
CRC	Committee on the Rights of the Child
EACJ	East African Community Court of Justice
ECCJ	ECOWAS Community Court of Justice
ECOWAS	Economic Community for West African States
EIA	environmental impact assessment
EU	European Union
ECHR	European Convention on Human Rights
ECtHR	European Court of Human Rights
FPIC	Free, Prior, and Informed Consent
GHG	Greenhouse gas(es)
GPI	Greenpeace International
HRC	United Nations Human Rights Committee
HRTB	human rights treaty bodies
IACHR	Inter-American Commission of Human Rights
IACtHR	Inter-American Court of Human Rights
IAHRS	Inter-American Human Rights System
ICAO	International Civil Aviation Organization
ICC	International Criminal Court
ICJ	International Court of Justice
ITLOS	International Tribunal for the Law of the Sea
IPCC	Intergovernmental Panel on Climate Change
IUCN	International Union for Conservation of Nature and Natural Resources

LDCS	Least Developed Countries
LNG	liquified natural gas
NDC	Nationally Determined Contribution(s)
NGO	Non-Governmental Organization
OAS	Organization of American States
OASTS	Organization of American States Treaty Series
OAU	Organisation of African Unity
OECD	Organisation for Economic Co-operation and Development
PISFCC	Pacific Islands Students Fighting Climate Change
RECS	regional economic communities
REDD+	Reducing Emissions from Deforestation and Forest Degradation
SDG	Sustainable Development Goal
SIDS	Small Island Developing States
SPC	The Pacific Community
SRFC	Sub-Regional Fisheries Commission
TANS	Transnational Advocacy Networks
TPNW	Treaty on the Prohibition of Nuclear Weapons
UK	United Kingdom
UKEF	UK's export credit agency
UN	United Nations
UNCLOS	United Nations Convention on the Law of the Sea
UNEP	United Nations Environment Programme
UNFCCC	United Nations Framework Convention on Climate Change
UNGA	United Nations General Assembly
UNTS	United Nations Treaty Series
USA	United States of America
VCLT	Vienna Convention on the Law of Treaties
WWF	World Wildlife Fund for Nature

Notes on Contributors

Editors

Tigre, Maria Antonia
is the Director for Global Climate Change Litigation at the Sabin Center for Climate Change Law at Columbia Law School. She previously worked as a Senior Attorney at the Environment Program of the Cyrus R. Vance Center for International Justice. She served as the Deputy Director for the Global Network for Human Rights and the Environment (GNHRE). She has authored numerous publications on regional and international environmental law, specifically focusing on environmental rights, the evolution of international environmental law, and climate litigation. Her research also encompasses the protection of the Amazon rainforest ecosystem. She has three sons.

Rocha, Armando
is a Professor of International Law, Law of the Sea, and Climate Change Law at *Universidade Católica Portuguesa* and researcher at the Católica Research Centre for the Future of Law. He is also an invited Professor at the Catholic University of Lille (France), member of the Young Scientists Seminar of the Academy of Sciences of Lisbon, member of the International Law Association Committee on the Protection of Persons at Sea, and coordinator of the Law Schools Global League research group on Environmental Regulation.

Authors

Carrillo Bañuelos, Jorge Alejandro
is a Climate Change and Human Rights Advisor at the Supreme Court of Mexico. He completed his LL.M. at Harvard Law School as a Fulbright Scholar. He holds an LL.B. (Hons.) from Centro de Investigación y Docencia Económicas (CIDE), Mexico. His academic research focuses on climate change litigation, environmental rights, and constitutional procedures. He has also collaborated with the Interamerican Association for Environmental Defense (AIDA) in climate change litigation cases.

Campbell, Austyn
is an international disputes lawyer at Gilbert + Tobin. Her practice focuses on issues of public and private international law, including matters before the

International Tribunal for the Law of the Sea and the International Court of Justice. Most recently, Austyn was part of the team that represented Timor-Leste before the International Tribunal for the Law of the Sea in the advisory proceedings on climate change, and advised Timor-Leste, Tonga, and Solomon Islands in preparing their written statements in the advisory opinion on climate change before the International Court of Justice.

Cohen, Miriam
is an Associate Professor and Canada Research Chair on Human Rights and International Reparative Justice at Université de Montréal Faculty of Law. She is Vicepresident of the Quebec Society of Internation al Law, a member of the Board of the Canadian Council on Internation al Law and a member of the Global Young Academy. She holds graduate degrees from Harvard Law School, Cambridge University, Université de Montréal and Leiden University. She has previously worked at the International Court of Justice and the International Criminal Court, and she has appeared as Counsel before the International Tribunal for the Law of the Sea, the Inter-American Court of Human Rights and the Supreme Court of Canada.

De Spiegeleir, Antoine
is a PhD Researcher in the Law Department of the European University Institute (Florence, Italy). Prior to his PhD, he worked as a Research and Teaching Assistant at the KU Leuven and Yale Law School. Antoine studied law and philosophy in Brussels, Leuven, and Zurich, and obtained an LL.M. School in 2022. His doctoral dissertation relates to storytelling in international adjudication.

Lupin, Dina
is a Associate Professor at the School of Law at the University of Southampton. They served as the Director of the Global Network for Human Rights and the Environment. Her research examines the role of fundamental legal values (such as human dignity) in the context of environmental decision-making. It uses feminist, queer, and decolonial theory in their analysis of Indigenous epistemic and social resistance to unjust environmental processes and practices. Previously Dina worked as a Post-doctoral researcher at the University of Vienna researching Indigenous rights and practices of resistance. Prior were based at the University of Tilburg researching civil society organisations working on sustainable development in Ethiopia

Main-Klingst, Lea
is a lawyer for international law and fundamental rights with ClientEarth, a legal environmental charity. She holds an LL.M. in Human Rights from University College London and an LL.M. in International Environmental Law from the George Washington University Law School. Prior to joining ClientEarth, she worked in public international law and human rights, including on cases before the International Court of Justice and the International Tribunal for the Law of the Sea. Lea has published on a variety of international law issues, including climate and environmental litigation, genocide, refugee law, and the law of the sea.

Marjanac, Sophie
is currently the Director of Legal Strategy at the Polluter Pays Project and is an environmental lawyer with diverse experience gained in the not-for-profit sector and private practice. She was at ClientEarth from 2015–2024, where she incubated the organisation's work on climate change litigation, leading its work to hold corporations to account for their environmental impacts. During her time at ClientEarth, she led a path-breaking human rights case on behalf of *Indigenous Torres Strait Islanders* (*Billy et al v Australia*), several cases seeking to hold companies to account for greenwashing, and a world-first claim against the Board of Directors of Shell plc. Sophie is an Australian-qualified lawyer (Victoria) and obtained a Bachelor of Law (first class honors) and Bachelor of International Studies (with distinction) from the University of New South Wales in 2009.

Medici-Colombo, Gastón
is a Lecturer in Public International Law at the University of Barcelona and Associate Researcher at the Tarragona Centre for Environmental Law Studies (CEDAT). Prior to joining the University of Barcelona, he worked as a Professor at the Barcelona Centre of International Studies (CEI, International Affairs) and as a lawyer in Spain and Argentina. His work focuses on environmental law, human rights and international courts.

Nanthakumar, Rohan
is a public and international lawyer at Blue Ocean Law, specializing in human rights, climate, environmental and constitutional law. He helps local communities, governments, international organisations and NGOs to devise and implement legal strategies in pursuit of environmental justice and the self-determination of peoples. Rohan has been instructed in all three of the climate change advisory opinions before the ITLOS, IACtHR and ICJ. He was a member

of the legal team and delegation to the Hague for the Republic of Vanuatu in the ICJ advisory proceedings. He has previously worked on litigation before domestic courts, engaged with the UN human rights system and the complaints process under the OECD Guidelines for Multinational Enterprises. He is also a Research Fellow in the Centre for Comparative Constitutional Studies at the University of Melbourne.

Narulla, Harjeevan S.
is a lawyer at Doughty Street Chambers who specializes in domestic and international climate change litigation, namely in the fields of human rights law, public international law, constitutional law, public law, corporate and commercial law, rights of Nature, and indigenous and First Nations law. He has been involved in climate litigation cases in more than 15 countries, across all continents, and he also provides advice on climate law and governance to governments, NGOs, and international inter-governmental organizations such as the UNFCCC. Harj was instructed in all three of the advisory opinions before the ICJ, IACtHR, and ITLOS, and presented Solomon Islands' case at the ICJ hearings in The Hague. Alongside his practice he has visiting academic roles in climate law and litigation at the University of Oxford and the London School of Economics.

Nekura, Ruth
is a human rights lawyer and socio-legal researcher whose work focuses on law reform, advocacy and strategic litigation. She is passionate about access to justice and invokes both structural and individual level analyses to challenge systemic inequality. She is an advocate of the High Court of Kenya. She holds an LL.M. in Human Rights Law and a PhD in Public International Law from the University of Cape Town. She works as an independent consultant providing technical support to grassroots, national and international civil society organizations.

Ollino, Alice
is an Assistant Professor in International Law at the University of Milano-Bicocca (Italy). She is the author of *Due Diligence Obligations in International Law* (CUP 2022). In 2019, she was awarded the ESIL Young Scholar Prize. Alice's research interests include general international law, international responsibility, and international human rights. She has published on a wide range of topics in national and international peer-reviewed journals. Alice has been a visiting Fellow at the Max Planck Institute for Comparative Public Law and International Law, a research fellow at the Centre for Studies and Research

of the Hague Academy of International Law, and a visiting researcher at the University of Geneva.

Papanicolopulu, Irini
is British Academy Global Professor of International Law at SOAS University of London. She is also a visiting professor at the Catholic University of Portugal and the University of St. Gallen (Switzerland) and has previously worked at the University of Oxford, the University of Glasgow, and the University of Milano-Bicocca. She is the author and editor of numerous publication addressing international law, the law of the sea, environmental law, and human rights law, including *International Law and the Protection of People at Sea* (OUP 2018) and the award-winning *Gender and the Law of the Sea* (Brill 2019). She is the Chair of the ILA Committee on Protection of People at Sea, Vice-Chair of COST Action Blue Rights and a member of the Coordinating Committee of the Interest Group on the Law of the Sea of the European Society of International Law. Irini advises states, international organisations, civil society organisations and business actors on issues of international law, the law of the sea, human rights law and environmental law.

Robertson, Claire
is an international lawyer at DLA Piper. She advises governments on public international law matters and dispute resolution between States on complex issues, including matters before the International Tribunal on the Law of the Sea and the International Court of Justice. Claire also advises governments on climate finance projects, in particular supporting ocean-related initiatives. Most recently, she was part of the teams that represented Timor-Leste before the International Tribunal for the Law of the Sea in the advisory opinion proceedings on climate change, and Timor-Leste, Tonga, Solomon Islands, and Zambia in the advisory opinion on climate change before the International Court of Justice.

Ann Samuel, Susan
Ann Samuel, Susan is an Indian lawyer and currently a PhD Researcher with University of Leeds, School of Politics and International Studies. She serves as Fellowship Officer of the Centre for International Sustainable Development Law (CISDL); and is a member of the International Union for Conservation of Nature–World Commission on Environmental Law (IUCN WCEL), and Global Network on Human Rights and Environment (GNHRE). She is a Priestley Climate Scholar with Priestley Centre for Climate Futures. Her research interests include Climate Law and Politics, Human Rights and Sustainable Development through a multidisciplinary lens.

Stewart, Melissa
is an Assistant Professor of Law at the University of Hawai'i at Mānoa, William S. Richardson School of Law. Her research combines theoretical and practical approaches to complex problems of law in the fields of international law, human rights, and international environmental law. She has held appointments at Georgetown University Law Center and the Center for Transnational Legal Studies in London. Prior to academia, she worked in private practice at Foley Hoag, LLP where she advised clients on matters related to international law, international environmental law, law of the sea, human rights, and corporate social responsibility.

Sthoeger, Eran
is a New York-based litigator, consultant and advisor on matters of public international law, including in matters relating to the law of the sea, human rights law, and also climate and environmental law. As such, his work experience includes working on several cases before the ITLOS, ICJ and arbitral tribunals. Apart from his activity as a litigator, he also conducts academic research in these fields and works as a Lecturer in international environmental law at Columbia University and Adjunct Professor at Brooklyn Law School.

Teles, Patrícia Galvão
is a member of the United Nations International Law Commission and of the Permanent Court of Arbitration. She is the Legal Advisor of the Portuguese Ministry of Foreign Affairs. Professor Galvão Teles is also Associate Professor of International Law at the Autonomous University of Lisbon, Co-Director of the Singapore CIL Academy of International Law and Global Senior Fellow at the Centre for International Law of the National University of Singapore. She is an Associate Member of the Institut de Droit International and a member of the Curatorium of The Hague Academy of International Law, having taught a special course in the Winter Session of 2024 on 'The Advisory Function of International Courts and Tribunals'.

Teixeira, Rita Guerreiro
is an Assistant Professor of Public International Law at Utrecht University, Department of International and European Law, and a member of the Utrecht Centre for Water, Oceans and Sustainability Law. Prior to joining Utrecht, Rita was a postdoctoral researcher at the Erik Castrén Institute, University of Helsinki, and a junior researcher at the Leuven Centre for Global Governance Studies. Her main research interests include international environmental law, international organisations, and law-making.

CHAPTER 1

The Role of Advisory Opinions in International Law in the Context of the Climate Crisis: An Introduction

Maria Antonia Tigre and Armando Rocha***

Abstract

This introductory chapter of 'The Role of Advisory Opinions in International Law in the Context of the Climate Crisis' explores the evolving landscape of international climate law at a pivotal moment marked by a surge in climate litigation and the landmark issuance of advisory opinions by international and regional courts and tribunals. Rooted in the context of decades of climate litigation primarily pursued at domestic levels, the shift to international courts and tribunals highlights an urgent need for clear and enforceable obligations on States to mitigate and adapt to climate change. Central to this inquiry are the Paris Agreement and UNFCCC, whose provisions, while vital, remain ambiguous and largely non-binding, prompting individuals, civil society, and States to seek legal clarity. By examining the growing influence of advisory opinions – including those recently delivered or forthcoming from the ITLOS, IACtHR, and ICJ – the book provides a comprehensive analysis of how international courts can clarify States' climate obligations. These non-binding opinions, positioned as 'Rosetta Stones' for interpreting States' responsibilities, illuminate a path forward by translating aspirational climate goals into actionable commitments. This chapter introduces the main topics and themes of the book, setting the stage for a critical conversation on the significance of this moment and the role of international law in addressing one of the world's most urgent challenges.

* *Sabin Center for Climate Change Law*, Columbia Law School, https://orcid.org/0000-0003-4308-1958, email: mb4913@columbia.edu.

** *Universidade Católica Portuguesa*, School of Law, Católica Research Centre for the Future of Law, https://orcid.org/0000-0002-8181-1512, email: armandorocha@ucp.pt.

Keywords

international climate law – climate litigation – advisory opinions – United Nations Framework on Climate Change (UNFCCC) – Paris Agreement – State obligations – climate change mitigation – greenhouse gas emissions – international courts – global climate governance

1 Introduction

In William Golding's *Lord of the Flies*, a group of children who survived an airplane accident are left alone on a remote island. The book has several lines of interpretation, one being the idea that a core element of a human community – of individuals or States – is the existence of clear and binding rules. When these rules are challenged ('Who cares?'), the answer is clear-cut: 'Because the rules are the only thing we've got!'[1]

The international community of States is also in need of clear and binding rules to reduce global emissions and concentration of greenhouse gas (GHG) emissions, thus avoiding the most hazardous consequences of climate change. To that end, States adopted the 1992 United Nations Framework on Climate Change (UNFCCC),[2] the 1997 Kyoto Protocol,[3] and the 2015 Paris Agreement.[4] The trio of treaties – together with other non-binding decisions adopted by the Conferences of the Parties (COPs) to the UNFCCC – form the 'UNFCCC legal complex,' which pursues the reduction of the concentration of GHG in the atmosphere[5] and, more specifically, to '[hold] the increase in the global average temperature to well below 2°C above pre-industrial levels and pursuing efforts to limit the temperature increase to 1.5°C above pre-industrial levels.'[6] Other norms of international law are also relevant in the context of climate change, although they are not directly concerned with their causes or consequences. Therefore, apart from the UNFCCC legal complex, the international law on climate change includes the principles of general environmental law

1 William Golding, *Lord of the Flies* [1954] (Faber & Faber 1983) 100.
2 1992 United Nations Framework Convention on Climate Change (adopted 9 May 1992, entry into force 21 March 1994) 1771 UNTS 107.
3 1997 Kyoto Protocol to the UNFCCC (adopted 11 December 1997, entry into force 16 February 2005) 2303 UNTS 162.
4 2015 Paris Agreement (adopted 12 December 2015, entry into force 4 November 2016) 3156 UNTS 79.
5 UNFCCC, art 2.
6 Paris Agreement, art. 2(1)(a).

(eg precaution, no-harm, or cooperation), rules and principles of the law of the sea, human rights law, or the rules and principles stemming from the treaties on the protection of the ozone layer.[7]

However, clarity and enforceability aren't exactly the hallmarks of international climate law. The lack of precision has spurred a shift toward international courts and tribunals to help pin down States' responsibilities for climate change action. In response, concerned individuals, civil society movements, and States have taken 'climate change' straight to the docket of major international and regional courts. In 2020, the first applications on human rights and climate change were filed before the European Court of Human Rights (ECtHR), and eventually decided in 2024.[8] Between December 2022 and March 2023, three requests for an advisory opinion were submitted to the International Tribunal for the Law of the Sea (ITLOS), the Inter-American Court of Human Rights (IACtHR), and the International Court of Justice (ICJ).[9] Furthermore, a request for an advisory opinion from the African Court on Human and Peoples' Rights (AfCtHPR) is being prepared,[10] as explained by Lupin and Nekura in Chapter 6. This pivot to advisory opinions is largely driven by three key reasons.

First, the UNFCCC and the Paris Agreement (ie the major climate treaties) lay down a set of non-, soft, or insufficiently characterized obligations at best.[11] For

7 1985 Vienna Convention for the Protection of the Ozone Layer (adopted 22 March 1985, entered into force 22 September 1988) 1513 UNTS 293; 1987 Montreal Protocol on Substances that Deplete the Ozone Layer (adopted 16 September 1987, entered into force 1 January 1989) 1522 UNTS 3.

8 *Duarte Agostinho and Others v Portugal and 32 Other States* (App No 39371/20) ECtHR [GC] 9 April 2024; *Verein KlimaSeniorinnen Schweiz and Others v Switzerland* (App No 53600/20) ECtHR [GC] 9 April 2024; *Carême v France* (App No 7189/21) ECtHR [GC] 9 April 2024. Although the ECtHR also has an advisory jurisdiction under Article 46 of the ECHR (Convention for the Protection of Human Rights and Fundamental Freedoms (adopted 4 November 1950, entered into force 3 September 1953) 213 UNTS 221) and Article 1 of Protocol 16 to the ECHR (adopted 2 October 2013, entered into force 1 August 2018, ETS No 214), it is unlikely that an advisory opinion on human rights and climate change will be requested *in lieu* of an individual application under Article 34 of the ECHR.

9 For a more comprehensive exploration of the trio of advisory opinion requests, see Maria Antonia Tigre, 'It is (Finally) Time for an Advisory Opinion on Climate Change: Challenges and Opportunities on a Trio of Initiatives' (2024) 17 *Charleston Law Review* 623. For a discussion on how the three requests interact through competition and dialogue, see Maria Antonia Tigre and Armando Rocha, 'Competition and dialogue between courts in the context of climate change advisory opinions,' (2023) 117 *AJIL Unbound* 289.

10 Tigre (n 14) 626.

11 Eg Lavanya Rajamani, 'The 2015 Paris Agreement: Interplay between Hard, Soft and Non-Obligations' (2016) 28(2) *Journal of Environmental Law* 337.

instance, Article 4 of the Paris Agreement – which is the bedrock of the entire building of the international law on climate change – sets out States' obligation to prepare, communicate and maintain, every five years,[12] a nationally determined contribution (NDC),[13] having in mind that each State's NDC will represent a progression over time and must reflect its highest possible ambition.[14] Apart from relying on a State's self-differentiation and self-assessment of its highest possible ambition, the wording of Article 4 of the Paris Agreement (including the variations in the verbal formulation) is the prime example of lack of clarity on States' obligations to mitigate and adapt to climate change.

Second, other rules and principles may be relevant in the context of, but were not devised for coping with the causes or consequences of climate change. As such, it is also unclear to what extent these rules and principles can be used as a source and tool to flesh out States' obligations in relation to climate change. This lack of clarity can ultimately lead to non-compliance – or, at the very least, under-compliance – with the overall goal of 'well below 2°C.' In fact, as we were finalizing this edited book in November 2024, data from the European Copernicus Climate Change Service confirmed that 2024 was set to be the hottest year on record.[15] The prediction is that we will surpass the 1.5°C temperature threshold – after 2023 had also set a record temperature rise of 1.48°C.

A *third* and final factor is the unlikelihood of a State-to-State dispute under the UNFCCC or the Paris Agreement in the coming years. Fear of retaliation or damaging diplomatic relations, and legal obstacles such as the unclarity of the legal background, the difficulty of establishing causation, or the lack of consent to jurisdiction pursuant to Articles 14 and 24 of the UNFCCC and the Paris Agreement, explain why States refrain from initiating judicial proceedings related to the causes or consequences of climate change. In this context, international courts' advisory jurisdiction is perceived as an opportunity for clarifying and developing the international law on climate change, without the risks and difficulties of contentious cases.

This background explains why international climate law is fertile ground for, and in need of, judicial development, as explored by Guerreiro Teixeira and Galvão Teles in Chapter 2. In other words, courts play a role in shaping international climate law when resolving disputes or issuing opinions on States' climate obligations. Choosing relevant rules and principles, interpreting them,

12 Paris Agreement, art 4(9).
13 ibid art 4(2).
14 ibid art 4(3).
15 Mark Poynting, *This year set to be first to breach 1.5C global warming limit*, BBC News (Nov. 7, 2024), https://www.bbc.com/news/articles/c1dpnxnvv2g0/.

and defining the precise scope of States' duties help bring the law into sharper focus. As such, advisory opinions, though non-binding, can serve as a 'Rosetta Stone' for decoding and clarifying States' obligations to tackle climate change, helping us translate lofty ambitions into actionable commitments for mitigation and adaptation.

As such, 2024–2025 marks an unprecedented moment in global climate litigation: as of November 2024, we are on the verge of having four of the world's most important international and regional courts and tribunals answering crucial legal questions on the (*ex ante* and *ex post facto*) responsibility of States for climate change. Whilst the ITLOS and the ECtHR have already made their pronouncements on international climate law – respectively, by means of an advisory opinion on climate-related obligations under the United Nations Convention on the Law of the Sea (UNCLOS)[16] and a ruling on States' obligation

16 United Nations Convention on the Law of the Sea (adopted 10 December 1982, entered into force 16 November 1994) 1833 UNTS 3. For short analyses of the ITLOS advisory opinion, see Korey Silverman-Roati and Maxim Bönnemann, *The ITLOS Advisory Opinion on Climate Change: An introduction into the joint blog symposium*, Climate Law Blog (May 22, 2024), https://blogs.law.columbia.edu/climatechange/2024/05/22/the-itlos-advisory-opinion-on-climate-change-an-introduction-into-the-joint-blog-symposium/; Jacqueline Peel, *Unlocking UNCLOS: How the ITLOS Advisory Opinion Delivers a Holistic Vision of Climate-relevant International Law*, Climate Law Blog (May 24, 2024), https://blogs.law.columbia.edu/climatechange/2024/05/24/unlocking-unclos-how-the-itlos-advisory-opinion-delivers-a-holistic-vision-of-climate-relevant-international-law/; Romany Webb, *The ITLOS Advisory Opinion and Marine Geoengineering: More Questions, Few Answers*, Climate Law Blog (May 24, 2024), https://blogs.law.columbia.edu/climatechange/2024/05/24/the-itlos-advisory-opinion-and-marine-geoengineering-more-questions-few-answers/; Armando Rocha, *A Small but Important Step: A Bird's-Eye View of the ITLOS' Advisory Opinion on Climate Change and International Law*, Climate Law Blog (May 27, 2024), https://blogs.law.columbia.edu/climatechange/2024/05/27/a-small-but-important-step-a-birds-eye-view-of-the-itlos-advisory-opinion-on-climate-change-and-international-law/; Christina Voigt, *ITLOS and the importance of (getting) external rules (right) in interpreting UNCLOS*, Climate Law Blog (May 29, 2024), https://blogs.law.columbia.edu/climatechange/2024/05/29/itlos-and-the-importance-of-getting-external-rules-right-in-interpreting-unclos/; Cymie Payne, *Finding Light in Dark Places: Specific Obligations for Climate Change and Ocean Acidification Mitigation*, Climate Law Blog (Jun. 4, 2024), https://blogs.law.columbia.edu/climatechange/2024/06/04/finding-light-in-dark-places-specific-obligations-for-climate-change-and-ocean-acidification-mitigation/; Marta Torre-Schaub, *Why Climate Science Matters for International Law*, Climate Law Blog (Jun. 6, 2024), https://blogs.law.columbia.edu/climatechange/2024/06/06/why-climate-science-matters-for-international-law/; Margaretha Wewerinke-Singh and Jorge E. Viñuales, *More than a Sink: The ITLOS Advisory Opinion on Climate Change and State Responsibility*, Climate Law Blog (Jun. 7, 2024), https://blogs.law.columbia.edu/climatechange/2024/06/07/more-than-a-sink-the-itlos-advisory-opinion-on-climate-change-and-state-responsibility/; Panos Merkouris, *'Relevant Rules' as Normative Environment:*

to protect the stability of the climate system pursuant to Articles 6 and 8 of the ECHR[17] – the IACtHR and the ICJ are expected to render their advisory opinions on climate change in 2025.

This moment in time marks a pivotal shift in international climate law. One advisory opinion has already been published, and two more are anticipated in 2025, each one adding weight to the collective push to define and enforce climate obligations at a global level. This book captures this critical juncture, aiming to spark a conversation on the role, importance, and far-reaching implications of these advisory opinions. This moment, however, is not happening in isolation; it reflects decades of mounting climate litigation and a steadily rising demand for accountability.[18] The escalating number of climate cases across domestic, regional, and international bodies shows a groundswell of concern over climate change and its relentless impacts. Until recently, climate litigation unfolded primarily in domestic courts, but the shift to international forums underscores an acknowledgment that climate change is a global issue requiring global solutions. This book invites readers to explore the significance of this turning point and to consider how advisory opinions may shape the path forward in addressing one of the most pressing challenges of our time.

This introductory chapter is structured as follows: Section 2 briefly discusses the advantages of the advisory route. Section 3 provides a brief overview of the three distinct requests for advisory opinions. Section 4 outlines the organization of the book, while Section 5 concludes the discussion and sets the stage for the chapters to come.

2 A Strategic Choice: Advantages of the Advisory Route

The requests for advisory opinions result from unparalleled advocacy work from States and civil society, who were concerned with the disappointing outcomes of negotiations at the COPs under the UNFCCC, as well as with the

---

Harmony vs Cacophony in the ITLOS Advisory Opinion on Climate Change, Climate Law Blog (Jun. 15, 2024), https://blogs.law.columbia.edu/climatechange/2024/06/15/relevant-rules-as-normative-environment-harmony-vs-cacophony-in-the-itlos-advisory-opinion-on-climate-change/.

17 For an overview of the decisions, see Maxim Bönnemann & Maria Antonia Tigre (eds.), *The Transformation of European Climate Litigation* (Verfassungsbooks, 2024).

18 See Michael Burger and Maria Antonia Tigre, *Global Climate Litigation Report: 2023 Status Review* (Sabin Center for Climate Change Law, Columbia Law School & United Nations Environment Programme 2023); Maria Antonia Tigre and Margaret Barry, *Climate Change in the Courts: A 2023 Retrospective* (Sabin Center for Climate Change Law, December 2023).

growing evidence that the global stocktake of States' NDCs remains short to meet the long-term temperature reduction goals of the Paris Agreement.[19] As a result, concerned States and civil society turned to the advisory jurisdiction of international and regional courts and tribunals as the most effective forum to provide an authoritative contribution to clarifying and advancing international climate law. Whilst Campbell, Robertson, and Sthoeger explain in detail the role of States in pursuing judicial clarification in the context of climate change in Chapter 9,[20] Narulla and Nanthakumar focus on how civil society movements pursued the same goal of clarification of what States' obligations to mitigate and adapt to climate change are in Chapter 10.[21]

As these authors explain, seeking an advisory opinion is not about involving courts and tribunals in the political negotiation process under the United Nations (UN), nor is it a substitute for negotiations within the COPs. Instead, it aims to clarify the legal obligations that underpin these political discussions. In this context, the trio of requests for advisory opinions is not a form of 'lawfare' but rather a genuine effort to provide an objective, depoliticized foundation for COP negotiations and climate litigation more broadly. By establishing a shared understanding of the legal framework applicable to climate change, these opinions can help ground the political process in a more explicit legal context.

The reason for resorting to advisory proceedings is straightforward: the rights-turn in climate litigation is linked to an upsurge of claims brought by the applicants into domestic courts or, at the supranational and international level, to the Court of Justice of the European Union, the ECtHR, the UN Human Rights Committee, or the UN Committee on the Rights of the Child. What these cases have in common is their inherently contentious nature: each was initiated through a petition or complaint against a State, raising specific legal issues that could impede a successful outcome, such as questions of standing, causation, attribution, redressability, or compliance with procedural requirements. Therefore, scholars have focused on the procedural requirements, challenges, and possible outcomes of climate change-related disputes. However, the lack of clarity with regards to the (bindingness of the) international climate law – hand in hand with fears of retaliation or damaging diplomatic

19 UNFCCC, 2023 Synthesis report on GST elements, Views on the elements for the consideration of outputs component of the first global stocktake, Synthesis report by the secretariat, FCCC/SB/2023/9 (4 October 2023), available at https://unfccc.int/sites/default/files/resource/SYR_Views%20on%20%20Elements%20for%20CoO.pdf. See also UNFCCC, *Outcome of the first global stocktake*, https://unfccc.int/topics/global-stocktake/about-the-global-stocktake/outcome-of-the-first-global-stocktake.

20 Chapter 9 in this book.

21 Chapter 10 in this book.

relations and the lack of consent to jurisdiction under Article 14 of the UNFCCC, Article 24 of the Paris Agreement or other regulations of international courts and tribunals or other adjudicatory bodies – means that the prospects for a State-to-State contentious case (necessarily at the level of international law) are extremely short, if at all. In this context, requesting an advisory opinion emerges as the most viable alternative – one that may also prove more effective for clarifying and developing the foundational principles of international climate law. This approach is both possible and advantageous because it avoids the complex factual context and procedural challenges that could 'muddle the waters' in contentious cases.

3 The Requests for Advisory Opinions

This section briefly explores the processes that resulted in the trio of requests for advisory opinions – bearing in mind that, as a process, they took place hand in hand with the diplomatic negotiations within the aegis of the COPs to the UNFCCC. However, a remarkable consequence of the trio of advisory opinions is that the primary outcomes in the international climate change law are, and will be, delivered not as a result of treaty negotiations or judicial dispute settlement, but rather from purely advisory proceedings. Advisory opinions are *prima facie* non-binding, but the judicial reputation of these bodies and the narratives they adopt explain why they can help unveil States' obligations under international law and further develop international climate change law, filling the blanks of a slow development under political processes. This idea is further explored in Section 4 of this Introduction, as well as by Guerreiro Teixeira and Galvão Teles in Chapter 2. The use of advisory opinions is not new in the recent history of international law. Still, the failure of dispute settlement mechanisms under the UNFCCC's legal complex means this is the first time that an entire block of international law is inaugurated and brought before three of the central international courts and tribunals simultaneously and through advisory opinions.

3.1 *The International Tribunal for the Law of the Sea*

Requesting an advisory opinion from ITLOS was not completely evident at first sight. In fact, the only reference in UNCLOS to the advisory jurisdiction of ITLOS is found in Article 191, which establishes that its Seabed Disputes Chamber can render an advisory opinion at the request of the Assembly or the Council of the International Seabed Authority on legal questions arising within the scope of their activities – ie questions regarding Part XI of UNCLOS ruling the exploitation of minerals in the International Seabed Area. However, Article 21 of ITLOS Statute (Annex VI to UNCLOS and thus having the same legal status as UNCLOS)[22] sets out that the jurisdiction of ITLOS comprises 'all matters specifically provided for in any other agreement which confers jurisdiction on the Tribunal.' In other words, since State consent is the basis of an international court's or tribunal's jurisdiction, the ITLOS' jurisdiction can be enlarged by means of an *ad hoc* treaty related to the purposes of UNCLOS. In the *Request for an Advisory Opinion submitted by the Sub-Regional Fisheries Commission* (*SRFC*),[23] ITLOS took the opportunity to espouse its understanding of this provision – and, namely, if it can be used for granting ITLOS an advisory competence.[24] In a nutshell, ITLOS concluded that States can enter a treaty in which they vest ITLOS with an advisory competence, provided that (i) the treaty relates to the purposes of UNCLOS; (ii) the treaty provides explicitly for the submission to ITLOS of a request for such an advisory opinion; (iii) the request is submitted by the body authorized by, or in accordance with, the latter treaty; and (iv) the opinion is given on a legal question (which, because ITLOS is a specialized international tribunal, must be a law of the sea question).[25] This understanding finds resonance in Article 138 of ITLOS Rules.

As such, during (but in parallel to) the 26th COP to the UNFCCC in Edinburgh (2021), the Governments of Antigua and Barbuda and Tuvalu signed the Agreement for the Establishment of the Commission of Small Island States on Climate Change and International Law (COSIS),[26] through which they created COSIS as a new international legal person.[27] COSIS' primary goal is to request an advisory opinion from ITLOS, according to Article 21 of ITLOS Statute[28] – therefore relying on Article 138 of ITLOS Rules and the understanding of the *SRFC Opinion*.

The COSIS Agreement was registered on the same day of adoption and entry into force and is open for accession to all Members of the Alliance of Small Island States.[29] If the urgency of climate change explains the speed of

22 UNCLOS, art 318.

23 *Request for an Advisory Opinion submitted by the Sub-Regional Fisheries Commission* (*SRFC*) (Advisory Opinion, 2 April 2015) ITLOS Case No 15 (*SRFC Opinion*).

24 ibid §§37–69.

25 ibid §60.

26 Agreement for the Establishment of the Commission of Small Island States on Climate Change and International Law (adopted and entered into force 31 October 2021) 3444 UNTS (COSIS Agreement).

27 ibid art 1(2).

28 ibid art 2(2).

29 COSIS Agreement, art 4(2). For a list of accessions, see <https://treaties.un.org/Pages/showDetails.aspx?objid=080000028o5c2ace>.

the registration and entry into force process, the pivotal role of small island States is also easy to understand. These States are more vulnerable to climate change-related consequences in the marine environment: sea level rise, for instance, threatens the very survival of such States, as was explicitly highlighted in the preamble of the COSIS Agreement.[30] For these States, facing the marine impact of climate change is a matter of urgency and of short- to medium-term survival. Their exposure and vulnerability towards marine factors also explain why small island States were keen on having ITLOS (as a specialized law of the sea international tribunal) making an authoritative pronouncement on States' obligations under UNCLOS in relation to the causes and consequences of climate change, emphasizing their obligations regarding the protection and preservation of the marine environment.

Accordingly, on December 12, 2022, COSIS lodged its request for an advisory opinion from ITLOS, where it asked what the States' specific obligations are under UNCLOS to prevent, reduce, and control pollution of the marine environment related to or resulting from excessive anthropogenic GHG emissions, as well as to protect and preserve the marine environment against the deleterious impacts resulting from climate change.[31] The request referred to, but was not limited to, States' obligations under Part XII of UNCLOS. On May 21, 2024, ITLOS rendered its advisory opinion.[32] This opinion is explored in more detail by Ollino and Papanicolopulu (Chapter 3). Still, it is worth mentioning that it was the first-ever pronouncement from an international court or tribunal on States' obligations to mitigate and adapt to climate change, having ITLOS adopted the innovative stance already espoused in prior advisory opinions related to the protection and preservation of the marine environment and natural resources.[33]

3.2 *The Inter-American Court of Human Rights*

The advisory competence of the IACtHR is established in Article 64 of the American Convention on Human Rights (ACHR), which sets out that members

30 COSIS Agreement, Preamble, §1.

31 The text of the request is available at <https://www.itlos.org/fileadmin/itlos/documents/cases/31/Request_for_Advisory_Opinion_COSIS_12.12.22.pdf>.

32 See also Maria José Alarcon and Maria Antonia Tigre, *Navigating the Intersection of Climate Change and the Law of the Sea: Exploring the ITLOS Advisory Opinion's Substantive Content*, Climate Law Blog (Apr. 24, 2023), https://blogs.law.columbia.edu/climatechange/2023/04/24/navigating-the-intersection-of-climate-change-and-the-law-of-the-sea-exploring-the-itlos-advisory-opinions-substantive-content/.

33 *Responsibilities and Obligations of States Sponsoring Persons and Entities with Respect to Activities in the Area* (*Request for Advisory Opinion Submitted to the Seabed Disputes Chamber* (Advisory Opinion, 1 February 2011) ITLOS Case No 17; SRFC Opinion (n 22).

of the Organization of American States (OAS), even if they are not parties to the ACHR,[34] and the organs listed in Chapter X of the Charter of the OAS,[35] can request an advisory opinion from the IACtHR regarding 'the interpretation of this Convention or of other treaties concerning the protection of human rights in the American [S]tates.'[36] As a result, although the requesting States or organs cannot ask the IACtHR about the interpretation of UNCLOS or the Paris Agreement, they can still request its advisory opinion regarding States' human rights obligations in relation to climate change under the ACHR. This conclusion stems from the fact that the IACtHR is a specialized international court, whose subject matter jurisdiction is limited to the interpretation and enforcement of the ACHR – although the interpretation and enforcement of the ACHR is an exclusive competence of the IACtHR also. Such a restrictive subject matter jurisdiction seems at odds with a request for an advisory opinion related to climate change, unless one bears in mind, one the one hand, the impacts of climate change on the effective enjoyment of human rights and, on the other hand, that systemic interpretation pursuant to the Vienna Convention on the Law of Treaties[37] implies that the ACHR's provisions are to be read in light of the entire building of international law, this including the UNFCCC and the Paris Agreement.

As such, requesting an advisory opinion from the IACtHR on what States' human rights obligations are to mitigate and adapt to climate change did not raise any concern. Therefore, on 9 January 2023, Chile and Colombia submitted a request for an advisory opinion from the IACtHR, seeking clarification regarding what such human rights obligations are in the context of climate change. In light of the subject matter jurisdiction of the IACtHR, the request focused on the obligations stemming from the ACHR and elaborated on a prior opinion from the IACtHR regarding human rights and the marine environment,[38] and the Inter-American Commission on Human Rights (IACmHR)'s

34 American Convention on Human Rights (adopted 22 November 1969, entered into force 18 July 1978) OAS Treaty Series No 36.

35 Charter of the Organization of American States (adopted 39 April 1948, entered into force 13 December 1951) 119 UNTS 3.

36 ACHR, art 64(1). Furthermore, at the request of a member State of the OAS, the IACtHR may provide that State with 'opinions regarding the compatibility of any of its domestic laws with the aforesaid international instruments.' (ibid, art 64(2)).

37 1969 Vienna Convention on the Law of Treaties (adopted 23 May 1969, entered into force 27 January 1980, 1155 UNTS 331, art 31(3)(c).

38 *The Environment and Human Rights (State Obligations in Relation to the Environment in the Context of the Protection and Guarantee of the Rights to Life and to Personal Integrity – Interpretation and Scope of Articles 4(1) and 5(1) of the American Convention on Human*

Resolution No. 3/2021.[39] While in OC-23/17, the IACtHR recognized the existence of a human right to a healthy environment as directly derived from Article 26 ACHR, in Resolution No. 3/2021, the IACmHR fleshed out States' obligations in the context of climate change. The scope of the pending request for an advisory opinion is very broad. It encompasses various legal issues such as obligations on mitigation, adaptation, loss and damage, common but differentiated responsibilities, cooperation among states, procedural matters, the protection of environmental defenders, and climate migration.

At the inception of this request for an advisory opinion from the IACtHR was an initiative by an international organization.[40] Since only member States and some organs of the OAS can lodge a request for an advisory opinion,[41] that organization approached Chile and Colombia, as both States had shown openness and political willingness to pursue such a request for an advisory opinion.[42] For instance, Chile and Colombia have been particularly active in pursuing international environmental goals, with Colombia being the requesting State of the landmark advisory opinion OC-23/17.[43] As Guerreiro Teixeira and Galvão Teles elaborated in Chapter 2, the turn to non-binding advisory opinions is explained by the authoritativeness of the court's pronouncement while avoiding any risk of retaliation or damage to diplomatic relations. But in the case of the request for an opinion lodged before the IACtHR, other factors help explain the turn to opinions: (i) the urgency of the climate situation favors advisory proceedings, which are much faster than contentious proceedings instituted by individuals (which need to go first through the IACmHR);[44] (ii) the need for using 'international tools' to establish a shared understanding of what are States' international obligations concerning climate change; (iii) the broader participation of States and civil society movements in advisory

Rights) Advisory Opinion OC-23/17, Inter-American Court of Human Rights Series A No 23 (15 November 2017).

39 IACmHR, Resolution No 3/2021, Climate Emergency: Scope of the Inter-American Human Rights Obligations' (31 December 2021).

40 According to Tomás Pascual (from the Chilean Ministry of Foreign Affairs), as reported to Maria Antonia Tigre: see n 14, 639.

41 ACHR, art 64(1).

42 Tigre (n 14) 639–640.

43 See also Maria Antonia Tigre, Natalia Urzola and Juan Sebastian Castellanos, *A Request for an Advisory Opinion at the Inter-American Court of Human Rights: Initial Reactions*, Climate Law Blog (Feb. 17, 2023), https://blogs.law.columbia.edu/climatechange/2023/02/17/a-request-for-an-advisory-opinion-at-the-inter-american-court-of-human-rights-initial-reactions/.

44 ACHR, art 44.

proceedings;[45] and finally (iv) the fact that requesting an opinion depends only on the State's Government and does not require any form of intervention of that State's Parliament or a judiciary.[46]

3.3 *The International Court of Justice*

Pursuant to the Charter of the United Nations[47] and the Statute of the ICJ,[48] the ICJ also holds jurisdiction to render advisory opinions. Nonetheless, contrary to what happens with ITLOS or the IACtHR, States are not entitled to request an advisory opinion from the ICJ. In fact, according to Article 96 of the UN Charter, only the General Assembly, the Security Council, or other UN organs or specialized agencies (provided that authorized by the General Assembly and that the question falls within their scope of activities) can lodge a request for an advisory opinion from the ICJ. However, although small island States and other concerned States could not request an advisory opinion from the ICJ on States' obligations regarding climate change, they could still lobby for creating a coalition vote that would secure the approval of such a request in the General Assembly.[49]

Furthermore, also in contrast with ITLOS or the IACtHR, the subject matter jurisdiction of the ICJ is broader since under Article 96 of the UN Charter, the ICJ can render an advisory opinion on any question of (i) international (ii) law (iii) whose interpretation is not an exclusive competence of other international court or tribunal. Accordingly, the ICJ's advisory jurisdiction is delimited negatively by excluding domestic or purely political questions or questions that fall in the exclusive jurisdiction of other international courts or tribunals (as is the case of the interpretation or enforcement of the ACHR). In a request for an advisory opinion, the requirement regarding a 'legal' question needs a few words since climate change mitigation and adaptation action are also political topics – and politically divisive issues. However, being political and legal topics simultaneously does not preclude the ICJ from rendering an advisory opinion on States' obligations regarding climate change. As the ICJ mentioned in the *Nuclear Weapons* opinion, 'The fact that this question also has political aspects, as, in the nature of things, is the case with so many questions which arise in international life, does not suffice to deprive it of its character as a

45 IACtHR Rules of Procedure, art 73.

46 Tigre (n 14) 640–641.

47 Charter of the United Nations (adopted 26 June 1945, entered into force 24 October 1945) 892 UNTS 119, art 96 (*UN Charter*).

48 Statute of the International Court of Justice (Annex to the UN Charter), arts 65–68 (*ICJ Statute*).

49 UN Charter, arts 18 and 96(1).

"legal question" and to "deprive the Court of a competence expressly conferred on it by its Statute".'[50]

With this background in mind, the grassroots movement to request an advisory opinion from the ICJ began in 2019, with an exercise proposed by Professor Justin Rose to law students at the Vanuatu campus of the University of South Pacific.[51]/[52] Already in 2021, Vanuatu announced its intention to fight for the approval, at the UN General Assembly, of a request for an advisory opinion from the ICJ;[53] and one year afterwards, Vanuatu had already secured a coalition at the General Assembly to support its initiative,[54] including the drafting of a resolution with the support also of law firms and advocacy groups.[55] Thus, on 29 November 2022, the core group of States (led by Vanuatu) sent to all UN member States a draft resolution for a request to the ICJ on States' obligations in relation to climate change.[56] On 23 January 2023 (after the requests to ITLOS and the IACtHR had been lodged), the core group sent a revised draft resolution, which incorporated the views from some member States.[57] And finally, on 20 February 2023, a final draft resolution was circulated among UN Member States,[58] and was supported by 18 core States and co-sponsored by more than 120 States[59] (including Antigua and Barbuda, Tuvalu, Chile, and Colombia, being the requesting States in the advisory proceedings before ITLOS and

50 *Legality of the Threat or Use of Nuclear Weapons* (Advisory Opinion) [1996] ICJ Rep 226, §13.

51 Tigre (n 14) 644 ff, where there is a detailed description of the youth movement that is responsible for the advisory opinion requested to the ICJ.

52 However, already in 2011, Palau had suggested for the first time requesting an advisory opinion from the ICJ on the topic of climate change. See UNGA, 16th Plenary Meeting Thursday, 22 September 2011, UN Doc A/66/PV.16 (Sep 22, 2011) available at <https://documents-dds-ny.un.org/doc/UNDOC/GEN/N11/508/71/PDF/N1150871.pdf?OpenElement>.

53 See Bernadette Carreon, 'Vanuatu to Seek International Court Opinion on Climate Change Rights' *The Guardian* (London, 25 September 2021) available at <https://www.theguardian.com/world/2021/sep/26/vanuatu-to-seek-international-court-opinion-on-climate-change-rights>.

54 Amy Gunia, 'Pacific Island Nations Are Bringing Their Climate Justice Fight to the World's Highest Court' Time (New York, 18 July 2022) available at <https://time.com/6197027/pacific-island-nations-vanuatu-climate-change/>.

55 Tigre (n 14) 650–652.

56 First Draft of UN Doc A/77/L.58.

57 Second Draft of UN Doc A/77/L.58.

58 Final Draft of UN Doc A/77/L.58.

59 UN General Assembly, *Request for an Advisory Opinion of the International Court of Justice on the Obligations of States in Respect of Climate Change*, UN Doc A/77/L.58 (1 March 2023) available at <https://documents-dds-ny.un.org/doc/UNDOC/LTD/N23/063/82/PDF/N2306382.pdf>.

the IACtHR). On 29 March 2023, the General Assembly (UNGA) resolution – requesting an advisory opinion from the ICJ on States' obligations in respect of climate change – was adopted by consensus.[60] In this request, the UNGA worked upon the subject matter jurisdiction of the ICJ, and asked the ICJ to pronounce on States' obligations in relation to climate change under the UN Charter, the International Covenant on Civil and Political Rights,[61] the International Covenant on Economic, Social and Cultural Rights,[62] the UNFCCC, the Paris Agreement, UNCLOS, general human rights law (including the non-binding Universal Declaration on Human Rights),[63] and the general principles of environmental law.[64]

4 Book Structure

This volume, *The Role of Advisory Opinions in International Law in the Context of the Climate Crisis*, is designed to provide a comprehensive view of the processes behind the trio of advisory opinion requests, the potential implications of these opinions, and their future impact on international law and climate governance. While two of these advisory opinions are forthcoming, this book's themes were crafted to ensure a timeless relevance. The chosen topics and analyses are structured not to be limited by the content of future advisory opinions, but rather to serve as a foundation upon which these impending opinions – and others that may follow – can build and enrich our understanding of climate law.

The book is organized into three sections, each exploring an essential facet of advisory opinions in shaping international law in response to the climate crisis.

The first section, *Advisory Opinions as Instruments of Climate Governance*, sets the stage by examining the foundational role advisory opinions play in the evolution of international law, particularly within the climate sphere. This section investigates how advisory opinions help clarify State obligations under

60 UNGA Res 77/276 (29 March 2023) UN Doc A/RES/77/276.

61 International Covenant on Civil and Political Rights (adopted 16 December 1966, entered into force 23 March 1976, 999 UNTS 171.

62 International Covenant on Economic, Social and Cultural Rights (adopted 16 December 1966, entered into force 3 January 1976) 993 UNTS 3.

63 UNGA Res 217A (III) (10 December 1948).

64 See also Maria Antonia Tigre and Jorge Alejandro Carrillo Banuelos, *The ICJ's Advisory Opinion on Climate Change: What Happens Now?*, Climate Law Blog (Mar. 29, 2023), https://blogs.law.columbia.edu/climatechange/2023/03/29/the-icjs-advisory-opinion-on-climate-change-what-happens-now/.

various jurisdictions, including the ICJ, ITLOS, IACtHR, and AfCtHPR, offering insights into the unique contributions of each body. By analyzing obligations under the UNFCCC legal framework, UNCLOS, the ACHR, and broader international legal principles, this section underscores the jurisdictional creativity that enables the recognition and enforcement of states' climate responsibilities, emphasizing the essential focus on climate justice in this expanding body of jurisprudence.

The second section, *Voices and Participation in Advisory Opinion Proceedings*, delves into the participatory nature of advisory proceedings, highlighting the roles of critical actors in framing and advancing climate-related obligations. This section explores how narrative tools are utilized within advisory proceedings to address systemic inequities and vulnerabilities, including the voices of states, civil society organizations, and diverse judicial perspectives. The section illustrates how these actors collectively enhance the legitimacy and influence of advisory opinions, helping to bridge the judiciary's role with the broader international community's goals in the fight against climate change.

The third section, *The Lasting Impact of Advisory Opinions*, considers the influence of advisory opinions beyond their immediate legal contexts, analyzing their effects on domestic litigation, national legal frameworks, and the case law of other international bodies. This section provides a forward-looking perspective, examining how advisory opinions can shape the future of international climate governance and impact domestic legal landscapes. By examining both the immediate and potential future impacts, this section underscores the enduring influence of advisory opinions on the evolution of climate governance at multiple levels.

Together, these sections offer a thorough exploration of advisory opinions as a transformative tool for addressing the climate crisis within the framework of international law. By weaving together insights from various perspectives, actors, and jurisdictions, this volume seeks to deepen the understanding of advisory opinions' potential to advance climate justice and promote global accountability. Each section is briefly discussed in the following chapters.

4.1 *Advisory Opinions as Instrument of Climate Governance*

Section I explores how advisory opinions function as tools of climate governance, shaping the development of international law, specifically climate change law, by clarifying States' responsibilities. Rita Guerreiro Teixeira and Patrícia Galvão Teles analyze the potential of advisory opinions for defining States' obligations toward climate action, providing a foundation for international legal standards. Alice Ollino and Irini Papanicolopulu examine the substantive contributions of the advisory opinion from ITLOS and how the

IACtHR and the ICJ could clarify climate-related obligations under international law. Melissa Stewart examines innovative uses of jurisdiction to reinforce these obligations within the pressing context of the climate emergency. Alejandro Carillo Bañuelos and Susan Ann Samuels discuss the collaborative role of various judicial bodies, including the ICJ, ITLOS, IACtHR, and AfCtHPR, in fostering a cohesive legal dialogue on climate issues. Lastly, Dina Lupin and Ruth Nekura focus on the African Human Rights System, emphasizing how civil society actors contribute to advisory proceedings on human rights and climate change, broadening the scope of climate accountability through regional frameworks.

Chapter 2, '*Advisory Opinions and the Development of International Law: an Opportunity for Climate Change Law?*', by Rita Guerreiro Teixeira and Patrícia Galvão Teles, discusses the role of international courts and tribunals in the judicial clarification and development of the international law on climate change. It supports the idea that 'the Court is not a legislative body. Its duty is to apply the law as it finds it, not to make it,'[65] as the ICJ expressly mentioned. In the *Nuclear Weapons* opinion, the ICJ further clarified that the role of courts 'is to engage in its normal judicial function of ascertaining the existence or otherwise of legal principles and rules,' meaning that 'it [only] states the existing law and does not legislate.'[66] However, 'the distinction between author and interpreter [is] more a matter of different aspects of the same process.'[67] In a legal system such as international law, where no centralized lawmaker exists, international courts and tribunals can enhance our understanding of the existing law by clarifying and developing its rules and principles. That is achieved by selecting the relevant facts and laws and eventually interpreting and applying these laws to those facts. In performing these mental operations, judges are not limited to the wording of law: they also carry their worldview and cultural imprint and contribute to flesh out what results from, and is implied in, every rule or legal principle. As a result, courts' contribution to the clarification and development of law is a natural 'collateral effect' of adjudication.[68]

65 *South West Africa (Liberia v South Africa)* (2nd Phase) [1966] ICJ Rep 6, §89.

66 *Legality of the Threat or Use of Nuclear Weapons* (Advisory Opinion) [1996] ICJ Rep 226, §18.

67 Ronald Dworkin, *Law's Empire* (Hart 1998) 229.

68 See, among others, Samantha Besson, 'Legal Philosophical Issues of International Adjudication', in Romano et al (eds), *The Oxford Handbook of International Adjudication* (OUP 2015) 413, 420–426; Armin von Bogdandy & Ingo Venzke, 'Beyond Dispute: International Institutions as Lawmakers (20211) 12 *German Law Journal* 979, 981; or Alan E Boyle & Christine M Chinkin, *The Making of International Law* (OUP 2007) 268.

Still, advisory opinions are not judgments, meaning they lack a binding character. Nonetheless, the authority to clarify and develop the law is rooted in the nature of the institution, not in the (binding) nature of the act. In other words, it results from how that institution is perceived by the players in the international legal system as an authoritative and knowledgeable court or tribunal, so that their findings (ie their clarifications and developments) are perceived as the best interpretation of the existing law. This same idea was entertained by ITLOS, which recognized the authoritativeness of the ICJ's advisory opinions. In the *Dispute concerning Delimitation of the Maritime Boundary between Mauritius and Maldives*,[69] one issue at stake was the non-binding character of the ICJ's advisory opinion on the *Legal Consequences of the Separation of the Chagos Archipelago from Mauritius in 1965*,[70] and namely whether the findings of the ICJ should be binding upon, or at least legally relevant to, ITLOS. In its judgment on the preliminary objections, ITLOS mentioned that although 'it is generally recognized that advisory opinions of the ICJ cannot be considered legally binding,' it still 'entails an authoritative statement of international law.'[71] As such, ITLOS 'finds it necessary to draw a distinction between the binding character and the authoritative nature of an advisory opinion of the ICJ. An advisory opinion is not binding because even the requesting entity is not obligated to comply with it in the same way as parties to contentious proceedings are obligated to comply with a judgment. However, judicial determinations made in advisory opinions carry no less weight and authority than those in judgments because they are made with the same rigour and scrutiny by the "principal judicial organ" of the United Nations with competence in matters of international law.'[72]

In this light, Chapter 2 explores how an advisory opinion rendered by ITLOS, the IACtHR, and the ICJ can contribute to clarifying and developing the international law on climate change, namely by fleshing out States' obligations and the fundamental principles of law relevant to the context of climate change – principles deriving from the UNFCCC legal complex, general international law, the law of the sea, or human rights law. In fact, if they are non-binding, the point of advisory opinions is actually to provide authoritative guidance on complex legal questions, offering clarity on international obligations.

---

69 *Dispute concerning Delimitation of the Maritime Boundary between Mauritius and Maldives in the Indian Ocean* (*Mauritius/Maldives*) (*Preliminary Objections*) (Judgment, 28 January 2021) ITLOS Case No 28 (*Maritime Boundary between Mauritius and Maldives*).

70 *Legal Consequences of the Separation of the Chagos Archipelago from Mauritius in 1965* (Advisory Opinion) [2019] ICJ Rep 95.

71 *Maritime Boundary between Mauritius and Maldives* (n 63) §202.

72 ibid §203.

Chapter 3, '*Climate-Related Obligations under the UNCLOS, the ACHR, and International Law in General*,' by Alice Ollino and Irini Papanicolopulu, discusses in more detail the substantive findings of ITLOS, the IACtHR, and the ICJ. As such, this chapter is not concerned with whether advisory opinions *can* develop international climate law but rather zooms in and focuses on *what are*, or *what can be*, the specific contributions of these international courts and tribunals. To that end, the chapter adopts a regime-based lens to flag the particular rules and principles from each legal regime that are more apt to be clarified or developed by ITLOS, the IACtHR, or the ICJ.

To that end, the chapter works upon the advisory opinion rendered by ITLOS on 21 May 2024.[73] It explores how ITLOS concluded that the emission of GHG and ocean warming fit in the concept of pollution of the marine environment,[74] thus triggering the application of Part XII, and Article 194 specifically, of UNCLOS. According to this provision, States bear the obligation to prevent, reduce, and control pollution of the marine environment, which can be qualified as a due diligence obligation,[75] ie an obligation of conduct whose performance can be assessed objectively by international law and which is subject to international judicial oversight. This obligation applies to the whole typology of sources of marine pollution, including land-based and vessel-sourced pollution. Moreover, Chapter 3 also analyzes how ITLOS interpreted the duty to protect, preserve, and ameliorate the marine environment in the context of climate change – an obligation that can be key in building coastal resilience and adapting to certain marine climate change-related impacts.

Although Chapter 3 was written before the IACtHR's and the ICJ's advisory opinions, it still explores the potential outcome of these opinions in human rights law and general international law (including environmental law and the UNFCCC legal complex). More particularly, Chapter 3 explores the potential use of 'positive obligations' to protect and secure the human rights of individuals in light of the deleterious effects of climate change. In fact, it is easy to frame climate change as a human rights issue, considering the pervasive consequences of climate change-related impacts on the effective enjoyment of human rights. The ECtHR highlighted this same idea in *Verein KlimaSeniorinnen Schweiz and Others v Switzerland*.[76] In this chapter, Ollino and Papanicolopulu explain what

73 *Request for an Advisory Opinion submitted by the Commission of Small Island States on Climate Change and International Law* (Advisory Opinion, 21 May 2024) ITLOS Case No 31 (*COSIS Opinion*).

74 Article 1(1)(4) of UNCLOS.

75 *COSIS Opinion* (n 69) §198.

76 *Verein KlimaSeniorinnen Schweiz and Others v Switzerland* (App No 53600/20) ECtHR [GC] 9 April 2024.

human rights are more likely to be mobilized in the advisory opinions (even though the full gamut of human rights may be affected by climate change-related effects), as well as what positive obligations promoting adaptation or mitigation can be flagged explicitly by the IACtHR or the ICJ on their opinions. To that end, Chapter 3 relies heavily on the case law of the ECtHR, the IACtHR, and UN treaty-based bodies to show a surprising coherence line among these bodies.[77] Furthermore, Chapter 3 explores in detail the obligations that stem from the principles of prevention of transboundary environmental harm and cooperation, as well as the obligations to mitigate and reduce GHG emissions that stem from the UNFCCC and the Paris Agreement.

Chapter 4, *'Jurisdictional Ingenuity in Pursuit of Promoting States' Obligations in the Context of the Climate Emergency,'* by Melissa Stewart, explains how international courts' and tribunals' jurisdiction (personal and subject matter) can be (and was) used strategically to pursuit climate justice through advisory opinions. It starts from Articles 14 of the UNFCCC and 24 of the Paris Agreement to highlight the limited potential use of these provisions and, thus, the limited potential for a State-to-State dispute settlement regarding climate change obligations. Thus, Chapter 4 explores the potential of 'jurisdictional ingenuity,' which means the pursuit of alternative jurisdictional avenues when direct means of dispute settlement are not available or are difficult to use. In particular, Stewart assesses how States have created a new international organization with the sole purpose of conferring advisory jurisdiction upon an existing tribunal and requesting an opinion from it, by resorting to diplomatic tools to secure a request for an advisory opinion that before was considered politically unrealistic; and by framing legal questions in a wording that may induce international courts and tribunals to open new avenues for future dispute settlement. In this regard, ITLOS's words cannot pass unnoticed when it stated that 'Article 2, paragraph 2, of the COSIS Agreement authorizes the Commission to request advisory *opinions* from the Tribunal.'[78] The use of the plural suggests ITLOS took the opportunity not only to clarify its advisory jurisdiction under the COSIS Agreement but also, and mostly, to highlight that it is open to receiving other requests for advisory opinions in the future.

Stewart highlights a design flaw and a design choice of international law. The shortcomings of international dispute settlement, namely in the realms of climate change and environmental law, result from an explicit and conscious

77 Concluding for the alignment, see also Armando Rocha & Rômulo Sampaio, 'Climate Change before the European and the Inter-American Court of Human Rights: Comparing Possible Avenues before Human Rights Bodies' (2023) 32(2) *RECIEL* 279.

78 *COSIS Opinion* (n 69) §141.

choice of States unwilling to discuss the interpretation and enforcement of climate and environmental agreements before a court of law. However, the lack of enforcement mechanisms under such treaties – or the lack of consent to jurisdiction, as under Article 14 of the UNFCCC and Article 24 of the Paris Agreement – does not necessarily mean that climate change is doomed to stay outside the courtroom. Cross-regime interaction and an ingenious understanding of the advisory jurisdiction of international courts and tribunals helped bring climate change into the docket of ITLOS, the IACtHR, and the ICJ – and may be used in the future for pursuing other alternative avenues of access to international courts and tribunals. The silver lining here is that the system may be flawed. Still, creativity and ingeniousness may be enough to bring climate change-related matters into the docket of international courts and tribunals.

Chapter 5, '*The Dialogue between the ICJ, the ITLOS, the IACtHR and the African Court*', by Susan Ann Samuels and Alejandro Carillo Bañuellos, examines the unique moment in climate litigation represented by the current surge in requests for advisory opinions from international courts and tribunals. It begins by analyzing the significance of having four major courts – the ICJ, ITLOS, IACtHR, and potentially the AfrCtHPR – involved in shaping legal obligations related to climate change through advisory opinions (hand in hand with the rulings already issued by the ECtHR). Each court operates within specific jurisdictional boundaries, covering areas such as international law, human rights, and the law of the sea. The chapter emphasizes how the diverse subject matter scopes of these courts and tribunals allow for a comprehensive interpretation of climate change-related obligations, reflecting both the fragmented yet interconnected nature of climate governance.

Specifically, Chapter 5 delves into the notion of judicial dialogue, exploring how ITLOS, the IACtHR, and the ICJ may interact formally and informally to create a more cohesive approach to international climate law. A comparative analysis of the advisory proceedings invites a discussion of how the courts and tribunals may share principles like due diligence, prevention, and obligations toward vulnerable groups affected by climate change. This dialogue can help bridge jurisdictional gaps and foster consistency across their opinions, encouraging a unified global response to the climate crisis. However, Chapter 5 also considers the practical limits of cross-institutional dialogue, addressing factors that may restrict or enable collaboration. For instance, it assesses how jurisdictional mandates, the range of participants, and the specific questions posed in each advisory opinion shape the extent of this interaction. By investigating these dynamics, the chapter underscores the potential and challenges of achieving coherent and impactful advisory opinions across different judicial regimes, ultimately aiming for a more integrated legal response to climate change.

Chapter 6, *'An Advisory Opinion on Human Rights and Climate Change in the African Regional Human Rights System,'* by Dina Lupin and Ruth Nekura, examines why the African human rights system is well-suited for an advisory opinion on States' human rights obligations in the face of climate change, highlighting two main factors: the severe impact of climate change on Africa's vulnerable populations and the progressive, cooperative framework of the African Charter on Human and Peoples' Rights.[79] Although Africa contributes minimally to global emissions, it faces severe threats from climate change affecting its development, food security, and human rights. The continent is particularly vulnerable to the impacts of climate change.

However, it also possesses a rich and diverse set of legal, policy, and regulatory mechanisms that could be instrumental in addressing climate-related harms and protecting human rights. For example, the African Charter recognizes an individual and collective (i) right to a satisfactory environment and (ii) economic, social, and cultural development (both of which have been recognized as creating climate change-related obligations for States. The Kampala Convention[80] recognizes climate change as a driver of internal displacement, and the AfCHR has recognized both States and corporate entities as duty bearers with respect to human rights obligations.

Lupin and Nekura, therefore, briefly introduce the African Human Rights System through its 'intricate framework of norms and institutions,' ie the African Commission on Human and Peoples' Rights (AfCmHPR), the African Committee of Experts on the Rights and Welfare of the Child, and the African Court on Human and Peoples' Rights (AfCtHPR). At the subregional level, they note the Economic Community for West African States (ECOWAS)'s Community Court of Justice (ECCJ) and the East African Community's Court of Justice (EACJ). While there haven't been any climate cases yet, a few examples of environmental and rights-based cases have been adjudicated before the AfCmHPR, the AfCtHPR, and the ECOWAS court, paving the way for climate cases.

Despite a progressive system, Lupin and Nekura observe that African States continue to engage in carbon-intensive and extractive activities. These actions are often linked to human rights violations, mass displacement, and violent conflicts with Indigenous and traditional communities. Furthermore, these States have not adequately addressed the impacts of climate change on

79 African Charter on Human and Peoples' Rights (adopted 27 June 1981, entered into force 21 October 1986) 1520 UNTS 217 (*African Charter*).

80 African Union Convention for the Protection and Assistance of Internally Displaced Persons (adopted 23 October 2009, entered into force 6 December 2012) 3014 UNTS 3.

human rights or made efforts to alleviate existing vulnerabilities, which would help make communities more resilient to climate change.

Within this context, Lupin and Nekura highlight the complex interplay of (i) promising laws and policies and (ii) vulnerable and impoverished communities, which highlights a significant gap in the efforts of states to address human rights threats adequately. This situation underscores the potential value of an advisory opinion from the AfCtHPR that clarifies the human rights responsibilities of States concerning climate change. Further, the AfCmHPR, the ECCJ, and the EACJ also have (underutilized) advisory jurisdiction, which could be leveraged for such an opinion on climate change-related responsibilities. The main problem is that standing to request advisory opinions in these mechanisms lies restrictively with duty bearers in the context of treaty obligations, ie member States or Council of Ministers, which may be reluctant to ask for further clarity in their obligations.

The AfCtHPR is the only international court that allows NGOs to request advisory opinions, in addition to the African Union (AU), all AU members (not only the ones that have ratified the AfCtHPR's Protocol), and AU organs. Still, the AfCtHPR's restrictive stance on standing provisions limits access for the most affected communities and civil society actors. Indeed, the authors note that the AfCtHPR's interpretation of 'African organizations recognized by the AU' has caused ambiguity and confusion, limiting the extent to which NGOs and civil society can access the AfCtHPR's advisory jurisdiction. Therefore, Lupin and Nekura argue that the urgency of climate change presents an opportunity for the Court to reconsider its approach to standing, potentially making it a more accessible institution. An advisory opinion on climate change, could, according to the authors, clarify crucial topics such as (i) mitigation of GHG emissions by carbon-intensive economies, (ii) procedural environmental rights that could further enable climate litigation, (iii) integration of rights-based standards into regional agreements and climate policies, (iv) climate refugees, (v) environmental rights of children, (vi) rights of Indigenous people, (vii) setting precedents for the expansion of climate litigation in domestic jurisdictions.

4.2 *Voices and Participation in Advisory Opinion Proceedings*

Section II delves into the voices that have guided and influenced the advisory opinions. Antoine De Spiegeleir delves into storytelling as a tool used by actors involved in the advisory opinions. Miriam Cohen provides a broad overview of participation and how the different actors have engaged with the judiciary. Austyn Campbell, Claire Robertson & Eran Sthoeger focus on the role of States in advisory opinions, while Harjeevan S. Narulla & Rohan Nanthakumar concentrate on the role of civil society.

Chapter 7, *'Storytelling in Advisory Proceedings on Climate Change,'* by Antoine De Spiegeleir, adopts a narrative-based perspective to explore the role of storytelling in climate change advisory opinions. This novel perspective draws attention not only to the legal substance of advisory opinion proceedings but also to their narrative makeup. The chapter argues that climate change proceedings, like all judicial processes, depend on the stories that legal actors construct and tell each other. Since storytelling has been demonstrated to shape public and institutional attitudes toward climate policy, it is paramount to understand better the narrative strategies used in climate change litigation.

De Spiegeleir paves the way for such an understanding by clarifying the links between climate change, storytelling, and international adjudication, as well as exploring international courts' multifaceted audiences and the role of other forms of judicial communications beyond judgments and advisory opinions. De Spiegeleir notably uses the examples of the amicus curiae brief submitted by the Avaaz Foundation to the IACtHR and the opening oral pleadings made by representatives of small island states before ITLOS. These examples illustrate how international courts function both as storytellers and as forums for others to tell stories. Ultimately, Chapter 7 provides a foundation for future research on the interplay between law, narrative, and climate change, underscoring the power of stories in the realm of international adjudication.

In Chapter 8, *'Participation in Climate Change Advisory Proceedings: Bridging the Gap between the Judiciary and the International Community,'* Miriam Cohen investigates the rules of participation governing the three international courts. Given the significance of the climate crisis and the strong role that civil society organizations have played in climate litigation more broadly, Cohen questions whether these procedural distinctions can limit the variety of arguments put before the courts, and therefore directly influence the outcome of the advisory opinions. As such, Cohen argues for a broader participation in advisory proceedings in fostering climate justice while also garnering their 'sociological legitimacy' and implementation.

Drawing on a wide array of international and regional treaties, as well as on principles of participatory democracy and participatory justice theory, Cohen emphasizes the importance of the active involvement of communities, Indigenous groups, NGOs, and other stakeholders in shaping policies, strategies, and adaptation/mitigation measures, including through advisory proceedings. Nonetheless, she notes that '[i]ssues such as power imbalances, representation, and the need for capacity-building' represent limitations.'[81] This became clear for small island developing States, for example, that had never before participated in any proceedings at the ICJ.

Advocates, therefore, organized 'writeshops' in Africa, the Caribbean, and the Pacific to encourage active participation of governments in these regions. These were held through a collaborative effort of governments, youth, and civil society organizations and in partnership with the African Union Commission, CariCom, and the Pacific Community, respectively.[82] These initiatives are intended to level the playing field and ensure that countries that have never before participated in ICJ proceedings have a chance to do so. This initiative, alongside a broad social media campaign and diplomacy work at the United Nations, helped garner unprecedented participation in the ICJ advisory opinion. For the first round, with the deadline of 22 March 2024, the ICJ received a record of 91 written statements.

More particularly, the ICJ received statements from 76 States, with five Scandinavian States (Denmark, Finland, Iceland, Norway, and Sweden) making a joint submission. Additionally, 14 European States participated.[83] Of these European submissions, five came from the Eastern European Group.[84] There were also submissions from 13 African States,[85] 21 from the Americas (19 from the Group of Latin American and Caribbean States (GRULAC),[86] along with the United States and Canada), and 31 from the Asia/Pacific region. This Asia/Pacific group includes 11 South Pacific nations,[87] three countries from the Gulf Cooperation Council (GCC),[88] as well as Australia and New Zealand.[89]

---

81 Miriam Cohen, Chapter 8, 207.

82 Available at <https://www.sprep.org/news/work-to-seek-an-advisory-opinion-on-climate-change-from-the-icj-hailed-as-a-success-story-of-collaboration>.

83 France, Germany, Netherlands, Liechtenstein, Portugal, Spain, Switzerland, and the United Kingdom.

84 Albania, Latvia, Romania, Russian Federation, and Slovenia.

85 Burkina Faso, Cameroon, Democratic Republic of Congo, Egypt, The Gambia, Ghana, Kenya, Madagascar, Mauritius, Namibia, Seychelles, Sierra Leone, and South Africa.

86 Antigua and Barbuda, Argentina, Bahamas, Barbados, Belize, Brazil, Chile, Colombia, Costa Rica, Dominican Republic, Ecuador, El Salvador, Grenada, Mexico, Peru, Bolivia, Saint Lucia, Saint Vincent & the Grenadines, and Uruguay.

87 Cook Islands, Federal States of Micronesia, Kiribati, Marshall Islands, Nauru, Palau, Samoa, Solomon Islands, Tuvalu, Tonga, Vanuatu.

88 Kuwait, Saudi Arabia, United Arab Emirates.

89 Remaining states include: Bangladesh, China, India, Indonesia, Islamic Republic of Iran, Japan, Nepal, Pakistan, Philippines, Timor Leste, Thailand, Republic of Korea, Singapore, Sri Lanka, Viet Nam.

Among those who submitted written statements, 12 were organizations.[90] The ICJ received submissions from the African Union, AOSIS, COSIS, the European Union, IUCN, Melanesian Spearhead Group, Organisation of African, Caribbean and Pacific States, Organisation of the Petroleum Exporting States, Pacific Islands Forum, Pacific Islands Forum Fisheries Agency, Parties to the Nauru Agreement Office, and the World Health Organisation.

Written comments in response to the original submissions were due in August 2024.[91] There were 62 submissions, 8 from organizations and 54 from States. Among the states that submitted written statements, ten were from Africa[92] and 21 from the Asia-Pacific region. The Asia-Pacific group included 12 South Pacific nations,[93] one Gulf Cooperation Council (GCC) member,[94] as well as Australia and New Zealand.[95] From the Americas, 17 states participated, with 16 submissions coming from the GRULAC[96] and one from the United States. Europe had a total of six submissions, with only two states representing Eastern Europe.[97]

The ICJ hearings are scheduled for December 2024. At the time of this writing, 100 oral statements were scheduled, 88 from States (including a joint statement from five Nordic States) and 12 statements from international organizations. Participation in the oral hearings has surged compared to the written phase, with several new states and organizations joining. Notably, 14 new states and one organization that had not joined the written phase have participated in the oral phase, including Côte d'Ivoire, Malawi, Maldives, Senegal, Sudan, and Zambia from Africa; Dominica, Guatemala, Jamaica, and Panama from the Americas; and Fiji, Myanmar, Palestine, and Syria from the Asia-Pacific region. Additionally, the Pacific Community has joined the hearings as a new organizational participant. Meanwhile, some previous contributors, including the Democratic Republic of Congo (DRC), Madagascar, and Argentina, as well as the Parties to the Nauru Agreement Office, opted not to participate

---

90 AOSIS, the Organisation of the Petroleum Exporting Countries, the Pacific Islands Forum Fisheries Agency and the World Health Organisation did not file statements.

91 https://www.icj-cij.org/sites/default/files/case-related/187/187-20240816-pre-01-00-en.pdf.

92 From the ones listed above, Ghana, Madagascar, and South Africa did not file statements.

93 From the ones listed above, Tonga did not file statements.

94 From the ones listed above, Kuwait and United Arab Emirates did not file statements.

95 Remaining states that did not file statements on this round include: China, India, Indonesia, Nepal, Thailand, Republic of Korea, Singapore.

96 From the ones listed above, Argentina, Bolivia, and Peru did not file statements.

97 From Eastern Europe, Russian Federation and Slovenia did not file statements. In addition, Germany, Liechtenstein, Portugal, Spain, Romania, and the five Nordern countries, Denmark, Finland, Iceland, Norway and Sweden, did not file statements.

in the oral phase. The regional breakdown of oral participation now includes 17 states from Africa, 33 from Asia-Pacific, 24 from the Americas, and 14 from Europe (with one joint submission from the five Nordic countries), alongside 12 organizations.

The IACtHR's advisory opinion received a record number of 255 written observations from 600 entities. The majority of submissions came from NGOs, totaling 76 submissions, followed by academic institutions with 71 submissions. Other notable contributors include individual members of civil society, with 44 contributions; communities, directly or together with NGOs, with 16 submissions; and States, which provided nine submissions.[98] Additionally, there were four submissions from Organs of the Organization of American States (OAS), 13 from international organs and bodies, 11 from NGOs collaborating with civil society or academic institutions, 10 from State bodies, and one from corporate actors.[99] The IACtHR held seven days of public hearings, with 176 participants (3 days in Barbados and four days in Brazil). Cohen notes that this large and diverse participation points to a strong connection between the international community and the judiciary, which will be able to benefit from the arguments in the multiple submissions.[100]

From 11 to 25 September 2023, the 21 Members of the ITLOS heard oral arguments from 35 States and three international organizations, which included a handful of States outside the 34 States and nine international organizations that filed written statements.

Chapter 9, '*The Role of States in the Requests for Advisory Opinions*,' by Austyn Campbell, Claire Robertson and Eran Sthoeger, discusses the participation of States in advisory proceedings from three different lenses: initiation, litigation, and implementation.[101] It examines the incentives that drive State participation, smaller nations' strategic use of advisory opinions, and the legal and political implications of States' contributions to these processes. The analysis begins by looking at States' deep interest in participating in advisory proceedings, particularly concerning climate governance and ongoing COP negotiations under the Paris Agreement. As the global legal landscape shifts in response to climate change, State involvement in such proceedings is increasingly critical to shaping international environmental law and policy.

98 Nine States submitted written observations to the IACtHR, namely: Costa Rica; Vanuatu; Barbados; Paraguay; Colombia;Chile; El Salvador; Brazil, and Mexico.

99 https://scholarship.law.columbia.edu/cgi/viewcontent.cgi?article=1222&context=sabin_climate_change.

100 Miriam Cohen, Chapter 8.

101 Chapter 9, Campbell et al.

A key theme in the chapter is the examination of the incentives that encourage State engagement in these advisory processes. Understanding the motivations behind States' participation sheds light on the complex dynamics in international legal consultations. States are often driven by the opportunity to influence legal outcomes, advance specific policy goals, and assert their positions within global governance frameworks. These incentives are crucial for understanding why States actively seek to shape advisory opinions and engage in deliberations. For example, they note that the increased use of advisory opinions related to this theme suggests a desire for a 'top-down approach,' in which States' climate obligations under international law are clarified.

The chapter also delves into the strategic use of advisory opinions by SIDS, which have utilized these legal tools to counterbalance the influence of more powerful nations. By leveraging advisory opinions, these States have managed to elevate their political and policy objectives on the global stage. Campbell, Robertson, and Sthoeger note that while SIDS and LDCs are often sidelined in international negotiations, the advisory opinions have provided them with an opportunity to challenge the *status quo*, and push for international climate action where other methods have failed. Therefore, they highlight how advisory opinions serve not only as legal instruments but also as powerful diplomatic tools in international relations. This manifests, for example, in how the States involved have drafted the requests (ie from consensus, such as how it was done in the ICJ proceedings, or by a smaller number of States, as was done in the ITLOS and IACtHR advisory proceedings).

In 'litigating' the advisory opinions, the authors discuss the role of States in (i) influencing procedural aspects, (ii) collaborating to focus the court or tribunal's attention on certain key issues, and (iii) the number and diversity of State representation. First, States have influenced the advisory opinions by requesting extensions of the originally set deadlines for submitting written statements. This procedural flexibility has allowed the wide range of participation noted above. Second, collaboration during the proceedings is crucial to ensure that critical areas of focus are covered in the advisory opinions ultimately published by the courts. For example, during the ITLOS oral proceedings, countries referenced other submissions, either by challenging them or showing the tribunal their similar interpretation of the law. This is especially important when the wording of the request is fairly open. Campbell, Robertson, and Sthoeger note that '[t]he Tribunal's explicit acknowledgment of the specific arguments advanced by States and international organizations demonstrates the role States play in shaping the findings of an advisory opinion,' and that '[t]his all demonstrates that advisory opinions can help to create sovereign equality through neutralizing "any power differences that may exist outside the courtroom".'[102] Third, the (impressive) number and diversity of States participating in the advisory proceedings (and in different stages) is crucial to reflect the universal impacts of climate change. The authors note the differences in rules of participation at the ICJ and ITLOS proceedings, and how these can bar smaller States from participation.

The chapter then discusses the role of States in the implementation of advisory opinions through a comparative analysis of the legal language used in other advisory opinions and recent climate-related proceedings before ITLOS and the ICJ. This analysis illuminates key similarities and differences in the way legal arguments are framed, providing insights into the evolving nature of environmental legal discourse.

Chapter 10, '*The Role of Civil Society in the Climate Change Advisory Proceedings*,' by Harjeevan Narulla & Rohan Nanthakumar, shifts our attention to the role of civil society, discussing the 'complex and shifting role' these stakeholders have played in the proceedings. The authors understand the concept of civil society to broadly include, environmental non-governmental organizations (NGOs), climate change activists and lawyers, scholars and academic or other research institutions, philanthropic funders, re-granters, Transnational Advocacy Networks (TANs), and specific cohorts or groups, in particular 'the Youth' and Indigenous peoples and communities.

The chapter first goes over the procedural rules of the three courts, ICJ, ITLOS, and IACtHR, discussing how civil society can participate in advisory proceedings. These resulted in no official participation of civil society in the ICJ advisory opinion and 10 civil society written statements on behalf of 13 civil society actors at ITLOS (with no opportunity for oral submissions). As noted, the IACtHR received written submissions from over 300 parties. Uniquely, civil society was also allowed – and encouraged – to make oral statements at the three hearings held in Barbados, and Brasília and Manaus in Brazil. These ranged from Global North and climate-focused organizations to Indigenous groups, Afro-descendant groups, and individuals, and organizations representing other vulnerable communities directly affected by climate change.

The analysis of civil society participation allows for five key conclusions from the authors regarding the role of civil society in climate litigation and its involvement in the climate change advisory proceedings. First, civil society is identified as a highly active participant in climate litigation. Through advocacy, legal action, and grassroots mobilization, civil society organizations have become a driving force in holding governments and corporations accountable

102 Chapter 9, Campbell et al.

for environmental harm. Their role extends beyond the courtroom, influencing public discourse and shaping the development of legal principles related to climate justice.

Second, the chapter highlights civil society's essential and strategic role in catalyzing the initiation of climate change advisory proceedings, and, therefore, in the development of international law. By pushing for these proceedings, civil society groups have played a pivotal role in bringing climate issues to the attention of international tribunals, demonstrating their capacity to influence global environmental governance. Their advocacy has been instrumental in ensuring that climate-related legal questions are addressed at the highest levels.

Third, despite formal technical and procedural limitations, civil society has found innovative ways to contribute directly and indirectly to the climate change advisory proceedings. Even when unable to formally participate as part of the case files, civil society groups have employed various strategies – such as providing amicus briefs, mobilizing public support, and influencing diplomatic channels – to make their voices heard. This highlights the resourcefulness of civil society in navigating complex legal processes and shaping outcomes. This participation is crucial because civil society submissions are often 'less constrained,' broader and bolder, often reflecting the perspectives of vulnerable groups disproportionately affected by climate change. As subject matter experts, civil society has developed briefs and resources that have facilitated knowledge sharing and broader participation among other actors, or organized events that facilitated conversations on legal arguments that would be at the core of the questions asked.[103] In this respect, the authors further note that 'It is also reasonable to assume that the vast collective corpus of publicly available legal submissions made before the IACtHR in particular, but also ITLOS and the ICJ, will inform and catalyse future climate litigation at the international, regional and domestic level.'[104] Furthermore, civil society has further campaigned, advocated, and raised awareness in climate cases and beyond.

103 See Katelyn Horne, Maria A Tigre & Michael B Gerrard, *Status Report on Principles of International and Human Rights Law Relevant to Climate Change* (Sabin Center for Climate Change Law 2023). Available at: https://scholarship.law.columbia.edu/faculty_scholarship/3924; Julia Neusner and Ama Francis, *Public Health and Human Health Implications of Climate Mobility*, June 2024. Available at: https://scholarship.law.columbia.edu/sabin_climate_change/227; Jessica Wentz, *Climate Change and Human Health: A Synthesis of Scientific Research and State Obligations Under International Law*, available at https://scholarship.law.columbia.edu/sabin_climate_change/223/ (May 2024).

104 Chapter 11, Narulla and Nanthakumar.

The fourth conclusion underscores civil society's ongoing role in championing the implementation of advisory opinions once they have been issued. These groups are well-positioned to advocate for the enforcement of international legal norms at the national and international levels. By pressuring governments and other actors to comply with advisory opinions, civil society can help translate abstract legal principles into concrete environmental protections.

Lastly, the chapter emphasizes that civil society will integrate advisory opinions into their broader climate litigation strategies. By using these opinions as legal precedents or persuasive authority in national courts and international forums, civil society can extend the impact of advisory opinions far beyond their immediate legal context. This strategic use of advisory opinions can amplify their influence, helping to clarify international law for states and driving long-term changes in environmental governance. Through these observations, the chapter illustrates the indispensable role that civil society plays in advancing climate justice and shaping the future of international environmental law.

4.3 *The Lasting Impact of Advisory Opinions: Domestic Dimensions*

Section IV begins to investigate what might happen after the advisory opinions have been published, discussing their long-lasting effects as the conclusions set forth are followed or replicated at the domestic level or across other international or regional adjudicatory bodies. Lea Main-Klingst and Sophie Marjanac examine how advisory opinions shape the jurisprudence of courts at the international, regional, and domestic levels, illustrating their broad legal and political impact on the development of climate-related legal norms and showing how these opinions serve as influential interpretative tools across jurisdictions, ultimately contributing to the evolution of international climate governance.

Gastón Medici-Colombo and Armando Rocha investigate how international advisory opinions subtly shape domestic legal frameworks despite their non-binding nature, analyzing how these opinions influence state practices through interpretative guidance on treaty obligations that may prompt legislative adjustments.

The confluence of the trio of requests, as noted by Main-Klingst and Marjanac, despite the advent of the Paris Agreement and the significant attendance at annual COPs, shows an acknowledgment that 'general international law (with relevant human rights and marine protection obligations) has an important role to play' in advancing global climate action and responding to the climate crisis.[105] But which role is this?

105 Main-Klingst and Marjanac, Chapter 12, 278.

In Chapter 11, '*The Downstream Impact of Advisory Opinions in the Case Law of Other International Bodies and Domestic Litigation*,' Lea Main-Klingst and Sophie Marjanac explore how different advisory opinions influence the jurisprudence of various courts, including international, regional, and domestic bodies, through a series of examples that illustrate the broad and lasting legal and political impact of AOs on the development of legal norms. The 'downstream impact' of advisory opinions on the case law of international bodies and domestic litigation can be substantial, though it varies significantly across jurisdictions. Advisory opinions are often used as interpretative tools by other courts and tribunals, with opinions from the ICJ generally seen as the most authoritative.

Main-Klingst and Marjanac argue that the advisory opinions will have 'legal implications across the globe.'[106] This includes 'influence, interpretation and application in other courts at national, regional, and international level,' which could likely be context specific.[107] The downstream impact of advisory opinions is essential for three reasons. First, the breadth, reach, and scope of the climate crisis makes these advisory opinions potentially more influential than previous advisory opinions. In particular, this significance relies on the new and insufficient legal responses to climate change, and its 'cross-pollination' and 'influence' across jurisdictions. Second, with scientific evidence of the growing impact of climate change on communities worldwide, these advisory opinions will guide answers on 'a range of (emerging) issues.' Third, the ever increasing demand for advisory opinions and dispute settlements from international courts and tribunals shows that they remain 'the seminal interpretants of international norms.' As such, they argue, their impact extends far beyond the limits of 'enforceability' or their 'binding character.' Indeed, they are 'authorative statements' on the law, contributing to shaping and advancing the international legal order, carrying normative force, formulating 'shared or community expectations,' ultimately contributing to preventing future disputes.

For example, advisory opinions from the ICJ have 'provided conclusive statements on customary international law, interpreted and clarified treaty provisions, made pronouncements on the law in the absence of a generally agreed rule,'[108] have furthered the public discourse, led to the creation of new UN bodies, have led to General Assembly resolutions in cases on non-compliance, and guided action at the EU level. This role is even strengthened

106 ibid, 279.
107 ibid, 279.
108 ibid, 281.

for the IACtHR, which has clarified that domestic courts consider not only the ACHR but also the interpretation by the IACtHR, when applying an international treaty.

Main-Klingst and Marjanac further explore overlapping themes in the trio of advisory opinions, discussing the risk of fragmentation in international environmental law, as well as their impact on domestic litigation. For example, the question of overlapping legal regimes arise as the three AOs seek to interpret the UNFCCC and the Paris Agreement within their respective legal regimes, ie international law more broadly (ICJ), UNCLOS (ITLOS) and ACHR (IACtHR). Significantly, ITLOS has clarified that separate regimes (ie UNCLOS and the Paris Agreement) could lead to different legal obligations related to climate change.[109] Furthermore, the ECtHR also applied the ECHR to climate harms in *KlimaSeniorinnen*.[110]

With respect to the questions asked, Main-Klingst and Marjanac highlight a few themes that may draw (similar or different) answers from the international courts, such as the issue of the common but differentiated responsibilities and respective capabilities (CBDR-RC) principle and burden-sharing necessary to achieve the temperature limit of the Paris Agreement, the role of scientific evidence in informing the obligations of States, States' obligations of due diligence, States' obligations to vulnerable countries and communities (such as children and future generations, Indigenous peoples, and women).

The concept of 'cross-fertilization' – where AOs influence regional human rights courts such as the European Court of Human Rights (ECtHR) – is explored in detail, especially in terms of how these courts translate advisory findings into binding judgments. Drawing on examples from other areas of international law, the authors show a pattern of cross-fertilization, further arguing that, given the novelty of the matter and its limited jurisprudence at the international level, cross-pollination is expected.

The authors then discuss the influence of advisory opinions in domestic climate litigation, contraposing examples in monist and dualist jurisdictions. In particular, the authors argue that advisory opinions can significantly influence systemic mitigation or framework cases when the jurisdiction has adopted a framework climate law or has otherwise a human rights legal framework that can be applied to climate action. Furthermore, the authors discuss how the

109 *Request for an Advisory Opinion Submitted by the Commission of Small Island States on Climate Change and International Law*, Case No. 31, International Tribunal for the Law of the Sea (21 May 2024) (COSIS Opinion), paras. 223–224.

110 *Verein KlimaSeniorinnen Schweiz and Others v Switzerland* App no. 53600/20 (ECtHR 9 April 2024).

ITLOS advisory opinion, for example, has already influenced international environmental law governing EIAs with respect to GHG emissions. These impacts go beyond affecting States directly; they also incorporate obligations to corporations as the requirements from ITLOS' advisory opinion are implemented at the national level through forthcoming regulation. These deliberations on AOs' influence on international climate governance will remain a central focus for future legal developments.

Chapter 12, '*The Impact on Domestic Law of Climate Change-Related Advisory Opinions: the Experience of the IACtHR and the ITLOS*,' by Gastón Medici-Colombo and Armando Rocha, explores the intricate relationship between international advisory opinions and their impact on domestic legal systems. The research question for this chapter seems odd at first sight since non-binding advisory opinions do not require specific enforcement for any State or party to the proceedings (if one may use the word 'party' in advisory proceedings). In other words, advisory opinions do not have an operative part or require any immediate State's action or omission. However, when an international court or tribunal clarifies and develops the law, its findings may entail a different reading of a State's international obligation, which, in turn, may imply a change in a State's domestic legislation to comply with that obligation. Yet, precisely because advisory opinions do not have a *dictum*, their impact on a State's domestic law is more difficult to detect, since changes in the domestic legislation resulting from an advisory opinion rendered by an international court or tribunal are often unacknowledged.

The chapter poses key questions on the challenges of incorporating these opinions into domestic law, underscoring the importance and limitations of advisory opinions in influencing state practices and legal frameworks. Key to their argument is the value of advisory opinions as interpretative tools of international treaties, which require an 'evolutionary reading to withstand the passage of time.'[111] In truth, they argue, these clarifications of States' obligations 'impact the fabric of international law.' Therefore, in their analysis, Medici-Colombo and Rocha researched and analyzed evidence of States' actions or inactions after an international court or tribunal rendered an advisory opinion.

Firstly, the authors discuss how international courts and tribunals interpret and clarify existing legal frameworks rather than creating new legal obligations or imposing duties on States. By doing so, these courts and tribunals are instrumental in revealing distinct aspects of international law, such as customary norms, while focusing on existing legal principles. As such, advisory opinions

111 Medici-Colombo & Rocha, Chapter 13, 307.

are positioned as a crucial tool for legal clarity, even if their findings are not binding. In the framework of the IACtHR, for example, advisory opinions are considered legally binding or quasi-binding given that they must be followed 'as part of the controlling legal substance in the exercise of conventionality control.'[112]

However, the more complex challenge lies in examining the domestic impact of these advisory opinions. The chapter delves into the complexities surrounding how States incorporate advisory opinions into their domestic legal systems, more often informally and without explicit acknowledgment. In the ACHR system, the practice of domestic courts varies depending on the constitutional order of each country, with a majority of States favoring this (quasi-)binding nature of IACtHR's case law, including advisory opinions. For the climate change advisory opinion, the foreseeable impact can be substantial, depending on how detailed the opinion is and how comprehensive the responses to all the questions posed to the court are. Based on the IACtHR's progressive interpretation of environmental law and rights as applied to the inter-American system,[113] it is likely that the impact will be 'disruptive' and reinforced in domestic climate litigation.[114]

The ITLOS has limited evidence of the impact of advisory opinions on the domestic legal framework. However, the advisory opinion on climate change recognized an obligation to adopt a national regulatory framework to reduce GHG emissions, thus requiring national implementation. This process of legal evolution is explored through specific examples such as the *Responsibilities and Obligations of Sponsoring States*[115] and the *SRFC*[116] advisory opinions, which demonstrate how international advisory opinions have shaped domestic legislation. In fact, the *Responsibilities and Obligations of Sponsoring States* is the prime example of how States are willing to make profound changes to their domestic law, although not acknowledging explicitly that these changes result from the findings espoused in ITLOS's advisory opinion.

112 ibid page 314.

113 Maria Antonia Tigre & Natalia Urzola,' The 2017 Inter-American Court's Advisory Opinion: changing the paradigm for international environmental law in the Anthropocene' (2021) 12(1) *Journal of Human Rights and the Environment* 24.

114 Medici-Colombo and Rocha, Chapter 13, page 319.

115 *Responsibilities and Obligations of States Sponsoring Persons and Entities with Respect to Activities in the Area* (*Request for Advisory Opinion Submitted to the Seabed Disputes Chamber* (Advisory Opinion, 1 February 2011) ITLOS Case No 17.

116 *Request for an Advisory Opinion submitted by the Sub-Regional Fisheries Commission* (*SRFC*) (Advisory Opinion, 2 April 2015) ITLOS Case No 15.

The chapter also acknowledges that while certain jurisdictions may integrate advisory opinions into their laws directly, others may not due to differing legal structures and constraints. By mapping these dynamics, the chapter offers a nuanced understanding of how international advisory opinions, while not directly enforceable, hold an informal but substantial influence over the evolution of domestic law.

5 Wrapping Up

As outlined in this introductory chapter, this edited book focuses on the transformative potential of international climate litigation, specifically through the lens of three landmark advisory opinions requested in 2022 and 2023. With one advisory opinion already published in May 2024 and two more anticipated in the first half of 2025, we find ourselves at a critical juncture. These advisory opinions will likely leave a lasting but nuanced impact, shaping climate litigation even without directly creating enforceable obligations for states or instantaneously reducing GHG emissions. By clarifying state obligations under international law – and potentially the responsibilities of other stakeholders, such as corporations – these opinions hold the potential to unify and strengthen the global legal framework on climate change. Their influence will likely ripple across international, regional, and domestic climate litigation cases for years to come, potentially sparking a new wave of cases similar to the surge that followed the Paris Agreement.

As Justice Ruth Bader Ginsburg once observed, 'Real change, enduring change, happens one step at a time.' These advisory opinions represent a significant step forward in the evolution of climate litigation, occurring at a moment when the world faces unprecedented environmental challenges, from rising sea levels to increasingly frequent floods and droughts. This book marks the first comprehensive analysis of the topic of climate change advisory opinions, serving as a foundation for what will undoubtedly be years of continued examination and debate.

Our concluding chapter outlines a future research agenda, offering a roadmap for legal scholarship as the remaining advisory opinions are published. We aim for this book to set the stage for ongoing discourse, sparking further analyses in blog posts, journal articles, and books that will dissect, interpret, and assess the long-term impact of these advisory opinions. By publishing this work while the courts are still deliberating, we intentionally position it as a springboard for deeper conversation.

The scope and diversity of perspectives in this book reflect our commitment to capturing a broad range of viewpoints. Our contributors include scholars, practitioners, NGO advocates, and international lawyers working alongside developing States – many directly engaged with the advisory opinions – offering both close-up and broad perspectives. This spectrum of insights enriches the analysis and broadens its relevance, ensuring that this book is a valuable resource for judges, lawyers, scholars, and policymakers alike. Judges, for example, will find crucial context for interpreting these advisory opinions as they navigate future climate litigation cases, while attorneys and academics will benefit from the multi-faceted insights presented here as they strategize future cases.

The following chapters delve into the specific dimensions of international climate litigation, including the unique legal pathways created by advisory opinions, the influence of cross-court dialogue, and the evolving role of civil society in these proceedings. Readers are invited to explore how these themes intertwine and examine the broader implications for international climate governance and accountability.

The 12 chapters that follow delve into the specific dimensions of international climate litigation, exploring the transformative potential of advisory opinions in international climate governance and examining their role in defining and reinforcing States' obligations within the climate crisis framework. It highlights how advisory opinions can shape international climate law, emphasizing the judiciary's power to clarify state responsibilities and contribute to a unified legal approach to climate accountability. Through an analysis of jurisdictional collaboration, the book underscores the importance of dialogue among international courts, demonstrating how cross-court interactions foster coherence in global climate jurisprudence.

Readers are invited to explore the different chapters to understand the different ways in which international courts and tribunals are interpreting States obligations in light of the climate crisis, and the potential of advisory opinions to address inequities within international law. By integrating storytelling and inclusive legal narratives, the book illustrates how advisory opinions can elevate marginalized voices, fostering climate justice on a global scale. Participation is also central to the discussion, focusing on the involvement of states, civil society, and the international community in advisory proceedings. The book examines how civil society engagement strengthens climate advocacy through legal mechanisms, emphasizing its crucial role in shaping international climate policy. Lastly, the book considers the downstream effects of advisory opinions on domestic legal systems, assessing how these international tools influence national policies and drive climate litigation. By examining the lasting impact of advisory opinions on both international and domestic frameworks, the book underscores their significance in building a cohesive, cross-jurisdictional response to the climate crisis.

In sum, this book aspires not only to illuminate the role of advisory opinions in the present but also to inspire future research on these decisions and contribute to a more profound understanding of the trajectory of international climate law. We hope it serves as a touchstone for all who seek to navigate and shape this dynamic and evolving field.

SECTION 1

Advisory Opinions as Instruments of Climate Governance

CHAPTER 2

Advisory Opinions and the Development of International Law: An Opportunity for Climate Change Law?

Rita Guerreiro Teixeira and Patrícia Galvão Teles***

Abstract

International courts and tribunals have played a crucial role in the development of international law, clarifying legal principles and rules, bridging gaps, solving conflicts, and maintaining coherence across legal regimes. With climate change emerging as a global crisis, courts have now been called upon to clarify states' obligations to protect the environment from the effects of climate change and the consequences of breaching them. By mid-2023, three requests for advisory opinions were pending before the International Court of Justice, the Inter-American Court of Human Rights, and the International Tribunal for the Law of the Sea. This chapter explores the potential of these advisory opinions to shape international climate law, focusing on the role of international courts and tribunals in legal development, their interpretative authority, and the opportunities and challenges these proceedings pose in addressing climate change.

Keywords

advisory opinions – climate change – judicial law-making – interpretative authority – international courts and tribunals

* Assistant Professor of Public International Law, Utrecht University. ORCID ID: 0000–0002-9013-9203.

** Member of the International Law Commission. Associate Professor, Autonomous University of Lisbon. ORCID ID: 0000–0001-8461-4445.

1 Introduction

International courts and tribunals are the interpreters per excellence of the international legal system, where they have been playing a key role in clarifying the content of the law, bridging gaps and solving conflicts of norms, and keeping coherence across legal regimes. While, strictly speaking, the role of the judiciary is to interpret and apply the law, few would disagree that the act of adjudication inevitably carries with it some element of law-making.[1] International law, just like any legal system, has an inherent degree of indeterminacy and applying the law requires, in many cases, first choosing among different meanings available to the interpreter. As mentioned by Judge Rosalyn Higgins, the 'very determination of specific disputes, and the provision of specific advice, does develop international law.'[2]

Accordingly, it is unsurprising that international courts have been called to intervene in one of the main crisis currently facing our societies and challenging the structure of international law: climate change. As of mid-2023, three requests for advisory opinions were pending before three international courts: the International Court of Justice (ICJ or the Court), the Inter-American Court of Human Rights (IACtHR) and the International Tribunal for the Law of the Sea (ITLOS). In these requests, each court was asked to clarify the content of states' obligations in relation to the prevention of climate change from the point of view of different fields of international law and what are the consequences of breaching them.

This chapter considers whether these advisory opinions offer decisive opportunities for the development of international climate change law, taking into account the role that the advisory jurisdiction of international courts and tribunals has played in international law. It starts by providing an overview of advisory procedures available before different international courts (section 2). Subsequently, it discusses the role that international courts and tribunals have played in the development of international law and factors that contribute to the authority of their judgments and opinions (section 3). Finally, it reflects on the opportunities and challenges posed by the pendency of three simultaneous requests for advisory opinions and speculates on possible outcomes of the proceedings and how they could contribute to catalyze more action in the fight against climate change (section 4).

1 See, eg, Alain Pellet and Daniel Müller, 'Article 38', in Zimmermann and others (eds), *The Statute of the International Court of Justice: A Commentary* (3rd edn, OUP 2019) §§324–326; Gleider Hernández, 'International Judicial Lawmaking', in Brölmann & Radi (eds), *Research Handbook on the Theory and Practice of International Lawmaking* (Edward Elgar 2016) 201; Alan Boyle & Christine Chinkin, *The Making of International Law* (OUP 2007) 268.

2 Rosalyn Higgins, *Problems and Process: International Law and How We Use It* (OUP 1995) 202.

2 Advisory Jurisdiction of International Courts and Tribunals

The power to render advisory opinions is a particular feature of certain international courts and tribunals, which does not find correspondence in several domestic legal systems in the world.[3] Unlike traditional contentious cases, advisory opinions do not (at least exclusively) apply existing legal rules to facts that have already occurred and gave rise to a dispute that the court must settle. Instead, they are forward-looking: in these proceedings, courts and tribunals are called upon to formulate general rules that should guide future action.

The origin of the advisory function in international law dates back to the Covenant of the League of Nations, which conferred upon the Permanent Court of International Justice (PCIJ) the powers to give advisory opinions 'upon any dispute or question referred to it by the Council or by the Assembly.'[4] Despite initial disagreements on the legal effects of these opinions,[5] it became clear through the practice of the PCIJ that they were meant to be non-binding, unlike decisions in contentious cases.

Today, five international courts and tribunals possess jurisdiction to issue advisory opinions: the ICJ, the ITLOS, and the three regional human rights courts in the Americas, Europe, and Africa.

2.1 *The International Court of Justice*

The ICJ may render advisory opinions on 'any legal question' at the request of the UN General Assembly, the Security Council or other organs of the UN and specialized agencies, when so authorized by the General Assembly and when

3 Anthony Aust, 'Advisory Opinions' (2010) 1 *Journal of International Dispute Settlement* 123, 124–125.

4 Covenant of the League of Nations (adopted 28 June 1919, entered into force 1 October 1920) League of Nations Official Journal (February 1920) 3, art 14. The PCIJ issued 27 advisory opinions in its 24 years of existence, all requested by the Council of the League of Nations.

5 Manley Hudson, who delivered a Hague Lecture on advisory opinions in 1925 and was appointed to the PCIJ in 1933, wrote that an advisory opinion 'is what it purports to be. It is advisory. It is not in any sense a judgment under Article 60 of the Statute, nor is it a decision under Article 59. Hence it is not in any way binding upon any State, even upon a State which is especially interested in the dispute or question to which the opinion relates.' Manley Hudson, *The Permanent Court of International Justice: A Treatise* (New York 1934) 455. Adopting an opposing view, Charles de Visscher, who also delivered a Hague Lecture on advisory opinions in 1929, wrote that the 'judicial character of the Court and of its advisory procedure means that within the limits of the question put to the Court on the judicial aspects of the dispute, the Council and, under certain circumstances, the interested states are bound by the opinion. The Court's opinion is in point of fact equivalent to a judgment and is binding.' Charles de Visscher, *Recueil des Cours de l'Academie de Droit International*,1929, vol I, 23 ff.

the question falls within the scope of competence of that body or agency.[6] The Court has so far delivered 28 advisory opinions and declined to exercise its advisory function in only one occasion – finding that it could not respond to the World Health Organization's (WHO) request for an *Advisory Opinion on the Legality of the Use by a State of Nuclear Weapons in Armed Conflict* as the question fell outside the mandate of the WHO.[7]

A central question in defining the advisory function of the ICJ has been the delimitation of the type of questions that can be subject to it. Whereas the scope of the advisory jurisdiction of the PCIJ was not clear in its early formulation,[8] this latter court clarified in the *Eastern Carelia* case that it would not issue a requested opinion if the question was 'not one of abstract law' but concerned directly the content of a dispute between two states and could only 'be decided by an investigation into the facts underlying the case.'[9] In those cases, the PCIJ found, 'answering the question would be substantially equivalent to deciding the dispute between the parties.' Eventually, the distinction between 'disputes', which should be the subject to contentious proceedings, and 'legal questions', which constitute the scope of advisory proceedings, became well established and was codified in the UN Charter and ICJ Statute.[10]

The ICJ has further detailed the scope of what constitutes a legal question and made it clear that it will not shy away from issuing a requested opinion simply because the question addressed has political aspects.[11] It has furthermore affirmed that 'in situations in which political considerations are prominent it may be particular necessary [...] to obtain an advisory opinion [...] as to the legal principles applicable.'[12] It is important to note that the Court is bound by the terms of the legal question submitted to it, even if it has developed a practice of determining the scope and meaning of the question, interpreting it

6 Charter of the United Nations (adopted 26 June 1945, entered into force 24 October 1945) 892 UNTS 119, art 96 (UN Charter).

7 *Legality of the Use by a State of Nuclear Weapons in Armed Conflict* (Advisory Opinion) [1996] ICJ Rep 66, §§21–22.

8 The Covenant of the Legal of Nations provided, in article 14, that 'The Court may also give an advisory opinion upon any dispute or question referred to it by the Council or by the Assembly.'

9 *Status of Eastern Carelia* (Advisory Opinion) PCIJ Series B No 5, at 28–29.

10 UN Charter, art 96(1); Statute of the International Court of Justice (adopted 26 June 1945, entered into force 24 October 1945) 892 UNTS 119, arts 38, 65(1).

11 *Accordance with International Law of the Unilateral Declaration of Independence in Respect of Kosovo* (Advisory Opinion) [2010] ICJ Rep 402 (*Kosovo Opinion*).

12 *Interpretation of the Agreement of 25 March 1951 between the WHO and Egypt* (Advisory Opinion) [1980] ICJ Rep 73.

when the question was unclear or vague,[13] and occasionally departing from the language of the question when it did not reflect the 'legal questions really in issue.'[14] In the *Kosovo Opinion*, while not reformulating the question, the Court significantly limited its scope by adopting a formalist interpretation according to which it found that the General Assembly only requested an opinion on whether or not the declaration of independence of Kosovo was in accordance with international law, and did not ask about the legal consequences of that declaration, namely for statehood.[15] These considerations underline the importance of clearly and carefully formulating the requests for advisory opinions.

2.2 *The International Tribunal for the Law of the Sea*

The advisory jurisdiction of ITLOS, now broadly undisputed, has been the subject of some controversy. The United Nations Convention on the Law of the Sea (UNCLOS) only provides for advisory jurisdiction of the Seabed Dispute Chamber[16] – neither Part XV of UNCLOS nor the ITLOS Statute establishing an explicit jurisdiction for the full Tribunal to issue advisory opinions. However, these powers have been derived from Article 138 of the Rules of the Tribunal, which establishes that '[t]he Tribunal may give an advisory opinion on a legal question if an international agreement related to the purposes of the Convention specifically provides for the submission to the Tribunal of a request for such an opinion,'[17] in combination with Article 21 of the ITLOS Statute of the Tribunal.[18]

ITLOS has clarified the relation between these two provisions in its advisory opinion on the *Request submitted by the Sub-Regional Fisheries Commission* (SRFC).[19] It explained that Article 138 of the Rules of the Tribunal 'does not establish the advisory jurisdiction of the Tribunal. It only furnishes the prerequisites that need to be satisfied before the Tribunal can exercise its advisory jurisdiction.'[20] Instead, the substantive legal basis of the advisory jurisdiction of the Tribunal is found in the combination of Article 21 of the Statute, which established jurisdiction for 'all matters specifically provided for in

13 *Application for Review of Judgment No 273 of the United Nations Administrative Tribunal* (Advisory Opinion) [1982] ICJ Rep 325, §46.

14 *Interpretation of the Agreement of 25 March 1951 between the WHO and Egypt* (n 12) §35.

15 *Kosovo Opinion* (n 11) §51.

16 United Nations Convention on the Law of the Sea (adopted 10 December 1982, entered into force 16 November 1994) 1833 UNTS 3, art 191.

17 International Tribunal for the Law of Sea, Rules of the Tribunal, ITLOS/8 (2009), art. 138.

18 Statute of the International Tribunal for the Law of the Sea, Annex VI to UNCLOS.

19 *Request for an Advisory Opinion submitted by the Sub-Regional Fisheries Commission (SRFC)* (Advisory Opinion, 2 April 2015) ITLOS Case No 15, §§ 59–60.

20 ibid, §59.

any other agreement which confers jurisdiction on the Tribunal,' and the relevant provisions of another international agreement that provide for this jurisdiction.[21]

The rendering by ITLOS of its first advisory opinion seems to have contributed to settle the question of whether it has competence to do so. Notably, whereas 13 states contested or questioned the advisory jurisdiction of the Tribunal in their statements submitted in the *SRFC* Opinion, only two states expressly contested this jurisdiction in the *Request for an Advisory Opinion submitted by the Commission of Small Island States* (*COSIS*) *on Climate Change and International Law*, in which the Tribunal clearly confirmed its jurisdiction to render advisory opinions.[22]

2.3 *Regional Human Rights Courts*

All three regional human rights courts have been conferred an advisory jurisdiction. The American Convention of Human Rights (ACHR) establishes that member states of the Organization of American States as well as the competent organs of that organization 'may consult the Court regarding the interpretation of this Convention or of other treaties concerning the protection of human rights in the American states.'[23] Furthermore, it provides for the possibility of states requesting advisory opinions on the compatibility of its domestic laws with the human rights instruments. This provided the IACtHR with an advisory function of a broad scope: it covers the interpretation of any treaty and domestic legislations (adopted or in draft form) as long as the question is directly related to the protection of human rights in states of the Inter-American system. The IACtHR has issued a total of 30 advisory opinions since its creation.

In similar terms to those of the Inter-American system, the Protocol Establishing the African Court of Human and Peoples Rights (ACtHPR) empowered this court to issue opinions 'on any legal matter relating to the Charter or any other relevant human right instruments,' excluding questions which are pending before the Commission.[24] Opinions can be requested by members states,

21 ibid, §58.

22 *Request for an Advisory Opinion submitted by the Commission of Small Island States on Climate Change and International Law* (Advisory Opinion, 21 May 2024) ITLOS Case No 31, §91 (*COSIS Opinion*).

23 American Convention on Human Rights (adopted 22 November 1969, entered into force 18 July 1978) OAS Treaty Series No 36, art 64.

24 Protocol on the Establishment of an African Court on Human and Peoples' Rights (adopted 9 June 1998, entered into force 25 January 2004) AU Doc OAU/LEG/EXP/AFCHPR/PROT (III), art. 4(1).

the Organization of African States or any of its organs, as well as other African organizations. The ACtHPR, which has only started its operations in 2004, has so far issued four advisory opinions.

The advisory function of the ECtHR is provided for in (i) article 47 of the European Convention of Human Rights (ECHR), at the request of the Committee of Ministers 'on legal questions concerning the interpretation of the Convention and the Protocols thereto,' and (ii) Protocol 16, which allows the highest courts of contracting parties to request 'advisory opinions on questions of principle relating to the interpretation or application of the rights and freedoms defined in the Convention or the protocols thereto' in the context of a case pending before them.[25] The ECtHR has issued 9 opinions to date.

3 Judicial Development of the Law

3.1 *A Law-Making Role for International Courts?*

A growing number of international courts and tribunals populate the international judicial space. With the exception of the ICJ, which is a court of general jurisdiction, each court or tribunal only has limited jurisdiction over certain areas of international law. On the one hand, this has raised concerns for the coherence of the legal system, as there is no centralized judicial function that can guarantee it. No court, not even the ICJ, has appellate jurisdiction and, hence, there is no mechanism to ensure systemic coherence between judgments from different courts.[26] On the other hand, there is a large number of judicial bodies whose pronouncements can contribute to the development of international law.[27]

Formally, judicial decisions are subsidiary means for the determination of applicable law and, thus, can only assist in the clarification of the content of legal rules, but do not constitute a formal or autonomous source of international law.[28] Moreover, international courts and tribunals can only exercise jurisdiction over a specific matter with the agreement of the parties to the dispute, which they confer either by joining a specific treaty system or issuing a declaration recognzsing the court's jurisdiction.[29] The ICJ has consistently

25 Protocol 16 to the ECHR (adopted 2 October 2013, entered into force 1 August 2018) ETS No 214, art 1.

26 Hernández (n 1) 202; Boyle and Chinkin (n 1) 263. Except, perhaps, judicial comity.

27 Boyle and Chinkin (n 1) 265.

28 ICJ Statute, art 38(2).

29 The ICJ and ITLOS depend on consent given by the parties in disputes, either through declaration, by an agreement to bring a case or through a compromissory clause in a treaty,

deferred to state consent and clarified that it would not overstep it[30] – a reasoning that it has also used to emphasize that it 'cannot legislate.'[31]

Nonetheless, the rulings of international courts and tribunals possess important interpretative authority in the international legal system.[32] Even if there is no formal rule of precedent in international law, and the judicial interpretation of applicable legal regimes in a given judgment is only binding for the parties in dispute, actors in the international system tend to follow previous judicial determinations. The ICJ case law, in particular, has been often invoked by the UN General Assembly, the International Law Commission, various international courts, and states.[33] Moreover, the UNGA stated in 1947 that 'it is [… …]] of paramount importance that the [ICJ] should be utilized to the greatest practical extent in the progressive development of international law.'[34] Similarly, the case law of human rights courts has shaped the evolution of human rights regimes and compelled states to make extensive changes to their domestic laws and policies.[35]

Well-known examples of courts' pronouncements that have been particularly significant for the development of international law include the pronouncement by the PCIJ of the principle according to which any breach of an international obligations gives rise to an obligation to make reparation, which constitutes the basis of the customary law regime of state responsibility.[36] Equally influential, the acceptance of the use of straight baselines for the determination of maritime zones in the *Anglo-Norwegian Fisheries* case

art 38(2) declarations or a special agreement – ibid, art 36; UNCLOS, arts 297–299. Within the human rights courts, the ECtHR has jurisdiction over the application of the ECHR (Convention for the Protection of Human Rights and Fundamental Freedoms (adopted 4 November 1950, entered into force 3 September 1953) 213 UNTS 221), art 32), whereas the jurisdiction of the IACtHR depends on a separate declaration by states (ACHR, art 62) and the jurisdiction of the ACtHPR depends on the ratification of the 1989 ACtHPR Protocol (art 34(6)).

30 Eg, *Armed Activities in the Territory of the Congo (New Application: 2002) (Democratic Republic of the Congo v Rwanda)* (Jurisdiction and Admissibility) (Judgment) [2006] ICJ Rep 6, §88.

31 *Fisheries Jurisdiction (United Kingdom v Ireland)* (Judgment) [1974] ICJ Rep 181, at 192.

32 Gleider Hernández, 'Interpretative Authority and the International Judiciary' in Bianchi, Peat &Windsor (eds), *Interpretation in International Law* (OUP 2015).

33 Se several examples infra; see also Hernández (n 1) 206–207.

34 UNGA Res 171(II) (1947) UN Doc A/519 ('Need for greater use by the United Nations and its organs of the International Court of Justice') 103, cited in Hernández (n 1) 203.

35 Boyle & Chinkin (n 1) 276–278; Dinah Shelton, 'The Boundaries of Human Rights Jurisdiction in Europe' (2003) 13 *Duke Journal of Comparative & International Law* 95.

36 *Case concerning the Factory at Chorzów (Germany v Poland), Jurisdiction* [1927] PCIJ Series A No 9, 22–25. 'Draft Articles on Responsibility of States for Internationally Wrongful Acts',

gave rise to supporting state practice following the judgment and was later codified in the Geneva Convention on the Territorial Sea and Contiguous Zone and now in the UN Convention on the Law of the Sea.[37]

The line between interpretation of existing rules and progressive development of the law is particularly blurred in relation to non-written law – namely customary international law and general principles – and this is where international courts and tribunals traditionally have had a more creative role. It is often practically difficult to distinguish the recognition of the existence of a customary rule and the determination of its content by an international court from its very coming into existence, and the ICJ has been referred to as 'ultimate arbiter' of the existence and content of custom.[38] Hence, while formally speaking the recognition of the existence of a rule of customary international law is not a constitutive element of that rule, it is that recognition that will be consistently invoked as evidence of its existence. Even when the ICJ has been criticised for its inconsistent (or totally absent) examination of state practice and *opinio iuris* as the constitutive elements of customary international law, its pronouncements still remained authoritative. An oft-cited example is the *Arrest Warrant* case, which did not cite any evidence of the two constituent elements of customary international law to support its conclusions that a minister of foreign affairs enjoys immunity before foreign criminal jurisdiction.[39] Nonetheless, that rule has not been questioned afterwards and has now been included in the Draft Articles on Immunity of State Officials from Foreign Criminal Jurisdiction adopted by the International Law Commission (ILC).[40]

adopted by the International Law Commission at its 53rd session, UN Doc A/RES/56/10 (2001), ch IV.E.1, art 31, Commentary (1).

37 *Fisheries Case* (*United Kingdom v Norway*) (Judgment) [1951] ICJ Rep 116.

38 Anthea Elizabeth Roberts, 'Traditional and Modern Approaches to Customary International Law: A Reconciliation' (2001) 95 *AJIL* 757, 772. See also Boyle & Chinkin (n 1) 278–279.

39 *Arrest Warrant of April 11, 2000* (*Democratic Republic of the Congo v Belgium*) (Judgment) [2002] ICJ Rep 3, §58.Another example of this inconsistency is the *Nicaragua* case, where the Court reversed the order of the two elements, first finding *opinio iuris* in the form of UNGA resolutions and then looking for state practice to support it (while discounting several instances of practice to the contrary) *Military and Paramilitary Activities in and against Nicaragua* (*Nicaragua v United States of America*) (Merits) (Judgment) [1986] ICJ Rep 14, §184. See discussion in Boyle & Chinkin (n 1) 280–282.

40 ILC, 'Immunity of State officials from foreign criminal jurisdiction – Texts and titles of the draft articles adopted by the Drafting Committee on first reading', UN Doc A/77/10 (2022), draft art 3.

A similar role is played by international courts and tribunals in the determination of whether a general principle of law exists in the international system and what is its content. In its ongoing work on general principles of law, the ILC has relied on various judicial decisions and opinions to provide examples of general principles that have been 'recognised by the community of nations'[41] and to identify the methodology used for the identification of such principles.[42]

There are several reasons why judicial determinations of international courts and tribunals carry significant weight in international law. First, international judicial decision-making follows pre-determined proceedings and methods that guarantee that courts do not exercise jurisdiction beyond what they were conferred and are assumed to lead to fair, well-balanced, and reasoned judgments. There are strict formal rules that govern the entire judicial process, from the procedures for appointment of judges, which should guarantee that they have the necessary legal expertise and are representative of the various legal cultures of the world, to rules about the conduction of procedures and rights of parties in disputes, and requirements for judges to provide reasons for their judgments.[43]

Second, the quality of reasoning contained in judgments contributes to their persuasiveness and authority, which determines the likelihood of them being cited in the future and influencing legal developments. As von Bogdandy and Jacob noted, 'legal scholars, advisers, other courts, and certainly not least the deciding court itself at a later point in time must be convinced of the soundness – broadly defined – of a prior decision.'[44] In international legal discourse, the persuasiveness of an argument is often associated with how well it can relate to the past applications and determinations of what the law is.[45] The emphasis that legal systems place on continuity and stability (and which

41 'Draft Conclusions on General Principles of Law, together with Commentaries thereto', adopted by the International Law Commission at its 74th session, UN Doc A/78/10 (2023), Draft conclusion 2.

42 See Marcelo Vásquez-Bermúdez, 'Second Report on General Principles of Law' (2021) International Law Commission 72nd session, UN Doc A/CN4/741, eg §§27, 36–39, 86–91.

43 See ITLOS Statute, arts 2, 24–30; ACHR, art 66(1); ICJ Statute, arts 2–4, 43, 56.

44 Armin von Bogdandy and Marc Jacob, 'The Judge as Law-Maker: Thoughts on Bruno Simma's Declaration in the Kosovo Opinion' in Ulrich Fastenrath and others (eds), *From Bilateralism to Community Interest: Essays in Honour of Bruno Simma* (OUP 2011) 822. See also Georg Schwarzenberger, *International Law as Applied by International Courts and Tribunals*, vol. 1 (Stevens and Sons 1957), 31, referring to the 'fulness and cogency of the reasoning' contained in a judgment as a factor of its potential for developing the law.

45 Ingo Venzke, 'Semantic Authority, Legal Change and the Dynamics of International Law' in Palmer Olsen & Capps (eds), *Legal Authority beyond the State* (CUP 2018) 123–124.

underlines notions of legal expectations and rule of law, also present in the international system) further reinforces the authority of past court decisions.

Third, international courts are agents of the international system, established with the function of clarifying the substance of international law. The ICJ is the 'principal judicial organ' of the UN[46]; the European, African, and Inter-American courts have 'supervisory jurisdiction'[47] over the fulfilment of obligations under their respective conventions and are primarily established to facilitate the attainment of their objectives;[48] ITLOS was established to solve disputes arising out of its interpretation and application of UNCLOS.[49] Accordingly, these courts enjoy a wide measure of authority in relation to the interpretation and application of their respective regimes. Furthermore, courts will often cite its previous case law, placing emphasis on continuity, consistency and predictability in the application of international law.[50] The ICJ has famously noted that 'while [previous] decisions are in no way binding on the Court, it will not depart from its settled jurisprudence unless it finds very particular reasons to do so.'[51]

A final word is due in relation to the often discussed question of the relative position of different international courts and tribunals. According to some, the ICJ enjoys a unique position in the international legal system as 'the most prestigious of all courts.'[52] It is true that, because of its status as the only court of general jurisdiction and the judicial organ of the UN, and its decades of existence, the ICJ has amassed an important measure of authority in the interpretation of general international law. It is the only international court whose findings can be potentially generalized beyond the specific legal circumstances of each case, as it decides 'in accordance with international law' and is, therefore, not limited to applicable law by the terms of the instruments establishing the court and delimiting its jurisdiction.[53] Nonetheless, other international

46 UN Charter, art 92.

47 ECHR, Preamble.

48 See Court Protocol to the African Charter, Preamble, §8; ACHR, art 3.

49 UNCLOS, arts 287–288.

50 The ICJ has noted that it does not render 'abstract justice but justice according to the rule of law; which is to say that its application should display consistency and a degree of predictability': *Continental Shelf (Libya v Malta)* (Judgment) [1985] ICJ Rep 13, 39, §45, cited in Pellet & Müller (n 1) §310.

51 *Application of the Convention on the Prevention and Punishment of the Crime of Genocide (Croatia v Serbia)* (Merits) (Judgment) [2015] ICJ Rep 3, §54.

52 Pellet & Müller (n 1) §316.

53 With the opposite reasoning, the ICJ has refused to generalise findings of arbitral tribunals to general international law: 'The Court notes that references to legitimate expectations may be found in arbitral awards concerning disputes between a foreign investor and

courts and tribunals have also played a relevant role in the clarification and development of their specific regimes. Hence, the various human rights courts have systematically adopted and broadened the scope of protection of human rights by adopting a dynamic interpretation of their respective conventions.[54] A notable development is the interpretation of human rights obligations to include obligations of states to protect the environment, despite the fact that only the African Charter on Human and Peoples Rights expressly mentions a right to a 'general satisfactory environment.'[55]

There is little doubt that, while not being endowed with law-making functions, international courts and tribunals have contributed significantly to improve our understanding of international law and influenced its development. This is true not only in relation to international judgments but also in relation to advisory opinions, which are the subject of the following section.

3.2 *In Particular: the Impact of Advisory Opinions*

Advisory opinions are, by definition, not binding. For that reason, their impact in subsequent international practice and legal developments depends on the recognition of their authority by relevant actors. The three factors discussed above of following consistent procedures, relying on high-quality reasoning, and embedding in the system are also relevant in respect to advisory opinions. In addition, the impact of advisory opinions is often strengthened by an express acceptance by the organ or institution that requested the opinion, which subsequently conforms its practice with its content.[56] The UN General Assembly, for instance, has the practice of receiving and affirming the opinions that it requests, creating also an opportunity for member states to display their support during debates.[57]

---

the host State that apply treaty clauses providing for fair and equitable treatment. It does not follow from such references that there exists in general international law a principle that would give rise to an obligation on the basis of what could be considered a legitimate expectation.' – *Obligation to Negotiate Access to the Pacific Ocean* (*Bolivia v Chile*) (Judgment) [2018] ICJ Rep 507, §162.

54 See supra note 35.

55 African Charter on Human and Peoples' Rights (adopted 27 June 1981, entered into force 21 October 1986) 1520 UNTS 217, art 24. See, for the ECtHR, European Court of Human Rights, 'Factsheet – Environment and the European Convention on Human Rights' <https://www.echr.coe.int/documents/d/echr/FS_Environment_ENG> accessed 4 November 2024; for the IACtHR, note 76 and corresponding text.

56 Hernández (n 1) 209; Karin Oellers-Frahm, 'Lawmaking Through Advisory Opinions?' (2011) 12 *German LJ* 1033, 1049.

57 See, as a recent example, UNGA Resolution 73/295 (22 May 2019) UN Doc A/RES/73/295 ('Advisory opinion of the International Court of Justice on the Legal Consequences of the Separation of the Chagos Archipelago from Mauritius in 1965'), affirming that Mauritius

International courts and tribunals have been conscious of the importance of not overstepping the limits of their advisory powers to maintain their legitimacy, and have expressly refrained from assuming an open-ended law-creating role. This judicial restraint is illustrated by the ICJ's advisory opinion on the *Legality of the Threat or Use of Nuclear Weapons*, where the Court refused to 'conclude definitively whether the threat or use of nuclear weapons would be lawful or unlawful' in extreme circumstances where the very survival of a State would be at stake, finding that the law was not clear on this point at that date.[58]

Still, advisory opinions of the various international courts have led to key developments in the international system.[59] The advisory opinions rendered by the ICJ are responsible for recognizing that the UN – and, consequently, other international organizations – possesses international legal personality,[60] and have clarified its powers and competences of its organs.[61] These pronouncements had constitutive effects for UN member states, as the organization subsequently operated in accordance with the findings in the advisory opinions.[62] Other influential advisory opinions have clarified key questions of treaty law in relation to the admissibility of reservations (at a time in which the question was not settled in international law)[63] and recognized a right to self-determination of non-self-governing territories and established consequences arising from its violation.[64]

---

has sovereignty over the Chagos Archipelago in accordance with the Chagos Advisory Opinion. See *Legal Consequences of the Separation of the Chagos Archipelago from Mauritius in 1965* (Advisory Opinion) [2019] ICJ Rep 95.

58 *Legality of the Threat or Use of Nuclear Weapons* (Advisory Opinion) [1996] ICJ Rep 226, §105(2)(E).

59 See additional illustrations in the chapter by Lea Main-Klingst & Sophie Marjanac in this volume.

60 *Reparations for Injuries Suffered in the Service of the United Nations* (Advisory Opinion) [1949] ICJ Rep 174.

61 Eg, *Certain Expenses of the United Nations (Article 17, paragraph 2, of the Charter)* (Advisory Opinion) [1962] ICJ Rep 151; *Effect of Awards of Compensation Made by the UN Administrative Tribunal* (Advisory Opinion) [1954] ICJ Rep 47.

62 Boyle & Chinkin (n 1) 296.

63 *Reservations to the Convention on the Prevention and Punishment of the Crime of Genocide* (Advisory Opinion) [1951] ICJ Rep 15. The guidelines developed by the Court constituted the basis for the regime later adopted in articles 19 to 23 of the Vienna Convention of the Law of Treaties, with a few differences – see William A Schabas, 'Genocide Convention, Reservations (Advisory Opinion)', *Max Planck Encyclopedia of Public International Law* (OUP 2021) §21 <https://opil.ouplaw.com/display/10.1093/law:epil/9780199231690/law-9780199231690-e136?prd=MPIL> accessed 4 November 2024.

64 *Legal Consequences for States of the Continued Presence of South Africa in Namibia (South West Africa) notwithstanding Security Council Resolution 276 (1970)* (Advisory Opinion) [1971] ICJ Rep 16, §52; *Western Sahara* (Advisory Opinion) [1975] ICJ Rep 12, §§54–59. This right was reaffirmed in the *Advisory Opinion on the Legal Consequences of the Construction*

The ICJ has often referenced its advisory opinions in subsequent cases and does not make any distinction between its judgments and opinions when it refers to previous case law. Its opinions have also been referred to by other international courts and tribunals. To mention but some examples, the International Criminal Tribunal for the Former Yugoslavia has referred to the *Namibia* advisory opinion[65] and a special chamber of ITLOS found that no dispute persisted concerning sovereignty over the Chagos Archipelago since Mauritius' sovereignty could 'be inferred from the ICJ's determinations' in its advisory opinion.[66]

The *Chagos* opinion further demonstrated how ICJ's opinions can have an important role in solving disputes between states, even though that is not their expressed function,[67] and even when they have been received unfavorably by affected states. Despite the rejection of the Court's findings by the United Kingdom – which, in the immediate aftermath of the opinion being issued, found that the court have failed to 'give sufficient regard to a number of legal and material factual issues' and made clear that it had 'no doubt about [its] sovereignty over the British Indian Ocean Territory' – ,[68] an agreement to return the Chagos islands to Mauritius was finally reached in October 2024.[69] Similarly, the findings in the *Wall* opinion, where the Court found that the construction of a wall in occupied Palestinian territory was illegal, were followed by the Supreme Court of Israel.[70]

---

of a Wall in the Occupied Palestinian Territory (Advisory Opinion) [2004] ICJ Rep 136), where the Court elaborated on the legal consequences for third states in relation to the violation of such right.

65 Prosecutor v Tadic, Decisions on the Defence Motion for Interlocutory Appeal on Jurisdiction, 2 October 1995, §§14–22.

66 *Dispute concerning Delimitation of the Maritime Boundary between Mauritius and Maldives in the Indian Ocean* (*Mauritius/Maldives*) (*Preliminary Objections*) (Judgment, 28 January 2021) ITLOS Case No 28, §246.

67 In its *Nuclear Weapons* opinion, the ICJ made it clear that '[t]he purpose of the advisory function is not to settle – at least directly – disputes between States, but to offer legal advice to the organs and institutions requesting the opinion.' *Nuclear Weapons* (n 58) §15.

68 United Nations General Assembly, Seventy-third session, 83rd plenary meeting, Wednesday, 22 May 2019, 10 a.m., New York [UN Doc A/73/PV.83], cited in Niko Pavlopoulos, 'Chagos (Advisory Opinion)', *Max Planck Encyclopedia of Public International Law* (Oxford University Press 2021) para 33 <https://opil.ouplaw.com/display/10.1093/law-epil/9780199231690/law-9780199231690-e2248?prd=MPIL> accessed 4 November 2024.

69 '*UK* and Mauritius Joint Statement, 3 October 2024' (*GOV.UK*) <https://www.gov.uk/government/news/joint-statement-between-uk-and-mauritius-3-october-2024> accessed 4 November 2024.

70 Israeli Supreme Court, Decision of 15 September 2005 in the case *Mara'abe v. Prime Minister of Israel* [2009] HCJ 7957/04, referenced in Oellers-Frahm (n 56) 1042.

The first advisory opinion of ITLOS, in addition to its substantive findings, made the key contribution of confirming that the full Tribunal has jurisdiction to render advisory opinions, despite questions having been raised in this respect by the majority of states that submitted written observations in the proceedings.[71] The fact that the majority of those objections have been abandoned in the context of the proceedings for an advisory opinion on the topic of climate change illustrate the recognition of the interpretative authority of this Tribunal.

Finally, among the human rights courts, the IACtHR has been the most proficuous in issuing advisory opinions, which have clarified both the scope of its own advisory competence and important substantive aspects of the human rights regime in the Americas. In *'Other Treaties' Subject to the Advisory Jurisdiction of the Court*, the IACtHR adopted a broad interpretation of the term 'other treaties concerning the protection of human rights in the American states' in article 64 of the ACHR to include not only human rights instruments but any provisions dealing with the protecting of human rights included in any international treaty.[72] This interpretation was confirmed in a subsequent advisory opinion, where it allowed the IACtHR to find jurisdiction to review provisions of the Convention on Consular Relations which confer human rights to individuals.[73]

Other IACtHR opinions clarified which human rights could not be derogated from even in emergency situations,[74] finding that migrant workers were entitled to non-discrimination and equality before the law, regardless of their legal status,[75] and clarified states' obligations in relation to the environment deriving from their human rights obligations.[76] Following the pattern common

71 See supra section 2.2.

72 *'Other Treaties' Subject to the Consultative Jurisdiction of the Court (art. 64 American Convention on Human Rights)*, Advisory Opinion OC-1/82, Inter-American Court of Human Rights Series A No 1 (24 September 1982).

73 *The Right to Information on Consular Assistance Within the Framework of the Guarantees of Legal Due Process*. Advisory Opinion OC-16/99, Inter-American Court of Human Rights Series A No 16 (1 October 1999). See, for more details, Oellers-Frahm (n 56) 1043.

74 *Habeas Corpus in Emergency Situations*, Advisory Opinion OC-8/87, Inter-American Court of Human Rights Series A No 8 (30 January 1987); *Judicial Guarantees in States of Emergency*, Advisory Opinion OC-9/87, Inter-American Court of Human Rights Series A No 9 (6 October 1987).

75 *Juridical Condition and Rights of Undocumented Migrants*. Advisory Opinion OC-18/03, Inter-American Court of Human Rights Series A No 18 (17 September 2003). See Oellers-Frahm (n 56) 1043–1044.

76 *The Environment and Human Rights (State Obligations in Relation to the Environment in the Context of the Protection and Guarantee of the Rights to Life and to Personal Integrity*

to international courts of referring to its previous case law, the IACtHR relied on previous opinions to determine that states obligations to protect the environment apply not only in relation to individuals within their territory, but also those under their authority or effective control.[77] It is noteworthy that, while these advisory opinions are non-binding, the IACtHR has found that national judiciaries of states that are parties to the American Convention must consider the interpretations made by this court.[78]

4 The Potential of the Advisory Opinions on Climate Change

Within a four-month period, between December 2022 and March 2023, three advisory opinions were requested from international courts and tribunals with the goal of clarifying states' obligations in relation to climate change. Two proceedings are currently pending: (i) a request for an advisory opinion from the ICJ on 'the obligations of States under international law to ensure the protection of the climate system and other parts of the environment from anthropogenic emissions of greenhouse gases' and the legal consequences of violating those obligations and causing 'significant harm to the climate system and other parts of the environment;' (ii) a request before the IACtHR on 'the scope of state obligations for responding to the climate emergency under the frame of international human rights law and, specifically, under the American Convention on Human Rights.'

ITLOS delivered its advisory opinion in April 2024, covering the specific obligations of state parties to the UNCLOS to protect the marine environment in the context of climate change. It found that state parties have an obligation to take all necessary measures to prevent, reduce, and control marine pollution from anthropogenic greenhouse gas emissions, and generally to protect the marine environment from climate change impacts and ocean acidification. These measures should be determined objectively, taking into account best available science and 'relevant international rules and standards contained in

– *Interpretation and Scope of Articles 4(1) and 5(1) of the American Convention on Human Rights*) Advisory Opinion OC-23/17, Inter-American Court of Human Rights Series A No 23 (15 November 2017).

77 ibid, § 73. *Rights and Guarantees of Children in the Context of Migration and/or Need of International Protection*. Advisory Opinion OC-21/14, Inter-American Court of Human Rights Series A No 14 (19 August 2014), §61

78 *Gender Identity, and Equality and Non-Discrimination of Same-Sex Couples*, Advisory Opinion OC-24/17, Inter-American Court of Human Rights Series A No 24 (24 November 2017), §26.

climate change treaties such as the UNFCCC and the Paris Agreement.'[79] This passage highlights the Tribunal's efforts of systemic integration of UNCLOS provisions on pollution of the marine environment with the wider normative environment of climate change law and obligations of emissions reduction and temperature targets. Simultaneously, ITLOS made it clear that compliance with obligations under the Paris Agreement is not enough for states to fulfil their specific obligations under UNCLOS in relation to protection of the marine environment.[80] They are required to adopt a stringent standard of due diligence and 'to take measures as far-reaching and efficacious as possible to prevent or reduce the deleterious effects of climate change and ocean acidification on the marine environment [...] given the high risks of serious and irreversible harm.'[81]

These three requests for advisory opinions were generally received with great enthusiasm, as an opportunity to clarify the international legal regime applicable to the protection of the environment and the prevention of the adverse effects of climate change, from the point of view of different legal fields. As discussed above, advisory opinions can be authoritative in international law and lead to key development of legal regimes and the adoption of new practices. It is hoped that clarifying states' international obligations will contribute for the adoption of more ambitious climate measures, that the opinions will lay down guiding principles that could accelerate and facilitate future climate negotiations, and that they could be relied on in future climate litigation, both at the national and international levels, that can pressure states to comply with their obligations when they are not doing enough. They can also contribute to bridge different international law regimes that all have implications for the environment and climate change, contributing to the coherence of the system – particularly if the ICJ and the IACtHR follow the lead of ITLOS.[82] In fact, the ITLOS advisory opinion, by dealing with the relation between obligations under the UNCLOS and the UNFCCC and the Paris Agreement, offered an example of how different treaty regimes can be integrated without fully converging them.[83] Finally, the international climate change field would particularly benefit from judicial interpretations that can further develop key concepts such as of due diligence, no harm, obligations to cooperation, causation,

79 *COSIS Opinion* (n 22) §§243, 400.
80 ibid, §§222–223.
81 ibid, §399.
82 On the potential for dialogue between the courts, see chapter by Susan Ann Samuel & Jorge Alejandro Carrillo Bañuelos in this volume.
83 See supra note 80 and corresponding text.

and the deference owed to science in determining necessary measures, and give them concrete meaning.

For these reasons, however, there are also inherent risks in these requests for advisory opinions. A central risk is the potential for further fragmentation and conflict among different legal regimes all dealing with (certain aspects of) climate change. International courts and tribunals will likely issue an opinion which is in line with their prior case law, ensuring consistency within their system, and this can result in different interpretation of similar legal standards. An example that has been put forward is how the IACtHR has adopted more developed criteria in detailing the due diligence standards in its previous case law than the ICJ and ITLOS.[84] However, it is not implausible that apparently similar concepts could have different meaning and requirements in different fields of law, and due diligence standards can be stricter and more developed under human rights law than other regimes.[85] Moreover, it is worth remembering that the ITLOS advisory opinion has substantially developed the requirements of due diligence in relation to the prevention of marine pollution from anthropogenic emissions and proposed strict standards, which might point towards a tendency for finding convergence between regimes rather than fragmentation of legal concepts. It remains to be seen how the other courts (particularly, the ICJ) will deal with the previous determinations of ITLOS on the matter.

Additionally, there is a risk that the findings in the two pending advisory opinions are not helpful, or not helpful enough, for consolidating the international climate regime. On the one hand, courts could be too cautious in their findings or narrow down the scope of the questions asked. This could particularly be the case in relation to the advisory opinion to be delivered by the ICJ: not only because this is the court that is asked for a determination of existing obligations under general international law (including those deriving from custom and general principles), but also because it has a practice of at times avoiding controversial issues in its advisory opinions.[86] Simultaneously, adopting a narrow interpretation of the questions asked could also be a strategy used to minimize overlaps across the three advisory opinions and, hence, contribute to coherent findings across jurisdictions.

84 Maria Antonia Tigre & Armando Rocha, 'Competing Perspectives and Dialogue in Climate Change Advisory Opinions' (2023) 117 *AJIL Unbound* 287, 288.

85 ibid 289.

86 This was notably the case in the *Nuclear Weapons* (n 58) and the *Kosovo Opinion* (n 11) – supra section 2.1. See Philippe Sands, 'Climate Change and the Rule of Law: Adjudicating the Future in International Law' (2016) 28 *Journal of Environmental Law* 19, 19–20.

On the other hand, the courts in question could lean towards the other end of the spectrum and actually provide very detailed answers to the questions asked, hypothetically going as far as establishing quantitative emission reduction targets, setting a formula for allocating fair shares of emissions among countries, or establishing a method for calculating compensation for the harms caused by climate change owed to small island states and individuals representing present and future generations. This could also constitute a problem as their advisory opinions could be rejected by states as overreaching beyond the courts' powers.[87] However, international courts and tribunals have consistently shown to be cognizant of the fact that their authority and the ability of their advisory opinions to influence the development of international law and shape behavior depends on perception of them acting exclusively within their scope of jurisdiction, providing continuity with past understandings of the law and not engaging in innovative law-making. Accordingly, this concern should not be overstated.

5 Conclusion

The requests for three advisory opinions on climate change is an historic moment in international law. They represent a renewed trust in the international legal system and in international courts and tribunals, which is particularly significant at a time in which international law and international negotiations are being heavily criticized for failing to deliver sufficient results to protect the world from the effects of climate change. These requests provide an opportunity for international courts to clarify the content of states obligations under international law in relation to combating climate change and to bring coherence across different legal regimes.

This chapter has demonstrated that international courts and tribunals can make important contributions to the development of international law, not only through their contentious proceedings but also by delivering highly influential advisory opinions that shape future action by international actors. The *COSIS Opinion* has led the way by interpreting obligations of protection of the marine environment within UNCLOS to also oblige states to prevent, reduce, and control anthropogenic greenhouse gas emissions which cause climate change and ocean acidification. It further reinforced the role of science ('the best available science') in determining the scope of states' obligations,

87 See this same concern in Daniel Bodansky, 'Advisory Opinions on Climate Change: Some Preliminary Questions' (2023) 32 *RECIEL* 185, 188.

clarifying that the high risk and seriousness of climate harm call for far reaching measures and applying a stringent standard of due diligence.

Even so, the role of judicial law-making should not be overstated. Any determinations that international courts make in relation to the content of international climate change law, particularly customary law, must be seen as evidencing existing rules rather than constituting new ones. Courts have been careful to base their argumentation on previous case law whenever possible and have not been openly disruptive of the status quo – bound as they are to respect the parameters of the international legal argument if they seek to have their determinations recognized by international legal actors. Furthermore, they are bound by the questions asked and the different legal regimes that they are called upon to apply, as well as constrained by their own previous case law. For these reasons, it is perhaps too hopeful to expect that the two remaining advisory opinions might quantify emissions targets or spell out mechanisms and formulas through which loss and damage can be compensated. Instead, the greatest potential of the climate change advisory opinions is likely to be their role in contributing to a 'change of consciousness.'[88] By highlighting existing obligations in relation to the protection of the environment, reducing emissions, and preventing significant harm, the advisory opinions can contribute to advance climate negotiations and promote the adoption of more ambitious legal regimes. They can catalyze much needed new action by states, international organizations, and other relevant actors to curb greenhouse gas emissions. And they can offer a 'beacon of hope'[89] that validates global climate activism and galvanizes further action to hold states accountable to their climate obligations, including through litigation and participation in policymaking at national and international level.

88 Sands (n 86) 26.

89 Margaretha Wewerinke-Singh, Ayan Garg &Jacques Hartmann, 'The Advisory Proceedings on Climate Change before the International Court of Justice' (2023) 102 *Questions of International Law* 23, 42.

CHAPTER 3

The Climate-Related Obligations under the UNCLOS, the ACHR, and International Law in General

Alice Ollino and Irini Papanicolopulu***

Abstract

This chapter examines the obligations arising from general international law, the United Nations Convention on the Law of the Sea and the American Convention on Human Rights, whose scope can encompass climate change issues. International obligations under UNCLOS already accommodate climate change challenges, as recently demonstrated by the ITLOS in the 2024 advisory opinion on climate change. Less clear is the extent to which the ACHR AND general rules of international law can constitute an effective tool to address climate change. The chapter analyses some structural features of obligations arising from these three different contexts, stressing how their due diligence nature along with the interpretative role of judge are key elements for successfully identifying climate-related duties.

Keywords

UNCLOS – ACHR – international obligations – climate change – advisory opinion – duty of prevention – due diligence – mitigation

1 Introduction

It has now become common knowledge that climate change is one of the most pressing challenges of our times and that the well-being of present and future

* Assistant Professor of International Law, University of Milano-Bicocca. (0009–0001-0608–1660).

** British Academy Global Professor of International Law, SOAS University of London. (0000–0003-2612–2404).

generations of humankind will depend on the international community's response to it.[1]

In international law, the framework of primary reference for addressing climate change is the treaty regime established under the 1992 United Nations Framework Convention on Climate Change (UNFCCC).[2] The Convention outlines the principles and general objectives of State parties toward the fight against climate change and establishes processes and institutions, such as the Conference of the Parties (CoP), to carry out future negotiations and adopt operational decisions. Since 1992, the UNFCCC has been followed by other international instruments. In 1997, the Kyoto Protocol was adopted to establish quantified emission limitations and reduction commitments for developed countries for a first period between 2008 and 2012, and then for a second period between 2013 and 2020.[3] In 2015, the parties to the UNFCCC adopted the Paris Agreement, which requires each party to 'prepare, communicate and maintain nationally determined contributions' that they intend to achieve to respond globally to climate change.[4]

While negotiation efforts have been intense, the UNFCCC framework and the most recent Paris Agreement present a number of shortcomings. The most significant probably concerns the nature and content of the commitments arising out of the treaties. As a framework convention, the UNFCCC only establishes general commitments of States to cooperate towards developing a law and governance structure based on general principles,[5] with the aim to further the ambitions of the community of States as a whole to avoid 'dangerous anthropogenic interference with the climate system.'[6] The Convention, however, does not include specific targets and timetables for States to achieve such objectives – despite the highly limited exception of Article 4(2) UNFCCC.

The Paris Agreement was established to provide more concrete obligations and commitments of State parties. Yet, despite the ambitious goals set by the Paris Agreement, the legal quality of its commitments remains a

1 UNGA, 'Obligations of States in Respect of Climate Change (Request for Advisory Opinion)' (1 March 2023) UN Doc. A/77/L.58, at 3.

2 United Nations Framework Convention on Climate Change (adopted 9 May 1992, entry into force 21 March 1994) 1771 *UNTS* 107.

3 Kyoto Protocol to the UNFCCC (adopted 11 December 1997, entry into force 16 February 2005) 2303 *UNTS* 162.

4 Paris Agreement (adopted 12 December 2015, entry into force 4 November 2016) 3156 *UNTS* 79.

5 UNFCCC, art 3.

6 ibid art 2.

point of contention. Many provisions in the Paris Agreement are not formulated as legally binding commitments, and only state that the parties 'should' strive toward the achievement of certain goals.[7] Some provisions are either addressed to the parties collectively[8] or they lack an addressee entirely and are expressed only as general statements of intent.[9] Even Article 4, which uses the term 'shall', is formulated in such a convoluted way – parties shall 'pursue domestic mitigation measures with the aim of achieving the objectives of [the NDCs]' – that some prominent legal scholars have questioned its legal force.[10] In a similar vein, many commentators have noted that the ambiguous manner in which commitments are articulated suggests a reading of the Paris Agreement as containing a 'spectrum of legal character,'[11] a continuum between hard obligations and non-obligations.

All these factors contribute to making the justiciability of the obligations arising out of the climate change treaty regime a difficult objective. One should also add that, unless States specifically consent to it, these treaties do not create compulsory dispute settlement procedures, and only provide for relatively weak compliance mechanisms.[12]

It is mostly because of the drawbacks of the treaty regime on climate change that States, civil society groups and legal scholars have attempted to explore the potential of relying on other rules of international law to address climate change concerns. The advisory proceedings before the International Court of Justice (ICJ), the International Tribunal for the Law of the Sea (ITLOS) and the Inter-American Court of Human Rights (IACtHR) are a reflection of this trend, as they tackle climate change hurdles outside the framework of the UNFCCC regime.

This chapter focuses therefore on the international obligations arising from general international law, the United Nations Convention on the Law of the Sea (UNCLOS) and the American Convention on Human Rights (ACHR) whose scope may encompass climate change issues. The chapter provides a general

---

7 James Crawford, 'The Current Political Discourse Concerning International Law' (2018) 81 *Modern Law Review* 1, 21.

8 Paris Agreement, arts 3 and 4(1).

9 ibid art 6.

10 Daniel Bodansky, 'The Paris Climate Change Agreement: A New Hope?' (2016) 110 *AJIL* 288, 295; Jutta Brunnée, 'Procedure and Substance in International Environmental Law' (2019) 450 *RCADI* 59.

11 Lavanya Rajamani, 'The 2015 Paris Agreement: Interplay Between Hard, Soft and Non-Obligations' (2016) 28 *Journal of Environmental Law* 337, 351.

12 See UNFCCC, art 14; Paris Agreement, art 24.

overview of the most salient climate-related obligations that pertain to these three areas and that have so far been addressed or are likely to be addressed by Courts in their respective advisory opinions.

A last caveat is necessary. This chapter only engages with the analysis of primary rules – whether treaty-based or general – whose application may be relevant in the context of climate change. This means that questions concerning State responsibility for violating such obligations and the correlative secondary rules are set aside. While the distinction between primary and secondary rules is not always clear-cut, this dogmatic approach explains why questions of compensation, damages and relevant principles applicable in the climate context (eg causality, the polluter pays principle, etc) are not part of the following discussion.

2 Climate-Related Obligations under UNCLOS

UNCLOS does not contain references to climate change. At the time when the Convention was negotiated and adopted, there was little scientific knowledge about climate change and its impacts, and it was not perceived as being an issue that needed to be addressed in the already complex negotiations. This gap becomes relevant today, when we have learned that GHG emissions cause acidification of the oceans and that the rise in the global temperature due to climate change produces heat waves, stratification and deoxygenation, and sea level rise, all of which have direct and indirect impacts on marine biodiversity, coastal communities and the planet.[13]

The absence of provisions specifically targeting climate change and its effects on the oceans, however, should not be taken to exclude the relevance of the UNCLOS in this field. On the contrary, the Convention contains numerous provisions that set out the duties of States in relation to protection and preservation of the marine environment and which can be used to address GHG emissions and the negative impacts of climate change on the oceans. The ITLOS has recently clarified the scope, nature and content of these obligations[14] and the following analysis will take into account its findings. Most of these provisions are to be found in Part XII UNCLOS, with other provisions being scattered in the other parts of the Convention.[15]

13 IPCC, *Special Report on the Ocean and Cryosphere in a Changing Climate* (CUP 2022).

14 *Request for an Advisory Opinion Submitted by the Commission of Small Island States on Climate Change and International Law* (Advisory Opinion, 21 May 2024) ITLOS Case No 31 (COSIS *Opinion*).

15 While this topic is extensively discussed in other chapters of this volume, it is worth recalling that UNCLOS, apart from its numerous substantial provisions, including those in Part XII, contains also procedural provisions, notably concerning binding dispute settlement.

2.1 *The Duty to Prevent, Reduce, and Control Pollution and Related Duties*

Part XII of UNCLOS contains a general obligation and other specific provisions that mandate States to prevent, reduce and control pollution of the marine environment.[16] The general duty, enshrined in Article 194 UNCLOS, is particularly broad, as it concerns pollution 'from any source', obliges States to take 'all necessary' measures, and applies to all activities under their jurisdiction and control.

The condition necessary to apply Article 194, and indeed any UNCLOS provision on pollution, is that a certain phenomenon falls within the definition provided by UNCLOS, according to which 'pollution of the marine environment' means:

> the introduction by man, directly or indirectly, of substances or energy into the marine environment, including estuaries, which results or is likely to result in such deleterious effects as harm to living resources and marine life, hazards to human health, hindrance to marine activities, including fishing and other legitimate uses of the sea, impairment of quality for use of sea water and reduction of amenities.[17]

As the ITLOS has authoritatively stated, GHG emissions into the atmosphere constitute pollution of the marine environment in accordance with this provision.[18] Climate change is caused by GHG emissions, such as carbon dioxide (CO_2), methane (CH_4), nitrous oxide (N_2O), hydrofluorocarbons (HFCs), perfluorocarbons (PFCs), sulphur hexafluoride (SF_6), and nitrogen trifluoride (NF_3). GHG are substances,[19] they are introduced by humans into the marine environment,[20] and they produce deleterious effects, including harm to living resources and marine life, hazards to human health, hindrance of activities, impairment of quality and reduction of amenities, both directly and indirectly, by causing an increase of heat which produces heat waves, deoxygenation, and

These provisions have been used to request an advisory opinion from the ITLOS, and have the potential to also trigger future inter-State litigation, especially if States do not comply with the obligations concerning protection of the marine environment, or the prevention, reduction, and control of marine pollution, ITLOS has pointed out in its advisory opinion.

16 UNCLOS, art 194(1) to (4).

17 UNCLOS, art 1(1)(4).

18 COSIS *Opinion* (n 14) §179.

19 ibid §§163–164.

20 ibid §§165–173.

sea level rise.[21] Notably, some of these GHG not only drive climate change, but may also have deleterious effects on the marine environment directly, as in the case of CO_2 which, absorbed by marine waters, is a direct cause of ocean acidification.

In this respect, it is relevant to note that the ITLOS adopted a broad concept of 'marine environment' in response to the narrow interpretation advanced by some States. The marine environment combines both spatial and material components[22] and it 'encompasses certain spaces beyond maritime zones' established by the UNCLOS.[23] This reading is in accordance with the general understanding, according to which the 'sea' for the law of the sea includes not only the water column, but also the seabed and subsoil underneath, as well as the airspace above. This is evident, for example, from the provisions dealing with freedom of the high seas, which include also overflight,[24] and those dealing with sovereign rights of the coastal state in its exclusive economic zone, which also include the production of energy from winds.[25]

Having established that GHG emissions are indeed a kind of pollution of the marine environment, the ensuing duties under Article 194(1) include three separate actions: prevention, reduction, and control. These are duties of due diligence[26] and together 'should be understood in the context of the comprehensive nature of the obligation' under this provision.[27] Action must be adopted at both the individual and the joint, multilateral, level, without there being a

21 ibid §§174–178.

22 ibid §166.

23 ibid §168.

24 UNCLOS, art 87(1)(b).

25 UNCLOS, art 56(1)(a).

26 COSIS *Opinion* (n 14) §234. See also *Responsibilities and Obligations of States Sponsoring Persons and Entities with Respect to Activities in the Area (Request for Advisory Opinion Submitted to the Seabed Disputes Chamber (Advisory Opinion, 1 February 2011)* ITLOS *Case No 17* §110 (*Responsibilities of Sponsoring States*). On due diligence in the context of the law of the sea, Irini Papanicolopulu, 'Due Diligence in the law of the Sea', in Krieger, Peters & Kreuzer (eds), Due Diligence in the International Legal Order (OUP 2020) 147; Doris König, 'The Elaboration of Due Diligence Obligations as a mechanism to Ensure Compliance with International Legal Obligations by Private Actors', *The Contribution of the International Tribunal for the Law of the Sea to the Rule of Law: 1996–2016* (Brill 2018) 83; Ida Caracciolo, 'Due diligence et le droit du mer', in Societé Francaise pour le Droit International (ed), *Le standard de due diligence et la responsabilité internationale* (Pedone 2018) 163. On the consequences of such qualification see *infra*, Section 5.

27 COSIS *Opinion* (n 14) §198.

priority between the two types of action.[28] Indeed, States must act both unilaterally and multilaterally to comply with their duties under Article 194.[29]

It is up to each State to decide the measures it needs to take to comply with Article 194, but these measures must be 'determined objectively'[30] on the basis of some factors: scientific knowledge, international rules and standards, and available means and the abilities of the State concerned.[31] The best available science should be used, as reflected, among other, in the IPCC reports, which point to the need to limit global warming to 1.5°C.[32] However, science alone cannot determine the content of necessary measures, and other factors need to be taken into account.[33]

States need also to take into account relevant international rules and standards, which include not only treaties to which they are parties, but also other hard and soft law instruments.[34] The precautionary approach applies, requiring States to adopt measures even if there is no scientific certainty.[35] Another significant principle, which the ITLOS has discussed in relation to geoengineering, is the duty not to transfer or transform one type of pollution into another.[36] The duty to test new technologies,[37] in combination with the duty not to transfer damage or hazards or transform one type of pollution into another,[38] plays a special role in addressing climate change. In the effort to reduce GHGs present in the atmosphere, some suggestions have been made to geoengineer the oceans to absorb more CO_2, for example by means of ocean fertilisation. These practices, however, might be harmful for the oceans and life in them and may also present other presently unknown consequences. In evaluating any such proposal, the precautionary principle/approach and the duties provided by Articles 195 and 196 UNCLOS must be seriously taken into account. The same applies to any measure which implies human intervention, for example to restore ecosystems or build resilience.

Other applicable rules include, first and foremost, the UNFCCC and Paris Agreement, and the ITLOS has clearly stated that they are both relevant in

---

28 ibid §201.
29 ibid §§201–202.
30 ibid§206.
31 ibid §207.
32 ibid §§208–210.
33 ibid §212.
34 ibid §214. See also §270.
35 ibid §213. See also *Responsibilities of Sponsoring States* (n 26) §131.
36 ibid §231.
37 UNCLOS, art 196.
38 UNCLOS, art 195.

interpreting and applying the UNCLOS. The temperature goal and the timeline set by the Paris Agreement, in particular, 'inform the content of necessary measures to be taken' under Article 194(1).[39] While this statement falls short of making such requirements compulsory for all UNCLOS parties, it is unmistakably a very strong statement in favour of the binding character of these requirements. In addition, as the Tribunal has added, compliance with the Paris Agreement alone is not sufficient to ensure compliance with Article 194 UNCLOS.[40] The threshold is therefore set high.

Finally, in determining the measures that need to be taken, there is 'a certain degree of flexibility' to accommodate the needs of States with limited means and capabilities. This flexibility, however, 'should not be used as an excuse to unduly postpone, or even be exempted from, the implementation of the obligation' under Article 194.[41] The ITLOS has carefully stroke the right balance between the need to underline the primary responsibility of developed States, while at the same time reminding all States that they do bear a responsibility to take measures to address climate change.

While Article 194(1) leaves States to determine what measures they need to take, guidance comes from its qualification as a due diligence obligation. Even before the 2024 Opinion, the ITLOS had identified a certain number of actions that are relevant in assessing compliance with a due diligence obligation: the adoption of laws and regulations;[42] the taking of administrative measures;[43] the exercise of a 'certain level of vigilance in their enforcement and the exercise of administrative control';[44] the enactment of enforcement measures, including 'boarding, inspection, arrest and judicial proceedings';[45] the proper marking of vessels;[46] the creation of monitoring mechanisms;[47] the investigation of any alleged violation and the duty to inform the affected state of the results;[48] the provision for sanctions 'sufficient to deter violations and

---

39 ibid §222.

40 ibid §223.

41 ibid §226.

42 *Responsibilities of Sponsoring States* (n 26) §119.

43 *Responsibilities of Sponsoring States* (n 26) §119; *Request for Advisory Opinion submitted by the Sub-Regional Fisheries Commission* (SRFC), Advisory Opinion, 2 April 2015, ITLOS Rep 4, §119 (SFRC).

44 *Responsibilities of Sponsoring States* (n 26) para 115, citing *Pulp Mills on the River Uruguay (Argentina v Uruguay)* [2010] ICJ Rep 14, §197.

45 *SFRC* (n 43) §§104–105.

46 ibid §137.

47 ibid §138.

48 ibid §139.

to deprive offenders of the benefits accruing from their' illegal activities.[49] The 2024 opinion further added that:

> the obligation of due diligence requires a State to put in place a national system, including legislation, administrative procedures and an enforcement mechanism necessary to regulate the activities in question, and to exercise adequate vigilance to make such a system function efficiently, with a view to achieving the intended objective.[50]

In addition to the general obligation to prevent, reduce, and control pollution of the marine environment under Article 194(1) UNCLOS, the Convention contains other provisions which set out specific duties of States with respect to pollution of the marine environment. Article 194(2) contains a similar yet separate provision identifying the duties of States with respect to transboundary pollution. While the analysis of this provision by the ITLOS mirrors that of Article 194(1) UNCLOS, the Tribunal stresses that the duty under 194(2) could be 'even more stringent' than under Article 194(1)[51] and expands upon the duties of States vis-à-vis private actors,[52] without however fully clarifying the scope of State's obligations. Reference to jurisdiction 'or' control in Article 194 UNCLOS means that the activities which should be regulated by the State include not only those in its territory and coastal zones, as well as by its vessels, but also any other activity which, although not necessarily falling within the State's *de iure* 'jurisdiction', is under its effective control. This control could extend, arguably, to objects, buildings, and processes operated by a national of the State, even if they are located outside the State's territory, coastal zones or vessels. Using climate change law language, the duty to prevent pollution of the marine environment under the UNCLOS substantiates the mitigation duties that States have under the UNFCCC and the Paris Agreement.

Apart from Article 194, further UNCLOS provisions deal with specific sources of pollution, identifying both the duties of States to legislate and their enforcement duties. In its Advisory Opinion, the ITLOS examined three sources of pollution: land-based activities,[53] vessels,[54] and atmospheric

49 ibid §138.
50 COSIS *Opinion* (n 14) §235.
51 ibid §256.
52 ibid §247.
53 ibid §§266–273 and 283–286.
54 ibid §§278–280 and 287–291.

pollution.[55] However, the Tribunal did not discuss pollution from seabed activities within[56] and beyond[57] national jurisdiction. The ITLOS examined extensively the relevant UNCLOS provisions addressing land-based and atmospheric pollution and clarified the specific duties that States have, as well as the relationship between national and international measures. In quite stark contrast, the discussion of duties with respect to pollution from vessels, is rather thin, and only addresses, very briefly, the duties of the flag States,[58] notwithstanding the specific provisions in the UNCLOS concerning duties and powers of coastal States and port States. The work of the IMO on Annex VI MARPOL is key in this respect, as are the delays that have characterised sometimes IMO's work. The advisory proceedings before ITLOS could have been an excellent opportunity to recall that not only States have duties, but also that intergovernmental organisations have the duty to fulfil their mandate – and States have the duty to help the organisation do so and not prejudice the adoption of the necessary rules and regulations.

Finally, the ITLOS identified three further duties linked with the obligations to prevent, reduce and control pollution. First, the obligation to cooperate, which requires States 'to cooperate, directly or through competent international organizations, continuously, meaningfully and in good faith, in order to prevent, reduce and control marine pollution' from GHG emissions.[59] This is an obligation of means but also an obligation 'of an ongoing nature.'[60] As the ITLOS notes, while the aim of this cooperation may be the adoption of a treaty or other normative instrument, the

> adoption of a particular treaty, such as the UNFCCC or the Paris Agreement, does not discharge a State from its obligation to cooperate, as the obligation requires an ongoing effort on the part of States in the development of new or revised regulatory instruments, in particular in light of the evolution of scientific knowledge.[61]

Second, obligations of technical assistance.[62] These include three categories of measures: the promotion of programmes of scientific, educational, technical

55 ibid §§274–277 and 283–286.
56 UNCLOS, arts 208 and 214.
57 UNCLOS, arts 209 and 215.
58 COSIS *Opinion* (n 14) §287.
59 ibid §321.
60 ibid §§306 and 311.
61 ibid §311.
62 ibid §326.

and other assistance to developing States;[63] the provision of appropriate assistance, especially to developing States, to minimise the major effects of climate change;[64] and the provision of appropriate assistance in the preparation of environmental assessments.[65] Other assistance may include financial assistance towards these aims.[66]

Third, obligations related to monitoring and environmental assessment.[67] The duty to monitor activities under the jurisdiction and control of States and to conduct environmental assessments[68] is particularly relevant to both identify the sources and trend of GHG emissions and to identify the effects of climate change over the oceans, their species and ecosystems. While these are procedural obligations, compliance with them is a factor for assessing also compliance with substantial obligations.[69]

2.2 *The Duty to Protect and Preserve the Marine Environment and Related Duties*

In addition to addressing pollution, Part XII of UNCLOS also more generally addresses protection and preservation of the marine environment. Article 192 UNCLOS provides for the general duty of States to protect and preserve the marine environment in apparently absolute terms and without mentioning any exception, condition, or limitation. Notwithstanding its broad language, this provision contains a legally binding obligation of due diligence;[70] in other words, '[w]hile article 192 imposes upon States a legal obligation, this provision is, at the same time, a statement of principle upon which the legal order for the protection and preservation of the marine environment under the Convention is based.'[71] It mandates States 'to ensure that non-State actors under their jurisdiction or control comply with' all measures they have adopted in compliance with their other duties.[72] The standard of due diligence under Article 192 is

63 ibid §332.

64 ibid §para 334. The comment of the ITLOS that '[t]his category appears to be of lesser relevance' is quite unfortunate, in light of the major impact of rising sea level on coastal communities.

65 ibid §335.

66 ibid §336.

67 ibid §367.

68 UNCLOS, arts 204 and 206. The duty to conduct EIAs has been considered as a direct duty in *Responsibilities of Sponsoring States* (n 26) §145.

69 COSIS *Opinion* (n 14) §345.

70 ibid §§385 and 397. See also *SFRC* (n 43) §120.

71 ibid §184.

72 ibid §396.

'stringent given the high risks of serious and irreversible harm to the marine environment by climate change impacts and ocean acidification.'[73]

The broad obligation of Article 192 is further specified and operationalised by numerous other obligations, which spell out in some detail what States need to do to protect and preserve the marine environment. Thus, all the provisions included in Part XII of UNCLOS can be considered as clarifications of the obligation under Article 192. At the same time, they are also self-standing legal obligations, which may be breached in their own rights and may therefore generate the international responsibility of the State.

Apart from the provisions on pollution addressed above, a number of other duties provided by Part XII are particularly relevant for climate change. First, the duty to protect fragile ecosystems and the habitats of endangered species requests States to go beyond general measures to address pollution and degradation, and to also adopt concrete measures targeted at these ecosystems and habitats.[74] The impact of climate change on corals, for example, requests States not only to adopt action to prevent the worsening of climate change, but also to adapt restoration and resilience building measures targeted specifically at them – measures that States might be required to adopt under this provision would fall in the 'adaptation' duties of States concerning climate change.

Second, duties relating to protection and preservation of marine living resources also come into play.[75] These include action by coastal States within their maritime zones, including the exclusive economic zone. In designing appropriate measures, coastal States are require to also take into account 'the impact of climate change and ocean acidification on marine ecosystems environmental stressors stock migration and the implications for vulnerable communities and specially affected developing states.'[76] They also include the obligation for States to take appropriate measures concerning living resources on the high seas,[77] as well as obligations to cooperate.

Finally, and quite interestingly, the ITLOS identified specific obligations relating to the introduction of alien species and requiring States to take adaptive measures to prevent reduce and control pollution from the introduction of non-indigenous species as a result of climate change impacts and ocean acidification which may cause significant and harmful changes to the marine environment.

73 ibid §399.
74 ibid §403.
75 ibid §§409–410.
76 ibid §414.
77 ibid §415.

3 International Human Rights and Climate-Related Obligations under the ACHR

From the perspective of mapping the international obligations set to address climate change and reduce GHG emissions, international human rights law does not add much to the current legal framework established under the UNFCCC framework, general international law, multilateral environmental agreements, and the international law of the sea. These regimes already identify the most important substantive obligations aimed at reducing the impact of climate change, mitigate its effects toward the environment and adapt to its consequences. However, international human rights law has proved an invaluable resource thanks to its capacity to verticalise the relationship between climate-related obligations and their correlative rights, by making individuals *right-holders* of climate-related obligations, and providing them with a forum to court litigation and quasi-judicial complaint mechanisms.[78]

The human rights-based approach to climate change has its limits, since applicants seeking to establish a State's failure to comply with obligations to mitigate or adapt to climate change will have to satisfy the requirements for admissibility before international human rights bodies – jurisdiction and 'victim' status being the most problematic.[79] That said, in the absence of an international court with competence over the UN climate treaties, construing cases on climate change through the lens of States' human rights obligations has been a game-changer in the field.

Obligations arising out of human rights treaties are typically divided into 'negative' and 'positive' human rights obligations. Negative human rights

78 *Duarte Agostinho and Others v Portugal and 32 Other States* (App No 39371/20) ECtHR [GC] 9 April 2024; *Verein KlimaSeniorinnen Schweiz and Others v Switzerland* (App No 53600/20) ECtHR [GC] 9 April 2024; Complaint in 'Mex M against Austria' (ECtHR, 25 March 2021); *Greenpeace Nordic v Norway*, Communicated Case No 34068/ 21 (ECtHR, 16 December 2021); Inter-American Commission on Human Rights, 'Petition Seeking Relief from Violations resulting from Global Warming caused by Acts and Omissions of the United States' (7 December 2005); Committee on the Rights of the Child, 'Decision adopted by the Committee on the Rights of the Child under the Optional Protocol to the Convention on the Rights of the Child on a communications procedure in respect of Communication No 104/2019' UN Doc No CRC/C/88/D/104/2019 (8 October 2021); Human Rights Committee, *Daniel Billy et al.* Views adopted by the Committee under article 5 (4) of the Optional Protocol, concerning communication No. 3624/201 Adopted by the Committee at its 135th session (27 June–27 July 2022).

79 *López Ostra v Spain* (App No 16798/90) ECtHR 9 December 1994; *Cordella and Others v Italy* (App No 54414/ 13) ECtHR 24 January 2019, §§100–109; Yevgeniy *Dmitriyev v Russia* (App No 17840/06) ECtHR 1 December 2020, §32.

obligations require States to 'respect' human rights, ie to refrain from committing human rights violations vis-à-vis individuals under their jurisdiction. Conversely, 'positive' human rights obligations require States to 'prevent' and 'protect' individuals from human rights violations by taking necessary measures to ensure the respect of human rights. Broadly speaking, obligations to prevent and protect from human rights violations are obligations of due diligence, since they require States to act to prevent and protect from human rights risks originating from private entities or from other 'external' sources – including environmental hazards.[80] Positive human rights obligations are the type of obligations at stake in the context of climate change. As the impact of climate change negatively affects human rights, under their human rights obligations, States may be required to take measures to avoid, adapt, or mitigate this impact.

Under the ACHR, a wide range of civil and political rights may be impacted by climate change. These include the right to life (art 4), the right to humane treatment (art 5), the right to fair trial (art 8), the right to privacy (art 11), freedom of expression (art 13), the rights of the child (art 19), the right to property (art 21), freedom of movement (art 22), the right to judicial protection (art 25), and eventually other economic, social, and cultural rights (art 26).[81] The request for an advisory opinion on Climate Emergency and Human Rights submitted to the IACtHR mentions most of them by building on the Court's previous jurisprudence.[82]

The Court has indeed already included environmental considerations in the interpretation of many of these rights.[83] In a landmark advisory opinion

---

80 Human Rights Committee, General Comment No 36, 'Article 6: Right to Life', UN Doc No CCPR/C/GC/36 (3 September 2019) §7.3; *Budayeva v Russia* (Apps Nos 15339/02, 21166/02, 20058/02, 11673/02 & 15343/02) ECtHR 20 March 2008, §§128–29.

81 An overview of the human rights that may be affected by climate change under the ACHR is offered by Inter-American Commission on Human Rights, 'Climate Emergency: Scope of the Inter-American Human Rights Obligations', Resolution 3/21, 31 December 2021.

82 Admittedly, while there is at least a reference to most of the rights listed above, the questions submitted before do not ask the Court to elaborate on the precise scope of each of these rights vis-à-vis climate change. Rather, questions are either very specific with regard to certain rights (eg access to information) or right-bearers (eg children) or they raise substantive issues that cut across several rights under the Convention. See for a critique Monica Feria-Tinta, 'An advisory opinion on climate emergency and human rights before the Inter-American Court of Human Rights' (2023) *QIL-Questions of International Law* 102, 45.

83 A cursory review of the jurisprudence of the Court is available in 'Cuadernillos de Jurisprudencia de la Corte Interamericana de Derechos Humanos: Derechos Económico, Sociales, Culturales y Ambientales', 22/2021 <https://www.diarioconstitucional.cl/wp-content/uploads/2021/08/6-08-CoIDH-Cuadernillos.pdf>, 22–28.

issued in 2017, the Court affirmed that Article 26 of the Convention, which establishes the progressive realisation of economic, social, and cultural rights, includes an autonomous right to a healthy environment.[84] The Court observed that a right to a healthy environment is a right with an individual and collective dimension. In its individual dimension, the right to a healthy environment requires a State to take steps to protect an individual against a risk of violation of their right to life, health, and personal integrity caused by environmental degradation.[85] In its collective dimension, this right constitutes a 'universal value' and is owed to present and future generations.[86] The collective dimension is especially relevant in relation to climate change, since it implies that States' obligations go beyond the protection from immediate environmental threats targeting specific (groups of) individuals, and extend to the adoption of measures to protect nature and the environment themselves for the benefit of humankind, including future generations.[87]

In order to discuss the scope of the climate-related human rights obligations deriving from these rights, a distinction between adaptation and mitigation measures is warranted.

3.1 *Human Rights Obligations that Promote Adaptation to Climate Change*

The rights protected under the ACHR are already interpreted in ways that may encompass States' positive obligations to promote measures that *adapt* to climate change. In relation to the right to life and personal integrity, for instance, there is consolidated consensus in international human rights practice that these rights require States to adopt an appropriate legal framework to deter any threat to the right to life or personal integrity and to establish effective judicial mechanisms capable of investigating and providing redress for any violation.[88] In addition, while States cannot be held responsible for *every* violation

84 *The Environment and Human Rights (State Obligations in Relation to the Environment in the Context of the Protection and Guarantee of the Rights to Life and to Personal Integrity – Interpretation and Scope of Articles 4(1) and 5(1) of the American Convention on Human Rights)* Advisory Opinion OC-23/17, Inter-American Court of Human Rights Series A No 23 (15 November 2017) §§47, 62.

85 ibid §59.

86 ibid.

87 ibid §62.

88 *Case of the 'Street Children' (Villagrán Morales et al) v Guatemala* (Merits) Inter-American Court of Human Rights Series C No 63 (19 November 1999), §144; *Case of the Pueblo Bello Massacre v Colombia* (Merits, Reparations and Costs) Inter-American Court of Human Rights Series C No 140 (31 January 2006) §120; *Case of the Sawhoyamaxa Indigenous*

of the right to life or personal integrity of *all* individuals under their jurisdiction, the positive obligation to protect life or personal integrity includes a State's duty to act and adopt all the necessary measures to prevent violations whenever state authorities knew, or should have known, of the existence of a situation of real and immediate risk to the life of targeted individuals (or groups thereof) and they could reasonably be expected to prevent or avoid that risk.[89] Similar considerations have been made about the scope of positive obligations correlated to other rights, including the right to a healthy environment, the right to food, the right to water, the right to cultural identity, the rights of children and the right to property.[90]

Transposed to the context of climate change, States have the obligation to adopt all the measures – legislative, administrative, judicial, and operational – necessary to address the environmental and social consequences of climate change that may result in violations of human rights protected under the Convention.[91] For instance, if the survival of a group of individuals residing in one coastal region under a State's jurisdiction is threatened by extreme weather events caused by sea-level rise and climate change, this State may be responsible for violating their right to life if it knew of the risk and failed to put in place adequate measures to prevent or minimize it – eg by installing early-warning systems to inform the local population, by relocating vulnerable groups from coastal areas to other regions, or by building coastal infrastructures aimed at managing environmental disasters.[92]

Generally speaking, significant climate change-induced environmental damage occurring in a State's territory and having the capacity to negatively affect the human rights of individuals under the State's jurisdiction would trigger preventive obligations and the adoption of necessary and adequate protective measures. In this respect, the IACtHR has already addressed in numerous cases the environmental impact that some activities carried under a State's jurisdiction or control bear on the human rights of certain individuals,

---

Community v Paraguay (Merits, Reparations and Costs) Inter-American Court of Human Rights Series C No 146 (29 March 2006) §153.

89 *Velásquez-Rodríguez v Honduras* (Merits) Inter-American Court of Human Rights Series C No 4 (29 July 1988) §172.

90 *Case of the 'Street Children'* (n 88) 88144; *Case of the Saramaka People v Suriname. Preliminary Objections* (Merits, Reparations and Costs) Inter-American Court of Human Rights Series C No 172 (28 November 2007) §91.

91 See Human Rights Committee (n 80) §62.

92 *Budayeva* (n 80) §§128–29; Öneryildiz *v Turkey* (App No 48939/99) ECtHR [GC] 30 November 2004; *Fadeyeva v Russia* (App No 55723/00) ECtHR 9 June 2005.

especially vulnerable groups like indigenous people.[93] In these cases, the 'source' of environmental risk was not climate change and consisted mainly of resource extraction activities carried out by private companies and authorized by the State.[94] However, one may argue that the same rationale would apply to significant climate change-induced environmental hazards known (or at least knowledgeable) by the State and threatening targeted individuals or vulnerable groups on its territory.

3.2 *Human Rights Obligations that Promote Mitigation of Climate Change*

Less clear is whether the interpretation of the scope of the obligations under the ACHR extends to the point of including a positive duty to reduce GHG emissions to prevent and protect from violations of human rights. Does prevention under the ACHR require States to act to achieve sufficient mitigation outcomes to effectively protect the human rights of individuals under their jurisdiction? What should mitigation measures in the context of human rights protection consist of?

The request for an advisory opinion on Climate Emergency and Human Rights asks the IACtHR precisely to clarify this point. Many of the questions posed to the Court regard the extent to which States' obligations to prevent human rights violations (whether general obligations to prevent or preventive duties vis-à-vis vulnerable groups) should be interpreted in light of the Paris Agreement and what activities and principles should inspire the action of mitigation.[95]

In a landmark decision issued by the European Court of Human Rights on April 2024, the Court has established that, under Article 8 of the European Convention on Human Rights, States parties to the Convention have a duty to adopt and effectively apply regulations and measures capable of *mitigating* the existing and potentially irreversible future effects of climate change.[96] Before this case, the response to this question by courts and international

93 *Case of the Kichwa People of Sarayaku v Ecuador* (Merits and Reparations) 27 June 2012, Inter-American Court of Human Rights Series C No 245 (27 June 2012); *Case of the Kaliña and Lokono Peoples v Suriname* (Merits, Reparations and Costs) Inter-American Court of Human Rights Series C No 309 (25 November 2015).

94 *Kaliña and Lokono* (n 93) §§217–230.

95 *Request for an advisory opinion on the Climate Emergency and Human Rights submitted to the Inter-American Court of Human Rights by the Republic of Colombia and the Republic of Chile*, questions A(1) and A(2)(A) A(2)(B).

96 *Verein KlimaSeniorinnen Schweiz v Switzerland* (n 78).

human rights bodies has been mixed.[97] With the *Verein KlimaS eniorinnen Schweiz* case, the ECtHR instead affirmed, for the first time, that States are under the positive obligation to adopt measures to mitigate climate change and that a margin of appreciation in the choice of means to fulfil such obligation is granted as long as States acts with the due diligence required of Article 8. According to the Court, such due diligence includes: the duty to adopt general measures to specifying a target timeline to reach carbon neutrality; the duty to set intermediate GHG emission reduction targets and to keep them updated; the duty to show evidence of compliance with these targets and to act in good time and in an appropriate and consistent manner.[98] In short, the Court has drawn on the global aims of the Paris Agreement to inform the extent of States' positive obligations under the ECHR.

The IACtHR's previous case law shows the potential to replicate the ECtHR's observations and incorporate a wide range of measures reflecting mitigation actions into the substance of positive obligations to protect human rights.

The Court is no stranger to the use of international environmental principle to formulate the scope of States' obligations to protect human rights. In the 2017 advisory opinion on Human Rights and the Environment, the IACtHR argued that the scope of the obligation to protect the right to life and integrity of individuals exposed to environmental damage must be assessed in light of principles of international environmental law. For a State to adopt all the necessary measures to protect the life of individuals facing potential environmental damage, a State is required to: adopt measures drawn from the general obligation to prevent significant harm or damage to the environment;[99] adopt measures informed by the precautionary principle;[100] comply with a duty to cooperate with other States with the view of avoiding or minimizing risks of environmental harm resulting in human rights violations.[101]

While the opinion did not concern climate change but transboundary environmental damage, the IACtHR has showed, however, a propensity to draw on legal principles belonging to a different regime – in this case, international environmental law – in order to expand the scope and meaning of State's positive obligation to protect human rights. There are therefore good reasons to believe that, following the ECtHR, the IACtHR could build on these arguments

---

97 See *Urgenda v Netherlands*, ECLI:NL:HR:2019:2007 (SC, 20 December 2019), English translation in (2020) 59 ILM 811. *Sacchi and others*, para 10.12. Daniel Billy (n 78) §4.3.

98 *Verein KlimaSeniorinnen Schweiz v Switzerland* (n 78), para 549–551.

99 ibid §§53–68.

100 ibid §§68–71.

101 ibid §§71–80.

and apply the same rationale to identify the measures States shall take to fulfil due diligence in relation to their positive human rights obligation to protect from climate change.

This conclusion may be further supported by the approach adopted by the IACtHR in relation to the concept of jurisdiction. In the advisory opinion on *Human Rights and the Environment*, the IACtHR argued that individuals whose rights are affected by transboundary environmental harm are under the jurisdiction of a State party if there is a causal link between the act originating in State territory and the human rights of persons outside of it.[102] Hence, if a State fails to prevent transboundary environmental damage, this may result in a breach of this State's obligations to ensure human rights and prevent violations. Such a conclusion may open the door to interpreting the obligations to protect human rights as including positive duties to mitigate GHG emissions. If a State can be responsible not only vis-à-vis the population on its territory but also persons affected by activities originating in State territory and causing transboundary environmental damage, this means that a State could, at least in theory, be blamed for human rights violations resulting from this State's impact on climate change – for instance, by manifestly failing to achieve reduction targets and by pursuing policies favouring pollution. *A fortiori*, a State's ability to achieve marginal reduction in GHG emission would instead be an indication of its compliance with, *inter alia*, human rights protective measures. The ECtHR has not gone this far in its interpretation of the reach of States' positive obligations under the Convention.[103]

4 Climate-Related Obligations under General International Law

Among the advantages that climate-related obligations under general international law offer with respect to treaty-based obligations is that States are bound by mitigation duties regardless of their consent to treaty commitments or unilateral declarations. Hence, a State withdrawing from climate change treaties could not cause unlimited amounts of GHG emissions and would still be bound by relevant rules under general international law.[104]

Yet, speaking of climate-related obligations under general international law presents challenges. A first problem concerns the identification of the

102 *Environment and Human Rights* (n 84) 103.
103 See *Duarte Agostinho* (n 78) §126.
104 See in detail Benoit Mayer, *International Law Obligations on Climate Change Mitigation* (OUP 2022) 88–90.

potentially relevant primary rules, an issue that is certainly not specific of international climate change law,[105] but which significantly affects this area. For instance, international environmental law is the primary source for the recognition of general rules applicable to the climate change context. While there are currently few doubts on the general nature of the duty to prevent environmental harm, questions remain on the exact contours and content of this rule, as well as whether certain environmental principles relevant for climate change would be applicable in this area. Secondly, issues of identification aside, the use of general international law to manage climate change problems requires one to assess how general rules apply to the specific sets of facts climate change brings about.[106]

Bearing this in mind, general international law retains the potential for addressing the climate change issue. It is possible to identify some customary obligations and general principles that may be used to address climate change-related problems.

4.1 *The Obligation to Prevent Transboundary Environmental Harm*

Under the obligation to prevent transboundary environmental harm, States have a duty to conduct their activities in a way that does not cause significant harm to the environment of other States or of areas beyond national control.

International courts and tribunals have upheld the customary status of the duty to prevent transboundary environmental harm.[107] Already in the 1996 Advisory opinion on *Nuclear Weapons*, the International Court of Justice (ICJ) recognized the 'general obligation of States to ensure that activities within their jurisdiction and control respect the environment of other States or of areas beyond national control.'[108] In *Pulp Mills,* the Court affirmed that 'the principle of prevention, as *a customary rule*, has its origins in the due diligence

105 As the recent ILC, works on the identification of customary international law and general principles of law have demonstrated, the methodology for the identification of these sources of law remains a contentious issue. See ILC 'Draft conclusions on identification of customary international law' (2018) ILC YB 2/II and 'Draft conclusions on general principles of law, together with commentaries thereto' (n 18).

106 See, for instance, the question on the interpretation of the obligation to prevent transboundary harm as applied to international watercourses in the *Dispute over the Status and Use of the Waters of Silala* (*Chile v Bolivia*) [2022] ICJ Rep 614, §§79–80.

107 *In the Matter of South China Sea Arbitration* (*Republic of the Philippines v The People's Republic of China*) PCA Case 2013–19 (2016) §941; *Award in the Arbitration regarding the Iron Rhine Railway between the Kingdom of Belgium and the Kingdom of the Netherlands* (*Belgium v The Netherlands*) 17 RIAA, §59.

108 *Legality of the Threat or Use of Nuclear Weapons* (Advisory Opinion) [1996] ICJ Rep 226, §29.

that is required of a State in its territory. It is "every State's obligation not to allow knowingly its territory to be used for acts contrary to the rights of other States".'[109] The Court did not infer the customary nature of the obligation to prevent environmental harm based on the rigorous two-steps approach required to identify custom,[110] but it relied on the application of a general principle of due diligence extrapolated from the *Corfu Channel* dictum and applied to the environmental context.[111] More recently, the ICJ has confirmed the customary status of prevention of environmental harm in the judgment in *Certain Activities*,[112] and in the 2022 judgment *Dispute over the Status and Use of the Waters of the Silala*.[113]

As to the *substance* of the general obligation to prevent environmental harm, it requires a State 'to use all the means at its disposal in order to avoid activities which take place in its territory, or in any area under its jurisdiction, causing significant damage to the environment of another State'.[114] States,[115] international courts and tribunals,[116] and scholars an obligation of conduct, hence a due diligence obligation.

The *due* diligence expected of a State to comply with prevention of transboundary environmental harm has been interpreted as implying a number of substantive and procedural duties. In *Certain Activities*, the ICJ established that 'to fulfil its obligation to exercise due diligence in preventing significant transboundary environmental harm,' a State planning on carrying out activities with the potential to negatively affect the environment of other States shall 'ascertain if there is a risk of significant transboundary harm' and, should this be the case, conduct an environmental impact assessment (EIA).[117] The Court continued by stating that 'in conformity with its due diligence obligation,' States also bear the *duties to notify* and *consult in good faith* with the potentially affected States if the EIA confirms that there is a risk of significant

109 *Pulp Mills* (n 44) §101 (emphasis added).

110 See ILC 'Draft conclusions on identification of customary international law', conclusion 2.

111 On this Yann Kerbrat, 'Le standard de due diligence, catalyseur d'obligations conven-tion-nelles et coutumières pour les Etats', in Cassella (ed), *Le standard de due diligence et la responsabilité internationale* (Pedone 2018) 27; Mayer (n 104) 98–101.

112 *Certain Activities Carried Out by Nicaragua in the Border Area* (*Costa Rica v Nicaragua*) [2015] ICJ Rep 665, §104.

113 *Waters of Silala* (n 106) §99.

114 *Pulp Mills* (n 44) §101; *Nuclear Weapons* (n 108) §29. See also ILC, 'Draft guidelines on the protection of the atmosphere' guideline 3.

115 See for instance the submissions of Chile and Bolivia in *Waters of Silala* (n 106).

116 *Pulp Mills* (n 44) §77. For a review of practice, see Alice Ollino, *Due Diligence Obligations in International Law* (CUP 2022) 90–97.

117 *Certain Activities Carried Out by Nicaragua* (n 112) §104.

transboundary harm.[118] In the recent *Waters of the Silala case*, the Court added that the duty of States *to cooperate* to manage the risk of significant transboundary harm is also part of the due diligence required to fulfil prevention.[119]

It should be noted that all these duties – to conduct an EIA, to notify, to consult and to cooperate – are discrete and self-standing (procedural) obligations, whose violation may trigger State responsibility. At the same time, such obligations 'complement'[120] and define with more precision the content of the general duty of due diligence required to fulfil the obligation to prevent transboundary environmental harm.

From this perspective, it is interesting to look at the way the UN General Assembly recently formulated the request for an advisory opinion on the *Obligations of States in respect of Climate Change*. In the submission before the ICJ, the General Assembly asks the Court to identify States' obligations under international law to ensure the protection of the climate and the environment from anthropogenic GHG emissions, 'having particular regard to', *inter alia*, 'the duty of due diligence' *and* 'the principle of prevention of significant harm to the environment.'[121] The request seems to imply that a duty of due diligence exists distinctively and separately from the general obligation to prevent transboundary environmental harm.

In our opinion, this formulation is confusing. There is no general and self-standing duty of due diligence in international law. Due diligence is an international standard of conduct that infuses international obligations interpreted through its prism with content, meaning, and rationale.[122] In relation to the general obligations to prevent transboundary environmental harm, invoking due diligence in the interpretation and application of such obligation allows exactly to identify and 'spell out' the concrete measures – mentioned above – which are understood as essential for a State to be compliant with its duty.

A plausible explanation for separating 'the duty of due diligence' and 'the principle of prevention' may be that, with the expression 'the duty of due diligence', the General Assembly is not *really* speaking of the existence of a general duty of due diligence. Rather, the Assembly is using this notion as a shorthand expression for the customary obligation of States 'not to knowingly allow their territory to be used for acts contrary to the rights of other States.'[123]

118 ibid.

119 *Waters of Silala* (n 106) §100.

120 ibid.

121 *Obligations of States in Respect of Climate Change* (*Request for Advisory Opinion*) 8.

122 Ollino (n 116) 44 ff.

123 See *Corfu Channel Case* (*UK v Albania*) (Merits) [1949] ICJ Rep 15, 22. On the use of the term of due diligence in this sense, see Ollino (n 116) 52–58.

Be as it may, the obligation to prevent transboundary environmental harm has so far been applied and adjudicated in bilateral disputes where a State causes harm to another State. However, this fact shall not impede an interpretation of this obligation as encompassing not only prevention in a State-to -State context, but also prevention *also* toward global and cumulative environmental harm affecting the international community as a whole – the type of harm caused by climate change. Already, in the *Nuclear Weapons* opinion, the ICJ conceptualised the duty of prevention as requiring action vis-à-vis the environment of other States as well as areas beyond national control.[124] Similarly, the ITLOS recognised in 2011 that prevention and due diligence toward environmental harm extend to the high seas and the Seabed Area.[125]

4.2 *The Obligation to Cooperate*

Customary international law points to a general obligation of States to cooperate with each other. This obligation arises in the UN Charter,[126] has been consistently referred to by UN General Assembly resolutions[127] and is reflected in several international treaties, including multilateral environmental agreements, UNCLOS, and human rights instruments. The preamble of UNFCCC also acknowledges that 'the global nature of climate change calls for the widest possible cooperation by all countries.'

On a general note, cooperation can be defined as the 'efforts of States to accomplish an objective by joint action, where the activity of a single State cannot achieve the same result.'[128] Yet, beside this very broad definition, it is difficult to identify the precise content of a general obligation of States to cooperate with each other. In relation to climate change, the substance of a general duty to cooperate could arguably be based on the interpretation of the obligation to cooperate as applied to international environmental law, where the principle has been established in treaty and customary international practice.[129]

124 *Nuclear Weapons* (n 108) §21.

125 *Responsibilities of Sponsoring States* (n 26).

126 Charter of the United Nations art 1(3).

127 See Declaration on Principles of International Law Concerning Friendly Relations and Cooperation among States in Accordance with the Charter of the United Nations, UNGA Res 625 (XXV) (24 October 1970); 'Report of the United Nations Conference on the Human Environment', principle 24; Report of the United Nations Conference on Environment and Development, principle 7.

128 Rüdiger Wolfrum, 'Cooperation, International Law of', in *Max Planck Encyclopedia of Public International Law* (OUP 2010) §2.

129 ILC, *Draft Articles on Prevention of Transboundary Harm from Hazardous Activities*, 2001, ILC YB II part 2, Article 4.

In this regard, one can identify at least two parameters against which cooperation should be assessed. The first is consultation *in good faith*, which is considered a fundamental premise for cooperation to be meaningful. For instance, in the *SRFC* 2015 opinion, the ITLOS affirmed the obligation to cooperate under Article 64(1) UNCLOS (requiring States' cooperation with a view at ensuring the conservation and sustainable management of shared fish stocks) is an obligation requiring good faith consultations that should be meaningful in the sense that substantial effort should be made by all States concerned.[130] The second is *negotiation*. An obligation to cooperate in good faith may entail, as part of the duties necessary to fulfil it, the obligation to negotiate relevant agreements.[131] Yet, whether this duty should be interpreted as requiring States *to bring negotiations to conclusion*[132] or only to make efforts to negotiate without guarantee of success is still debated.[133]

Given its poorly understood nature and content, it is therefore unlikely a broad obligation to cooperate established under general international law could add much to the current climate change international legal framework.

4.3 *The Precautionary Principle*

On a very general note, precaution differs from prevention in relation to the type of risk entailed. Prevention presupposes action toward risks that are, at least, identifiable by the State, ie risks that are known or should/could be known by the State. Precaution, on the contrary, applies when there is lack of scientific certainty about a risk.[134] Under Principle 15 of the Rio Declaration, 'where there are threats of serious or irreversible damage, lack of full scientific certainty shall not be used as a reason for postponing cost-effective measures to prevent environmental degradation.'

In the *Responsibilities of Sponsoring States* opinion, the ITLOS hinted at the existence of a *customary* obligation providing for a precautionary approach,

130 *SRFC* (n 43) §201.

131 *Nuclear Weapons* (n 108) §46; *Pulp Mills* (n 44) §145; *Lac Lanoux*, Award (16 November 1957), 12 RIAA 281, §1.

132 *Obligations Concerning Negotiations Relating to Cessation of the Nuclear Arms Race and to Nuclear Disarmament* (*Marshall Islands v India*) (Admissibility) [2016] ICJ Rep 833, §261.

133 *Dispute Concerning Delimitation of the Maritime Boundary Between Ghana and Côte d'Ivoire in the Atlantic Ocean* (Judgment, 23 September 2017) ITLOS Case No 23, §604.

134 For an overview of precaution in the context of international environmental law, see Patricia Birnie, Alan Boyle & Catherine Redgwell, *International Law and the Environment* (3rd edn, OUP 2007) 152–8; for a distinction between prevention and precaution and what it implies for international law, see Makane Moïse Mbengue, *Essai sur une théorie du risque en droit international public* (Pedone 2009) 75–95, 159–78.

which would apply in situations where scientific evidence concerning the scope and potential negative impact of the activity in question is insufficient, but where there are plausible indications of potential risks.[135] In other circumstances, courts and tribunals have cautiously opted for referring simply to the precautionary approach, without specifying whether the latter shall be seen as a general principle of international law or a customary obligation.[136]

Be it as it may, the application of the precautionary approach may be considered part of the due diligence required by a State to fulfil its primary rules, including climate-change related obligations. In the 2011 *Responsibilities of Sponsoring States* opinion, the Seabed Dispute Chamber noted that the precautionary approach is an integral part of the sponsoring State's due diligence obligation to prevent damage that might result from the activities of contractors that they sponsor. In other words, a sponsoring State would fail to meet its obligations of due diligence if it disregarded risks linked to the activities which are not certain according to scientific evidence but still potentially plausible.

4.4 *A General Obligation to Mitigate Climate Change?*

198 States are parties to the UNFCCC. The Paris Agreement is also almost universally accepted, with 195 States being party to it. States have also widely acknowledged and reiterated in various fora their commitment to cooperate to address climate change,[137] thus making it clear that the international legal framework regarding climate change is of fundamental importance for the international community.

This may bring one to query the extent to which the current UNFCCC framework reflects customary international law. Indeed, while instruments under the UNFCCC are not codification treaties, the ILC has recognized that treaties may play an important role in developing customary international law.[138]

The problem with recognizing general obligations arising out of the climate change regime relates mainly to the identification of their content. On the one hand, the almost universal acceptance of the UNFCCC and the Paris Agreement shows that States consider it urgent and necessary to combat climate change and to keep the temperature rise limited to preferably 1.5°C degree. On the other hand, the legal content of these instruments and the relatively weak obligations arising from them bring one to question the real commitment of States into this fight.

135 *Responsibilities of Sponsoring States* (n 26) §131.
136 *Pulp Mills* (n 44).
137 See for an overview, Mayer (n 104) 101–104.
138 See ILC 'Draft conclusions on identification of customary international law', conclusion 6.

Arguably, if a customary rule exists, this would not go beyond the recognition that States need to take measures to mitigate climate change with the view of maintaining the global temperature goal set by the UNFCCC.[139] In other words, a general obligation to mitigate climate change could be seen as reflected by the specific commitments taken by States. However, besides those measures already ingrained in customary environmental law and incorporated into the principle of prevention, it would be difficult to define with more precision what this general obligation may entail.

5 Observations and Conclusion

The analysis conducted above allows us to identify some shared characteristics of States' climate-related obligations across different areas and advance a few general considerations on their underlying nature and potential.

The legal regimes considered – the law of the sea, international human rights law, general international law – provide for many rules that were not originally conceived or adopted to specifically target climate change. However, through a process of interpretation, their content is now understood – or *could* be understood – as including climate-change related duties.

A first consideration is that, in these obligations, the existence of specific duties towards climate change is often inferred by their due diligence nature. In other words, measures requiring States to mitigate or adapt to climate change are typically conceptualised as part of the due diligence required of a State to fulfil a certain obligation – even if the latter does not expressly mention or was not originally intended to address climate change.

This point warrants further elaboration. From a theoretical standpoint, due diligence is an identifier for certain classes of primary rules.[140] It is an international standard of conduct that serves the interpretation of obligations that have, *by nature*, a flexible and open-ended content, ie obligations of conduct. Obligations of conduct are duties requiring a State to display best effort toward the achievement of a given result, without the guarantee of success. They are opposed to obligations of result.[141] For instance, in relation to the obligation

139 Paris Agreement art 4(2).

140 Generally, on the role and use of due diligence in international law, see Krieger, Peters & Kreuzer (n 26); Samantha Besson, 'La "Due Diligence" en Droit International' (2020) 409 *RCADI* 153; Ollino (n 116) 44 ff.

141 Admittedly, the distinction and definition of obligations of result and obligations of conduct is not clear-cut and has no unique meaning in international law. See Pierre-Marie Dupuy, 'Reviewing the Difficulties of Codification: On Ago's Classification of Obligations

to prevent transboundary environmental harm, States are not required to succeed in preventing transboundary environmental harm at all costs and in every circumstance.[142] A State's responsibility for violating the general duty of prevention of environmental harm does not arise just because the latter has occurred. States are '*only*' required to take the necessary and appropriate measures at their disposal to ensure that transboundary environmental harm will not occur. As the ITLOS aptly put it in the COSIS Opinion, it is 'thus the conduct of the State, not the result which would be entailed by the conduct, that will determine whether the State has complied with its obligation.'[143]

For obligations depicted as 'of conduct', understanding exactly which measures are required of States to comply is no easy task, given their largely vague and open-ended substance.[144] Invoking the standard of due diligence serves exactly this purpose. Using due diligence to construe obligations of conduct means indeed that certain legal and factual parameters linked to this notion – eg reasonableness, knowledge of the circumstances, power, capacity to act, resource capabilities, among others – will be taken into account to determine with more precision conduct expected of a State in a particular case.[145]

In many instances, the recognition that an obligation is *only* of a due diligence nature implies that its substance will be perceived as rather weak.[146] For example, in the climate change context, when scholars point to the due diligence character of many obligations contained in the UNFCCC and the Paris Agreement, they wish to emphasize the relative weak nature in comparison with obligations of result. The argument goes as follows: although due diligence concretises the scope and substance of certain international obligations, its content remains flexible, since States will always maintain a certain margin of appreciation in choosing means and measures deemed sufficient to comply with the standard.[147]

---

of Means and Obligations of Result in Relation to State Responsibility' (1999) 10 *EJIL* 371; Antonio Marchesi, 'The Distinction Between Obligations of Conduct and Obligations of Result Following its Deletion from the Draft Articles on State Responsibility', in *Studi in onore di Gaetano Arangio-Ruiz* (Editoriale Scientifica 2004) vol 2, 827.

142 COSIS *Opinion* (n 14) §254.

143 ibid §233.

144 For a review and examples see Ollino (n 116) 97 ff.

145 On the legal and factual parameters that may inform the notion of due diligence, see ILA Study Group on Due Diligence in International Law, 'Due Diligence in International Law – Second Report' (Johannesburg 2016) 6 ff; Ollino (n 115) 131 ff.

146 Ollino (n 115) 3 ff.

147 COSIS *Opinion* (n 14) §257.

However, at times using due diligence to 'harness' the substance of certain obligations achieve the opposite outcome – ie it provides the interpreter with the opportunity not just to 'clarify' the scope of the obligation but, potentially, to expand it. This way, primary rules originally conceived as obligations with a rather weak and open-ended content may turn into obligations requiring more stringent and specific measures. Such an outcome may be achieved through different legal techniques, of which the following are mere examples:

1. the 'spelling' out of discrete and more stringent duties based on the understanding that 'measures that are considered sufficiently diligent at a certain moment in time may become not diligent enough in light of different changes;'[148]
2. the so-called 'proceduralization' of the standard of due diligence, ie the progressive replacement of the factual or para-legal parameters that make up this notion (reasonableness, capacity, etc) with specific legal measures and discrete obligations;[149]
3. recourse to evolutive or systemic interpretation to substantiate what is 'sufficiently diligent' at a certain time and within a certain context.[150]

The recent ITLOS' COSIS Opinion, the IACtHR's interpretation of a right to a healthy environment and the ECtHR's decision in the *Verein KlimaSeniorinnen Schweiz* have shown that such is the approach followed by the tribunals. By resorting to one or a combination of these techniques, the 'spelling out' of what is 'due' in relation to certain obligations has been enlarged to include also climate change concerns.

A good example is the ITLOS' COSIS Opinion and international law. Here the Tribunal made use of both systemic interpretation (iii) and the understanding of due diligence as a variable concept (i) to incorporate duties to mitigate climate change into State's obligations to prevent and reduce marine pollution. In relation to (i), the Tribunal acknowledged that while States shall prevent marine pollution according to their capabilities,[151] they would fail to fulfil due diligence should they not consider the 'best available science' currently at disposal. In determining the meaning of 'best available science', the Tribunal expressly referred to rules external to UNCLOS (iii), noting that the best capabilities and the best available science should be determined according to 'international rules and standards contain in climate change treaties.'[152] To prove

148 *Responsibilities of Sponsoring States* (n 26) §117.

149 Ollino (n 116) 232 ff.

150 ibid.

151 COSIS *Opinion* (n 14) §240.

152 ibid §§ 212–224 and 243.

that due diligence shall not necessarily be synonymous of 'weak substance', the ITLOS noted that 'an obligation of due diligence should not be understood as an obligation which depends largely on the discretion of a State or necessarily requires a lesser degree of effort to achieve the intended result (...). In many instances, an obligation of due diligence can be highly demanding.'[153]

While the ITLOS, the ECtHR and the IACtHR all have dealt with the substance of due diligence in relation to treaty-based obligations, it is worth considering whether a similar approach could be transposed to the general obligation to prevent transboundary environmental harm. As noted above, it is difficult to determine, at the state of the art, whether a customary obligation to mitigate climate change exists and what its content entails.

In this regard, an alternative to recognizing a discrete general obligation to mitigate climate change would be to incorporate general duties of mitigation into the due diligence required of States to fulfil the obligation to prevent transboundary environmental harm. This could be done by the ICJ in the advisory opinion on climate change and international law. The Court could, for instance, read the existence of a duty to mitigate climate change or take steps that address its impact as part of the measures that are now considered necessary to comply with the general obligation to prevent and the due diligence expected of it.[154] As we have shown, the very nature of due diligence allows for interpretations that may progressively expand, change and specify the meaning of what is 'due' in a certain context. Furthermore, given the universally accepted recognition by States of the need to mitigate climate change, it would be plausible for the ICJ to adopt an evolutive interpretation of due diligence and the principle of prevention, and incorporate a duty of mitigation into the progressive understanding of what is 'due' in the environmental context.

This approach would have the advantage of allowing the ICJ to refrain from engaging with an analysis of whether an obligation to mitigate climate change has now reached the status of customary international law. Instead, the Court would use its interpretative power to enlarge the scope of due diligence in the environmental context and elaborate further on its meaning.

One final point worth mentioning regards the primary role played by international judicial and quasi-judicial practice in the process of 'spelling out' progressively due diligence and the specific measures required of States in relation to their obligations of conduct. From a general standpoint, it is clear that the task of solidifying the substance and scope of 'vague' obligations by

153 ibid §257.

154 The ICJ embarked into a similar mission in *Certain Activities Carried Out by Nicaragua* (n 112); see Ollino (n 116) 243 ff.

invoking international standards (such as due diligence) is typically performed by courts and tribunals.[155] To this end, advisory opinions are extremely effective in reaching this goal: despite the nature of due diligence obligations as highly contextualized and 'depend[ent] on the circumstances of the case,'[156] advisory opinions allows courts to specify, a priori and in general terms, conduct expected of States in complying with their duties.

However, this process is not devoid of ambiguities. When courts and tribunals solidify the meaning of what is 'due' by providing substance to obligations of conduct, due diligence becomes the catalyser for the development of standards and duties which, as legal rather than factual parameters, can apply *in abstracto* to all States bound by the primary rule (of due diligence) beyond the circumstances of a single case. From a strict positive stand, one may not deny that, in such a situation, courts and tribunals may de facto create new legal rules going well beyond what originally conceived by States.

Acknowledgement

While this contribution stems from the joint efforts of the authors, for the purpose of Italian public procedures the authors declare that Alice Ollino has written Sections 3, 4, and 5, whilst Irini Papanicolopulu has written Section 1 and 2.

155 Ollino (n 116) 232 ff.

156 *Case Concerning Application of the Convention on the Prevention and Punishment of the Crime of Genocide* (*Bosnia Herzegovina v. Serbia and Montenegro*) (*Merits*) [2007] ICJ Rep 43, §430.

CHAPTER 4

Jurisdictional Ingenuity in Pursuit of Promoting States' Obligations in the Context of the Climate Emergency

*Melissa Stewart**

Abstract

Time is running out to avoid the most devastating consequences of climate change. States are falling short of the stated goal of the Paris Agreement to hold the increase in global temperature to 'well below' 2°C. For some States, climate change poses an existential threat. In the face of limited jurisdictional pathways to pursue direct accountability against the States most responsible for climate change, States are pursuing creative solutions to seek progress before international courts and tribunals. The requests for advisory opinions submitted to the International Court of Justice, the International Tribunal on the Law of the Sea, and the Inter-American Court of Human Rights are illustrative of what I term 'jurisdictional ingenuity;' meaning the pursuit of alternative jurisdictional avenues when direct pathways to dispute resolution under the relevant legal framework are weak or unavailable. Jurisdictional ingenuity is also the creation of jurisdictional pathways. The effect of jurisdictional ingenuity may facilitate future pathways for dispute resolution the domestic, regional, or international level. In the context of the climate emergency, jurisdictional ingenuity is a survival mechanism that may contribute to the future security of all.

Keywords

advisory opinions – climate change – dispute resolution – international law – jurisdiction – small island states.

* Assistant Professor of Law at the William S. Richardson School of Law, University of Hawaiʻi at Mānoa. ORCID No. 0000–0003-4842-3654.

1 Introduction

There can be no doubt that the reality of climate change is no longer a dire warning about the future. It is here. Climate change is more than the gradual warming of the earth's atmosphere. It will usher in a complete reshaping of our natural world. The climate crisis poses risks for all of humanity. States are already experiencing devastating losses caused by increased frequency and severity of disasters, such as cyclones, catastrophic flooding, and wildfires. For a discrete number of States at risk of losing the entirety of their territory due to sea level rise, the threat is existential.[1] Tragically, those States that are most at risk for experiencing the adverse impacts of climate change tend to be the least responsible for its cause.[2]

The Paris Agreement was seen as a breakthrough in the global community's efforts to fight climate change. Despite the initial optimism surrounding the agreement, States are falling far short of meeting the stated goal to hold the increase in global temperature to 'well below' 2°C and pursue efforts to limit the increase to 1.5°C. The Paris Agreement offers limited pathways to pursue accountability for the failure of States to meet their existing pledges under the agreement or for failing to make pledges sufficient to meet the aims of the agreement.[3] States have thus far been reluctant to consent to compulsory dispute resolution before the ICJ to resolve disputes over the interpretation or application of the UNFCCC and the Paris Agreement, and other dispute resolution mechanisms envisioned in these treaties have yet to be operationalized.

In the face of these obstacles and with time running out to avoid the most devastating consequences of climate change, States are pursuing creative solutions in an effort to move the needle forward on climate change before it is too late. Nowhere is this clearer than in the requests for advisory opinions from the ICJ, ITLOS, and the IACtHR, and a potential future request to the AfCHPR.[4]

---

1 Melissa Stewart, 'Cascading Consequences of Sinking States' (2023) 59 *Stanford JIL* 131.

2 Margaretha Wewerinke-Singh, 'The Rising Tide of Rights: Addressing Climate Loss and Damage Through Rights-Based Litigation' (2023) 12 *Transnt'l Env't L* 537, 538.

3 Progress has been made on the establishment of the Paris Agreement Implementation and Compliance Committee (a mechanism envisioned in Article 15 of the Paris Agreement). However, this mechanism is designed only to 'encourage compliance' in a way that is 'transparent, non-adversarial and non-punitive.' This type of 'managerial model' of compliance is distinct from an 'enforcement model' of compliance. See Abram Chayes & Antonio Handler Chayes, *The New Sovereignty: Compliance with International Regulatory Agreements* (Harvard University Press 1996); Andrew T Guzman, 'A Compliance-Based Theory of International Law' (2002) 90 *California LR* 1823, 1830; Tim Stephens, *International Courts and Environmental Protection* (CUP 2009) 104–105.

4 Benoit Mayer & Harro van Asselt, 'The Rise of International Climate Litigation' (2023) 32 *RECIEL* 175, 176.

While advisory opinions have addressed issues of common concern,[5] never before have the questions been so urgent and ambitious in their vision for potential impact. Nor has there ever been this number of simultaneous requests focused on a common cause that were submitted or contemplated in such a wide range of jurisdictions.

These efforts are illustrative of what I term 'jurisdictional ingenuity', meaning the pursuit of alternative jurisdictional avenues when direct pathways to dispute resolution under the relevant legal framework are weak or unavailable under international law. Jurisdictional ingenuity is also the creation of jurisdictional pathways. In the case of the climate change advisory opinion requests, this can be observed in at least three ways. First, through the creation of a new international organization for the purpose of conferring jurisdiction on an existing tribunal.[6] Second, by utilizing diplomatic tools to achieve an advisory opinion request that was previously out of reach. Third, by framing the legal questions in the requests in such a way that the forthcoming advisory opinions have the potential to create further avenues of dispute resolution.

Deploying jurisdictional ingenuity through multiple requests for advisory opinions on the obligations of States in the context of climate change has many potential benefits as well as risks. The expected opinions to be issued in relatively short succession may lead to cross-regime interaction that may result in a more comprehensive approach to addressing the climate crisis than if action had been pursued through the climate regime alone.[7] However, there is also a risk that decisions will produce fragmented or contradictory outcomes that cause confusion, or worse yet, hinder progress towards solving the climate crisis.[8]

Jurisdictional ingenuity in the context of the climate emergency is a survival mechanism. For States that face an existential threat from climate change, jurisdictional ingenuity is just one strategy among many to confront the crisis. Deployed by small States, jurisdictional ingenuity is one way in which they

5 *Legality of the Threat or Use of Nuclear Weapons* (Advisory Opinion) [1996] ICJ Rep 226.

6 Agreement for the Establishment of the Commission of Small Island States on Climate Change and International Law (adopted 31 October 2021, entered into force 31 October 2021) 3447 UNTS (*COSIS Agreement*).

7 Christina Voigt, 'The Power of the Paris Agreement in International Climate Litigation' (2023) 32 *RECIEL* 237.

8 Daniel Bodansky, 'Advisory Opinions on Climate Change: Some Preliminary Questions' (2023) 32 *RECIEL* 185; Benoit Mayer, 'International Advisory Proceedings on Climate Change' (2023) 44 *Michigan JIL* 41; Melissa Stewart, 'Climate Change Advisory Opinion Requests: Risk and Reward' (*Lawfare*, 24 March 2023) <www.lawfaremedia.org/article/climate-change-advisory-opinion-requests-risk-and-reward> accessed 14 January 2024; Maria Antonia Tigre & Armando Rocha, 'Competing Perspectives and Dialogue in Climate Change Advisory Opinions', 117 *AJIL Unbound* 287, 288–289. See also, Susan Ann Samuel & Jorge Alejandro Carrillo Bañuelos, Chapter 4 in this book.

counteract the 'asymmetr[ies] of power' among the community of states.[9] In the end, it may contribute to the future security of all of humanity.

2 Jurisdictional Pathways under the Climate Change Regime

The UNFCCC was adopted in May 1992 and came into force in March 1994. Together with the 1997 Kyoto Protocol and the 2015 Paris Agreement, it constitutes the legal framework governing climate change under international law ('climate change regime' or 'climate change framework').[10] This chapter focuses on the jurisdictional provisions of the UNFCCC and the Paris Agreement as the relevant legal frameworks for the resolution of disputes between States regarding their obligations in the context of climate change.[11] As this chapter is focused on jurisdictional pathways for the resolution of disputes between States, it distinguishes dispute resolution procedures from compliance mechanisms and enforcement as while they are interrelated, they remain distinct.

The UNFCCC initially envisioned both non-adversarial procedures as well as traditional State-to-State dispute resolution procedures. Article 13 of the UNFCCC provides for the potential 'establishment of a multilateral consultative process' that would be 'available to Parties on their request, for the resolution of questions regarding the implementation of the Convention.'[12] During negotiations for the UNFCCC, this cooperative procedure was thought to be more appropriate for addressing the collective challenges of climate change.[13] According to Daniel Bodansky, the COP could have designed the multilateral consultative process to allow for individuals, international organizations, or NGOs to have standing to participate in the process.[14] A Multilateral Consultative Committee was considered at COP4 and COP5, but was never implemented

9 See Douglas Guilfoyle, 'Small States, Legal Argument, and International Disputes' (*CIL Dialogues,* 7 July 2023) <https://cil.nus.edu.sg/blogs/small-states-legal-argument-and-international-disputes/> accessed 14 January 2024; see also Douglas Guilfoyle, 'Litigation as Statecraft: Small States and the Law of the Sea,' (2023) 1 *British YIL* 1.

10 Daniel Bodansky, 'The History of the Global Climate Change Regime', in Luterbacher & Sprinz (eds), *International Relations and Global Climate Change* (MIT Press 2001) 32–35.

11 Voigt (n 7) 238.

12 UNFCCC, art 13.

13 Daniel Bodansky, 'The United Nations Framework Convention on Climate Change: A Commentary' (1993) 18 *Yale JIL* 451, 547.

14 ibid, 548.

due to a failure of the parties to reach an agreement on its precise composition.[15] Although the consultative process might be revived in the future, the possibility seems unlikely due to its extended period of 'dorman[cy].'[16]

Article 14 of the UNFCCC outlines the provisions for the settlement of disputes between State Parties on its interpretation or application. It was initially drafted to complement the multilateral consultative process outlined in Article 13, which, as explained above, has yet to be implemented. Under Article 14, States must first seek to settle disputes through negotiation or another peaceful means of dispute settlement. Should negotiation fail to resolve a dispute within twelve months, States can request the establishment of a conciliation commission and submit their dispute to conciliation. Alternatively, should both parties have recognized one of the compulsory dispute mechanisms outlined in Article 14, namely the submission of a dispute to the ICJ or arbitration, States can submit their disputes using the compulsory procedures. Article 14 was drafted as a compromise to accommodate the disparate views of State parties, some of which preferred non-mandatory and non-binding procedures, others of which preferred mandatory and binding procedures.[17]

Under Article 24 of the Paris Agreement, the dispute resolution provisions of Article 14 of the UNFCCC apply *mutatis mutandis* to the Paris Agreement. While a panel of experts is currently developing a conciliation annex that was considered in advance of COP28,[18] the COP has yet to adopt the required additional procedures on conciliation or compulsory arbitration envisioned by Article 14 of the UNFCCC.[19] The Solomon Islands and Tuvalu have consented to compulsory arbitration pursuant to Article 14 and only one State, the Netherlands, has consented to compulsory arbitration *and* the compulsory jurisdiction of

15 Xueman Wang & Glenn Wiser, 'The Implementation and Compliance Regimes under the Climate Change Convention and its Kyoto Protocol' (2002) 11 *RECIEL* 181, 186; Clara Reichenbach, 'The Missing Dispute Resolution Mechanisms in International Climate Change Agreements' (2022) 3 *Global Energy Law & Sustainability* 129, 134.

16 Roda Verheyen & Cathrin Zengerling, 'International Dispute Settlement', in Carlarne, Gray and Tarasofsky (eds), *The Oxford Handbook of International Climate Change Law* (OUP 2016) 419.

17 Daniel Bodansky, Jutta Brunnée & Lavanya Rajamani, *International Climate Change Law* (OUP 2017) 115.

18 'ICCA Launches Panel of Experts to Develop a Paris Agreement Conciliation Annex' (*ICCA*, 10 February 2023) <www.arbitration-icca.org/icca-launches-panel-experts-develop-paris-agreement-conciliation-annex.> accessed 14 January 2024.

19 Catherine Amirfar & Merryl Lawry White, 'The Paris Agreement's Conciliation Annex: If Not Now, Then When?' (*ASIL Insights*, 15 September 2021) <www.asil.org/insights/volume/25/issue/17> accessed 14 January 2024.

the International Court of Justice.[20] The Netherlands is also the only State to renew its declaration under Article 24 of the Paris Agreement.[21] No State has yet invoked the dispute settlement procedures outlined in Article 14.[22]

Given the lack of State consent to compulsory arbitration or the compulsory jurisdiction of the ICJ, conciliation is the default method of dispute resolution for the vast majority of States should negotiation fail. A conciliation commission may be created at the request of one of the parties to a dispute pursuant to the basic procedures established under Article 14(6). However, in the absence of a conciliation annex, it is unclear what procedures would apply beyond the number of members to be appointed to a conciliation commission and by whom.[23] The absence of clear procedures may act as a 'disincentive' to the resolution of a dispute through conciliation as the parties would have to first negotiate the applicable procedures.[24] Furthermore, any decision by the conciliation commission would not be legally binding as it only has the authority to issue a 'recommendatory award' for parties to 'consider in good faith.'[25]

Should that fail, the secondary mechanisms for the resolution of the dispute are not currently available as the mechanism for compulsory arbitration has not been established and only one State has agreed to the compulsory jurisdiction of the ICJ. As the negative impacts of climate change accelerate, States experience devastating effects that result in the loss of life and enormous economic losses. The current structure and implementation of the UNFCCC and Paris Agreement leave impacted States without clear pathways for the resolution of disputes on the interpretation and application of the conventions most applicable to confronting the challenge of climate change.

States have pushed for alternatives to conciliation or inter-State dispute resolution mechanisms to provide some measure of redress for losses suffered due to the adverse impacts of climate change or to secure greater compliance

20 UNFCCC, Declarations by Parties <https://unfccc.int/process-and-meetings/the-convention/status-of-ratification/declarations-by-parties> accessed 14 January 2024.

21 Amirfar & White (n 19).

22 Bodansky, Brunnée & Rajamani (n 17) 115; Reichenbach (n 15) 129; Maria Antonia Tigre & Margaretha Wewerinke-Singh, 'Beyond the North-South Divide: Litigation's Role in Resolving Climate Change Loss and Damage Claims' (2023) 32 *RECIEL* 439, 442.

23 The Paris Agreement Draft Conciliation Annex was presented to 50 state representatives in November 2023. 'The ICCA Panel of Experts Engages with States on the Paris Agreement Draft Conciliation Annex' (*ICCA*, 29 November 2023) <www.arbitration-icca.org/icca-panel-experts-engages-states-paris-agreement-draft-conciliation-annex> accessed 14 January 2024.

24 Reichenbach (n 15) 143.

25 UNFCCC, art 14(6).

with State pledges for the nationally determined contributions.[26] Small island developing States have advocated for such measures for over three decades.[27] This includes the Alliance of Small Island States' proposal for an International Insurance Pool.[28] While insurance is envisioned as a potential area of cooperation under Article 8(4)(f) of the Paris Agreement and Article 4(8) of the UNFCCC, parties have yet to bring such a mechanism to fruition. There was much optimism following the agreement to establish a Loss and Damage Fund at COP27.[29] However, there is skepticism that it will meet the anticipated need of $300 billion per year by 2030.[30] Even with the agreement to establish a Loss and damage fund, there remains strong pushback from developed States that they accept any liability for the adverse impacts of climate change or have a legal obligation to finance the fund.[31]

Faced with this reality that a direct pathway to dispute resolution under the climate framework is weak or unavailable, States have exercised jurisdictional

26 Arthur Wyns, 'COP27 Establishes Loss and Damage Fund to Respond to Human Cost of Climate Change' (2022) 7 *The Lancet* 21 <www.thelancet.com/journals/lanplh/article/PIIS2542-5196(22)00331-X/fulltext> accessed 14 January 2024; Maxine Burkett, 'Reading Between the Red Lines: Loss and Damage and the Paris Outcome' (2016) 6 *Climate Law* 118.

27 M.J. Mace & Roda Verheyen, 'Loss, Damage and Responsibility after COP21: All Options Open for the Paris Agreement' (2016) 25 *RECIEL* 197, 198.

28 Vanuatu, Draft Annex Relating to Article 23 (Insurance) for Inclusion in the Revised Single Text on Elements Relating to Mechanisms (A/AC.237/WG.II.Misc.13) Submitted by the Co-Chairmen of Working Group II, Negotiation of a Framework Convention on Climate Change (17 December 1991) A/AC.237/WG.11/CRP.8 <www.aosis.org/an-insurance-mechanism-for-the-consequences-of-sea-level-rise/> accessed 14 January 2024.

29 Wyns (n 26).

30 'What you Need to Know about the COP27 Loss and Damage Fund' (*UN Environment Program*, 29 November 2022) <www.unep.org/news-and-stories/story/what-you-need-know-about-cop27-loss-and-damage-fund> accessed 14 January 2024. Operationalization of the new funding arrangements, including a fund, for responding to loss and damage referred to in paragraphs 2–3 of decisions 2/CP.27 and 2/CMA.4 (UNFCCC, 13 December 2023) <https://unfccc.int/documents/636558> accessed 14 December 2023. Nina Lakhani, '$700m Pledged to Loss and Damage Fund at COP28 Covers Less than 0.2% Needed' *The Guardian* (Dubai, 6 December 2023) <www.theguardian.com/environment/2023/dec/06/700m-pledged-to-loss-and-damage-fund-cop28-covers-less-than-02-percent-needed> accessed 14 December 2023.

31 The United States deputy special envoy for climate at the State Department, Sue Biniaz, was recently quoted as saying she was 'violently opposed' to the idea that the USA and other high emitting or developed countries have 'a legal obligation to pay into the fund.' Valerie Volcovici, 'US Seeks Focused, Efficient Fund for Climate Disasters' (*Reuters*, 23 August 2023) <https://www.reuters.com/sustainability/sustainable-finance-reporting/us-seeks-focused-efficient-fund-climate-disasters-2023–08–23/> accessed 14 January 2024.

ingenuity to seek clarity on the obligations of States under international law through alternative jurisdictional avenues. The ICJ provides one potential avenue as a court of general jurisdiction, but as will be explained below, pursuing a case on climate change before the ICJ is politically risky and, at the present moment, may be of limited utility.

The contentious jurisdiction of the ICJ is based on State consent.[32] Disputes come to the court through special agreement in which parties specifically refer matters to the Court, through treaties and conventions that provide for the jurisdiction of the ICJ, or through the compulsory jurisdiction of the court if both States have recognized the same obligation.[33] Under the compulsory jurisdiction of the court, a State could submit a dispute related to '(a) the interpretation of a treaty; (b) any question of international law; (c) the existence of any fact which, if established, would constitute a breach of an international obligation; (d) the nature or extent of the reparation to be made for the breach of an international obligation.'[34]

With respect to climate change, it is unlikely that a large emitter State would agree to a special agreement to resolve a dispute regarding the adverse impacts of climate change.[35] The most relevant treaties that provide for the jurisdiction of the ICJ in their dispute resolution clauses are the UNFCCC and the Paris Agreement, although there are potentially others that could be used.[36] As outlined above, only the Netherlands has consented to the compulsory jurisdiction of the ICJ pursuant to either the UNFCCC or the Paris Agreement.

Currently, only 74 States have deposited declarations under the optional clause of Article 36(2) of the Statute of the ICJ recognizing its general compulsory jurisdiction.[37] Among those, most have included what Aloysius Llamzon describes as 'eviscerUnatory caveats.'[38] While it is possible that a State

32 Statute of the International Court of Justice (adopted 26 June 1945, entered into force 24 October 1945) 892 UNTS 119 (*ICJ Statute*) arts 36 & 37; Jonathan Charney, 'Compromissory Clauses and the Jurisdiction of the International Court of Justice' (1987) 81 *AJIL* 855.

33 ICJ Statute, art 36.

34 ICJ Statute, art 36.

35 Andrew L. Strauss, 'Climate Change Litigation: Opening the Door to the International Court of Justice', in Burns & Osofsky (eds), *Adjudicating Climate Change: State, National, and International Approaches* (CUP 2009) 340.

36 For example, writing in 2009, Andrew Strauss argued that Friendship, Commerce, and Navigation (FCN) or similar treaties could potentially provide a path for the ICJ to exercise jurisdiction over a climate change related dispute. ibid 345.

37 'Declarations Recognizing the Jurisdiction of the Court as Compulsory' (*ICJ*) <www.icj-cij.org/declarations> accessed 14 January 2024.

38 Aloysius P. Llamzon, 'Jurisdiction and Compliance in Recent Decisions of the International Court of Justice' (2007) 18 *EJIL* 815, 817.

that recognizes the compulsory jurisdiction of the ICJ could bring a dispute concerning climate change against any State that also accepts this obligation, there are obstacles to pursuing that strategy. With the exception of the Marshall Islands, very few small island States have deposited a declaration with the ICJ recognizing its compulsory jurisdiction. That obstacle is easily surmountable for small island States as any State may deposit a declaration with the UN Secretary-General at any time. However, only one of the three largest emitter States recognizes the ICJ's compulsory jurisdiction: India. Other large emitter States that accept the ICJ's compulsory jurisdiction include Australia, Canada, Germany, Japan, Mexico, Poland, and the United Kingdom.[39] So, any State would be limited in the available respondent States should it decide to institute proceedings before the ICJ pursuant to Article 36(2).

In 2002, Tuvalu briefly considered suing the United States and Australia for their failure to join the Kyoto Protocol.[40] While Tuvalu stated at the time that it would pursue a case before the ICJ, it is unclear how it would have obtained jurisdiction for such a dispute.[41] It could have accepted the compulsory jurisdiction of the ICJ and pursued a case against Australia, but the United States withdrew its consent for such jurisdiction in 1985.[42]

A contentious case would present enormous challenges and significant political risks for any State pursuing this strategy.[43] A State could bring a case alleging another State failed in its obligation to prevent the adverse impacts of climate change or contributed to climate change. However, as described by Philippe Sands, the obligations under the UNFCCC are 'crushingly vague,' making it 'impossible to argue that any particular provision gives rise to a cause of action.'[44] Written on the eve of the negotiations of the Paris Agreement, Sands'

---

39 Daniel Bodansky, 'The Role of the International Court of Justice in Addressing Climate Change: Some Preliminary Reflections' (2017) 49 *Arizona State LJ* 689, 711.

40 Richard C. Paddock, 'A Nation on Edge of Extinction' (*The Washington Post*, 24 November 2002) <www.washingtonpost.com/archive/politics/2002/11/24/a-nation-on-edge-of-extinction/3b32c521-3664-46fa-8625-516e7fb05765/> accessed 12 June 2023.

41 Rebecca Elizabeth Jacobs, 'Treading Deep Waters: Substantive Law Issues in Tuvalu's Threat to Sue the United States in the International Court of Justice' (2005) 14 *Pacific Rim L & Pol'y J* 103.

42 United States, Notification of Termination of No 3 Declaration Recognizing as Compulsory the Jurisdiction of the ICJ (received 7 October 1985, effective 7 April 1986) 1408 UNTS 270 Annex A <https://treaties.un.org/doc/Publication/UNTS/Volume%201408/v1408.pdf#page=286> accessed 14 January 2024.

43 Bodansky (n 39) 708.

44 Philippe Sands, 'Climate Change and the Rule of Law: Adjudicating the Future in International Law' (2016) 28 *JEL* 19, 28. See also, Tim Stephens, 'See You in Court? A Rising Tide of International Climate Litigation' (*The Interpreter* 30 October 2019) <https://www

assessment would likely apply to that agreement as well given the intention of States to avoid liability under that treaty.

It is not clear under international law that historic GHG emissions or current failures to adopt more ambitious nationally determined contributions would constitute a breach of an international obligation. Much of the historic emissions occurred prior to the signing of the Paris Agreement or the UNFCCC. Actions that occurred prior to these agreements coming into force could not constitute noncompliance with obligations under the respective agreements, and States that are not currently parties do not have obligations pursuant to the agreements absent an argument that any obligations are reflective of customary international law. Compelling arguments have been made that other principles of international environmental law, such as the 'no harm rule,' are applicable in the context of climate change.[45] Further arguments have been made that failure to reduce emissions following the ratification of the UNFCCC *could* amount to an internationally wrongful act under Articles 2 and 4.2 of the UNFCCC,[46] although this perspective is 'without consensus.'[47] Even if a State could demonstrate these actions constituted a breach of an international obligation, there would be issues in determining attribution and causation related to any specific harm given the global contributions to the underlying causes of climate change.

Concerns about attribution and causation aside, an authoritative interpretation of the obligations of States with respect to climate change under international law could help to clarify what action or inaction by States constitutes a breach of an international obligation. This could reduce the uncertainty to some extent as to the utility of a potential contentious case interpreting obligations under the UNFCCC, the Paris Agreement, or more broadly under international law before the ICJ. As the next section explains, advisory opinions seeking such an answer could potentially provide this essential interpretation in an area where, to date, there has yet to be a State-to-State dispute.[48]

.lowyinstitute.org/the-interpreter/see-you-court-rising-tide-international-climate-litigation> accessed 22 March 2024.

45 See eg Benoit Mayer, 'The Relevance of the No-Harm Principle to Climate Change Law and Politics' (2016) 19 *APJEL* 79.

46 Christina Voigt, 'State Responsibility for Climate Change Damages' (2008) 77 *Nordic JIL* 1, 7.

47 ibid, 7. See also Stephens (n 3) 68–69. Although the decision in the ITLOS Advisory Opinion lends credence to this perspective, as explained below.

48 Annalisa Savaresi, 'Inter-State Climate Change Litigation: 'Neither a Chimera nor a Panacea', in Alogna, Bakker & Gauci (eds), *Climate Change Litigation: Global Perspectives* (Brill Nijhoff 2021) 366; Dapo Akande, Naomi Hart & Mubarak Waseem, 'Climate Change and

3 Jurisdictional Ingenuity through Requests for Advisory Opinions

The pursuit of advisory opinions in multiple jurisdictions is an example of what I am terming jurisdictional ingenuity, as it corresponds to a pursuit of alternative jurisdictional avenues when direct pathways to dispute resolution under the relevant legal framework are weak or unavailable.

Jurisdictional ingenuity as a strategy is distinct from forum shopping in that it focuses on jurisdiction creation or lowering the barriers to accessing potential jurisdictional pathways as compared to selecting between existing and competing jurisdictions.[49] Although as employed in the context of the climate change advisory opinion requests, it raises some similar concerns, such as potentially inconsistent opinions from different courts and tribunals and risk of fragmentation.[50]

Jurisdictional ingenuity is also distinct from what Laurence Helfer has termed 'regime shifting,' which attempts to 'mov[e] treaty negotiations, lawmaking initiatives, or standard setting activities from one international venue to another.'[51] Parties engaged in jurisdictional ingenuity as described are not attempting to shift the regime from one international venue to another. Rather, they are seeking out jurisdictional pathways to influence the *existing* regime, in this case, the climate framework. This is not to say that there is no risk that jurisdictional ingenuity could contribute to regime shifting. However, on its own, jurisdictional ingenuity does not constitute a regime shift.

Framing this strategy as 'ingenuity' is a purposefully positive framing. The States that are pursuing this strategy have provided leadership on combating climate change for decades.[52] While the positive framing is reflective of jurisdictional ingenuity in the context of climate change, an examination of other examples of this jurisdictional strategy would be a valuable comparison,

---

Proceedings before the ICJ and ITLOS' (*Essex Court Chambers*, 20 October 2022) <essexcourt.com/publication/climate-change-in-law-current-perspectives-week-9/> accessed 14 January 2024.

49 Forum shopping has been observed in international environmental law. Typically, this occurs when there is a 'range of fora' in which a State might bring a dispute. Stephens (n 3) 275–279. That type of range of fora for State-to-State dispute resolution is currently lacking in the context of climate change.

50 Joost Pauwelyn & Luiz Eduardo Salles, 'Forum Shopping before International Tribunals: (Real) Concerns, (Im)Possible Solutions' (2009) 42 *Cornell ILJ* 77, 83.

51 Laurence R. Helfer, 'Regime Shifting: The TRIPs Agreement and New Dynamics of International Intellectual Property Lawmaking' (2004) 29 *Yale JIL* 1, 14.

52 Margaretha Wewerinke-Singh, 'Litigating Human Rights Violations Related to the Adverse Effects of Climate Change in the Pacific Islands', in Lin & Kysar (eds), *Climate Change Litigation in the Asia Pacific* (CUP 2020) 109.

although it is outside of the scope of this chapter. For the purposes of this chapter, general questions about the value of state-to-state dispute resolution are deferred for another day.[53]

The following will explore three illustrative avenues of jurisdictional ingenuity in the context of climate change. First, the creation of an international organization to confer jurisdiction on an existing tribunal. Second, the utilization of diplomatic tools to achieve an advisory opinion request on climate change that was previously out of reach. Third, the framing of the legal questions in the requests to create future avenues of dispute resolution.

3.1 *The Creation of an International Organization for the Purpose of Conferring Jurisdiction on an Existing Tribunal*

A remarkable illustration of jurisdictional ingenuity in the context of climate change is the creation of an international organization for the purpose, at least in part, of requesting an advisory opinion of ITLOS. The Commission of Small Island States on Climate Change and International Law ('COSIS') was established through an agreement executed by Antigua and Barbuda and Tuvalu on October 31, 2021.[54] According to the agreement, the mandate of COSIS is

> to promote and contribute to the definition, implementation, and progressive development of rules and principles of international law concerning climate change, including, but not limited to, the obligations of States relating to the protection and preservation of the marine environment and their responsibility for injuries arising from internationally wrongful acts in respect of the breach of such obligations.[55]

The agreement is comprised of only four articles. The activities of COSIS outlined in the agreement are to assist other Small Island States in the promotion and progressive development of international law on climate change, appoint experts and advisors, and, most importantly, the agreement authorizes COSIS to request advisory opinions from ITLOS 'on any legal question within the scope of the [UNCLOS].'[56]

53 See eg Vaughan Lowe, 'The Function of Litigation in International Society' (2021) 61 *ICLQ* 209; Benedict Kingsbury, 'Is the Proliferation of International Courts and Tribunals a Systemic Problem?' (1999) 31 *NYU Journal of Int'l Law & Policy* 679.

54 COSIS Agreement (n 10).

55 ibid, art 1.

56 ibid, art 2.

The advisory jurisdiction of the full tribunal of ITLOS has not been without controversy.[57] UNCLOS does not explicitly confer advisory jurisdiction on the full tribunal of ITLOS, only on the Seabed Disputes Chamber.[58] The origins of the Tribunal's advisory jurisdiction can be found in Article 21 of the Statute of the Tribunal, and Article 138 of the Rules of the Tribunal. Article 21 of the Statute establishes that '[t]he jurisdiction of the Tribunal comprises all disputes and all applications submitted to it in accordance with this Convention and all matters specifically provided for in any other agreement with confers jurisdiction on the tribunal.'[59] Article 138 of the Rules provides that the 'Tribunal may give an advisory opinion on a legal question if an international agreement related to the purposes of the Convention specifically provides from the submitted to the Tribunal of a request for such an opinion.'[60]

In the *Request for an Advisory Opinion Submitted by the Sub-Regional Fisheries Commission* (*SRFC*), 23 States submitted written statements that objected to ITLOS exercising its advisory jurisdiction in that case on the grounds that UNCLOS does not contain an explicit reference to the advisory jurisdiction of ITLOS. Despite these concerns, ITLOS determined that it has advisory jurisdiction pursuant to Article 288 of UNCLOS, Article 21 of the Statute of the Tribunal, and Article 138 of the Rules of Procedure.

While ITLOS did exercise its advisory jurisdiction, the separate declaration of Judge Cot highlighted some of the weaknesses in the Tribunal's approach, calling the reasoning 'convoluted' and 'unpersuasive,' and its interpretation 'misguided.'[61] He highlighted the need to elaborate a clear jurisdictional framework for when ITLOS will exercise its advisory jurisdiction and warned of the 'dangers of abuse and manipulation' by States 'seek[ing] to gain an advantage over third States' through the execution of a bilateral or multilateral agreement.[62]

57 Rozemarijn J. Roland Holst, 'Taking the Current When it Serves: Prospects and Challenges for an ITLOS Advisory Opinion on Oceans and Climate Change' (2023) 32 *RECIEL* 217, 217–218.

58 UNCLOS, art 191.

59 Statute of the International Tribunal for the Law of the Sea (Annex VI to UNCLOS) (*ITLOS Statute*) art 21.

60 International Tribunal for the Law of the Sea Rules of the Tribunal (adopted 28 October 1997) ITLOS/8 (*ITLOS Rules*) art 138.

61 *Request for an Advisory Opinion submitted by the Sub-Regional Fisheries Commission* (*SRFC*) (Advisory Opinion, 2 April 2015) ITLOS Case No 15, Declaration of Judge Cot, §§2–3, 13 (*SRFC Opinion*).

62 ibid, §9.

Where others might see a danger of 'abuse and manipulation'[63] or a 'shortcut,'[64] the governments of Antigua and Barbuda and Tuvalu saw an opportunity. What they could not achieve as State Parties to the UNCLOS, they accomplished with the stroke of a pen. The COSIS Agreement was executed on the eve of COP26 in 2021 and the request for an advisory opinion was submitted a little over a year later on December 12, 2022.[65] The COSIS Agreement does little more than authorize the organization to request an advisory opinion from ITLOS.[66] The substance of the request was for an advisory opinion on the obligation of States under UNCLOS to, inter alia, 'prevent, reduce, and control pollution of the marine environment' resulting from climate change and 'protect and preserve the marine environment in relation to climate change impacts.'[67]

Whether the full tribunal of ITLOS had advisory jurisdiction was a live issue in the case.[68] While many States and international organizations submitted written statements that ITLOS had jurisdiction to render an advisory opinion,[69]

63 ibid. See also Richard Barnes, 'An Advisory Opinion on Climate Change Obligations Under International Law: A Realistic Prospect? (2022) 53 *Ocean Development & IL* 180, 193 & 202.

64 Alina Miron, 'COSIS Request for an Advisory Opinion: A Poisoned Apple for the ITLOS?' (2023) 38 *Int'l J Marine & Coastal L* 249.

65 *Request for an Advisory Opinion submitted by the Commission of Small Island States on Climate Change and International Law* (Institution of Proceedings, 12 December 2022) (Pending) <www.itlos.org/en/main/cases/list-of-cases/request-for-an-advisory-opinion-submitted-by-the-commission-of-small-island-states-on-climate-change-and-international-law-request-for-advisory-opinion-submitted-to-the-tribunal/> accessed 9 February 2024.

66 Although COSIS has already engaged in activities beyond the ITLOS request. It also submitted written statements in the advisory opinion requests submitted to the International Court of Justice and the Inter-American Court. Statement of Gaston Alfronso Browne, Prime Minister of Antigua and Barbuda, on behalf of COSIS in the ITLOS Advisory Opinion Oral Proceedings. Verbatim Record 11 Sept 2023, 10 AM pg 5.

67 *Request for an Advisory Opinion submitted by the COSIS* (n 65).

68 Compare Armando Rocha, 'The Advisory Jurisdiction of the ITLOS in the Request Submitted by the Commission of Small Island States' (*Climate Law,* 12 April 2023) <https://blogs.law.columbia.edu/climatechange/2023/04/12/the-advisory-jurisdiction-of-the-itlos-in-the-request-submitted-by-the-commission-of-small-island-states/> accessed 8 February 2024 with Donald R. Rothwell, 'Climate Change, Small Island States, and the Law of the Sea: The ITLOS Advisory Opinion Request' (*ASIL Insights*, 12 May 2023) <https://www.asil.org/insights/volume/27/issue/5> accessed 10 March 2024.

69 *Request for an Advisory Opinion submitted by the COSIS* (n 65); ibid, Written Statement of New Zealand; ibid, Written Statement of Germany; ibid, Written Statement of Mauritius.

several States objected[70] or submitted substantive statements without prejudice to their position on the advisory jurisdiction of the full tribunal.[71] Even if they did not object, many States expressed the view that it was important for the Tribunal to elaborate on the basis of its jurisdiction and under what circumstances the conditions of jurisdiction will be met.[72]

In its Advisory Opinion of May 21, 2024, ITLOS found that it had jurisdiction to issue an Advisory Opinion in the case pursuant to Article 21 of the Statute and the COSIS Agreement.[73] It relied on the *SRFC Advisory Opinion* to outline that its jurisdiction includes 'all "matters" … specifically provided for in any other agreement which confers jurisdiction on the Tribunal,' and that the COSIS Agreement meets that requirement.[74] In addition to statements provided by States during the written and oral proceedings in support of the exercise of jurisdiction, the Tribunal noted that States recently concluded the Agreement under the United Nations Convention on the Law of the Sea on the conservation and sustainable use of marine biological diversity of areas beyond national jurisdiction (BBNJ). The convention specifically allows the BBNJ COP to request an advisory opinion from ITLOS.[75] Given that the agreement was adopted by consensus, it provides strong evidence that State parties to UNCLOS consider that they may confer advisory jurisdiction on ITLOS through a separate agreement.[76]

70 *Request for an Advisory Opinion submitted by the COSIS* (n 65), Written Statement of the Federative Republic of Brazil, para 9; Written State of the People's Republic of China, §25.

71 For example, Australia submitted a statement 'without prejudice to Australia's position on the advisory jurisdiction of the Tribunal' that cited to their written statement in the *SRFC* case. *Request for an Advisory Opinion submitted by the COSIS* (n 69), Written Statement of Australia. The written statement in the *SRFC* case argued that the Tribunal may not have advisory jurisdiction at all given it cannot be found in UNCLOS, and if it does, it should be limited to the interpretation and application of the "other agreement" that confers advisory jurisdiction on the Tribunal, and not UNCLOS. *Request for Advisory Opinion submitted by the Sub-Regional Fisheries Commission* (n 65), Written Statement of Australia.

72 See eg *Request for an Advisory Opinion submitted by the COSIS* (n 65), Written Statement of Poland; ibid, Written Statement of Norway; ibid, Written Statement of Italy; ibid, Written Statement of Germany.

73 *Request for an Advisory Opinion Submitted by the Commission of Small Island States on Climate Change and International Law* (Advisory Opinion, 21 May 2024) ITLOS Case No 31, §§88–89, 109 (*COSIS Opinion*).

74 ibid, §§85–88.

75 Art 47(7).

76 See *COSIS Opinion* (n 73) §92. However, Mossop has described the provision in the BBJN as 'circumscribed.' Joanna Mossop, 'Dispute Settlement Provisions in the Agreement for Biodiversity Beyond National Jurisdiction' (2024) 1 *Portuguese J of Int'l L* 98, 110.

ITLOS did not directly address the concerns about the exercise of its advisory jurisdiction expressed by Judge Cot in the *SRFC Advisory Opinion*, a point that was noted in the Declarations of Judges Kulyk and Kittichaisaree. Judge Kulyk wrote that ITLOS could have further elaborated on the grounds for its exercise of advisory jurisdiction.[77] Judge Kittichaisaree wrote separately to dismiss the concerns that this was an agreement executed for the 'sole purpose' of requesting an advisory opinion or that COSIS was not a truly international organization.[78]

What may now see obvious was not necessarily evident at the time the COSIS Agreement was executed. While it was certainly possible that ITLOS would exercise its advisory jurisdiction in this case, it was not guaranteed when the request for an advisory opinion was submitted, much less when the COSIS agreement was concluded. The Creation of the Commission is a powerful example of jurisdictional ingenuity as the creation of jurisdictional pathways as well as the leadership of small-island states.

3.2 *The Utilization of Diplomatic Tools to Open a Jurisdiction Pathway*

Jurisdictional ingenuity in the context of climate change has involved utilizing diplomatic tools to achieve an advisory opinion request on climate change that was previously out of reach. The idea that states might utilize international adjudication to address issues related to climate change is not new.[79] Neither is the idea of seeking an advisory opinion from the ICJ. Yet, to date, there has not been a state-to-state dispute related to climate change. Until the March 2023 General Assembly Resolution, efforts to request an advisory opinion on climate change from the ICJ had failed to come to fruition.

In 2011, Palau, together with the Marshall Islands, announced that it would call on the UN General Assembly 'to seek, on an urgent basis … an advisory opinion from the [ICJ] on the responsibilities of States under international law to ensure that activities emitting [GHG] that are carried out under their jurisdiction or control do not damage other States.'[80] Although Palau had built a coalition of small island and other interested states,[81] it was reportedly pressured by the United States to drop the initiative.[82] It never came to the floor of

77 ibid, Declaration of Judge Kulyk.

78 ibid, Declaration of Judge Kittichaisaree, §§4–10.

79 Bodansky (n 39) 689.

80 Address by Johnson Toribiong, President of the Republic of Palau, UN GAOR 66th Session, 16th Plenary Meeting at 26, 27, UN Doc A/66/PV.16 (22 September 2011).

81 Mayer (n 8) 63.

82 Maxine Burkett, 'A Justice Paradox: On Climate Change, Small Island Developing States, and the Quest for Effective Legal Remedy' (2013) 35 *Univ Haw LR* 633, 635.

the UN General Assembly. This was apparently not the first time a small island state considered proposing an advisory opinion request. An 'undisclosed small island State' was considering such an endeavor as early as 1997.[83]

The current ICJ advisory opinion request illustrates the potential when multilateral diplomacy fueled by grassroots advocacy comes to fruition.[84] In 2019, a group of law students from eight Pacific Island countries founded the Pacific Islands Students Fighting Climate Change (PISFCC).[85] PISFCC started a campaign to persuade states to seek an Advisory Opinion from the ICJ on the issue of climate change and human rights, a call first answered by Vanuatu.

Vanuatu worked over the course of several years with a 'Core Group' of States to gain diplomatic support for a UN General Assembly Resolution on a 'Request for an advisory opinion of the [ICJ] on the obligations of States in respect of climate change.'[86] It sought input from a wide range of stakeholders in framing the legal question to be included in the draft resolution. While the content of the question has not been without its detractors,[87] the efforts to reach some sort of consensus appear to have paid off. The resolution was adopted on March 29, 2023, with 132 co-sponsors. It was the first request for an advisory opinion from the UN General Assembly to be adopted by consensus.[88] According to Vanuatu, this sends 'a strong and unambiguous signal that

83 Bodansky (n 8) 185, note 18.

84 The request for an advisory opinion on the legality of the threat or use of nuclear weapons was fueled by a similar, if not larger, effort by civil society. The World Court Project, a non-governmental organization that lobbied the World Health Organization and General Assembly for the advisory opinion requests, was supported by 700 organizations around the world. John Burroughs, *The Legality of the Threat or Use of Nuclear Weapons: A Guide to the Historic Opinion of the International Court of Justice* (Lit Verlag 1998) 9.

85 '"Beginning of a New Era": Pacific Islanders Hail UN Vote on Climate Justice' *The Guardian* (29 March 2023) <www.theguardian.com/world/2023/mar/30/un-vote-on-climate-justice-pacific-island-change-crisis-united-nations-vanuatu> accessed 9 February 2024.

86 *Request for an Advisory Opinion of the International Court of Justice on the Obligations of States in respect of Climate Change*, UNGA Res 77/276 (29 March 2023) UN Doc A/RES/77/276.

87 Philippa Webb, 'EJIL : The Podcast! Episode 18 – "Be Careful What You Ask For"' (28 February 2023) <https://www.ejiltalk.org/ejilthe-podcast-episode-18-be-careful-what-you-ask-for/> accessed 17 March 2024, 15:35–15:36. (Philippe Sands, on the danger of drafting the question too broadly, 'I'm afraid the drafts that are circulating and that which has gone to ITLOS are so open ended, that the room for mischief [by the Court] is very significant.')

88 Although no State called for a vote, Member States still voiced concerns during the debate. The representative of the United States expressed that addressing shared goals related to climate change was best achieved through diplomatic means rather than a judicial process. 'General Assembly Adopts Resolution Requesting International Court of Justice Provide Advisory Opinion on States' Obligations Concerning Climate Change' (*United*

nations are united in their commitment to abide by existing climate obligations under international law.'[89]

Through the use of diplomatic tools for this advisory opinion request, the ICJ may contribute to the normative development of international law on climate change on a faster timetable than would be possible had they waited for a future State-to-State dispute to arrive through the underutilized dispute settlement mechanism of the UNFCCC or the compulsory jurisdiction of the ICJ. Of course, while the ITLOS decision was generally received positively, it remains to be seen if the ICJ opinion will help or hinder the ability of States to address the threat of climate change.

3.3 *Framing the Legal Questions to Create Future Avenues of Dispute Resolution*

The legal questions in the requests for advisory opinions also represent jurisdictional ingenuity. In this way, jurisdictional ingenuity can be synergistic and may contribute to the systemic integration of climate change law.[90] In this context, the legal questions are framed in such a way that they will open the doors to future avenues of dispute resolution across regimes. Or, in the words of Margaretha Wererinke-Singh, the opinions have the potential to 'mak[e] international law more actionable through climate litigation.'[91]

The ITLOS advisory opinion provides evidence of jurisdictional ingenuity as a way to connect disparate areas of law as well as create future pathways for dispute resolution. UNCLOS was negotiated well before climate change was recognized by the General Assembly as a "common concern" in 1988.[92] It was

Nations, 29 March 2023) <https://press.un.org/en/2023/ga12497.doc.htm> accessed 9 February 2024.

89 'ICJ Resolution' (*Vanuatu ICJ Initiative*) <www.vanuatuicj.com/resolution> accessed 9 February 2024.

90 See eg Damilola S. Olawuyi, 'Harmonizing International Trade and Climate Change Institutions: Legal and Theoretical Basis for Systemic Integration' (2014) 7 *L & Dev Rev* 107, 118; Spyridon Aktypis, Emmanuel Decaux, and Bronwen Leroy, 'Systemic integration between climate change and human rights at the United Nations?' in Quirico & Boumghar (eds), *Climate Change and Human Rights: An International and Comparative Law Perspective* (Taylor & Francis 2015) 232; Ottavio Quirico, 'Systemic Integration Between Climate Change and Human Rights in International Law?' (2017) 35 *Neth Q Hum Rts* 31, 44. See also Samuel & Carrillo Bañuelos (n 8).

91 Statement by Margarethe Wewerinke-Singh, Doughty Street Chambers, 'Advisory Opinions on climate change before the ICJ, IACtHR and ITLOS' (17 November 2023) 35:50 – 44:20 <https://youtu.be/oz3ddbraOBo?si=5nf-XKkM_wWmj_KW> accessed 9 February 2024.

92 UNGA Res 43/53 (6 December 1988) UN Doc A/43/755 ('Protection of Global Climate for Present and Future Generations of Mankind').

adopted in 1982, a full decade before the UNFCCC was open for signature.[93] UNCLOS does not mention climate change or the emission of GHG. However, the 'constitution for the ocean' has been described as a 'living treaty'[94] subject to 'evolutive interpretation.'[95]

The question posed to ITLOS was phrased in such a way to bridge the gap between UNCLOS and the climate change regime. It asked the tribunal for an advisory opinion on the obligation of State parties to UNCLOS to (a) 'prevent, reduce and control pollution of the marine environment' from the effects of climate change, including through ocean warming and sea level rise, and ocean acidification, which are caused by greenhouse gas emissions into the atmosphere, and (b) 'to protect and preserve the marine environment in relation to climate change impacts, including ocean warming and sea level rise, and ocean acidification.' In short, one of the main issues the question posed to the Tribunal was to address the open question of whether the emission of GHG constitutes 'pollution of the marine environment' within the meaning of UNCLOS and what specific obligations flow from that potential threshold determination.

In terms of the applicable law, neither the COSIS Agreement nor the request for the advisory opinion mentions either the UNFCCC or the Paris Agreement. The request for the advisory opinion was submitted pursuant to UNCLOS and involves the interpretation and application of UNCLOS. However, the interpretation of the legal questions seemed to necessitate reference to the UNFCCC and the Paris Agreement. Indeed, many States in their written submissions expressed that the UNFCCC and the Paris Agreement were the 'primary instruments' to guide the interpretation of the obligations of States in relation to climate change.[96] Other States suggested that ITLOS was permitted to refer to the UNFCCC and related agreements pursuant to Part XII of UNCLOS,[97] but clarified that it was limited to determining the obligations under UNCLOS and not under related treaties.[98]

---

93 See also Millicent McCreath, 'The Potential for UNCLOS Climate Change Litigation to Achieve Effective Mitigation Outcomes', Lin & Kysar (n 56) 122.

94 Jill Barret & Richard Barnes (eds), *Law of the Sea: UNCLOS as a Living Treaty* (British Institute of International and Comparative Law 2016).

95 Lianne P. Baars, 'The Salience of Salt Water: An ITLOS Advisory Opinion at the Ocean-Climate Nexus' (2023) 38 *Int'l J Marine & Coastal L* 1, 2.

96 See, eg *Request for an Advisory Opinion submitted by the COSIS* (n 65), Written Statement of Norway; ibid, Written Statement of the European Union.

97 See eg *Request for an Advisory Opinion submitted by the COSIS* (n 65), Written Statement of the Republic of Korea, §16.

98 See eg *Request for an Advisory Opinion submitted by the COSIS* (n 65), Written Statement of Canada, §61.

In its opinion, the Tribunal confirmed that UNCLOS is considered a 'living instrument' with flexible rules of interpretation that can be read with reference to the text of the instrument itself in addition to other 'external rules' of international law.[99] Specifically, it found that the global climate change regime, including the UNFCCC and the Paris Agreement, were particularly relevant external rules in responding to the request, but that they were not *lex specialis*.[100] To fully bridge the gaps between the two regimes, the Tribunal determined that GHG emissions constitute "pollution of the marine environment" within the meaning of Article 1, paragraph 1, subparagraph 4 of UNCLOS.[101] This is significant as the Tribunal found that State parties to UNCLOS have specific obligations to 'prevent, reduce and control pollution of the marine environment' under Article 194 of the treaty.[102]

Prior to the current advisory opinion effort or even the creation of COSIS, Alan Boyle, among others,[103] argued that UNCLOS provided a viable pathway for the settlement of disputes on the obligations of States to protect and preserve the marine environment from the effects of climate change.[104] A State could bring a case against another state party to UNCLOS alleging its lack of compliance with the pollution control obligations of UNCLOS. As Boyle pointed out, there are challenges in pursuing this effort. One is the enormous financial resources required to pursue arbitration. The other was the indeterminacy of the meaning of pollution under UNCLOS.[105] While some argued that it was clear that climate change and the emission of GHG constitute pollution within the meaning of UNCLOS,[106] that issue had yet to be determined until ITLOS issued its advisory opinion.

---

99 *COSIS Opinion* (n 73), §§130–131.

100 ibid, §§137 & 224.

101 ibid, §179.

102 The Tribunal elaborated on these obligations, finding that States have 'specific obligations to take all necessary measures to prevent, reduce and control marine pollution from [GHG] emissions.' Ibid, para 243. See also, Melissa Stewart, 'What to Watch for Following Historic Climate Opinion from "The Oceans Court"' (4 June 2024) *Just Security* <https://www.justsecurity.org/96365/oceans-court-climate-opinion/> accessed August 7, 2024.

103 See eg McCreath (n 93) 122; William C. G. Burns, 'Potential Causes of Action for Climate Change Damages in International Fora: The Law of the Sea Convention' (2006) 2 *McGill Int'l J. Sustainable Development L & Pol* 27.

104 Alan Boyle, 'Litigating Climate Change under Part XII of the LOSC' (2019) 34 *Int'l J Marine & Coastal L* 458.

105 Alan Boyle & Navraj Singh Ghaleigh, 'Climate Change and International Law Beyond the UNFCCC', in Carlarne, Gray, Tarasofsky (eds), *The Oxford Handbook of International Climate Change Law* (OUP 2016) 46.

106 McCreath (n 93) 123, who argues that 'it is now generally accepted that several of the causes and effects of climate change can be considered pollution of the marine environment.'

While the advisory opinion is not binding on State Parties to UNCLOS, it does have 'legal effect.'[107] The conclusion that GHG emissions constitute 'pollution' within the meaning of UNCLOS provides the substantive link between the climate regime and the law of the sea. This lowers at least one barrier to entry and easing the burden for States that may wish to pursue a contentious case pursuant to UNCLOS.

The determination that GHG emissions constitutes 'pollution' potentially opens other avenues for State-to-State dispute resolution related to climate change outside of the dispute settlement regime of UNCLOS. As explained by Steve Lorteau, this type of 'state-as-polluter' litigation is in some ways a well-worn path under international law.[108] ITLOS elaborated on the due diligence obligations of States in context of climate change, finding that the standard 'is stringent, given the high risks of serious and irreversible harm to the marine environment' from GHG emissions.[109] The Tribunal also found that states have specific obligations to ensure that GHG emissions within their jurisdiction and control do not cause transboundary harm. In this context, the obligation is 'even more stringent … because of the nature of transboundary pollution,' in that pollution from one state that spreads beyond its jurisdiction has the potential to 'cause damage to other States and their environment.'[110] The opinion also noted that a State may incur international responsibility if it 'fails to comply' with the obligation to 'take all necessary measures to prevent, reduce and control marine pollution from anthropogenic GHG emissions, *including measures to reduce such emissions*.'[111] Thus, the opinion may make it easier in the future for a State to establish that another State failed to comply with its obligation of due diligence to prevent transboundary harm from GHG emissions.

If the ICJ opinion builds on the ITLOS opinion, it could open the door to future state to state dispute resolution even wider. The legal question in the request for an advisory opinion from the ICJ is much broader than the request submitted to ITLOS. As a court of general jurisdiction, the ICJ has the opportunity to interpret the question with reference to any body of international law.

107 *Dispute concerning Delimitation of the Maritime Boundary between Mauritius and Maldives in the Indian Ocean* (*Mauritius/Maldives*) (*Preliminary Objections*) (Judgment, 28 January 2021) ITLOS Case No 28, §§202–205.

108 Steve Lorteau, 'The Potential of International "State-as-Polluter" Litigation' (2023) 32 *RECIEL* 259.

109 *COSIS Opinion* (n 73) §243.

110 ibid, §258.

111 ibid, §286 (emphasis added)

The chapeau paragraph of the legal question was intentionally capacious in its inclusion of sources and general principles of international law.[112]

According to counsel for Vanuatu, the legal question in the request for an advisory opinion from the ICJ is framed in such a way as to offer the court an opportunity to provide an avenue for States to pursue compensation for climate harms, including those caused by past actions.[113] Under paragraph (b), the question asks, '[w]hat are the legal consequences under these obligations for States where they, by their acts and omissions, *have caused* significant harm' to the climate and the environment?[114] Julian Aguon, counsel to Vanuatu, recently described that part of the legal question as being 'the home for reparations.'[115] While it does not seem likely that the ICJ will find that historic emissions prior to the UNFCCC constitute an internationally wrongful act[116] or that historic emitters have an obligation to make reparations for damage caused by climate change, it does seem to be the hope of many behind the effort that an advisory opinion will open a pathway for such potential future action.[117] These do not appear to be isolated hopes. Counsel for Vanuatu wrote elsewhere that '[a]n advisory opinion from the ICJ on the issue of compensation could set the stage for further international litigation …"[118]

---

112 The chapeau paragraph listed the 'Charter of the United Nations, the International Covenant on Civil and Political Rights, the International Covenant on Economic, Social and Cultural Rights, the United Nations Framework Convention on Climate Change, the Paris Agreement, the United Nations Convention on the Law of the See, the duty of due diligence, the rights recognized in the Universal Declaration of Human Rights, the principle of prevention of significant harm to the environment and the duty to protect and preserve the marine environment.' UNGA Res 77/276 (n 86).

113 Statement by Margaretha Werewinke-Sing, saying the legal question will give the ICJ the opportunity to have 'due regard for past, present, and future.' Doughty Street Chambers, 'Advisory Opinions on climate change before the ICJ, IACtHR and ITLOS' (17 November 2023) 35:50 – 44:20 <https://youtu.be/oz3ddbraOB0?si=5nf-XKkM_wWmj_KW> accessed 9 February 2024.

114 UNGA Res 77/276 (n 86) (emphasis added).

115 UH Better Tomorrow Speaker Series, 'Julian Aguon: An Indigenous Pursuit of Climate Justice' (31 October 2023) 1:00:00 – 1:14:30 <www.youtube.com/watch?v=mabawiuyvD4> accessed 9 February 2024.

116 Under Article 13 of the Draft Articles on the Responsibility of States for Internationally Wrongful Acts, 'An act of a State does not constitute a breach of an international obligation unless the State is bound by the obligation in question at the time the act occurs.' See 'Draft Articles on Responsibility of States for Internationally Wrongful Acts', adopted by the International Law Commission at its 53rd session, UN Doc A/RES/56/10 (2001).

117 See also, Benoit Mayer, 'Climate Change Reparations and the Law and Practice of State Responsibility' (2017) 7 *Asian JIL* 185; Voigt (n 46) 1.

118 Margaretha Wewerinke-Singh, Julian Aguon & Julie Hunter, 'Bringing Climate Change before the International Court of Justice: Prospects for Contentious Cases and Advisory Opinions', Alogna, Bakker & Gauci (n 48).

With respect to the ICJ, it is possible that an advisory opinion could clarify how existing bodies of law and general principles of international law relate to the climate regime, such as the concept of due diligence or the relationship between the 'no harm' rule and the obligations of States with respect to climate change. Even the non-binding interpretation in an advisory opinion could help lower the barrier for States contemplating pursuing interstate dispute resolution as a result of less uncertainty in the legal landscape.

Jurisdictional ingenuity in the context of climate change may be synergistic in another way. It may allow for further climate litigation to move forward at the regional or domestic level in jurisdictions that incorporate international law.[119] Several landmark decisions on climate change have come from regional[120] and domestic courts[121] and progressive articulation of the obligations of States in respect of climate change could lead to future litigation to push States to adopt more ambitious climate targets.

4 Potential Risks of Jurisdictional Ingenuity in the Context of Climate Change

As explained above, jurisdictional ingenuity can open up legal pathways through alternative jurisdictional avenues when direct pathways to dispute resolution are weak or unavailable. Jurisdictional ingenuity can also be synergistic by approaching litigation strategy in such a way as to create future pathways for dispute resolution. Jurisdictional ingenuity is not without risks, however. Generally speaking, jurisdictional ingenuity can lead to fragmentation in the law. With respect to climate change, it has the potential to clarify obligations in a less progressive way than hoped for by its advocates and could potentially undermine future progress within the climate regime.

Jurisdictional ingenuity has the potential to lead to fragmentation in the law.[122] This is particularly true where, as here, the strategy is pursued through

119 Bodansky (n 8) 185.

120 *Verein KlimaSeniorinnen Schweiz and Others v Switzerland* (App No 53600/20) ECtHR [GC] 9 April 2024.

121 District Court of the Hague (DC), *Urgenda Foundation v The State of the Netherlands*, Case No. C/09/456689 / HA ZA 13–1396, 24 June 2015.

122 'Fragmentation of International Law: Difficulties arising from the Diversification and Expansion of International Law', Report of the Study Group of the International Law Commission, adopted at its 58th session, UN Doc A/CN.4/L.682 (2006); Martti Koskenniemi & Päivi Leino, 'Fragmentation of International Law? Postmodern Anxieties' (2002) 15 *Leiden JIL* 553; Yuval Shany, 'No Longer a Weak Department of Power? Reflections on the Emergency of a New International Judiciary' (2009) 20 *European JIL* 73, 87.

simultaneous advisory opinion requests in multiple jurisdictions with overlapping subject matter jurisdiction.[123] For example, the legal questions submitted to the ICJ touch on States obligations under international human rights law and the law of the sea, the subject matter jurisdiction of the IACtHR and the ITLOS, respectively. There is a risk that these tribunals will interpret the obligations of States under these overlapping bodies of a law in a way that is inconsistent, creating a more muddied legal landscape rather than clarifying the law.[124] Conflicting opinions might lead to States choosing the least common denominator through which to demonstrate their compliance with international law.

The concern about fragmentation is not unique to jurisdictional ingenuity,[125] nor is it a new concern in the field of environmental law. As explained by Tim Stephens, 'jurisdictional competition' between various multilateral and bilateral agreements related to international environmental law has led to forum shopping, simultaneous proceedings, and successive proceedings in international environmental law.[126]

While proponents of the advisory opinion requests are hopeful that it will lead to much needed positive action on climate change, it is not at all clear that the opinions will result in such an outcome.[127] An opinion at the ICJ that merely confirms that States have a duty of due diligence or an obligation to cooperate under customary international law is unlikely to change the status quo.[128] It would further entrench the notion that international environmental obligations are framed in terms of 'conduct and not of result.'[129] Even a seemingly progressive opinion announcing that States have an obligation under international law to compensate States for loss and damage caused by climate

123 See Stephens (n 3) 272–273; Tigre & Rocha (n 8) 287–288.

124 The timelines of the expected opinions appear to lessen this concern somewhat as the opinions may be issued sequentially with sufficient time for the subsequent opinion to consider the previous decision.

125 ILC, 'Fragmentation of International Law' (n 122); Koskenniemi & Leino (n 122).

126 Stephens (n 3) 272–286.

127 British Institute of International and Comparative Law, 'Promoting Climate Justice through International Law: Climate Litigation & Climate Advisory Opinions' 6 <https://www.biicl.org/documents/163_event_report_climate_advisories_litigation_15_march.pdf> accessed 10 March 2024.

128 Law Report, 'Vanuatu's Push for International Court Action on Climate Change' 12 July 2022 <https://www.abc.net.au/listen/programs/lawreport/vanuatu-climate-court/13965770> accessed 22 February 2024.

129 Martti Koskenniemi, 'Peaceful Settlement of Environmental Disputes' (1991) 60 *Nordic JIL* 73, 77. This is reflective of Tim Stevens concern with the ITLOS opinion, that it is lacking in clarity as to 'precisely what the obligation *is* under Article 194.' ANZSIL-OIELIG ITLOS AO Webinar (28 May 2024) 41:15–41:25 <https://tinyurl.com/3pxckanr> accessed 17 March 2025.

change might not result in more ambitious climate action.[130] As Daniel Bodansky has explained, it could 'threaten to blow up the negotiations' under the climate regime if States are seen to have circumvented the multilateral process under the UNFCCC.[131] There is also the possibility that the ICJ could divert from the ITLOS advisory opinion and announce that States do not have obligations beyond which they have agreed to under the UNFCCC and the Paris Agreement, a result that could stifle progress for years if not decades to come.

5 Conclusion

Jurisdictional ingenuity in the context of the climate emergency has the potential to transform the legal landscape. For States that are at risk of losing the entirety of their territory due to sea level rise, it is an attempt to avoid the most severe consequences of climate change before it is too late.[132] Although there are risks of fragmentation in the law and there is no guarantee of a positive result, there is potential for substantive outcomes that will lead to future progress on addressing the dire threat of climate change.

---

130 Bodansky (n 8) 185. Law Report, 'Vanuatu's Push for International Court Action on Climate Change' 12 July 2022 <https://www.abc.net.au/listen/programs/lawreport/vanuatu-climate-court/13965770> accessed 22 February 2024 (Douglas Guilfoyle describing such an outcome as 'radical.')

131 Bodansky (n 8) 185. See also 'Special Online Briefing with Secretary John Kerry, Special Presidential Envoy for Climate, and Monica Medina, Assistant Secretary of State for Oceans and International Environmental and Scientific Affairs' (US Department of State 3 March 2023) <https://www.state.gov/special-online-briefing-with-secretary-john-kerry-special-presidential-envoy-for-climate-and-monica-medina-assistant-secretary-of-state-for-oceans-and-international-environmental-and-scientific-aff/> with Secretary Kerry describing Vanuatu's Advisory Opinion effort as 'sort of just jumping ahead and going to court.'

132 Stewart (n 8).

CHAPTER 5

The Role of Advisory Opinions in International Law in the Context of the Climate Crisis

The Dialogue between the ICJ, the ITLOS, the IACtHR, and the AfCtHPR

Susan Ann Samuel and Jorge Alejandro Carrillo Bañuelos***

Abstract

The 'quartet' of requests for advisory opinions marks an unprecedented moment in global climate change litigation. These initiatives can provide an opportunity to clarify the legal obligations of States, enhance coherence in the international legal system, and ultimately lead to more ambitious action on climate change. However, the contribution of the regional and international courts to the clarification and development of international law depends, to some extent, on their ability to render coherent advisory opinions. Judicial dialogue can serve that purpose. The ICJ, the ITLOS, the IACtHR, and the AfCtHPR will probably not ignore the work of each other but rather try to pursue a dialogue among themselves. How can these courts dialogue, and through what means? What are the potential limits of this cross-regime and cross-institution interaction? This chapter considers the different advisory proceedings on climate change to explore how they can create or limit opportunities for judicial dialogue.

Keywords

advisory opinions – climate litigation – International and regional courts – judicial dialogue

* University of Leeds, https://orcid.org/0000-0002-1362-4571.

** Supreme Court of Mexico, https://orcid.org/0009-0001-5736-3836.

1 Introduction

The current 'quartet of requests for advisory opinions'[1] marks an unprecedented moment in global climate change litigation, 'with the world's highest courts weighing in on the legal rights and duties related to the climate crisis.'[2] Three requests for advisory opinions to the International Court of Justice (ICJ), the International Tribunal for the Law of the Sea (ITLOS), and the Inter-American Court of Human Rights (IACtHR) were submitted within a period of six months. Additionally, it is observed that an initiative of African civil societies and community-based organizations is about to request an advisory opinion from the African Court of Human and Peoples' Rights (AfCtHPR).[3] 'When it rains, it pours,' as Bodansky rightly expressed it.[4] Whether by the surge of global climate change litigation,[5] the tardiness of climate negotiations,[6] or the rise of climate movements[7] – the importance and urgency for international law to intervene in interpreting norms, principles, and standards are now more crucial than ever.

The *Global Climate Litigation Report: 2023 Status Review* highlights that 'people are increasingly turning to the courts to combat the climate crisis.'[8] As of September 8, 2023, the global climate change litigation databases included more than 2,400 cases filed in over seventy jurisdictions. This increasing number of legal cases can be attributed, to some extent, to 'the – still – inadequate'[9] level of climate ambition worldwide and the failure to achieve the long-term

1 See 'Advisory Opinions on Climate Change: An Overview | Columbia Climate School' <https://www.climate.columbia.edu/events/advisory-opinions-climate-change-overview> accessed 17 June 2023.

2 Maria Antonia Tigre, 'It Is (Finally) Time for an Advisory Opinion on Climate Change: Challenges and Opportunities on a Trio of Initiatives' (2024) 17 *Charleston Law Review* 623.

3 ibid.

4 Daniel Bodansky, 'Advisory Opinions on Climate Change: Some Preliminary Questions' (2023) 32 *RECIEL* 185.

5 As of May 2022, the Sabin Center for Climate Change Law's database recorded over 2000 cases pertaining to climate change that had been filed in national and international courts and tribunals.

6 Bodansky (n 4).

7 Louis J Kotzé & Henrike Knappe, 'Youth Movements, Intergenerational Justice, and Climate Litigation in the Deep Time Context of the Anthropocene' (2023) 5 *Environmental Research Communications* 025001; Susan Ann Samuel, '"Greening" International Law en route to Agenda 2030: The Role of Youth in Enhancing the Soft Power of Climate Justice' (2024) 33 *Yearbook of Int'l Environmental Law* 3.

8 United Nations Environment Programme, *Global Climate Litigation Report: 2023 Status Review* (UNEP 2023) IX.

9 Tigre (n 2) 625.

temperature goals and objectives of the Paris Agreement.[10] The 'almost stagnant level' of the aggregate effect of Nationally Determined Contributions (NDCs) implementation also highlights an urgent need for a significant increase in the level of ambition.[11] This situation has created the premise for an emerging trend of litigation.[12]

Much of the climate litigation to date has come at the domestic level,[13] aiming to compel national action on climate change mitigation and adaptation.[14] Furthermore, there is increasing reliance on tort, constitutional, or human rights law in domestic courts to interpret international law in a manner that mandates governments to strengthen their efforts in mitigating or adapting to climate change.[15] In contrast, in the international scenario, the voluntary nature of adjudication is an obstacle to inter-state litigation, particularly considering that 'most large greenhouse gas (GHG) emitters do not accept the compulsory jurisdiction of the ICJ and show no interest in referring a climate-related case to an international court.'[16]

Then why a turn to international courts? And why requesting advisory opinions? For some of the main proponents, international courts and tribunals can provide an authoritative interpretation of States' rights and obligations and lead States to take more ambitious action on climate change.[17] In this context, advisory opinions may offer several advantages in contrast with contentious

10 United Nations Environment Programme, *Emissions Gap Report 2022: The Closing Window – Climate crisis calls for rapid transformation of societies* (UNEP 2022) XVI.

11 UNFCCC, 'Nationally determined contributions under the Paris Agreement – Synthesis report by the Secretariat' (14 November 2023) UN Doc FCCC/PA/CMA/2023/12, §153.

12 UNFCCC, 'Decision 1/CP.26, Glasgow Climate Pact, in U.N. Climate Change Conference, Rep. of the Conference of the Parties to the Paris Agreement on Its Third Session, 2, UN Doc. FCCC/CP/2021/12/Add.1'; See, *generally*, United Nations Environment Programme, *Emissions Gap Report 2021: The Heat Is On—A World of Climate Promises Not Yet Delivered* (UNEP 2021).

13 Daniel Bodansky, 'The Role of the International Court of Justice in Addressing Climate Change: Some Preliminary Reflections' (2017) 49 *Arizona State LJ* 689, 699.

14 See Laura Melrose, 'Emerging Trends in Australian Climate Change Litigation: Bringing the Heat' (2022) 47 *Alternative Law Journal* 187; Millicent McCreath, 'The Potential for UNCLOS Climate Change Litigation to Achieve Effective Mitigation Outcomes', in Kysar & Lin (eds), *Climate Change Litigation in the Asia Pacific* (Cambridge University Press 2020); Bridie Butterfield, 'The Potential Role of Climate Change Litigation in Furthering the Mitigation Objectives of the Paris Agreement' (2018) 21 *Asia Pacific Journal of Environmental Law* 29; Benoit Mayer, 'Prompting Climate Change Mitigation through Litigation' (2023) 72 *ICLQ* 233.

15 Benoit Mayer, 'International Advisory Proceedings on Climate Change' (2023) 44 *Michigan JIL* 41.

16 ibid.

17 ibid 45.

cases. For instance, some scholars argue that advisory proceedings have the potential to circumvent the resistance of States that are major GHG emitters. Moreover, an advisory opinion could be 'less controversial than a contentious case, for example concerning state responsibility for harms associated with the impacts of climate change.'[18] These opinions can also avoid delicate issues intrinsic to disputes, such as causation and attribution.[19] Advisory opinions could also better reflect the global nature of climate change,[20] allow the participation of State and non-State actors,[21] and avoid narrow rules on intervention that apply to contentious proceedings.[22]

Advisory opinions also carry great 'legal weight and moral authority.'[23] The limited binding force of these opinions has minimal consequences in a legal system where enforcement is already challenging. Furthermore, the authoritative nature of advisory opinions and the norm-building character of the courts are significant in catalyzing political will.[24] Courts acknowledge that both advisory opinions and judgments are considered 'judicial decisions' and serve as subsidiary means for determining rules of law[25] and initiating

18 Annalisa Savaresi, Kati Kulovesi & Harro van Asselt, 'Beyond COP26: Time for an Advisory Opinion on Climate Change?' (*EJIL: Talk!*, 17 December 2021) <https://www.ejiltalk.org/beyond-cop26-time-for-an-advisory-opinion-on-climate-change/> accessed 15 August 2023.

19 See Penelope Ridings, 'An ICJ Advisory Opinion on Climate Change: Can It Assist in Driving Ambition?' (31 October 2021) <https://peneloperidings.com/wp48/index.php/2021/11/01/an-icj-advisory-opinion-on-climate-change-can-it-assist-in-driving-ambition/> accessed 9 July 2023.

20 See David Freestone, Richard Barnes & Payam Akhavan, 'Agreement for the Establishment of the Commission of Small Island States on Climate Change and International Law' (2022) 37 *Int'l Journal of Marine & Coastal Law* 1; Rüdiger Wolfrum, 'Advisory Opinions: An Alternative Means to Avoid the Development of Legal Conflicts?', in Ruiz Fabri (ed), *International Law and Litigation: A Look Into Procedure* (Nomos 2019) 99, 106.

21 Eg Statute of the International Court of Justice (adopted 26 June 1945, entered into force 24 October 1945) 892 *UNTS* 119, art 36 (*ICJ Statute*); Rules of the International Tribunal for the Law of the Sea, adopted on 1 October 1 1997, ITLOS/8/Rev.1, art 133 (*ITLOS Rules*).

22 See, for example, on intervention: ICJ Statute, arts 62–63; United Nations Convention on the Law of the Sea (adopted 10 December 1982, entered into force 16 November 1994) 1833 UNTS 3 (UNCLOS, Annex VI (Statute of the International Tribunal for the Law of the Sea), arts 31–32; and on *amicus curiae*, ICJ Statute, art 34(2); ITLOS Rules, art 84.

23 International Court of Justice, 'Advisory Jurisdiction' <https://www.icj-cij.org/advisory-jurisdiction> accessed 9 July 2023.

24 See Alain Pellet & Daniel Müller, 'Article 38' in Zimmermann & Tams (eds), *The Statute of the International Court of Justice: A Commentary* (OUP 2019).

25 ICJ Statute, art 38(1)(d).

a trickle-down effect on subsequent judicial decisions made by other courts, including domestic ones.[26]

In this context, advisory opinions represent an opportunity to clarify the legal obligations of States in respect to climate change. Tigre notes that this clarification can 'enhance coherence within the overall legal system, particularly in areas that have been excessively fragmented.'[27] Similarly, Bodansky argues that an advisory opinion from an international court such as the ICJ could clarify and elaborate the relevant norms of international law in the context of climate change.[28] However, the contribution of these regional and international courts to the clarification and development of international law 'depends on rendering decisions that are coherent.'[29]

Providing 'coherent' advisory opinions may be challenging in light of the differences between the ICJ, the ITLOS, the IACtHR, and the AfCtHPR. For example, Bodansky describes how the requests for advisory opinions on climate change differ significantly with respect to the jurisdiction of the themes they cover under international law.[30] The ICJ's advisory jurisdiction covers international law matters.[31] This allows the ICJ to determine the obligations of States under climate change treaties such as the UNFCCC and the Paris Agreement, the UNCLOS, human rights law treaties, and customary international law.[32]

When it comes to the ITLOS, the request of the Commission of Small Island States on Climate Change and International Law (COSIS) centers solely on the obligations under the UNCLOS. In contrast, the IACtHR is authorized to provide advisory opinions regarding the American Convention on Human Rights (ACHR) and other treaties related to the safeguarding of human rights within the American States.[33] The jurisdiction of AfCtHPR is also quite nuanced. This court has the authority to furnish a legal opinion concerning the African Charter on Human and Peoples' Rights or any pertinent human rights instruments.[34]

---

26 See Georges Abi-Saab, *Les Exceptions Préliminaires Dans La Procedure De La Court Internationale* (Pédone 1967); Robert Kolb, *The Elgar Companion to the International Court of Justice* (Elgar 2016) 277; Hugh Thirlway, *The International Court of Justice* (OUP).

27 Tigre (n 2) 708.

28 Bodansky (n 13) 712.

29 Maria Antonia Tigre & Armando Rocha 'Competing Perspectives and Dialogue in Climate Change Advisory Opinions' (2023) 117 *AJIL Unbound* 287, 291.

30 Bodansky (n 4).

31 ICJ Statute, art 65(1).

32 Bodansky (n 4).

33 ACHR, art 64(2).

34 African Court on Human and Peoples' Rights, 'Jurisdiction' (*African Court on Human and Peoples' Rights*) <https://www.african-court.org/wpafc/jurisdiction/> accessed 11 August 2023.

Despite these differences in jurisdiction and expertise, courts still have several areas of opportunity to discuss the same issues or to analyze the same norms. For instance, the Paris Agreement will probably play a relevant role in all the advisory proceedings, 'either directly regarding its interpretation or application, or indirectly where it may inform the interpretation of other international agreements.'[35] Similarly, the questions posed in these advisory proceedings will probably allow the courts to provide an opinion on common issues such as the duty of due diligence, the principle of prevention, and the obligations of States towards persons, groups, or communities that are injured or especially affected by climate change. Lastly, several State and non-State actors will participate in more than one advisory proceeding, suggesting that the arguments in the *amicus curiae* briefs submitted before these international courts and tribunals will probably follow a relatively coherent line.

Accordingly, the ICJ, the ITLOS, the IACtHR, and the AfCtHPR will probably not ignore the work of each other but rather try to pursue a dialogue among themselves. Judicial dialogue seems both inevitable and highly beneficial in this context – particularly in terms of coherence and consistency in the international legal system. However, how can these courts dialogue, and through what means? What are the potential limits of this cross-regime and cross-institution interaction? This chapter engages a comparative analytical approach that considers the different advisory proceedings to explore how they can create or limit opportunities for judicial dialogue. Such analysis also intends to illustrate how judicial dialogue happens or may happen across these courts – evoking a coherent line of decision and positing the relevance of finding a common denominator in legal proceedings in response to the climate crisis.

The chapter is divided into two sections. First, it assesses the concept of judicial dialogue and explores the existing venues for this dialogue in the international legal system. This section highlights that the ICJ, the ITLOS, the IACtHR, and the AfCtHPR can and should engage in formal and informal dialogue. These international courts may use the lessons from others, facilitating coherence and consistency among the advisory opinions on climate change. Second, this chapter analyzes the limits of the cross-regime and cross-institution interaction and whether and how they affect the advisory proceedings. In particular, this section illustrates how the scope of the dialogue between the courts could be determined by (a) the jurisdiction *ratione materiae*, (b) the actors that participate in advisory proceedings, and (c) the questions posed.

35 Christina Voigt, 'The Power of the Paris Agreement in International Climate Litigation' (2023) 32 *RECIEL* 237, 238.

2 Judicial Dialogue and Climate Change

Judicial dialogue can be broadly defined as the communication between judicial authorities.[36] This communication entails, for instance, the practice of domestic and international courts of 'using the reasoning of other courts to construct a better interpretation of a legal norm.'[37] This dialogue relies on 'reciprocal deference' and it can be practiced between domestic courts, between international courts, or between domestic and international courts.[38] Some scholars observe that, as such, judicial dialogue occurs without a central institution establishing uniform criteria among different courts.[39]

Some authors also argue that the concept of judicial dialogue specifically refers to the influence courts receive from foreign legal sources, distinct from merely citing those sources and independently constructing jurisprudential standards.[40] In contrast, authors such as Sandholtz highlight the relevance of citation in judicial dialogue as a means to bring legitimacy and foster a coherent line of interpretations between courts.[41] Sandholtz also stresses how the deliberate exchange of ideas among courts through judicial dialogue is "purposeful" by exploring how when human rights courts engage in judicial dialogue they perceive themselves as integral to and actively contributing to a worldwide legal framework for human rights.[42]

The dialogue between courts is becoming increasingly frequent,[43] particularly because globalization 'has opened the door to greater interaction between national and supranational judicial institutions.'[44] According to Ferrer Mac-Gregor, 'an isolationist attitude seems to be at odds with the contemporary *modus operandi* of domestic and international courts.'[45] Scholars

---

36 Elżbieta Karska & Karol Karski, 'Judicial Dialogue in Human Rights: Introductory Remarks' (2019) 21 *Int'l Community Law Review* 391.

37 Eduardo Ferrer Mac-Gregor, 'What Do We Mean When We Talk About Judicial Dialogue?: Reflections Of A Judge Of The Inter-American Court Of Human Rights' (2017) 30 *Harv HRJ* 89, 91.

38 ibid.

39 Manuel Eduardo Góngora-Mera, 'Diálogo Policéntrico', in Mac-Gregor, Martinez & Figueroa (eds), *Diccionario de Derecho Procesal Constitucional y Convencional* (PJF-CJF-IIJ-UNAM 2014) 586; Ferrer Mac-Gregor (n 37) 90.

40 Ferrer Mac-Gregor (n 37) 91.

41 Wayne Sandholtz, 'Human Rights Courts and Global Constitutionalism: Coordination through Judicial Dialogue' (2021) 10 *Global Constitutionalism* 439, 452.

42 ibid 439.

43 Anne-Marie Slaughter, 'A Typology of Transjudicial Communication' (1994) 29(1) *University of Richmond LR* 99.

44 Ferrer Mac-Gregor (n 37) 91.

45 ibid.

have also observed some of the benefits judicial dialogue can offer to international law, including the development of customary international law through state practice[46] and the enforcement of international legal norms.[47] This dialogue can also help avoid the risk of conflicting views or standards in legal decisions,[48] promote a 'spirit of systemic harmonization,' and ultimately 'refine' international law.[49] For instance, Tigre and Rocha highlight that 'international courts often refer to other courts' decisions to inform their perspectives and avoid conflicts with their rulings.'[50] Judicial dialogue seems highly beneficial in this context.

Literature around judicial dialogue is extensive,[51] for instance, in the context of human rights law.[52] However, judicial dialogue in climate litigation has received less attention. In 2007, Osofsky highlighted that climate litigation did not fit neatly into the mainstream discussion of judicial dialogue, considering that courts in these cases 'do not often engage in direct dialogue with one another because subnational and national litigation in common law legal systems focuses on context-specific precedent.'[53] However, the increasing number

46 Philip Moremen, 'National Court Decisions as State Practice: A Transnational Judicial Dialogue' (2006) 32 *North Carolina JIL* 259.

47 Eyal Benvenisti & George W Downs, *Between Fragmentation and Democracy: The Role of National and International Courts* (CUO 2017) Chapters 5 and 6.

48 Voigt (n 35), to whom a 'Paris-aligned interpretation' is a trigger of international litigation and the requests for advisory opinions on climate change.

49 *Al-Dulimi and Montana Management Inc v Switzerland* (App No 5809/08) ECtHR 21 June 2016, §140, apud Anne Peters, 'The Refinement of International Law: From Fragmentation to Regime Interaction and Politicization' (2017) 15 *Int'l J Constitutional Law* 671.

50 Tigre & Rocha (n 29) 289.

51 See, generally, Anne-Marie Slaughter (n 43); Francis G Jacobs, 'Judicial Dialogue and the Cross-Fertilization of Legal Systems: The European Court of Justice' (2003) 38 *Texas IL Journal*; Melissa A Waters, 'Mediating Norms and Identity: The Role of Transnational Judicial Dialogue in Creating and Enforcing International Law' (2005) 93 *Georgetown Law Journal* 487; Philip Moremen (n 46); Allan Rosas, 'The European Court of Justice in Context: Forms and Patterns of Judicial Dialogue' (2007)1 *European J Legal Studies* 1; Janne E Nijman & André Nollkaemper (eds), *New Perspectives on the Divide Between National and International Law* (OUP 2007); Ricardo Lorenzetti, 'Global Governance : Dialogue between Courts' (European University Institute 2010); David Law and Wen-Chen Chang, 'The Limits of Global Judicial Dialogue' (2011) 86 *Washington LR* 523; André Nollkaemper, 'Conversations Among Courts: Domestic and International Adjudicators', in Romano, Alter & Shany (eds), *The Oxford Handbook of International Adjudication* (OUP 2013) 523; Ferrer Mac-Gregor' (n 37).

52 Karska & Karski (n 36); Madalina Moraru, Galina Cornelisse & Philippe De Bruycker (eds), *Law and Judicial Dialogue on the Return of Irregular Migrants from the European Union* (Hart Publishing 2020).

53 Hari M. Osofsky, 'Climate Change Litigation as Pluralist Legal Dialogue' (2007) 26 *Stanford Environmental LJ* 181, 192.

of global climate litigation cases[54] 'continues to bash holes in the view of domestic legal systems as hermetically sealed units.'[55] Affolder and Dzah note that several domestic climate litigation cases are inspired by litigation in other countries, and that the decisions in these cases 'are indicative of transjudicial influences and sometimes even dialogue on climate change.'[56] Cross-citation and cross-fertilization are not surprising in this context, considering 'the intensely transnational nature of both climate change and climate change litigation.'[57]

The transnational dimension of several climate change litigation cases can be attributed, to some extent, to the use of international instruments such as the Paris Agreement in domestic litigation.[58] This climate treaty has played a critical role in some of these cases[59] and, according to Affolder and Dzah, has allowed domestic courts to consider 'how courts in other jurisdictions have interpreted national obligations under that treaty.'[60] For instance, domestic courts have interpreted and applied the Paris Agreement's temperature and time targets[61] in cases such as *Urgenda*,[62] *Gloucester*,[63] and *Greenpeace Norway*.[64] Despite the differences between legal systems, these decisions exemplify how courts are approaching the question of what is required of a country to meet its goals under the Paris Agreement.[65] This information may be relevant for analyzing new climate litigation cases in other jurisdictions, even if a court 'distinguishes' and concludes that a specific foreign case has no direct

54 The database of the Sabin Center for Climate Change Law documented over 2000 legal cases concerning climate change that had been lodged in both national and international courts and tribunals; 190 of which were filed in the last 12 months.

55 Natasha Affolder & Godwin E.K. Dzah, 'The Transnational Exchange of Law Through Climate Change Litigation' in Sindico, McKenzie, Medici-Colombo & Wegener (eds), *Research Handbook on Climate Change Litigation* (Elgar 2024) 207.

56 ibid.

57 ibid.

58 ibid 11.

59 David Hunter, Wenhui Ji & Jenna Ruddock, 'The Paris Agreement and Global Climate Litigation after the Trump Withdrawal' (2019) 34 *Maryland JIL* 224, 225.

60 Affolder & Dzah (n 55) 11.

61 Brian J. Preston, 'The Influence of the Paris Agreement on Climate Litigation: Legal Obligations and Norms (Part I)' (2021) 33 *JEL* 1, 31–32.

62 *Urgenda Foundation v The State of the Netherlands* (*Ministry of Infrastructure and the Environment*) [2015] ECLI:NL:RBDHA:2015; The State of the Netherlands (*Ministry of Infrastructure and the Environment*) *v Urgenda Foundation* [2018] ECLI:NL:GHDHA:2018; *The State of the Netherlands* (*Ministry of Economic Affairs and Climate Policy*) *v Stichting Urgenda* [2019] ECLI:NL:HR:2019.

63 *Gloucester Resources Limited v Minister for Planning* [2019] NSWLEC 7.

64 *Greenpeace Nordic v The State of Norway* (*represented by the Ministry of Petroleum and Energy*), Case No 23–099330TVI-TOSL/05.

65 Affolder & Dzah (n 55) 8.

bearing on the legal case at hand.[66] In any event, this information on global climate change litigation can provide courts with opportunities to dialogue, engage in comparative legal research, and consider the work of other courts.

Judicial dialogue can also occur between international courts. These judicial bodies play a relevant role in 'clarifying and developing the understanding of existing rules and obligations'[67] under international law. That is why the dialogue between international courts and tribunals can enhance coherence in the international legal system.[68] This is particularly important in light of the recent upsurge in requests for advisory opinions on climate change.[69] These simultaneous requests before the ICJ, the ITLOS, and the IACtHR provide an opportunity to clarify the legal obligations of States to mitigate or adapt to climate change. However, as illustrated by Tigre and Rocha, the contribution of these courts to the clarification and development of international law 'depends on rendering decisions that are coherent.'[70] Judicial dialogue can serve that purpose.

As noted above, there are several interpretations of the concept of judicial dialogue. For example, Law and Tushnet distinguish between transnational and domestic judicial dialogue. The former describes 'exchanges among courts and judges that belong to different national and international legal regimes,'[71] while the latter refers to the 'interaction between courts and other branches of government, particularly legislatures.'[72] Transnational judicial dialogue, in turn, can occur 'in literal sense when judges communicate and network with each other, but also in a figurative sense when judges engage in comparative legal research and consider each other's work.'[73] Figurative judicial dialogue can involve emulating, endorsing, criticizing, or rejecting foreign law. Law and Tushnet note that this dialogue is not necessarily explicit and, accordingly, it does not require a citation to a foreign authority.[74]

Some scholars also distinguish between vertical and horizontal judicial dialogue. Vertical judicial dialogue can describe a hierarchical interaction that occurs when courts are formally obligated to respond to decisions by other courts.[75] In the typology of Slaughter, vertical judicial dialogue takes place

66 ibid 7–8.
67 Tigre & Rocha (n 29) 287.
68 Tigre (n 2) 708.
69 Tigre & Rocha (n 29) 287.
70 ibid 291.
71 David S Law & Mark Tushnet, 'The Politics of Judicial Dialogue', in Tushnet & Kocherov (eds), *Research Handbook on the Politics of Constitutional Law* (Elgar 2023) 286.
72 ibid.
73 ibid.
74 ibid 4.
75 ibid 8.

between national and supranational courts.[76] In contrast, horizontal judicial dialogue 'takes place between courts of the same status, whether national or supranational, across national or regional borders.'[77] In this non-hierarchical interaction, courts are not bound to follow or take account of one another's jurisprudence.[78] Similarly, courts do not necessarily have to acknowledge this dialogue using citations.[79] Slaughter also distinguishes the degree of engagement of the courts. For example, courts can engage in a 'direct dialogue' when the communication is initiated by one court and responded to by another. In some instances, the dialogue between courts can also be identified as a 'monologue', considering there may not be any intention to actually communicate with a foreign counterpart.[80]

Lastly, judicial dialogue can be described as formal and informal. Formal dialogue can occur through judgments when courts consider the views of other courts. In contrast, informal dialogue can describe meetings and conversations among judges.[81] This distinction can coincide with the concepts of figurative and literal transnational judicial dialogue. For instance, Law and Tushnet note that the most visible venues for judicial dialogue in a literal sense include seminars, scholarly meetings, and international and regional organizations of constitutional and apex courts.[82] These venues can also be considered informal.[83] Similarly, the situations in which courts issue a decision or opinion considering what their counterparts have said or done in other jurisdictions can be described as figurative dialogue and formal dialogue.

This typology can illustrate the available venues for judicial dialogue in the context of the advisory opinions on climate change. The ICJ, the ITLOS, and the IACtHR can engage in both formal and informal dialogue. For example, members of these courts could explore opportunities to participate in 'informal' meetings. A case in point is the recent 'Dialogue among Regional Human Rights Courts' held in San José, Costa Rica, from May 25 to 26, 2023. In this meeting, the IACtHR, the AfCtHPR, and the ECtHR shared experiences and identified challenges in the protection of human rights.[84] These courts discussed,

76 Slaughter (n 43) 106.

77 ibid 103.

78 ibid.

79 ibid.

80 ibid 112–113.

81 Joint Committee on Human Rights, House of Commons and House of Lords, 'The Government's Independent Review of the Human Rights Act (8 July 2021) §66.

82 Law & Tushnet (n 71) 4.

83 Joint Committee on Human Rights (n 81) §67.

84 IACtHR 'Press release 35/23, Dialogue between the Regional Human Rights Courts' (30 May 2023) <https://www.corteidh.or.cr/docs/comunicados/cp_35_2023_eng.pdf> accessed 5 August 2023.

among other topics, the role of courts in climate change litigation.[85] The three regional courts also adopted the San José Declaration (II), recognizing the importance of strengthening coordination and having 'a permanent dialogue and consultation mechanisms to exchange experiences, knowledge, and best practices in the interpretation and application of their respective regional human rights instruments.'[86] This declaration arguably provides a venue for judicial dialogue in the context of advisory opinions on climate change, particularly in the case of the IACtHR and the AfCtHPR.

The ICJ, the ITLOS, and the IACtHR can also engage in formal dialogue. For example, the IACtHR can consider and reflect on prior decisions and opinions of the ICJ, the ITLOS, and the AfCtHPR to inform its analysis of the legal obligations of States under the ACHR. The IACtHR engaged in this form of judicial dialogue in its advisory opinion OC-23/17 on human rights and the environment. The court expressly considered decisions from the ICJ to analyze the obligation to prevent transboundary environmental harm.[87] In this context, Tigre and Rocha highlight that some of these regional and international courts have already engaged in dialogue in previous cases.[88] For instance, due diligence 'was first mentioned by the ICJ in the *Pulp Mills* case and later developed consistently by the ICJ and the ITLOS – including its derivative obligations, such as the duties to conduct an environmental impact assessment, or to exercise a certain level of vigilance.'[89] Accordingly, to enhance coherence in the advisory opinions on climate change, the ICJ, the ITLOS, and the IACtHR can 'resort to each other's prior decisions on related topics (e.g., due diligence or precaution) and consider states' and non-state actors' observations before other courts to analyze the commonalities among them.'[90]

85 Michael Gerrard, 'I Was Happy to Speak about Global Climate Litigation Today in San Jose, Costa Rica to a Joint Meeting of the Judges of the Inter-American, European and African Human Rights Courts. @IACourtHR https://T.Co/FF7JKBF4Yx' <https://twitter.com/MichaelGerrard/status/1662310673425088514> accessed 9 July 2023.

86 AfCtHPR, European Court of Human Rights, and IACtHR, 'San José Declaration (II)' (26 May 2023).

87 *The Environment and Human Rights (State Obligations in Relation to the Environment in the Context of the Protection and Guarantee of the Rights to Life and to Personal Integrity – Interpretation and Scope of Articles 4(1) and 5(1) of the American Convention on Human Rights)* Advisory Opinion OC-23/17, Inter-American Court of Human Rights Series A No 23 (15 November 2017) §§95–103.

88 Tigre & Rocha (n 29) 289–290.

89 ibid 290.

90 ibid 289.

On 21 May 2024, the ITLOS confirmed this conclusion in its advisory opinion on climate change and international law.[91] The tribunal expressly considered previous judgments and advisory opinions from the ICJ. For instance, the ITLOS considered the *Advisory Opinion on the Legality of the Threat or Use of Nuclear Weapons*[92] to interpret the term 'marine environment' in Article 1(1)(4) UNCLOS, concluding that this concept 'combines both spatial and material components.'[93] Similarly, the ITLOS quoted the *Pulp Mills on the River Uruguay*[94] and the *Gabčíkovo-Nagymaros*[95] cases to analyze the obligation of due diligence.[96]

Unsurprisingly, judicial dialogue can also consider the available advisory opinions on climate change. Tigre and Rocha note that 'simultaneous requests do not mean that the opinions will also be rendered simultaneously.'[97] For instance, the ITLOS issued its advisory opinion on 21 May 2024,[98] while the IACtHR is expected to issue its opinion around the second half of 2025, and the ICJ at the beginning of 2026.[99] Therefore, the IACtHR and the ICJ will probably have the opportunity to consider and reflect on at least one prior advisory opinion on climate change. That would also be the case if the AfCtHPR receives a request and renders an advisory opinion. That is why Tigre and Rocha also argue that 'as one court renders its [advisory] opinion, others can adjust and incorporate the views expressed in prior opinion(s) by another court.'[100]

91 *Request for an Advisory Opinion submitted by the Commission of Small Island States on Climate Change and International Law* (Advisory Opinion, 21 May 2024) ITLOS Case No 31 (*COSIS Opinion*).

92 *Legality of the Threat or Use of Nuclear Weapons* (Advisory Opinion) [1996] ICJ Rep 226.

93 *COSIS Opinion* (n 91) §62.

94 *Case Concerning Pulp Mills on the River Uruguay* (*Argentina v Uruguay*) (Merits) ICJ Rep 14.

95 *Gabčikovo-Nagymaros Project* (*Hungary v Slovakia*) (Merits) [1997] ICJ ICJ Rep 7.

96 *COSIS Opinion* (n 91) §§84, 132.

97 ibid.

98 Center for International Environmental Law (CIEL), 'Climate Opinion Awaited as Historic Hearings Conclude at ITLOS' (CIEL, 25 September 2023) <https://www.ciel.org/news/climate-opinion-awaited-as-historic-hearings-conclude-at-itlos/> accessed 14 April 2024.

99 ibid.

100 ibid 289.

3 Limits of the Cross-Regime and Cross-Institution Interaction

The ICJ, the ITLOS, the IACtHR, and the AfCtHPR can engage in formal and informal dialogue. This dialogue can enhance coherence in the advisory opinions on climate change and, ultimately, the international legal system. However, even if formal and informal venues for judicial dialogue are fully operational, the interaction between regional and international courts could face several constraints. In particular, the scope of the dialogue between these courts could be determined by (a) the jurisdiction *ratione materiae*, (b) the actors that can participate in advisory proceedings within each court, and (c) the formulation of the questions posed. This section will address each of these potential limitations to determine how they impact judicial dialogue and how courts may overcome them.

3.1 *Subject Matter Jurisdiction*

The differences between the subject matter jurisdiction of the ICJ, the ITLOS, the IACtHR, and the AfCtHPR can limit the opportunities for judicial dialogue. This argument assumes that courts would not have incentives to establish some form of judicial dialogue if they are not going to give an opinion on matters or issues that are, to some extent, coincidental. Jurisdiction is particularly relevant in this context, considering that it can determine whether or not a court has the authority to address a particular question and to interpret or apply certain international agreements. The advisory opinions on climate change were requested before one specialized human rights court, one law of the sea specialized court,[101] and a court that can entertain 'any question of international law.'[102]

These differences between jurisdiction *ratione materiae*, norms, and regimes have been well-documented in the context of the advisory opinions on climate change. For instance, Mayer and van Asselt have pointed out that, considering the subject matter jurisdiction of ITLOS and the IACtHR, '[c]limate change would respectively have to be approached through the lenses of the law of the sea and human rights law.'[103] In this context, Holst notes that the ITLOS would not 'extend jurisdiction *ratione materiae* to other areas of international law, unless this would be truly incidental to the interpretation and application of

101 ITLOS Statute, art 21.

102 ICJ Statute, art 36.

103 Benoit Mayer & Harro van Asselt, 'The Rise of International Climate Litigation' (2023) 32 *RECIEL* 175, 177.

UNCLOS.'[104] Similarly, Rocha and Sampaio highlight that a regional and specialized human rights court would not find infringements of climate treaties or order States to comply with these treaties.[105]

3.1.1 The Jurisdiction of the ICJ

In principle, the ICJ would not face these limitations. The ICJ has 'both general and universal jurisdiction: it is open to all Member States of the United Nations and, subject to the provisions of its Statute, may entertain any question of international law.'[106] Accordingly, in the context of the advisory opinion on climate change, the ICJ would not be constrained to analyze and clarify the obligations of States considering just one regime or international instrument. On the contrary, the ICJ has been asked to render an opinion considering several principles of law and international agreements, including the UNFCCC, the Paris Agreement, UNCLOS, the Universal Declaration of Human Rights, the International Covenant on Civil and Political Rights, and the International Covenant on Economic, Social and Cultural Rights.[107]

As illustrated in the previous paragraph, the ICJ has been asked to interpret general human rights instruments. This can incentivize the ICJ, the IACtHR, and the AfCtHPR to establish some form of judicial dialogue and even to reach a common ground that might inform their respective advisory proceedings. The ICJ is not a specialized human rights court,[108] and it would benefit from the experiences and perspectives developed through the extensive human rights case law of the IACtHR and the AfCtHPR.

The ICJ has played a more modest role in interpreting and applying international human rights treaties, which can be explained, for instance, with the lack of access of individuals to the ICJ. Individuals can only form the subject of proceedings if a State, exercising its right of diplomatic protection, takes up the case of one of its nationals and invokes against another State the wrongs

104 Rozemarijn J. Roland Holst, 'Taking the current when it serves: Prospects and challenges for an ITLOS advisory opinion on oceans and climate change' (2022) 32 *RECIEL* 217, 220–221.

105 Armando Rocha & Rômulo Sampaio, 'Climate Change before the European and Inter-American Courts of Human Rights: Comparing Possible Avenues before Human Rights Bodies' (2023) 32 *RECIEL* 279, 289.

106 *ICJ Handbook* (ICJ 2019) 5, <https://www.icj-cij.org/sites/default/files/documents/handbook-of-the-court-en.pdf> accessed 9 July 2023.

107 UNGA Res A/77/L.58 (1 March 2023).

108 James Crawford & Amelia Keene, 'Interpretation of the human rights treaties by the International Court of Justice' (2020) 24 *Int'l J Human Rights* 935.

which its national claims to have suffered.[109] Furthermore, compromissory clauses accepting the jurisdiction of the ICJ in human rights treaties are rare.[110]

Despite these structural limitations, the ICJ can play a relevant role by incorporating human rights into its jurisprudence, as can be seen in the *Diallo*,[111] the *Bosnia Genocide*,[112] or the *Belgium v Senegal* cases.[113] The *Diallo* case is particularly relevant in this context, not only because it involved the interpretation of human rights treaties but also because the ICJ considered the interpretations of the Human Rights Committee and the jurisprudence and practice of the IACtHR, the African Commission on Human and Peoples' Rights, and the ECtHR.[114] This receptiveness may prove to be particularly useful for the advisory opinion on climate change. The ICJ can make use of the multiple resolutions from the UNGA or the Human Rights Council; general comments, recommendations, and statements by United Nations human rights treaty bodies; and other soft law instruments that highlight the link between human rights and climate change.[115] These documents have identified, analyzed, and concretized several obligations in respect of climate change. The jurisprudence of the IACtHR and the AfCtHPR can also play a significant role, namely if the ICJ is able to consider judgments and opinions of other judicial bodies, including the advisory opinion OC-23/17 on human rights and the environment issued by the IACtHR,[116] or even the opinions rendered by the ITLOS and the IACtHR.

3.1.2 Jurisdiction of the IACtHR and the AfCtHPR

Subject matter jurisdiction would not necessarily limit judicial dialogue between regional human rights courts either. Both the IACtHR and the AfCtHPR have jurisdiction to interpret and apply their respective regional human rights instruments. The IACtHR has jurisdiction over all matters relating to the interpretation and application of the ACHR, as well as other treaties

109 ICJ, *Handbook* (n 101) 33.

110 Crawford & Keene (n 103) 936.

111 *Ahmadou Sadio Diallo* (*Republic of Guinea v Democratic Republic of the Congo*) (Merits) [2010] ICJ Rep 639.

112 *Application of the Convention on the Prevention and Punishment of the Crime of Genocide* (*Bosnia and Herzegovina v Serbia and Montenegro*) [2007] ICJ Rep 43, §§228–230, 327–328.

113 *Questions relating to the Obligation to Prosecute or Extradite* (*Belgium v Senegal*) (Merits) [2012] ICJ Rep 422, §101.

114 Crawford & Keene (n 171) 941; *Ahmadou Sadio Diallo* (n 113) §§66–68.

115 *Request for an Advisory Opinion of the International Court of Justice on the Obligations of States in respect of Climate Change*, UNGA Res 77/276 (29 March 2023) UN Doc A/RES/77/276, available at <https://www.icj-cij.org/sites/default/files/case-related/187/187-20230412-app-01-00-en.pdf>.

116 Advisory Opinion OC-23/17 (n 87).

concerning the protection of human rights in the American states.[117] The wording 'other treaties' includes specialized human rights treaties adopted by the OAS and non-regional human rights treaties ratified by the American States.[118] Similarly, the jurisdiction of the AfCtHPR extends to all disputes concerning the interpretation and application of the African Charter on Human and Peoples' Rights (ACHPR), the Protocol to the ACHPR on the establishment of an AfCtHPR, and 'any other relevant Human Rights instrument ratified by the States concerned.'[119] The AfCtHPR can also provide advisory opinions on any legal matter relating to the ACHPR or 'any other relevant human rights instruments.'[120]

The similarities between the regional human rights instruments that grant jurisdiction to the IACtHR and the AfCtHPR, as well as the open-ended language that allows the interpretation of any other international instruments that might be relevant for a specific case or proceeding, create an ideal scenario for judicial dialogue. These specialized human rights courts can 'exchange experiences, knowledge and best practices in the interpretation and application of their respective regional human rights instruments.'[121] This possibility was expressly recognized in the San José Declaration (II), signed by the IACtHR, the AfCtHPR, and the ECtHR in May 2023. This declaration recognizes the importance of strengthening judicial dialogue to bolster the protection of human rights and access to justice. These human rights courts even discussed the importance of climate change litigation at the 'Dialogue among Regional Human Rights Courts' in which the declaration was adopted.[122]

3.1.3 Jurisdiction of the ITLOS

The limits of informal judicial dialogue related to subject matter jurisdiction may be more challenging in the case of the ITLOS, which holds jurisdiction over any dispute concerning the interpretation or application of UNCLOS and 'over all matters specifically provided for in any other agreement which confers jurisdiction on the Tribunal.'[123] The COSIS Agreement provides an example of

117 ACHR, art 64(1).

118 *"Other Treaties" Subject to the Consultative Jurisdiction of the Court (art. 64 American Convention on Human Rights)* Advisory Opinion OC-1/82, Inter-American Court of Human Rights Series A No 1 (24 September 1928). See also Mayer (n 15) 75.

119 Protocol to the African Charter on Human and Peoples' Rights on the Establishment of an African Court on Human and Peoples' Rights (adopted 10 June 1998) art 3(1).

120 ibid art 4(1).

121 San Jose Declaration (n 86).

122 ibid.

123 ITLOS Statute, art 21.

the latter, as it authorizes the COSIS to request advisory opinions 'on any legal question' within the scope of UNCLOS.[124] In this context, the Tribunal 'cannot extend jurisdiction *ratione materiae* to other areas of international law, unless this would be truly incidental to the interpretation and application of UNCLOS.'[125] However, the ITLOS must still read the Convention in the light of 'other relevant rules of international law not incompatible with UNCLOS.'[126] That includes, for instance, the UNFCCC or the Paris Agreement.[127]

3.1.4 Systemic Integration and Judicial Dialogue

As noted above, the differences between the subject matter jurisdiction of the regional and international courts have been well-documented in the context of the advisory opinions on climate change. These differences are instrumental in determining the international agreements and norms that may be interpreted and applied by each court. For instance, the regional human rights courts would focus on human rights law instruments while the ITLOS would focus on the interpretation and application of UNCLOS.[128] However, the fact that these courts have a specialized jurisdiction and the authority to interpret and apply certain international agreements does not mean they cannot consider or analyze norms and instruments from different regimes. This possibility can derive from established methodologies of treaty interpretation,[129] including systemic integration under Article 31(3)(c) of the Vienna Convention on the Law of Treaties.[130]

The Paris Agreement can illustrate the importance of systemic integration in the context of the advisory opinions on climate change. In fact, as the most comprehensive multilateral climate treaty, the Paris Agreement will become legally relevant in all international advisory proceedings on climate change.[131] This treaty not only contains an 'almost universal consensus on the science-based 'direction of travel' to address climate change,'[132] but also several

124 Agreement for the Establishment of the Commission of Small Island States on Climate Change and International Law (adopted 31 October 2021, entered into force 31 October 2021) 3447 UNTS (COSIS Agreement).

125 Holst (n 99) 220–221.

126 ibid 221.

127 ibid.

128 Mayer & van Asselt (n 98) 177.

129 Voigt (n 35) 243.

130 Vienna Convention on the Law of Treaties (adopted 23 May 1969, entered into force 27 January 1980, 1155 UNTS 331) (VCLT) art 31(3)(c).

131 Voigt (n 35) 238.

132 ibid.

normative elements that might be relevant in the interpretation of obligations contained in other treaties or even in customary international law.[133] For instance, Voight highlights the importance of Articles 2(1)(a), 4(1), 4(2), and 4(3) for the interpretation of international agreements such as UNCLOS and the ECHR.[134] These provisions establish (i) the level of mitigation ambition in the NDCs, (ii) the requirements of progression and highest possible ambition, and (iii) the pursuit of domestic mitigation measures with the aim of achieving the objectives in the NDCs.[135] These elements in the Paris Agreements are particularly relevant for informing the interpretation of other international agreements, including the ACHR, the Protocol of San Salvador, and the Escazú Agreement on access rights. For instance, the IACtHR would have the opportunity to interpret the 'principle of progressivity' or progressive realization of human rights law[136] considering these treaties and the normative requirements of progression and 'highest possible ambition' contained in Article 4(3) of the Paris Agreement.

The IACtHR has interpreted the principle of progressivity as a mandate to broaden the scope and protection of rights to the greatest extent possible until they are fully effective.[137] The Court has also interpreted this principle as a non-regression clause to prevent backsliding in human rights protection.[138] This analysis can be linked with Article 4(3) of the Paris Agreement and, particularly, the requirements of progression and highest possible ambition.[139] If a court reviews the compatibility of a specific government action with the ACHRs using the principle of progressivity, the standard of review is not only one of progressivity and non-regression, but also 'the highest possible

133 ibid 243.
134 ibid 239.
135 ibid.
136 ACHR, art. 26; Additional Protocol to the American Convention on Human Rights in the Area of Economic, Social, and Cultural Rights (adopted 17 November 1988, entered into force 16 November 1999, OAS Treaty Series No 69) (San Salvador Protocol) art. 1; Regional Agreement on Access to Information, Public Participation and Justice in Environmental Matters in Latin America and the Caribbean (adopted 4 March 2018, entered into force 22 April 2021, 3398 UNTS) (Escazú Agreement) art. 3.
137 *Case of Cuscul Pivaral et al v Guatemala* (Preliminary Objection, Merits, Reparations and Costs). Inter-American Court of Human Rights, Serie C No 378 (14 May 2019) §§81 & 142.
138 ibid §143.
139 Maria Antonia Tigre & Jorge Alejandro Carrillo Bañuelos, 'The ICJ's Advisory Opinion on Climate Change: What Happens Now?' (29 March 2023). <https://blogs.law.columbia.edu/climatechange/2023/03/29/the-icjs-advisory-opinion-on-climate-change-what-happens-now/> accessed 14 April 2023.

ambition' under Article 4(3).[140] Furthermore, 'given that this provision of the Paris Agreement refers to the NDC in general terms, a possible interpretation would be that the ratcheting mechanism [of Article 4(3)] extends to any action that integrates the NDC and not only its overall objectives.'[141] This new analysis could be linked, in turn, with Article 4(2) and the pursuit of domestic mitigation measures to achieve the objectives of such NDCs.

This example intends to illustrate the importance of the Paris Agreement for interpreting other treaties and norms. Since the request for an advisory opinion on climate change expressly referred to the obligations that derive from the Escazú Agreement and the Paris Agreement,[142] the IACtHR has the opportunity to interpret the ACHR, the Protocol of San Salvador, and the Escazú Agreement in light of the Paris Agreement. Systemic integration is not unusual in the Inter-American jurisprudence, as can be evidenced by the advisory opinion OC-23/17, where the IACtHR interpreted the concept of 'significant harm' having in mind the UNFCCC, the Convention on Biological Diversity, the case law of the ICJ, and the International Law Commission's draft articles on the prevention of transboundary harm from hazardous activities.[143] Following this precedent, the IACtHR will probably consider the Paris Agreement to inform the interpretation of the aforementioned human rights treaties. The Preamble of the Paris Agreement may be particularly relevant for this analysis, considering that it asks States to 'respect, promote and consider their respective obligations on human rights' when taking action to address climate change.[144] This paragraph has already been invoked in climate litigation cases to identify the Paris Agreement as a human rights treaty, analyze the links between human rights and climate change, and inform the interpretation of human rights obligations.[145]

The ITLOS advisory opinion on climate change also illustrates the importance of climate change treaties such as the Paris Agreement for informing

---

140 Jorge Alejandro Carrillo Bañuelos, *Climate Action in the Mexican Courts: The Unexpected Role of the Paris Agreement in Domestic Litigation* (LL.M. thesis, Harvard University 2022) 60.

141 ibid.

142 *Request for an Advisory Opinion on the Climate Emergency and Human Rights submitted to the Inter-American Court of Human Rights by the Republic of Colombia and the Republic of Chile* (9 January 2023) available at <https://www.corteidh.or.cr/docs/opiniones/soc_1_2023_en.pdf> accessed 12 August 2023.

143 ibid §134.

144 Paris Agreement (adopted 12 December 2015, entered into force 4 November 2016, 3156 UNTS 107) Preamble.

145 For instance, *PSB et al v Brazil* (*on Climate Fund*), Federal Supreme Court of Brazil (1 July 2022) <https://climatecasechart.com/non-us-case/psb-et-al-v-federal-union/> accessed 12 August 2023.

the interpretation of other international agreements. The advisory opinion emphasizes that Article 31, paragraph 3(c), of the Vienna Convention on the Law of Treaties 'requires that account be taken, together with the context, of any relevant rules of international law applicable in the relations between the parties.'[146] According to the ITLOS, this method of interpretation ensures that treaties 'do not operate in isolation but are interpreted and applied within the framework of the entire legal system prevailing at the time of the interpretation.'[147] The Tribunal also concluded that 'coordination and harmonization between the Convention and external rules are important to clarify, and to inform the meaning of, the provisions of the Convention and to ensure that the Convention serves as a living instrument.'[148] According to the ITLOS, these relevant external rules may be found in 'the UNFCCC, the Kyoto Protocol, the Paris Agreement, Annex VI to MARPOL, Annex 16 to the Chicago Convention, and the Montreal Protocol, including the Kigali Amendment.'[149] For instance, the ITLOS considered the global temperature goal and the timeline for emission pathways outlined in the Paris Agreement to 'inform the content of necessary measures to be taken under article 194, paragraph 1, of [UNCLOS].'[150]

This discussion on jurisdiction and systemic integration is particularly relevant for judicial dialogue. Although the differences between the jurisdiction of the ICJ, the ITLOS, the IACtHR, and the AfCtHPR can reduce the opportunities for informal judicial dialogue, there are still several areas of opportunity to discuss the same issues or to analyze the same norms. Systemic integration enhances these opportunities, as illustrated by the potential role of the Paris Agreement in the interpretation of other international agreements and norms. This "Paris-aligned'[151] interpretation would not only enhance legal consistency between diverse parts of international law, but also 'provide a positive feedback loop towards effective implementation' of the treaty.[152]

3.2 *Actors That Can Participate in the Advisory Proceedings*

One of the potential benefits of having a 'quartet of initiatives' is that certain actors can participate in more than one advisory proceeding. In this context, it could be argued that each court or tribunal would receive similar inputs if the same actors are authorized to participate in the proceedings. Arguably, even if

146 ITLOS (n 91) 52.
147 ibid.
148 ibid 51.
149 ibid 53.
150 ibid 80.
151 Voigt (n 35) 239.
152 ibid 237.

the questions posed and the jurisdiction of each court vary, submissions from the same actor would follow a relatively coherent line. Simultaneous participation and consistency in the submissions could provide, in turn, a common ground for judicial dialogue and foster consistent results in the advisory opinions.

However, the rules that govern the participation of these actors are relatively different between courts. For instance, States and international organizations are the main participants in advisory proceedings before the ICJ in opposition to courts such as the IACtHR. The ICJ 'draws up a list of those States and international organizations likely to be able to furnish information on the question and notifies them (…) that it is prepared to receive, within a specified time-limit, written statements relating to the question, or to hear oral statements.'[153] This list determines the opportunity to participate in written and oral proceedings and to comment on the statements made by other States or organizations.[154]

The States in the list are usually members of the organization requesting the opinion, but any interested State may ask the ICJ for the opportunity to take part in the proceedings.[155] International organizations can also participate, but the ICJ rarely authorizes organizations other than the one that has asked for the opinion.[156] Furthermore, if a non-governmental international organization submits a written statement on its initiative, it will be treated as a publication readily available and not as part of the case file.[157] This submission may also be referred to by the States and intergovernmental organizations participating in the proceedings.[158]

The Statute and the Rules of the ICJ are relatively different from those governing advisory proceedings in other courts and tribunals. The IACtHR is a good example. Any member of the Organization of American States (OAS) can request an advisory opinion from the Court.[159] Once the request has been submitted, the Presidency of the IACtHR can invite or authorize 'any interested party' to present written submissions, considering the expertise or area of work of such party.[160] The IACtHR is also empowered to conduct oral proceedings.[161] The advisory opinion OC-23/17 on human rights and the

153 ICJ, *Handbook* (n 101) 85.

154 ibid 85–86.

155 ibid 85.

156 ibid.

157 ICJ, Practice Direction (No XII), <https://www.icj-cij.org/practice-directionsf> accessed 9 July 2023.

158 ibid.

159 ACHR, art 64.

160 Rules of Procedure of the Inter-American Court of Human Rights (adopted 16 November 2009) art 73(3).

161 ibid art 73(4).

environment illustrates the wide variety of actors that can participate in proceedings before the IACtHR. In this case, the Court received 51 written statements, and more than half were submitted by international and national organizations, non-governmental organizations, and academic institutions. The IACtHR even received 20 written statements submitted by individual members of non-governmental organizations.[162] Several representatives of these organizations also participated in the oral proceedings.[163]

The Rules of Procedure of the AfCtHPR are similar in this aspect. Under Rule 83, the Registrar can invite observations from member States of the African Union, the African Union Commission, relevant African Union organs, and '[a]ny other relevant entities.'[164] The rule does not expressly determine the type of entity that can present observations, and it does not require that entity to have a particular expertise. This broad wording has allowed non-governmental organizations to contribute to advisory proceedings.[165]

The rules of the ITLOS are more aligned with those of the ICJ. Under Article 133 of the Rules of the Tribunal, the Registrar must give notice of the request for an advisory opinion to all States Parties.[166] Furthermore, the Seabed Disputes Chamber, or its President if the Chamber is not sitting, shall identify the intergovernmental organizations which are likely to be able to furnish information on the question.[167] Both State Parties and organizations are invited to present written statements. These rules also apply in advisory proceedings before the plenary of the Tribunal.[168] If the ITLOS receives a written statement from other actors, including non-governmental organizations, it would not be part of the case file.[169] However, the statement will be accessible to the public along with the written statements submitted pursuant to articles 138 and 133 of the Rules of the Tribunal.[170]

162 Advisory Opinion OC-23/17 (n 87) §6.
163 ibid §9.
164 Rules of Court, African Court on Human and Peoples' Rights (adopted 1 September 2020) rule 83.
165 Bizimana Jean D'Amour, 'Missed Opportunities: Participation of NGOs in Advisory Proceedings of the African Court on Human and Peoples' Rights' (2022) 22 *Human Rights Law Review* 1.
166 Rules of the Tribunal, ITLOS (adopted 28 October 1997), art 133.
167 ibid art 133(2).
168 ibid art 138.
169 'Advisory Proceeding' (International Tribunal for the Law of the Sea: Advisory Proceedings) <https://www.itlos.org/en/main/jurisdiction/advisory-proceedings/> accessed 12 August 2023.
170 ibid.

The differences between the rules that govern advisory proceedings in these courts may prevent some actors from participating in more than one proceeding. For instance, NGOs that submitted a written statement to the IACtHR would not have the same opportunity before the ICJ, regardless of whether it holds the knowledge or expertise to furnish information on the questions posed. This scenario would not be beneficial for judicial dialogue, assuming that the existence of uniform submissions can encourage or facilitate dialogue between the courts.

Nonetheless, several actors can still participate in more than one advisory proceeding. In the case of the advisory opinion on climate change, the President of the ICJ allowed[171] the United Nations and its member States to submit written statements.[172] Some of these States will also have the opportunity to submit statements before the ITLOS, the IACtHR, and the AfCtHPR. Furthermore, as of March 2024, the ICJ had already authorized the participation of the International Union for Conservation of Nature (IUCN), the COSIS, the European Union, the African Union, the Organization of the Petroleum Exporting Countries, the Pacific Community, the Pacific Islands Forum, the Alliance of Small Island States, the Nauru Agreement Office, the World Health Organization, the Melanesian Spearhead Group, the Forum Fisheries Agency, and the Organisation of African, Caribbean and Pacific States. Some of these actors will have a relevant role in other advisory proceedings on climate change.

Curiously, the United Nations, the IUCN, the COSIS, the Pacific Community, and the African Union were also invited to submit written statements pursuant to Article 133(3) of the Rules of the ITLOS,[173] and they can also submit statements before the IACtHR, considering the open-ended language used in Article 73(3) of the Rules of the Court.[174]

---

171 ICJ Statute, art 66(2).

172 ICJ Order, 'Fixing of Time-limits: Presentation of the written statements and written comments on those statements' (20 April 2023) <https://www.icj-cij.org/sites/default/files/case-related/187/187-20230420-ORD-01-00-EN.pdf> accessed 5 August 2023.

173 *Request for an Advisory Opinion submitted by the Commission of Small Island States on Climate Change and International Law* (Advisory Opinion, 21 May 2024) ITLOS Case No 31, available at <https://www.itlos.org/en/main/cases/list-of-cases/request-for-an-advisory-opinion-submitted-by-the-commission-of-small-island-states-on-climate-change-and-international-law-request-for-advisory-opinion-submitted-to-the-tribunal> accessed 12 August 2023.

174 Rules of Procedure of the Inter-American Court of Human Rights (adopted 16 November 2009) art 73(3). In 2017, this language allowed the IUCN's World Commission on Environmental Law (WCEL) to participate in the written and oral proceedings conducted as part of the advisory opinion OC-23/17. 'Advisory Opinion (OC-23/17)—Inter-American Court

Additionally, it must be noted that the communication among scholars, lawyers, non-governmental organizations, groups, communities, and applicants has been particularly intense regarding climate litigation. The participatory process that led to the adoption of the UNGA resolution requesting an advisory opinion on climate change is a recent example of this strong communication, considering that it involved informal consultations with UN member States and the active engagement of more than 1,500 civil society and youth groups.[175] This suggests that the arguments being incorporated in written statements submitted before international courts could also follow a similar line, thus providing a common ground for informal judicial dialogue, and contributing to consistent results in the advisory opinions.

3.3 *The Questions*

Differences in the questions posed before the courts could also limit judicial dialogue. If each of these courts is presented with different questions, it would make little sense for them to engage with each other and exchange points of view, insofar as they would have to address substantially different issues. These regional and international courts 'are bound by the request submitted to them, which means that even if they can rephrase the question, courts still need to answer what is specifically asked of them.'[176] Different questions 'can lead to different answers, and it should not be surprising if a question on states' obligations under a human rights treaty leads to a different answer than a question on states' obligations under the UNCLOS.'[177] This is closely related to subject matter jurisdiction. As noted above, the ITLOS has been asked to specify the obligations of State Parties to the UNCLOS, while the IACtHR has been asked to determine the obligations of States under the ACHR.

However, it is important to consider that some of the questions are not entirely different and can give courts enough space to analyze the same issues. For example, the ICJ has been asked to determine the obligations of States under international law to reduce GHG emissions in light of the principle of prevention,[178] but one of the questions posed to the IACtHR also refers to the principle

of Human Rights' (15 November 2017) <https://www.elaw.org/IACHR_CO2317> accessed 12 August 2023, para 6.

175 Tigre & Carrillo (n 134).

176 Tigre & Rocha (n 29) 290.

177 Ibid.

178 *Request for an Advisory Opinion of the International Court of Justice on the Obligations of States in respect of Climate Change*, UNGA Res 77/276 (29 March 2023) UN Doc A/RES/77/276, available at <https://www.icj-cij.org/sites/default/files/case-related/187/187-20230412-app-01-00-en.pdf>, accessed 11 August 2023.

of prevention and its relationship with the enjoyment of human rights.[179] Similarly, the questions posed will probably allow the courts to provide an opinion on issues such as intergenerational justice, the obligations of States towards future generations, the duty of due diligence in the context of climate change, and the obligations of States towards persons, groups, or communities that are injured or especially affected by or are particularly vulnerable to the adverse effects of climate change. This could provide an incentive for judicial dialogue.

4 Conclusion

The 'quartet' of requests for advisory opinions on climate change has provided the ICJ, the ITLOS, the IACtHR, and the AfCtHPR with an opportunity to clarify the legal obligations of States, enhance coherence in the international legal system, and lead to more ambitious action. The coherence between advisory opinions is particularly important to achieve these goals. These advisory opinions will be articulated considering the particular expertise, subject matter jurisdiction, and rules of procedure of each court. However, courts still have several areas of opportunity to analyze the same international instruments (such as the Paris Agreement) and to discuss the same issues, rules, and obligations (such as the duty of due diligence). Judicial dialogue can be instrumental in this context. The communication between these courts can create consistency in the advisory opinions and provide an opportunity for each court to benefit from the experience of the others, as well as find a common denominator in the process.

In other words, even though the differences between the ICJ, the ITLOS, the IACtHR, and the AfCtHPR can reduce the opportunities for judicial dialogue, the jurisdiction of each court and the questions posed in the advisory opinion requests leave enough room to discuss similar issues and even reach common ground. This is an evolving process, and it is yet to be determined whether these regional and international will engage in judicial dialogue and what will be the scope of this communication. However, this highlights how further research may consider the impact this formal and informal judicial dialogue has on the advisory opinions on climate change, as well as the impact that the first advisory opinion to be issued would have on judicial dialogue for the rest of the advisory proceedings.

179 *Request for an advisory opinion on the Climate Emergency and Human Rights submitted to the Inter-American Court of Human Rights by the Republic of Colombia and the Republic of Chile* (n 137).

CHAPTER 6

An Advisory Opinion on Human Rights and Climate Change in the African Regional Human Rights System

Dina Lupin and Ruth Nekura***

Abstract

While African countries are some of the most vulnerable to the impacts of climate change, despite contributing the least to global emissions, it is a continent with a rich and progressive regional human rights system. The African Charter on Human and Peoples' Rights was ground-breaking both in its recognition of environmental human rights and in its embracing of the collective rights of peoples. The African Charter, more than any other regional human rights instrument, is built on principles of solidarity, compassion and co-operation across borders and a recognition that a satisfactory environment is a human right. These are all features that should make the African human rights system uniquely responsive to climate change and, for this reason, should make the African Court of Human Rights uniquely positioned to hand down an advisory opinion on the obligations of African states in response to climate change. There is, however, a significant obstacle to the Court handing down such an opinion: it has taken an unusually restrictive approach in its interpretation of the standing provisions, all but blocking access to the Court for non-state parties. In this chapter we argue that the context of climate change merits consideration of the potential and impact of an advisory opinion and this might be a necessary and important opportunity for the Court to reconsider its jurisprudence on standing. This, we argue, could have significant beneficial impacts both for the practice of the Court as an accessible and inclusive institution, and on regional responses to climate change.

* Associate Professor at the University of Southampton Law School, D.Lupin@soton.ac.uk, https://orcid.org/0000-0002-6531-8066.

** Human Rights Lawyer, Consultant at Initiative for Strategic Litigation in Africa (ISLA), https://orcid.org/0000-0003-0716-0704.

© KONINKLIJKE BRILL BV, LEIDEN, 2025 | DOI:10.1163/9789004730618_007

Keywords

climate change – African Charter on Human and Peoples' Rights – African Court on Human and Peoples' Rights – Standing – Advisory opinion

1 Introduction

There are many factors that make the African human rights system ideal for an advisory opinion on the human rights obligations of states in relation to climate change. One of those factors is the significant impact that climate change is having in African countries and the heightened vulnerability and reduced resilience of many communities and peoples living in Africa. Despite contributing the least to global warming and having some of the lowest emissions globally, climate change is a considerable threat to most African countries, undermining development gains, pushing up poverty levels, threatening food security, and posing significant risks to stability and the realization of human rights. This points to the urgent need for clear laws and appropriate action by states to secure the rights of their populations, build resilience, and respond to climate threats.

A second factor that makes the African human rights system ideal for an advisory opinion on climate change is the progressive and ground-breaking nature of its approach to the intersection of human rights and the environment. The African Charter on Human and Peoples Rights is, as Winks has argued, a covenant of compassion. 'The African Charter is the first and only binding international instrument that directly recognizes the solidarity rights of peoples: to existence, equality, self-determination, sovereignty over natural resources, peace, development and environment.'[1] The African Charter, more than any other regional human rights instrument, is built on principles of solidarity, compassion and co-operation across borders and a recognition that a satisfactory environment is a human right. These are all features that should make the African human rights system uniquely responsive to climate change. Setting out the human rights obligations of African states in response to climate change would meaningfully advance the unique African human rights agenda.

There is, however, one crucial problem. A request for an advisory opinion is most likely and most appropriately going to be brought by communities and

1 Benjamin Elias Winks, 'A Covenant of Compassion: African Humanism and the Rights of Solidarity in the African Charter on Human and Peoples' Rights' (2011) 11 *African Human Rights Law Journal* 447, 453.

civil society actors facing the impacts of climate change. These groups can directly attest to the human rights impacts of the climate crisis, will benefit from human rights action by states, and are not put off by some of the international politics and disputes that might discourage states from making such a request.[2] Indeed, a coalition of African communities, civil society organizations and lawyers are already working on a request. However, the African Court on Human and Peoples' Rights (AfCtHPR) has taken an unusually restrictive approach in its interpretation of the standing provisions in relation to advisory opinions, all but blocking access to the Court for non-state parties.

Despite this significant barrier, in this chapter we argue that the context of climate change merits consideration of the potential and impact of an advisory opinion and this might be a necessary and important opportunity for the Court to reconsider its jurisprudence on standing. In section 2, we begin with a brief overview of the African human rights system and the key institutions discussed in this chapter. In section 3, we discuss climate change in the region and how issues related to climate change are already being addressed at a regional and sub-regional level. In section 4, we turn to advisory opinions and discuss the opportunities and challenges associated with bringing requests for an advisory opinion before the AfCtHPR. In section 5, we look at the need and significance of an advisory opinion on human rights obligations related to climate change were a request to be made to the AfCtHPR. Such a request, we argue, could have significant beneficial impacts both for the practice of the Court as an accessible and inclusive institution, and on regional responses to climate change.

2 The African Human Rights System – A Short Introduction

The African human rights system consists of an intricate framework of norms and institutions. The main normative instrument of the African human rights system is the African Charter on Human and People's Rights 1982 (African Charter).[3] Other key instruments include the Protocol to the African Charter on Human and People's Rights on the Rights of Women in Africa 2003 (Maputo

2 Bizimana Jean D'Amour, 'Missed Opportunities: Participation of NGOs in Advisory Proceedings of the African Court on Human and Peoples' Rights' (2022) 22 *Human Rights Law Review* 1.

3 African Charter on Human and People's Rights (adopted 27 June 1981, entered into force 21 October 1986) 1520 UNTS 217.

Protocol),[4] the African Charter on the Rights and Welfare of the Child 1990 (African Children's Charter),[5] the Protocol to the African Charter on Human and Peoples' Rights on the Establishment of the AfCtHPRs (AfCtHPR's Protocol),[6] the African Union Convention for the Protection and Assistance of Internally Displaced Persons (Kampala Convention),[7] the Protocol to the African Charter on the Rights of Persons with Disabilities,[8] and the Protocol to the African Charter on the Rights of Older Persons.[9]

Three main institutions make up the African human rights interpretive and adjudicative mechanism, namely the African Commission on Human and Peoples' Rights (AfCHPR), the African Committee of Experts on the Rights and Welfare of the Child, and the AfCtHPR. In this chapter, we focus on the role of the Commission and the Court.

The AfCHPR is a quasi-judicial body established by the African Charter with a twin mandate of protecting and promoting human rights. Under its protection mandate, the AfCHPR can receive and determine Communications on alleged violations of the African Charter. It can also conduct investigative visits for the purpose of protecting human rights. Anyone, including individuals and NGOs in Africa and beyond can bring a complaint to hold state parties to the African Charter accountable on the basis of the rights under the Charter. The AfCHPR is the most accessible human rights mechanism in Africa because the African Charter enjoys universal ratification on the continent. Its promotional mandate includes state reporting, conducting promotional visits, issuing general comments and resolutions. The AfCHPR has special mechanisms including special rapporteurs, working groups, and specialized committees and has been operational for 37 years, during which it has developed significant jurisprudence on environmental related rights (discussed further below).

4 Protocol to the African Charter on Human and People's Rights on the Rights of Women in Africa (adopted 1 July 2003, entered into force 25 November 2005) 3268 UNTS 1.

5 African Charter on the Rights and Welfare of the Child (adopted 11 July 1990, entered into force 25 November 1999) CAB/LEG/24.9/49 (1990).

6 Protocol on the Establishment of an African Court on Human and Peoples' Rights (adopted 9 June 1998, entered into force 25 January 2004) AU Doc OAU/LEG/EXP/AFCHPR/PROT (III).

7 African Union Convention for the Protection and Assistance of Internally Displaced Persons (adopted 23 October 2009, entered into force 6 December 2012) 3014 *UNTS* 3.

8 Protocol to the African Charter on the Rights of Persons with Disabilities (adopted 29 January 2018, not yet in force).

9 Protocol to the African Charter on the Rights of Older Persons (adopted 31 January 2016, not yet in force).

The AfCtHPR was established to complement the protection mandate on the AfCHPR.[10] The Court's findings are binding, not recommendations, as is the case for the AfCHPR. The AfCtHPR's decisions are also final and not subject to appeal. The Court's mandate is mainly protective, with a limited promotional mandate. While the Court has unfettered jurisdiction to interpret the African Charter, as well as any other ratified human rights instrument, under its contentious jurisdiction, the Court can only hear cases submitted against countries that have ratified the Court's Protocol. On standing, cases can be submitted to the AfCtHPR by state parties, the AfCHPR and African intergovernmental organisations. Further, NGOs with observer status before the African Commission and individuals can also submit cases but only against states that have made a declaration accepting the competence of the AfCtHPR to receive such cases in accordance with Article 34(6) of the AfCtHPR Protocol.[11] As of now, eight countries have deposited this declaration, namely Burkina Faso, Malawi, Mali, Ghana, Tunisia, The Gambia, Niger and Guinea Bissau. Four African States – Rwanda, Côte d'Ivoire, Benin and Tanzania (where the seat of the AfCtHPR is) made the declarations but withdrew between 2016 and 2020. Therefore, while the AfCtHPR is arguably a strong platform to remedy human rights violations and develop normative standards on the basis of the widest possible range of existing global human rights instruments, it is also the least accessible mechanism.

At the sub-regional level, there are two judicial organs of regional economic communities (RECs) established within their respective treaty frameworks. The Economic Community for West African States (ECOWAS) has a Community Court of Justice (ECCJ), which has jurisdiction to determine cases of violation of human rights that occur in any ECOWAS member state. All ECOWAS member states are *ipso facto* parties to the Court's Statue by virtue of being members of the regional economic community. While there is no specific sub-regional human rights instrument, litigants before the ECCJ have leveraged the courts competence to determine human rights cases and invoked a wide range of regional and international human rights instruments.[12] A unique feature of the ECCJ, different from other regional and international judicial bodies, is that this sub-regional court does not require exhaustion of domestic

10 Protocol to the African Charter on Human and Peoples' Rights on the Establishment of an African Court on Human and Peoples' Rights (adopted 10 June 1998, entered into force 25 January 2004) UNTS.

11 AfCtHPR Protocol, art 5.

12 Solomon Ebobrah, 'The Uneven Impact of International Human Rights Law in Africa's Subregional Courts', in Olsen & Lund (ed), *The Making of iCourts* (Nomos 2022) 441.

remedies. Some have argued that this is an opportunity for deploying climate change litigation with a human rights approach in the context of West African states.[13]

The East African Community has a Court of Justice (EACJ) established under its Treaty to ensure adherence to the Community law in its interpretation and application. The EACJ does not have a clear jurisdiction on human rights despite the fact that the treaty requires 'adherence to universally acceptable principles of good governance, democracy, the rule of law, observance of human rights and social justice'[14] as conditions for admission to the EAC, and alludes to the promotion of sustainable use of the environment and ensuring the protection of the environment. There is a suspended jurisdiction to determine human rights violations due to the provision that the Court 'shall have such other original, appellate, human rights and other jurisdiction as will be determined by the [EAC] Council at a suitable subsequent date'.[15] There are instances where the Court has creatively managed its jurisdiction to accommodate human rights. For instance, in the *Katabazi* case the EACJ stated that 'it will not abdicate from exercising its jurisdiction of interpretation … merely because the reference includes allegation of human rights violation.'[16] In practice, the EACJ is known to respond more favorably when matters before it are framed as issues of governance and rule of law rather than as violations of human rights.[17] The EACJ has been described as a 'cautious but activist adjudicator willing to push the boundaries of its jurisdiction to accommodate what it probably considers to be deserving cases of human rights violations.'[18]

3 Climate Change and Vulnerability in Africa

Africa is disproportionately vulnerable to the impacts of climate change, although the nature and severity of those impacts are not uniform across the

13 Muyiwa Adigun,'A Human Rights Approach to Climate Litigation before the ECOWAS Court' (2023) 26 *Environmental Law Review* 16.

14 Treaty for the Establishment of the East African Community (EAC Treaty) (adopted 30 November 1999, entered into force 7 July 2000) 2144 UNTS 255 (as amended on 14 December 2006 and 20 August 2007) arts 6(d) and 7(2).

15 EAC Treaty, art 27(2).

16 *Katabazi et al v Secretary General of the East African Community and Attorney General of the Republic of Uganda*, Case No 1/2007.

17 East Africa Court of Justice, *Court Manual: A Practical Guide to the Law and Practice of the East African Court of Justice* (2020).

18 Ebobrah (n 12).

continent. Even if globally states do achieve the ambitious aspiration set out in the Paris Agreement to keep heating to 1.5°C, climate change will continue to have significant impacts across the African continent.

In its Sixth Assessment Report, the IPCC reported that the African continent has experienced higher levels of warming than the global average.[19] The impacts of this heating on human rights is apparent and severe. Droughts in eastern and southern Africa have caused acute food and water insecurity, increasing the number of people facing hunger as a result of food shortages and price spikes.[20] Food insecurity will only get worse as warming has significant impacts on labor in the agricultural sector, especially on outdoor workers. A growing number of Africans have been displaced by climate impacts and this has far-reaching implications for the human rights of those displaced and those who host displaced peoples.

These impacts must, of course, be understood through an intersectional and contextual lens.[21] Food insecurity, health deterioration, loss of work,[22] loss of land, loss of access to clean water and other climate impacts interact with social, economic and political conditions, exclusions and oppressions. These impacts exacerbate existing inequalities and threaten both the substantive and procedural human rights of those who are already marginalized.[23]

Many communities in Africa are subject to multi-dimensional vulnerability. As the IPCC has found:

> High levels of poverty, lack of access to basic services (human rights to water and sanitation), poor governance and conflict are important factors that characterise vulnerability and systemic human vulnerability in particular … These context conditions within a country or region limit the access to effective adaptation options particularly for the poor and marginalised groups.[24]

---

19 Christopher Trisos et al, 'Africa', in Hans-Otto Pörtner et al (eds), *Climate Change 2022: Impacts, Adaptation and Vulnerability. Contribution of Working Group II to the Sixth Assessment Report of the Intergovernmental Panel on Climate Change* (CUP 2022).

20 IPCC, Hoesung Lee et al (ed), *Climate Change 2023: Synthesis Report. Contribution of Working Groups I, II and III to the Sixth Assessment Report of the Intergovernmental Panel on Climate Change* (IPCC 2023).

21 Anna Kaijser & Annica Kronsell, 'Climate Change through the Lens of Intersectionality' (2014) 23 *Environmental Politics* 417.

22 'Africans are disproportionately employed in climate-exposed sectors: 55–62% of the sub-Saharan workforce is employed in agriculture and 95% of cropland is rainfed.' IPCC (n 13) 1289.

23 ibid 485.

24 ibid 1195.

Across the continent, communities and states lack the resources and tools with which to face these overwhelming impacts. Resilience to climate change will require, among other things, updating and redesigning infrastructure across the continent (including sanitation, water, health, transport, communications and energy infrastructure) so that these systems can survive and continue to provide essential services to the communities that depend on them. Climate change on the continent compounds and aggravates existing threats to human rights in circumstances where states are already unable or unwilling to address development and rights needs.

3.1 *African Regional Law and Policy on Human Rights and Climate Change*

3.1.1 Environmental and Climate Law in the African Human Rights System

While Africa as a continent faces heightened vulnerability to the impacts of climate change, it is also a continent with a rich and diverse body of legal, policy and regulatory mechanisms and tools that could be of significant value in addressing climate harms and threats to human rights. Most African states are party to international law on human rights and various agreements on climate change, including the United Nations Framework Convention on Climate Change (UNFCCC), the Kyoto Protocol, and the Paris Agreement.

The African human rights system includes a number of instruments that are significant in regard to climate change. These include the African Charter, the Kampala Convention, as well as group-specific rights texts such as the Charter on the African Children's Charter, the Maputo Protocol, the African Youth Charter (2006), the Protocol on the Rights of Persons with Disabilities in Africa (2018), among others. Only the Kampala Convention specifically refers to climate change,[25] although the realization of all of these regional agreements, policies and goals are affected by its impacts.

The African Charter is one of the few regional human rights instruments that recognizes the right to a satisfactory environment (art 24) as well as a right to economic, social and cultural development (art 22). As Addaney and others have argued, 'The provision on the right to environment reflects the recognition that a satisfactory environment is significant for economic, social and cultural development as well as the realization of other human rights in

25 Article 5(4) requires states to take measures to protect and assist persons who have been internally displaced due to natural or human-made disasters, including climate change.

Africa.'[26] Both provisions have been interpreted by the African Commission as vulnerable to climate change impacts and as creating climate change related obligations on states.[27]

Another important feature of the Charter is that it protects both individual and collective rights. This is significant in the African context because of the high number of Indigenous and traditional communities whose collective identities are threatened by climate change. In addition, the Kampala Convention expressly recognises climate change as a driver of internal displacement and Article 5 requires State parties to 'take measures to protect and assist persons who have been internally displaced due to natural or human made disasters, including climate change.'

A further feature of the African rights system that makes it uniquely suited to address climate wrongs is that the AfCHPR has recognized that not only States are duty bearers when it comes to human rights obligations. Corporate entities also owe a duty to rights holders under Article 27 of the African Charter, which creates duties for both individuals and states that 'the rights and freedoms of each individual shall be exercised with due regard to the rights of others, collective security, morality and common interest.'[28]

In addition to a useful human rights framework for responding to and recognizing the impacts of climate change on human rights in Africa, a number of other normative interventions, initiatives and working groups engage directly with climate change and its impact on rights. For example, the ACHPR has adopted resolutions that seek to develop understanding, research and action on the link between climate change and human rights in Africa.[29] Currently,

---

26 Michael Addaney, Chantelle Gloria Moyo & Thabang Ramakhula, 'Human Rights, Regional Law and the Environment in Africa: Legal and Conceptual Foundations', in Addaney & Jegede (eds), *Human Rights and the Environment under African Union Law* (Springer 2020) 13.

27 ACHPR/Res153 (XLVI) 09: Resolution on Climate Change and Human Rights and the Need to Study its Impact in Africa.

28 African Charter on Human and Peoples' Rights (adopted 27 June 1981, entered into force 21 October 1986) (1982) 1520 UNTS 217, art 27. See also African Commission on Human and People' Rights, 'State Reporting Guidelines and Principles on Articles 21 and 24 of the African Charter relating to Extractive Industries, Human Rights and the Environment', adopted at the 62nd Ordinary Session of the African Commission on Human and Peoples' Rights (25 April-9 May 2018).

29 Including the African Commission of Human and Peoples' Rights, ACHPR/Res153 (XLVI) 09: Resolution on Climate Change and Human Rights and the Need to Study Its Impact in Africa (25 November 2009) and African Commission on Human and Peoples' Rights '271: Resolution on Climate Change in Africa', adopted at the 55th ordinary session of the African Commission on Human and Peoples' Rights held in Luanda, Angola (28 April–12 May 2014).

under the African Commission Resolution No 153 ACHPR/Res.153(XLVI)09, a committee is conducting an investigation into climate change and human rights in Africa and has produced a zero draft report (at the time of writing, the report has just completed a comments phase).

The Zero draft report has identified a number of key issues in African rights law at the intersection of climate change and human rights. Despite the recognition that climate change disproportionately affects already vulnerable and oppressed groups, the Zero Draft notes that these groups are not sufficiently addressed in existing AU law and policy on climate change. Although women and girls are uniquely vulnerable to climate impacts, for example, 'gender-responsive measures, including reference to aspects of sexual and reproductive health and rights, and its intersection with human rights are not extensively reflected in official documents.'[30]

Together, these components of the African human rights systems offer a number of useful approaches, principles and tools for understanding and addressing the relationship between climate change and human rights on the continent and work is being done to recognize critical gaps in the law. As Jegede argues, these developments in the African human rights system 'are indicative of a system that recognizes the potential link of climate change to human rights.'[31] However, the exact contours of this relationship and the specific obligations and duties associated with it, as well as the legal and political measures that need to be taken to address gaps, still need to be fully expressed.

Beyond human rights tools and instruments, there is some evidence of a human rights approach to the environment in other areas of AU law. The 2003 African Convention on the Conservation of Nature and Natural Resources (Conservation Convention) was revised in 2003 to reflect Article 24 in the African Charter and emphasises the right to a satisfactory environment.

In 2009, the African Union Summit adopted the Nairobi Declaration on the African Process for Combating Climate Change;[32] and in 2014, the AU adopted a Draft Continental Strategy on Climate Change. Both documents are addressed at identifying continent-wide concerns related to climate change and the Strategy provides guidance to states on addressing the impacts. In 2015, the African Adaptation Initiative was launched to facilitate pan-African collaboration for climate adaptation and to address the problem of adaptation

30 Zero Draft (2023) 6–7.

31 Ademola Oluborode Jegede, 'Should a Human Right to a Safe Climate Be Recognized Under the AU Human Rights System?', in Addaney & Jegede (n 26) 57.

32 Nairobi Declaration on the African Process for Combating Climate Change, ALLAFRICA (May 29, 2009).

finance. A focus of this initiative has been on climate information services, the development, availability and accessibility of climate knowledge at institutional and individual levels.

Recently, the African Union Climate Change and Resilient Development Strategy and Action Plan (2022–2032) was published.[33] The Strategy aims at building resilience and achieving low-emission, sustainable economic growth. It includes a number of guiding principles that speak to a human-rights sensitive approach, namely: 1. A People Centred Approach 2. Conserving and restoring natural capital 3. Aligning plans and priorities 4. Leave no one behind/a just transition 5. Evidence and practice 6. African-led and African-owned 7. Whole of economy approach 8. Intersectionality 9. Common but differentiated approach.

3.1.2 African Case Law

Although there are a growing number of climate change cases making their way into domestic courts in Africa,[34] to date, there have been very few cases before the African human rights system that directly address the issue of climate change. The African Charter does, however, create opportunities for litigating on climate issues that are not readily available in other regions. Importantly, the inclusion of a right to a generally satisfactory environment in Article 24, for example, makes it possible for the AfCtHPR to 'directly review a State's compliance with its obligations to respect and protect the human right to a healthy environment, which can encompass climate change issues.'[35]

The Article 24 right has been adjudicated by the AfCHPR in the matter of *Social and Economic Rights Action Centre and the Centre for Economic and Social Rights v Nigeria* in 2002 (the SERAC case).[36] The case related to Nigeria's responsibility for destructive and rights violating oil extraction activities by the state and the company Shell in Ogoniland in the Niger Delta. In that case, the African Commission found that rights that have an environmental

33 African Union, *African Union Climate Change and Resilient Development Strategy and Action Plan* (2022–2032), available at <https://au.int/sites/default/files/documents/41959-doc-CC_Strategy_and_Action_Plan_2022-2032_08_02_23_Single_Print_Ready.pdf>.

34 Jovan Mugga, Joyeeta Gupta & René Lefeber, 'Shaping Africa's Climate Action through Climate Litigation: An Impact Assessment' (2023) 26 *Recht in Afrika* 26.

35 Yusra Suedi & Marie Fall, 'Climate Change Litigation before the African Human Rights System: Prospects and Pitfalls: Practice Note: GNHRE Climate Litigation in Global South Project' (2023) *Journal of Human Rights Practice* huad024, 3.

36 *SERAC v Nigeria* (Decision) Comm No 155/96 (AfCHPR, Oct 27, 2001) available at <https://africanlii.org/akn/aa-au/judgment/achpr/2001/35/eng@2001-10-27>.

dimension create an array of obligations on states that are both procedural and substantive in nature.[37]

In the *SERAC* case, the Commission considered allegations of violations of a number of rights, including rights to life, health and to a satisfactory environment. In relation to the environmental right, the Commission identified a number of specific rights-based duties. The state must take 'reasonable and other measures to prevent pollution and ecological degradation, to promote conservation, and to secure an ecologically sustainable development and use of natural resources'[38] and to do this, it must ensure proper monitoring of environmental impacts, conduct environmental and social impact studies, ensure affected communities' rights to access to information about their environment.[39] In the *SERAC* case, not only did the Nigerian government fail in regard to all of these duties, but it employed a sustained programme of brutal violence against the Ogoni people to suppress any opposition or demands for rights protections. It should be noted that no reference to climate change was made in either the pleadings or the decision.

In the *Ogiek* case,[40] the AfCtHPR adjudicated on a case in which an Indigenous People, the Ogiek community, were being forcibly removed from their land in the Mau Forest by the Kenya Forest Service. The AfCtHPR had handed down a decision on the merits in 2017, finding that Kenya had violated Articles 1, 2, 8, 14, 17(2) and (3), 21 and 22 of the Charter.[41] In 2022, the AfCtHPR handed down its judgment on reparations. Both decisions are significant in their recognition of Indigenous Peoples and of the importance of the relationship between Indigenous Peoples and their land, culture, laws and traditions. Indigenous Peoples, the Court determines, are uniquely vulnerable by virtue of their traditional ways of life and close connection to and dependence on their land. They have been 'the subject and easy target of deliberate policies of exclusion, exploitation, forced assimilation, discrimination and other forms of persecution, whereas some have encountered extinction of their cultural distinctiveness and continuity as a distinct group.'[42]

---

37 See the discussion of this case in Suedi & Fall (n 35); Elinor Buys and Bridget Lewis, 'Environmental Protection through European and African Human Rights Frameworks' (2022) 26 *The International Journal of Human Rights* 949.

38 *SERAC* (n 36) §52.

39 ibid §53.

40 *The Matter of African Commission on Human and Peoples' Rights v Republic of Kenya* (Reparations) App No 006/2012 (June 23, 2022).

41 *The Matter of African Commission on Human and Peoples' Rights v Republic of Kenya* (Merits) App No 006/2012 (May 26, 2017).

42 ibid §180.

Although the Ogiek case is not directly about climate change or the environmental right, the judgment highlights the particular vulnerability of Africa's Indigenous Peoples and the duties of states to recognize and protect them and 'to attune their legal systems to accommodate Indigenous peoples' rights to property such as land.' The AfCtHPR's finding that the survival of Indigenous Peoples depends on the protection of their rights to land and natural resources points to the importance of understanding and developing mechanisms to address those things that threaten Indigenous land and resource rights, including climate change. Despite this significant judgment, the Zero Draft finds that Indigenous Peoples across the continent are experiencing the 'indirect impact of climate change due to expropriation of lands for development and related activities which have implications for climate change.'[43]

Although this chapter is focused on the AU and not the sub-regions, one important case in East Africa is worth mentioning. In 2023, the ECOWAS court upheld the right to a healthy environment in the matter of *Adou Kouame and Others v Cote d'Ivoire*.[44] In that case, the court found that the state had allowed mining activities by a private company that had adversely affected plantations, forests, rivers and sites of ancestor worship. Importantly in this case, the court ordered compensation in money as well as requiring the state to take measures to ensure that a healthy environment was rapidly restored and ongoing environmental degradation was stopped and the perpetrators held accountable.

3.1.3 Good Law is Not Enough

This discussion of African human rights law reveals that the African human rights and broader regional law system boasts some important legal tools and policies that put nations in good standing to pursue strong protections of human rights in the face of climate change. However, the reality of policy and state practice rarely aligns with this promising legal framework. States in Africa continue to pursue carbon-intensive and extractive activities as key components of their economic growth plans. This is not only an emissions problem (Africa remains a relatively minor emitter compared with global North economies) but a human rights one. Extractive industries on the continent have long been associated with grave human rights violations, mass displacement and violent engagements with Indigenous and traditional communities.[45]

---

43 Zero Draft, §29.

44 *Adou Kouame and Others v Cote d'Ivoire*, Case No ECW/CCJ/APP/08/21 (Judgment) Nov 30, 2023 (ECW/CCJ/JUD/46/23).

45 As is apparent in the *SERAC* case and in the case of *IHRDA v Democratic Republic of Congo*, involving a massacre in the city of Kilwa. See *Institute for Human Rights and Development*

In addition, African states have failed to address the impacts of climate change on human rights, or to address existing vulnerabilities (including food shortages, lack of access to water and sanitation, and lack of housing) to make communities more resilient to climate change. This failure is, in many cases, not a failure of policy. Across the continent, African states have adopted climate change laws, strategies and plans. For example, the Nigerian Federal Government has spent billions of Naira from the ecological fund on projects that attempt to address soil erosion, flooding, desertification, drought and other environmental degradation resulting from climate change. However, high levels of internal displacement, caused by environmental, economic and political conditions, has rendered thousands of people homeless and this number is likely to grow substantially over the coming years. Nigeria has failed to address its existing housing crisis, and growing numbers of people are living in informal settlements in climate-vulnerable areas. As growing numbers of people are displaced by changing and extreme weather events (it is projected that 150 million could be permanently displaced in Africa), states have done too little to make provision for these displaced communities or for the communities that do and will receive them.

Last, adaptation and mitigation measures have also been the source of human rights violations on the continent. Carbon markets and forest carbon projects, for example, have often been conceptualized and implemented without the participation of those whose lands are affected by these schemes, resulting in further displacement and vulnerability. For example, the REDD+ programme (Reducing Emissions from Deforestation and Forest Degradation in Developing Countries) adopted under the UNFCCC process was meant to be a means through which finance could be channeled to developing countries that undertook activities aimed at conserving forest carbon stocks, reducing forest degradation and deforestation, managing forests sustainably and enhancing forest carbon stocks. Across the African continent, however, REDD+ programmes have been implemented without the consultation of Indigenous Peoples whose lands and ways of life are impacted, and often harmed, by these programmes. The Sengwer community in Kenya, for example, has faced repeated forced removals from their land in the Embobut Forest, in part as a result of a World Bank funded REDD+ project.

This complex matrix of promising (but far from perfect) laws and policies, highly vulnerable and impoverished communities, and states failing to take remotely adequate measures to address threats to human rights (often

in Africa (IHRDA) *and Others v Democratic Republic of Congo* (Decision) Comm No 393/10 (AfCHPR, June 18, 2016).

aggravating or perpetrating those threats) all point to the potential value of an advisory opinion by the AfCtHPR clarifying the human rights duties of states in the context of climate change. It is to an advisory opinion, and the barriers to obtaining such an opinion, that we now turn.

4 Taking a Judicial Route: An Advisory Opinion on Climate Change and Human Rights from the AfCtHPR

4.1 *Advisory Opinions and African Judicial Organs*

Before turning focus to the AfCtHPR's advisory jurisdiction, which is our main interest, it is important to highlight that some of the other African regional and sub-regional organs also have advisory jurisdiction. The AfCHPR can issue advisory opinions as part of its mandate to interpret the Charter, submit opinions and make recommendations to governments.[46] Such requests can be made by a State party, an institution of the Organisation of African Unity (OAU) or an African organization recognized by the OAU. The AfCHPR has clarified this advisory mandate under Rule 127 of its rules of procedure on 'interpretation and advisory opinions' which indicates that where the Commission receives requests for interpretation of the Charter it shall transmit a copy thereof and notify States Parties, the AfCtHPR and any other interested entity of its decision or advisory opinion in response to such a request. However, this is a grossly underutilized advisory mechanism. The AfCHPR has only ever issued one advisory opinion in 2007 on the UN Declaration on the Rights of Indigenous People.[47] This advisory opinion was self-invoked by the AfCHPR to provide clarity following a series of controversial debates on the Declaration, including within the AU Assembly of Heads of States who raised concerns about the content of the declaration.

The ECCJ also has an advisory competence which allows the court to, at the request of Member States, or the Executive Secretary, and any other institution of the Community, issue a legal opinion on matters that require interpretation of the provisions of the Treaty.[48] This allows the Court to play an important role in the prevention of conflicts or disputes and to interpret the provisions of

46 African Charter, art 45 (1) and (3).

47 *Advisory Opinion of The African Commission On Human And Peoples' Rights on The United Nations Declaration on The Rights of Indigenous Peoples, Adopted by the African Commission on Human and Peoples' Rights* (Advisory Opinion) 30 May 2007, available at <https://www.iwgia.org/images/publications/Advisory_Opinion_ENG.pdf>

48 ECOWAS Protocol on The Community Court of Justice A/P.l/7/91, 1991, art 10.

the Treaty. The EACJ's advisory jurisdiction can be invoked by the EAC Council of Ministers or a Partner State.[49] In addition, national courts and tribunals can seek an interpretation or application of the Treaty or on questions of the validity of the regulations, directives, decisions or actions of the EAC, and the EACJ can issue preliminary rulings to such national courts.[50]

The advisory jurisdictions of these bodies are potential avenues that can be used to interpret state obligations in the context of climate action. However, they remain underutilized. This may be due to limited access in terms of *locus standi*, but also because it is not in the interest of those who have standing to expand normative clarity on treaty-based obligations, especially human rights obligations. In the mechanisms discussed above, access to the advisory jurisdiction is limited to duty bearers in the context of treaty obligations, such as member states or council of ministers.

Jean D'Amour argues that when standing in advisory proceedings is exercised exclusively by states or organs of intergovernmental bodies, they may be reluctant to make requests for advisory opinions for political motives.[51] Therefore, such underutilization should not be surprising. The two reported instances where the EACJ received requests for advisory opinions are telling in terms of the kinds of issues states or organs of intergovernmental bodies would be interested in. One involved interpretation regarding the principle of rotation in the nomination of leaders of EAC, especially in the context where a state withdraws one nominee in an existing position in order to qualify for nominating for another (higher) position.[52] The second involved the question of variable geometry and whether consensus in decision-making among member states implies unanimity.[53] These examples show that states and organs of intergovernmental bodies are often interested in using advisory mechanisms to interpret operational questions which are really about power. It is hardly about normative clarification for the advancement of human rights protection.

---

49 EAC Treaty, art 36.

50 ECOWAS Protocol on The Community Court of Justice, art 34.

51 D'Amour (n 2).

52 *Request by the Council of Ministers of the East African Community pursuant to Articles 14(4) and 36 of the Treaty and Rule 75(4) of the East African Court of Justice Rules of Procedure 2013*, Advisory Opinion No 1 of 2015, available at <https://www.eacj.org/?cases=request-for-an-advisory-opinion-no-1-of-2015-in-the-matter-of-a-request-by-the-council-of-ministersof-the-east-african-community-for-an-advisory-opinionmade-pursuant-to-articles-14-4-and-36-of-t>.

53 *Request by the Council of Ministers of the East African Community pursuant to Articles 14 (4) and 36 of the Treaty*, Advisory Opinion No 1 Of 2008, available at <https://www.eacj.org/?cases=application-no-1-of-2008-advisory-opinion-of-the-court>.

This is the same experience with the AfCtHPR advisory opinion jurisdiction as we will see below.

4.2 *Bringing Advisory Opinion Requests to the AfCtHPR – Problems and Potential*

The AfCtHPRt's identity has mostly developed through its contentious jurisdiction and some have argued its advisory jurisdiction has been significantly neglected.[54] Yet, from the moment this Court became operational, there were optimistic analyses that the advisory jurisdiction would increase access to and engagement with the Court.[55] This hope was because the AfCtHPRt is the only international court that allows a wide range of organizations, including NGOs, to make requests for advisory opinions.

However, at the time of writing this chapter, the Court's statistics show that of the 342 applications received, only 15 are requests for advisory opinion.[56] Of the 15 requests, only two have been brought by states.[57] Two have been brought by organs of the AU,[58] and the rest, a majority of over 70% of the advisory opinions, have been brought by NGOs.

All the requests brought by NGOs have been struck out, except two,[59] as a result of a restrictive interpretation by the Court on the standing rules and on what NGOs need to do in order to access the AfCtHPRt.[60] In this part of

54 Chidi Anselm Odinkalu, 'Advice without Consent? Assessing the Advisory Jurisdiction of the African Court on Human and Peoples' Rights' (2023) 45 *Human Rights Quarterly* 365.

55 AP Van der Mei, 'The Advisory Jurisdiction of the African Court on Human and Peoples' Rights' (2005) 5 *African Human Rights Law Journal* 27.

56 African Court on Human and People's Rights Website accessed at <https://www.african-court.org/cpmt/advisory-finalised>.

57 *Request for Advisory Opinion No 001/2011 Requested by the Republic of Mali, Request for Advisory Opinion No 002/2011*, Requested by Advocate Marcel Ceccaldi on Behalf of Libya.

58 Advisory Opinion No 002/2013 (Dec 5, 2014) *On the Standing of the African Committee of Experts on the Rights and Welfare of the Child before the African Court on Human and Peoples' Rights, Requested by the African Committee of Experts on the Rights and Welfare of the Child;* Advisory Opinion No 001/2021 (Jul 16, 2021) *On the application of the principle of regional rotation in the election of the bureau of the Pan African Parliament* (PAP), *requested by* PAP.

59 Advisory Opinion No 001/2020 (Jul 16, 2021) *On the right to participate in the government of one's country in the context of an election held during a public health emergency or a pandemic, such as the Covid-19 crisis, requested by Pan African Lawyers Union* (PALU); Advisory Opinion No 001/2018 (Dec 4, 2020) *On the compatibility of Vagrancy Laws with the African Charter on Human and Peoples' Rights and other human rights instruments applicable in Africa, requested by Pan African Lawyers Union* (PALU).

60 Decision on Request for Advisory Opinion No 002/2016 (Sep 28, 2017) *On the consistency with the African Charter on Human and Peoples' Rights of the Draft Model Law on Mining*

the chapter, we discuss the potential and challenges in the law and practice of bringing advisory opinions, and then turn to how climate change could provide a context for re-thinking the importance of widening instead of restricting access to the advisory jurisdiction of the AfCtHPR.

Under Article 4(1) of the AfCtHPR's Protocol, the AfCtHPR may provide an advisory opinion on any legal matter relating to the Charter or any other relevant human rights instruments.[61] It goes on to provide that advisory opinions may be requested by the African Union (AU), any organs of the AU, all AU Member States, and any African organization recognized by the AU.[62]

The expansive standing provisions for advisory proceedings before the African Court provide a number of unique opportunities. First, the criteria which includes *all* AU member states, means that any of the 55 AU member states can make a request for an advisory opinion, not only the 34 member states that have ratified the Court's Protocol.[63] This is broader than standing in contentious cases, which is limited to state parties to the AfCtHPR Protocol.[64] Further, the organs of the AU allowed to bring requests for advisory opinion are also more expansive. They include those specified in the AU Constitutive Act, as well as the African Commission and the Committee of Experts. This is more than the number of organs which can engage in the contentious

on Community Land in Africa, requested by L'Association Africaine de Defense des Droits de l'Homme, §§33–35; Decision on Request for Advisory Opinion No 001/2016 (Sep 28, 2017) *On State Obligations under Article 6(d) of the Protocol to the African Charter on Human and Peoples' Rights on the Rights of Women in Africa requested by Centre for Human Rights, University of Pretoria, Federation of Women Lawyers, Kenya, Women's Legal Centre, Women Advocates Research and Documentation Centre and Zimbabwe Women Lawyers Association*, §§46–49; Decision on Advisory Opinion No 002/2014 (Sep 28, 2018) *On Institution of legal action before the African Commission on Human and peoples' Rights or the African Court on Human and Peoples' Rights following an unconstitutional change of government, Requested by Rencontre Africain pour la Defense des Droits de l'Homme* (RADDHO), §§35–38; Decision on Advisory Opinion No 001/2013 (May 26, 2017) *On the meaning of an African Organisation Recognised by the African Union and whether extreme, systemic and widespread poverty is a violation of certain provisions of the African Charter on Human and Peoples' Rights, In particular, Article 2 thereof which prohibits discrimination based on 'any other status', Requested by Socio-Economic Rights and Accountability Project* (SERAP).

61 AfCtHPRt Protocol, art 4(1).

62 ibid.

63 Status List of ratifications for the AfCtHPR Protocol, accessed at <https://au.int/sites/default/files/treaties/36393-sl-PROTOCOL_TO_THE_AFRICAN_CHARTER_ON_HUMAN_AND_PEOPLESRIGHTS_ON_THE_ESTABLISHMENT_OF_AN_AFRICAN_COURT_ON_HUMAN_AND_PEOPLES_RIGHTS_0.pdf>.

64 AfCtHPR Protocol, art 5.

proceedings, as the Protocol only mentions the AU Commission and the African Commission.[65]

Another key opportunity is that 'any African organisations recognised by the AU' is included as a category of persons who can access the court's advisory jurisdiction. We are particularly interested in this category of personal jurisdiction because it opens up potential avenues for diverse climate justice actors, including NGOs, to engage with the advisory mechanism of the AfCtHPR. Allowing NGOs to engage in advisory proceedings is a unique feature in comparison to other regional or international courts which typically limit access to member states and intergovernmental bodies.

4.2.1 An 'African Organisation'

In considering the meaning of 'African Organisation', the Court has interpreted the word 'organization' under Article 4 of the Court's Protocol to include both *inter-governmental* and *non-governmental* organizations.[66] In terms of what 'African' means, the Court has found that an organization is 'African' if it is 'registered in an African State, has structures at the sub-regional, regional or continental level *or* undertakes its activities beyond the territory where it is registered, as well as any organizations in the diaspora recognized as such by the AU.'[67] The Court's interpretation can be taken to mean any NGO, whether local, regional or international, as long as it is registered in an African country, and has *either* 'structures at the sub-regional, regional or continental level' *or* has 'activities beyond the territory' of registration. Unfortunately, this means that local NGOs who operate within one African country are excluded. The Court's recognition of 'organizations in the diaspora' as part of the definition also provides an opportunity for collaboration among international organizations, African diaspora and organizations in the continent to leverage expertise in climate litigation and share lessons that have been learned elsewhere.

4.2.2 'Recognition by the African Union'

The Court's interpretation of what it means for NGOs to be 'recognized by the AU' is more restrictive. In the SERAP Advisory Opinion, the court construed 'recognition' to mean that an NGO must have observer status before the AU or a Memorandum of Understanding with the AU.[68] This reasoning severely limits the access of NGOs for a number of reasons. First, the Criteria for Granting

65 ibid.
66 Advisory Opinion No 001/2013 requested by SERAP decision (n 59) §§46–47.
67 ibid §48.
68 ibid §§52–64.

Observer Status to NGOs[69] by the AU is despotic, burdensome, impractical and does not reflect the reality of how NGOs exist and operate in the continent. For instance, the Criteria requires that at least two-thirds of the NGOs resources must come from members' contributions.[70] The majority of NGOs in, or operating in, Africa are not membership organizations, and even where they are, they do not raise the majority of their funds through membership contributions. In practice, to secure such AU Observer Status, NGOs or groups need to be sponsored by one or more states, and 'if it is a diaspora organization, then it is required to have the support of at least two states.'[71] This process seems counterproductive and paradoxical given that the reason civil society groups would want to access the AfCtHPR's advisory mechanism is to strengthen normative clarity for purposes of enhancing accountability and state compliance with their human rights obligations. Requiring NGOs to first negotiate state sponsorship in order to be 'recognized' as having standing to access the court, defeats the purpose of civil society which is to act as checks for imbalances of power as part of advocating for State accountability. This practice only enables the foregrounding of Government Organised NGOs (GONGOs), which are government-sponsored NGOs known to mimic civil society and thrive in authoritarian regimes by advancing state political interests.

Further, many NGOs are not aware of the AU Criteria for Granting Observer Status not only because finding AU decisions is generally difficult, but because the finalized version of the Criteria is not publicly accessible. The closest one can come to accessing the Criteria is to locate the *Draft* Criteria which was discussed in a report by the Permanent Representatives' Committee (PRC) and legal experts in a 2005 meeting.[72] From the deliberations, it is clear that a number of revisions were still needed for the draft Criteria to be finalized. Although there is information that the Executive Council later took a decision to adopt the Draft Criteria in 2006, the finalized Criteria is not provided in the record.[73]

Some commentators have argued that to avoid the difficulties associated with these stringent criteria for granting observer status, NGOs should pursue

69 Draft Criteria for Granting African Union Observer Status to Non-Governmental Organisations (NGOs) Annex IV of the *Report of the PRC And Legal Experts On Various Legal Matters* EX.Cl/195 (VII), Annex IV.

70 As above, section 1, art 7.

71 Odinkalu (n 54).

72 Report of the PRC And Legal Experts On Various Legal Matters EX.Cl/195 (VII), Annex IV. Executive Council Seventh Ordinary Session 28 June-2 July 2005 Sirte, Libya.

73 Decision on the Criteria For Granting Observer Status And A System Of Accreditation Within The AU Doc EX.Cl/195(VII), EX.Cl/Dec. 230 (VII).

the alternative avenue of signing an MoU with the AU.[74] However, this is not a better or easier avenue for civil society organizations to pursue, because there are no clear guidelines or regulations on the process that NGOs should follow to acquire such an MoU with the AU. The fundamental challenge here is the lack of a defined and systematic way through which any NGO can acquire such an MoU in order to be 'recognized' by the AU. The only NGO that has succeeded in doing so is the Pan African Lawyers Union (PALU). In PALU's instance, the AfCtHPR relies on a confirmation by the AU Commission's Legal Counsel that PALU and the AU signed an MoU and noted that 'the signing of an MoU is an accepted way by which the AU recognizes non-governmental organizations.'[75]

Following PALU's example would essentially require that each NGOs seeks out personal and individual ways of approaching the AU Commission to negotiate an MoU. Such a process is unjust, not only because it is fraught by vagueness, but because it would likely require personal or at least direct professional connections within the AU to get a favorable outcome. This is a kind of privilege that most NGOs simply do not have.

The lack of clear, concrete, systematic and widely accessible guidance about how to obtain such 'recognition by the AU' causes confusion about CSOs eligibility, undermining their ability to contribute effectively to engaging the AfCtHPR under article 4(1). The restrictive interpretation by the Court can also discourage CSOs from participating in the system, thus limiting the scope of human rights discourse and protection.

Scholars have analyzed the kind of interpretation that the AfCtHPR applied in reaching this restrictive conclusion and found that the Court applied a simplistic 'textual analysis' as opposed to a purposive or dynamic interpretation that takes into account the context of a Treaty.[76] This kind of interpretation is not in line with the Vienna Convention on the Law of Treaties which provides that 'a treaty shall be interpreted in good faith in accordance with the ordinary meaning to be given to the terms of the treaty in their context, and in light of its object or purpose.'[77] A purposeful interpretation would be one which, for example, acknowledges that 'recognition by the AU' includes 'recognition by any organ of the AU.'[78] The NGOs who have made requests for advisory opinion

74 D'Amour (n 2).

75 Advisory Opinion No 001/2018, requested by Pan African Lawyers Union (PALU) (n 60).

76 Lilian Chenwi, 'The Advisory Proceedings of the African Court on Human and Peoples' Rights' (2020) 38 *Nordic Journal of Human Rights* 61; D'Amour (n 2).

77 Vienna Convention on the Law of Treaties (adopted 23 May 1969, entered into force 27 January 1980) 1155 UNTS 331), art 31(1).

78 Anthony Jones, 'Form over substance: The African Court's restrictive approach to NGO standing in the SERAP Advisory Opinion' (2017) 17 *African Human Rights Law Journal* 320.

have observer status before the African Commission, which is an organ of the AU. Thus, the argument from NGOs has always been that they have standing because they have recognition by an organ of the AU. However, the AfCtHPR has consistently rejected this argument and maintained that recognition by an organ of the AU does not amount to recognition by the AU. Scholars[79] have argued that this interpretation is contrary to the International Law Commission's Draft Articles on Responsibility of International Organisations (DARIO) which provides that the conduct of an organ of an international organization shall be considered the conduct of that organization under international law.[80]

4.3 *The Importance of Climate Change as a Context for Widening the Court's Approach to 'Recognition by the AU' as a Condition of Standing Title*

The discussion above has shown that the AfCtHPR's interpretation of 'recognition by the AU' has caused ambiguity and confusion that has limited the extent to which NGOs and civil society can access the advisory jurisdiction. The context of climate change presents an opportunity to re-think and widen this restrictive interpretation due to the nature of human rights violations in this context and the actors involved.

NGOs and other civil society collectives have grassroots structures that best position them to know and respond to climate-related human rights issues in the most remote areas, more than any other institutions.[81] Because of the nature of their work, NGOs can easily identify legal questions that need normative clarification through advisory opinions. Therefore, NGOs' standing in advisory proceedings is a feature of the African human rights system that has great potential for normative clarification and development that is transformative for the most vulnerable African communities.

An advisory opinion on climate change is best brought by constituents of rights holders likely to be most affected in the context of climate change. This includes NGOs who work directly with Indigenous and local communities, supporting their resilience. Bizimana reminds us that it would be naïve to keep expecting that African states or inter-governmental organs are sufficient to file advisory requests. Most advisory requests are triggered by the failure of states to fulfill their human rights commitments, therefore 'states would not be

79 D'Amour (n 2).

80 ILC, 'Draft Articles on the Responsibility of International Organisations, with commentaries' (2011) II *Yearbook of the International Law Commission*, art 6.

81 D'Amour (n 2).

willing to expose themselves by initiating processes that would identify their responsibility more than ever.'[82]

Advisory opinions are also a unique opportunity for advancing climate justice because the influence and reach of an advisory opinion is much wider.[83] Such proceedings deal with legal questions of widespread interest. The normative development or clarity that arises from advisory opinions have the potential to result in wide scale application and impact as opposed to a specific situation or set of facts as is the case for contentious cases. Although advisory opinions are not binding, they can serve a critical role in the elucidation and development of international law as well as providing clarity on the nature of state obligations. The persuasive nature of advice can sometimes be superior to force and coercion, thus advisory opinions may even be more important in international relations than judgments.[84] Given the wide unlimited material jurisdiction of the advisory mechanism under Article 4(1) of the AfCtHPR Protocol, this would be an opportunity to invoke a wide range of human rights instruments, including non-binding soft law, to clarify the nature and scope of state obligations in the context of climate change.

In addition to bringing advisory opinions, there is an opportunity for climate justice scholars, NGOs, activists and lawyers to engage the AfCtHPR as *amicus curiae* in advisory proceedings in ways that link substantive rights analysis with procedural rights on access. This may include providing guidance and comparative perspectives on rules of treaty interpretation that expand instead of restricting access to judicial and quasi-judicial bodies.

In 2015, the African Union, through the Executive Council, initiated a process of reviewing and harmonizing the accreditation criteria for NGOs.[85] Although this process has been going on parallel to the ongoing AU Reform process, it has not been consultative, and it is unclear the extent to which users of human rights mechanisms have been consulted or engaged with the process. This is another prime opportunity for engagement because the Criteria that will result from this process could strengthen or weaken CSOs engagement with the human rights mechanisms, including the advisory jurisdiction of the AfCtHPR.

82 D'Amour (n 2) 14.

83 Chenwi (n 76).

84 Teresa Mayr & Jelka Mayr-Singer, 'Keep the Wheels Spinning: The Contributions of Advisory Opinions of the International Court of Justice to the Development of International Law' (2016) 76 *ZaöRV* 425.

85 Executive Council Decision EX/CL 890 (XXVII) of June 2015.

5 The Potential Impact of an AO on Climate Change – Developing Regional Responses

In the previous sections, we outlined some of the significant hurdles to a civil society advisory opinion application. We also argued, however, that the context of climate change and human rights, and the need for broad participation by those most affected by climate harms, might merit greater advocacy and pressure on the court to reconsider its very limited interpretation of the standing requirements.

In this section, we put aside the thorny issue of standing and procedure to consider the kinds of issues that an advisory opinion could and should address, were the Court to consider the substantive legal questions and what kinds of problems it might encounter in outlining rights obligations on African states.

5.1 *Possible Problems or Concerns Related to an Advisory Opinion on Human Rights and Climate Change in Africa*

Climate litigation has often focused on the failures of states to take sufficiently ambitious steps to meet their climate mitigation obligations under international law or in order to avoid human rights impacts. African states, however, are not historically responsible for the causes of climate change and most still make negligible contributions to global emissions (although a small number of states do significantly contribute). The fact that African states will bear the costs of climate change impacts, without benefitting from the industrialisation that caused it and without having meaningfully contributed to its causes, may make the question of African state duties and burdens in the context of climate change a fraught one. In the context of international climate change negotiations, African and other Global South countries have demanded the transfer of funds, technology and skills from the Global North. This is not just a demand for accountability and for developed states to address the harm they have caused, it is also a necessary component of making climate responses affordable for the poorest states. While states have agreed to this transfer of funds, action to actually make the funds, skills and technology available to African states has been slow, and most African states lack the necessary resources to rapidly and meaningfully address climate change impacts.

However, the fact that African states have not historically contributed to the causes of climate change cannot be an argument that excuses those states from addressing the impacts of climate change on human rights on the continent. Given Africa's history of colonial occupation and ongoing inequalities in our global financial systems, there are few human rights issues which are not bound up in complex, historical and ongoing dynamics of oppression and control between the global North and South.

Climate change as a driver of inequality and suffering is tied up with the range of other factors that makes so many of Africa's communities vulnerable, including regulatory, social, institutional, and political failings. While African states are not responsible for the GHGs that have caused climate change, they are not immune to responsibilities for the heightened vulnerability of their populations.

In addition, while only a small number of African states are significant emitters of GHGs, the degradation of the environment is embedded in the economic development of most African states, especially through the intensification of resource extraction. Extractive activities have far-reaching impacts on the environment and the AfCHPR has noted that the rate of destruction of the African environment and ecosystem by extractive industries is a major concern.[86] Environmental and ecological destruction reduce both the environment's and people's resilience and adaptability in the face of climate change, making both even more vulnerable to its impacts.

5.2 *Critical Issues an Advisory Opinion on Human Rights and Climate Change in Africa Might Address*

While there may be many critical questions related to international emissions, historical responsibility, and global finance related to climate change that an advisory opinion might not be able to address, the AfCtHPR could address a number of crucial climate related human rights issues on the continent. We discuss a few of these next.

5.2.1 Mitigation

While Africa, as a continent, has historically contributed little to the causes of climate change, this has begun to change in recent years. A number of African countries have growing, carbon-intensive economies. South Africa, in particular, sits among the 20 top emitters in the world and Nigeria's economic growth means it too is rising in the rankings of high emitting countries.[87]

---

86 African Commission on Human and Peoples' Rights Res No 321 (November 18, 2015) pmbl, discussed in Michael Addaney, Ademola Oluborode Jegede & Miriam Z Matinda, 'The Protection of Climate Refugees under the African Human Rights System: Proposing a Value-Driven Approach Section II: Articles Related to the Theme of the Year 2019: "Refugees, Returnees and Internally Displaced Persons: Towards Durable Solutions to Forced Displacement in Africa"' (2019) 3 *African Human Rights Yearbook* 242.

87 Jegede (n 24).

The AfCtHPR has the opportunity to consider the duties and obligations of higher emitting states within the context of the region, looking not only at state's obligations to their own populations, but also considering the obligations of states to each other's populations. The Court might look beyond human rights law in this regard, understanding human rights in a broader legal context. The Conservation Convention makes 'environmental management a common duty of African states (in addition to individual state action).'[88] The idea of collective state duties in the face of a shared crisis, even where the causes of that crisis are not shared, is an important one in an African context. This opens up the possibility for greater regional collaboration and cooperation in relation to mitigation of climate impacts, including those activities that aggravate the impacts of climate change, such as environmental destruction through extractive activities.

5.2.2 Access to Environmental Information, Participation, and Access to Justice

A critical gap in regional level law relates to the right to participation in environmental matters. Currently, there is no African treaty that is the equivalent of the Aarhus Convention or the Escazú Agreement. The African Convention on the Conservation of Nature and Natural Resources does reflect Rio Principle 10, setting a path for the potential development of law in this area. In addition, Article 16 of the Conservation Convention requires signatories to adopt measures to ensure the dissemination of environmental information, to ensure public participation in decision-making and access to justice in environmental matters.

In the *SERAC* case, discussed above, the Commission interpreted Article 24 (the right to a satisfactory environment) as creating an obligation on states to 'monitor threatened environments, require environmental and social impact studies, provide relevant information to the communities exposed to hazardous materials and activities, and ensure meaningful opportunities for individuals to participate in the decision-making affecting their communities.'[89] In Resolution 153, the African Commission specifically mentions free, prior and informed consent as a key principle that must be included in any adopted text on climate change.

While there is a good foundation for rights to participation, the context of climate change merits proper consideration and articulation of rights in this

88 Addaney, Moyo & Ramakhula (n 26) 11.

89 Jonas Ebbesson, 'Public Participation', in Bodansky, Brunnée & Hey (eds), *The Oxford Handbook of International Environmental Law* (OUP 2007).

regard. A crucial area in which growth is needed is access to justice in environmental matters (arguably including through greater standing for NGOs to request advisory opinions from the AfCtHPR). Oniemola has argued for the importance of not just recognizing rights to access to justice, but also for the creation of 'an enabling environment for climate litigation in African states.'[90]

5.2.3 The Integration of Human Rights Standards into Future African Regional Agreements and Conventions

In its Resolution 153, the African Commission expresses concern about the 'lack of human rights safeguards in various draft texts of the conventions under negotiation' which the Commission finds 'could put at risk the life, physical integrity and livelihood of the most vulnerable members of society notably isolated Indigenous and local communities, women, and other vulnerable social groups.' (Preamble)

The advisory opinion could be a means through which African states are encouraged to center human rights considerations in their ongoing policy work on climate change at both the domestic level and in international negotiations. At the international level, states have resisted the adoption of rights language into UNFCCC documents and agreements. Many states have been reluctant to accept an overlap between human rights and climate change law. The AfCtHPR could take the opportunity to encourage a policy shift on the part of the African Union's negotiating team on climate change, making Africa an advocate for rights based approaches at the international level.

5.2.4 Development of a Framework to Protect the Rights of Climate Refugees

There is no explicit protection for climate refugees in international law or in African regional law. While Africa has an instrument for internally displaced persons, which refers to displacement as a result of climate change, this instrument does not apply to those who cross state borders.[91] This is a critical area in need of policy development and a framework for state cooperation and this will become an increasingly urgent issue on the continent.

Addressing forced displacement requires a human rights approach that can take into account the differentiated social identities of those who are displaced and respond appropriately. Research has found that women, forced to move

90 Peter Kayode Oniemola, 'A Proposal for Transnational Litigation against Climate Change Violations in Africa Limits and Potential of Human Rights in Pursuit of Climate Justice' (2020) 38 *Wisconsin International Law Journal* 301, 324.

91 Addaney, Jegede & Matinda (n 86).

due to extreme weather conditions and changing access to food and water, face an increased risk of gender-based violence.[92] Displacement impacts older people, children, people with disabilities, LGBTQ+ communities in multiple ways and responding to these threats requires attention to the unique conditions, risks, and vulnerabilities of these groups.[93]

5.2.5 Recognition of the Environmental Rights of Children, Especially in Light of the CRC's General Comment

The African Charter on the Rights and Welfare of the Child (1990) requires 'the development of respect for the environment and natural resources' by children through education, but does not include any provisions that directly recognize or protect children's rights to a healthy or satisfactory environment nor does it address the unique vulnerability and rights of children in the context of climate change.

Through an advisory opinion, the AfCtHPR has an opportunity to consider the recent General Comment No 26, adopted by the Committee on the Rights of the Child (CRC) on children's rights and the environment (GC 26),[94] and to develop a framework for advancing and protecting children's rights in an African context. The African Charter on the Rights of the Child offers a crucial foundation, but both the threats to children's rights as a result of climate change and the agency and activism of children on the continent demand better recognition.

Crucially, an advisory opinion presents an opportunity for the encouragement of better mechanisms to ensure the rights of children on the continent to be heard at both the domestic and regional level.

The importance of children's participation in law-making is recognized in the African Committee of Experts on the Rights and Welfare of the Child's 'African Agenda for Children 2040',[95] which calls for dedicated processes for

---

92 'How Climate Change Could Drive an Increase in Gender-based Violence' (*Nature* 14 July 2022).

93 C McLeod, H Barr & K Rall, 'Does Climate Change Increase the Risk of Child Marriage: A Look at What We Know and What We Don't with Lessons from Bangladesh and Mozambique' (2019) 38 *Columbia Journal of Gender Law* 96; HRC, 'Analytical study on the promotion and protection of the rights of older persons in the context of climate change, Report of the Office of the High Commissioner for Human Rights' A/HRC/47/46 (OHCHR Older persons study report).

94 Committee on the Rights of the Child, 'General Comment No 26 (2023) on children's rights and the environment, with a special focus on climate change', UN Doc No CRC/C/GC/26, 22 August 2023.

95 <https://au.int/sites/default/files/newsevents/agendas/africas_agenda_for_children-english.pdf>, accessed on 09/04/2024.

children's participation at both national and in monitoring and accountability for the Agenda at AU level. However, the Agenda includes only a fleeting reference to climate change and does not seem to envision general opportunities for children to participate in broader AU decision-making. The Court might also consider how to facilitate and enable children's participation in Court and Commission proceedings on climate change.

5.2.6 Understanding the Threats to Indigenous Peoples and Encouraging Greater Protection

The Court and Commission already have considered and developed important jurisprudence on the rights of Indigenous Peoples, especially in the context of forced removals. The unique vulnerability of Indigenous Peoples on the continent needs to be better recognised, understood and addressed, especially in relation to Indigenous children and women about whom there is very little disaggregated data.[96]

Climate change poses a profound threat to Indigenous ways of life, livelihoods, cultures and identities, especially for those who live in close and familial relationships to the environment.[97] However, Indigenous Peoples are also holders of critical knowledge about the environment and hold expertise on adaptation and resilience building in the face of environmental and social change. As Oguamanam has argued, African countries have been at the forefront of promoting Indigenous knowledge in international fora, including in negotiations on climate change, but this knowledge is still 'treated marginally in key instruments, perhaps as a legacy of colonially entrenched contempt for Indigenous knowledge systems.'[98]

Indigenous Peoples and Indigenous knowledge need to be better recognized in the AU's climate change law and policy-making in response to climate change.

5.2.7 Setting a Precedent for African Climate Litigation

Of the more than 2300 climate litigation cases that have been filed,[99] less than twenty have been filed in Africa (and of those, ten were filed in South Africa, and the remaining cases have been filed in just four countries). There are

96 Zero Draft, §30.

97 Ademola Oluborode Jegede, *The Climate Change Regulatory Framework and Indigenous Peoples' Lands in Africa: Human Rights Implications* (Pretoria University Law Press, 2016).

98 Chidi Oguamanam, 'A Critical Examination of the African Legal Framework for Indigenous Knowledge' (2023) 67 *Journal of African Law* 1.

99 This number comes from the Sabin Centre's Database of climate litigation. See <https://climatecasechart.com/> accessed on 9 May 2024.

many possible reasons why so few cases have been instituted on the continent, including limiting legal frameworks and constraining standing requirements, as well as limited resources to fund such litigation. An advisory opinion by the AfCtHPRt, however, could set a useful precedent for more litigation. First, by articulating the duties that African states have, the Court could set a precedent, providing litigators with the necessary legal scaffolding with which to build future cases. Second, the case might inspire more African communities and civil society organizations to seek judicial remedies for climate harms. Third, the case might attract the attention of international funders and supporters to address some of the financial and other resources barriers to litigation.

6 Conclusion

In this chapter, we have argued that an advisory opinion on the human rights obligations of African states in the context of climate change could be enormously significant in shaping the region's policy and structure responses to the unique and devastating impacts on the continent. However, the system for requesting an advisory opinion from the Court creates a significant barrier to community-based and civil society organizations bringing such a request. In the context of climate change, this is particularly problematic as it is exactly these groups who are best placed to bring such a request and to provide the Court with the information it needs.

This chapter has outlined alternatives and options for other avenues but has also sought to emphasize the unique context of climate change on the continent, the enormous potential value of an advisory opinion in bringing together disparate legal instruments and policy initiatives at the regional level, and has argued that the Court has an opportunity to widen its interpretation of the standing provision.

SECTION 2

Voices and Participation in Advisory Opinion Proceedings

CHAPTER 7

Storytelling in the Advisory Proceedings on Climate Change

*Antoine De Spiegeleir**

Abstract

This chapter introduces storytelling as a novel perspective to study international advisory proceedings on climate change at the ICJ, the IACtHR, and ITLOS. It suggests that, despite their lack of binding character, or perhaps precisely because of it, advisory proceedings could contribute to meaningful climate action by weaving compelling climate change stories. This requires quite a bit of conceptual unpacking around 'climate change storytelling' and the role of international courts in this process both as storytellers and as arenas for others to tell stories. The chapter discusses two specific examples of climate change storytelling drawn from the amicus brief submitted by the Avaaz Foundation to the IACtHR and the opening oral pleadings made by representatives of small island states before ITLOS. It ends on a call to explore further the space for climate change storytelling in international adjudication.

Keywords

narrative – storytelling – (non-legal) effects of adjudication – court communication – separate opinions – oral proceedings – audience – amicus briefs – small island states representatives

1 Introduction

The two climate change advisory opinion requests pending before the International Court of Justice (ICJ) and the Inter-American Court of Human Rights (IACtHR) as well the recent climate change advisory opinion rendered by the International Tribunal for the Law of the Sea (ITLOS) bring the advisory

* PhD Researcher, Law Department, European University Institute (FWO Fellow), antoine.despiegeleir@eui.eu, https://orcid.org/0000-0002-6409-6668.

 | DOI:10.1163/9789004730618_008

function of international courts to our attention once again. Assuredly not a panacea, these opinions may nevertheless make a noteworthy contribution to climate change law and the climate action movement, as is analyzed in several contributions to this edited volume. In this chapter, I introduce storytelling as a novel perspective to study these pending advisory proceedings and suggest that, despite their lack of binding character, or perhaps precisely because of it, advisory proceedings could contribute to meaningful climate action by weaving compelling climate change stories.

The claim that courts and other legal actors tell stories is not new.[1] But why care about storytelling, even if it takes place in a legal setting? The reason, in the words of Peter Brooks, is that storytelling 'appears to be one of our large, all-pervasive ways of organizing and speaking the world—the way we make sense of meanings that unfold in and through time.'[2] If this is so, then storytelling in a legal setting has the potential to shape the stories we tell each other to 'speak the world' and impact our shared understandings of this world and our relationship to it.[3] This is especially relevant to climate change: how we understand and frame this unprecedented wave of cross-sectoral changes that are often unpredictable matters considerably to how we experience this wave of changes and shapes our capacity to react to it.[4]

This chapter has four sections. I begin by introducing the idea of 'climate change storytelling.' Both proponents and opponents of climate change understand the power of storytelling and have been using it for decades to advance their respective agendas. If many instances of storytelling could be said to relate at least loosely to climate change, this chapter focuses on 'purposive' climate change storytelling, ie, storytelling for the evident purpose of shaping the

1 The 'law and narrative movement' owes much to Robert Cover's 1983 exploration of the inseparability of law and narratives: Robert M Cover, 'The Supreme Court, 1982 Term—Foreword: Nomos and Narrative' (1983) 97 *Harvard Law Review* 4.

2 Peter Brooks, 'The Law as Narrative and Rhetoric' in Peter Brooks and Paul Gewirtz (eds), *Law's Stories: Narrative and Rhetoric in the Law* (Yale University Press 1996) 14. On storytelling and collective action, see generally Frederick Mayer, *Narrative Politics: Stories and Collective Action* (OUP 2014).

3 Comp. Clifford Geertz, *Local Knowledge: Further Essays in Interpretive Anthropology* (Basic Books 1983) 173, 184 (pointing out that law is 'a distinctive manner of imagining the real').

4 Eg Robin Kundis Craig, 'Learning to Live with the Trickster: Narrating Climate Change and the Value of Resilience Thinking' (2016) 33 *Pace Environmental Law Review* 351, 352; Tom Griffiths, 'Weather and Mind Games: Why Can't We Talk about Climate Change?' (2013] *Griffith Review* 246, 255 (labeling climate change as 'the colossal story of our time'); and Chad J McGuire and Devon Lynch, 'Competing Narratives of Climate Change' (2017) 19 *Environmental Practice* 218 (including the literature cited therein).

audience's understanding of or attitude toward climate change. Next, I present the claim that advisory proceedings before international courts can and do serve as sites of storytelling. 'Official' stories woven by courts have a peculiar role to play in the climate change storytelling space, and yet they have been almost completely ignored in the literature thus far. Besides, court proceedings as narrative forums enable multiple actors to tell their stories. This chapter looks at two examples: the amicus brief submitted by the Avaaz Foundation to the IACtHR; and the opening oral pleadings made by representatives of small island states before ITLOS. The analysis of these two examples alerts us to two important teachings flowing from the adoption of a narrative analysis lens. First, it indicates the significance of the varied audiences of the ICJ, the IACtHR, and ITLOS. Second, it highlights the storytelling potential of forms of judicial communications other than 'official' rulings and opinions, such as press releases, annual reports, and the ambiguous category of writing referred to in this chapter as 'separate opinions,' ie all types of opinions and declarations appended to a court's ruling by individual judges. These two lessons are addressed in turn, and a short conclusion follows.

2 Storytelling for and against the Climate

In recent years, the word 'narrative' has made its way into most fields of research outside of narrative theory, its disciplinary home.[5] In law, too, interest in narrative has been burgeoning.[6] For all the engouement around it, the term narrative often remains vague and indeterminate. The literature sometimes suggests distinguishing between 'story' (one or more events), 'narrative discourse' (the way the story is conveyed), and 'narrative' (the combination of story and narrative discourse).[7] This trio of concepts is helpful to make clear what is the level of description one operates at—the content, the form, or both, as it were. This trio of concepts undergirds my reflections in this chapter, but I chose to use a fourth term to describe the object of my inquiry, namely, 'storytelling.' I have

5 For a critical take on this 'narrative imperialism,' see James Phelan, 'Editor's Column: Who's Here? Thoughts on Narrative Identity and Narrative Imperialism' (2005) 13 *Narrative* 205 210 (noting that 'those of us who champion narrative and narrative theory should worry at least as much about claiming too much for their powers as about claiming too little').

6 For a helpful overview, see Greta Olson, 'Narration and Narrative in Legal Discourse' in Peter Hühn (ed), *Handbook of Narratology* (de Gruyter 2014).

7 See notably H Porter Abbott, *The Cambridge Introduction to Narrative* (CUP 2021) 18 (and chapter 2 on 'Defining Narrative').

two reasons for this choice. First, I want to avoid the confusion that the word 'narrative' continues to carry since it is being used in so many different ways in legal and non-legal scholarship. Second, I am specifically interested in stories that are told for the evident purpose of shaping the audience's understanding of or attitude toward climate change, a quality better conveyed by the term storytelling as it is used in general conversation. Let us now look at two examples of purposive climate change storytelling.

The movie *Don't Look Up*, which was directed by Adam McKay and features numerous Hollywood super-stars such as Leonardo Di Caprio and Jennifer Lawrence, is a telling illustration of the use of (audiovisual) storytelling for conveying an action-oriented message about the climate crisis. The movie tells the story of a group of scientists who discover an unknown comet set to collide with Earth in six months and which could potentially lead to humanity's extinction. They are faced with skepticism, disengagement, and mockery by both politicians and the media. Eventually, they succeed in convincing the United States government to put forward a plan to divert the comet from its earth-bound trajectory using nuclear weapons. But this plan is suddenly aborted after Peter Isherwell, the billionaire CEO of 'BASH Cellular,' realizes that the comet is made of rare-earth elements worth trillions of US dollars. The new plan, which is not supported by the scientific community, consists of an interception meant to enable the United States (and not other major powers) to mine the comet for profit. As is expected, the plan fails, and humanity is doomed. As this quick summary shows, climate change is not addressed in *Don't Look Up*. Still, the analogy does not require extraordinary powers of imagination, and the movie's satirical take on collective denial is a clear indictment of our collective response to the climate crisis as well as a strong call to do better.[8]

On the other end of the spectrum, the—much lesser-known—children's book entitled *Petro Pete's Big Bad Dream* tells the story of a lovable little boy, Petro Pete, who has a terrible nightmare.[9] After bidding his affectionate dog good night, Pete is seemingly transported to a parallel universe. Everything there looks pretty much the same as it does in Pete's real life, except for a lot of ordinary objects that have somehow gone missing. No clothes for school, no

8 Cara Buckley, 'Don't Just Watch: Team Behind "Don't Look Up" Urges Climate Action' *The New York Times* (11 January 2022).

9 Carla Schaeperkoetter, *Petro Pete's Big Bad Dream* (OERB (Oklahoma Energy Resources Board) 2016).

toothbrush or comb, no school bus, and someone even removed Pete's bicycle's tires! Adorable Pete is forced to run to school in his pajamas and face his classmates' puzzled questioning. Luckily, Mrs. Rigwell's science class saves the day. We soon learn that what Petro Pete is missing is all by-products of petroleum. Pete has just the time to realize that footballs are also made from petroleum before he wakes up in his bedroom and realizes with a deep sigh of relief that all his cherished petroleum by-products are back where they belong, that is to say, everywhere. This children's book was published in 2016 and made available to Oklahoma's pupils thanks to the generosity of the Oklahoma Energy Resources Board. This Board is an agency of the state of Oklahoma 'funded voluntarily by Oklahoma's oil and natural gas producers and royalty owners.'[10] One of its purported missions is to 'educate Oklahomans about the vitality, contributions and environmental responsibility of the oil and natural gas industry.'[11] A public education mission the Board evidently takes to heart, especially when it comes to younger and—cynics would add—more impressionable members of the public.[12]

Admittedly, *Don't Look Up* and *Petro Pete's Big Bad Dream* are cliché examples of storytelling in favor of or against climate change action.[13] But they are helpful in highlighting the pervasiveness of climate change stories. Key to both examples is the sequencing of disparate events they embody: the actions and connections they emphasize, as well as all the other potential actions and connections they leave out. This sequencing or 'emplotment' is what distinguishes stories from a simple series of events or happenings; it is 'the design and intention of narrative, what shapes a story and gives it a certain direction or intent of meaning.'[14]

10 See <https://oerb.com/about/>.

11 As quoted on the first page of *Petro Pete's Big Bad Dream* (n 9).

12 For decades, the oil and natural gas industry has been using stories of all sorts in its far-reaching efforts to influence the public's perception of its activities. See notably Geoffrey Supran and Naomi Oreskes, 'Assessing ExxonMobil's Climate Change Communications (1977–2014)' (2017) 12 Environmental Research Letters 084019; and Geoffrey Supran and Naomi Oreskes, 'Addendum to "Assessing ExxonMobil's Climate Change Communications (1977–2014)" Supran and Oreskes (2017 Environ. Res. Lett. 12 084019)' (2020) 15 *Environmental Research Letters* 119401.

13 For another (less cliché) example, see the project entitled 'We Still Have a Chance' at the University of Exeter: <https://greenfutures.exeter.ac.uk/we-still-have-a-chance/>.

14 Peter Brooks, *Reading for the Plot: Design and Intention in Narrative* (Vintage Books 1985) xi. See also, among many others, Andreea Deciu Ritivoi, 'Explaining People: Narrative and the Study of Identity' (2009) 1 *Storyworlds: A Journal of Narrative Studies* 25, 33.

Scientists, too, pay increasingly more attention to how storytelling shapes attitudes and beliefs about the climate. A recent study in the United States examined the impact of the general public's exposure to the personal story of an individual whose fishing and hunting grounds are negatively impacted by climate change.[15] This personal story was shared on hundreds of radio stations across the United States and shown to have a positive effect on global warming beliefs and risk perceptions among these radios' audiences. This is also true for fictional stories. In another recent study, readers' attitudes and beliefs about climate change were found to be affected positively after their being exposed to climate fiction, or 'cli-fi,' ie, a genre of fiction that deals with the theme of climate change.[16]

All in all, it is argued that purposive climate change storytelling impacts our beliefs and attitudes toward climate change policymaking. If this is so, then we must think critically about the stories we create, amplify, or suppress, and about who are the actors involved in this process. The remainder of this chapter takes a closer look at the narrative function of the ICJ, the IACtHR, and ITLOS, understood as climate change storytellers and arenas for climate change storytelling, simultaneously.

3 Advisory Proceedings on Climate Change as Sites of Storytelling

Not all climate change stories are told in blockbuster movies or children's books. Many engage in storytelling on the theme of climate change in their daily lives, and so do institutions through their collective voices. This chapter focuses on an understudied family of institutional climate change storytellers: international courts. As storytellers, these courts are indubitably an intriguing species. Although they are legal actors tasked with solving legal disputes and answering legal questions, they cannot avoid engaging with climate change storytelling in the course of their activities. The 'official' climate change stories they produce themselves or enable others to produce warrant scrutiny.

To understand the implications of this claim, we must go back to the question of the effects of (international) adjudication. Saying that advisory

15 Abel Gustafson and others, 'Personal Stories Can Shift Climate Change Beliefs and Risk Perceptions: The Mediating Role of Emotion' (2020) 33 *Communication Reports* 121.

16 Matthew Schneider-Mayerson and others, 'Environmental Literature as Persuasion: An Experimental Test of the Effects of Reading Climate Fiction' (2023) 17 *Environmental Communication* 35. On cli-fi, see Matthew Schneider-Mayerson, 'Climate Change Fiction' in Greenwald Smith (ed), *American Literature in Transition, 2000–2010* (CUP 2017).

opinions differ from judgments in that they are not binding is not saying much.[17] International lawyers seem to hold unanimously that advisory opinions carry a certain authority or prestige regardless of their advisory nature, and it would be 'almost blasphemous' to call this authority or prestige into question.[18] In an international legal system where enforcement is extremely weak and where the line between hard and soft law is blurred, we can even argue that the non-binding character of advisory opinions is of little consequence to their effects.[19]

However, it is unclear what exactly lies behind the idea that advisory opinions have 'legal weight and moral authority,'[20] 'persuasive authority,'[21]

---

17 To say a little more, it is possible to make an advisory opinion binding through a convention: Charles N Brower and Pieter HF Bekker, 'Understanding "Binding" Advisory Opinions of the International Court of Justice' in Andō, McWhinney % Wolfrum (eds), *Liber Amicorum Judge Shigeru Oda (Vol. 1)* (Kluwer 2002).

18 Teresa F Mayr & Jelka Mayr-Singer, 'Keep the Wheels Spinning: The Contributions of Advisory Opinions of the International Court of Justice to the Development of International Law' (2016) 76 *ZaöRV* 425, 430 (writing about the ICJ). In as early as 1938, Leland Goodrich remarked that 'the statement that advisory opinions are purely advisory is formalistic, perhaps even naïve' (Leland M Goodrich, 'The Nature of the Advisory Opinions of the Permanent Court of International Justice' (1938) 32 *AJIL* 738, 758).

19 Comp., among others, Manfred Lachs, 'Some Reflections on the Contribution of the International Court of Justice to the Development of International Law' (1983) 10 *Syracuse Journal of International Law and Commerce* 239, 249. ITLOS expressed a similar view with regard to advisory opinions rendered by the ICJ: '[J]udicial determinations made in advisory opinions carry no less weight and authority than those in judgments because they are made with the same rigour and scrutiny by the "principal judicial organ" of the United Nations with competence in matters of international law' (*Dispute concerning Delimitation of the Maritime Boundary between Mauritius and Maldives in the Indian Ocean* (*Mauritius/Maldives*) (*Preliminary Objections*) (Judgment, 28 January 2021) ITLOS Case No 28, §203). See also Michael Bothe, 'Legal and Non-Legal Norms—A Meaningful Distinction in International Relations?' (1980) 11 *Netherlands YIL* 65, 85 (noting that 'it appears from the international practice that obligations which are clearly non-legal are still taken seriously by states').

20 Anxhela Mile, 'Emerging Legal Doctrines in Climate Change Law—Seeking an Advisory Opinion from the International Court of Justice' (2021) 56 *Texas International Law Journal* 59, 68. The expression 'legal weight and moral authority' is used by the ICJ itself on its website: 'Despite having no binding force, the Court's advisory opinions nevertheless carry great legal weight and moral authority. They are often an instrument of preventive diplomacy and help to keep the peace. In their own way, advisory opinions also contribute to the clarification and development of international law and thereby to the strengthening of peaceful relations between States' (<https://www.icj-cij.org/advisory-jurisdiction>).

21 Daniel Bodansky, 'An ICJ Advisory Opinion on Climate Change: Ten Questions and Answers' (2022) *Center for Climate and Energy Solutions* 3.

or similar expressions.[22] This may have to do with the concept of authority itself, which serves as placeholder for a variety of concerns in international law scholarship and is seldom spelled out.[23]

I propose to take a different route and rely on Thomas Stoddard's distinction between the rule-shifting and culture-shifting effects of the law, which he developed in relation to the American civil rights movement.[24] 'The law,' Stoddard argues, 'is not now, and never has been, simply a set of formal rules; it is also the most obvious expression of a society's values and concerns, and it can and ought to be used to improve values and concerns.'[25] Focusing on litigation, the two obvious goals pursued by participants in an adjudicative process are the enforcement of existing rules and the alteration of these rules if necessary—for instance, to determine how human rights obligations look like when applied to a new set of factual circumstances. But litigation can serve two additional goals, following Stoddard's framework: it can aim to 'express a new moral ideal or standard' and 'to change cultural attitudes and patterns.'[26] These two additional goals embody the culture-shifting role of litigation. Importantly, rule-shifting and culture-shifting can go hand-in-hand: formal application of the rules may contribute to cultural change.

If we apply this two-fold approach to our study of advisory proceedings on climate change, we can easily recognize, first, that advisory proceedings have rule-shifting capabilities. It has virtually never been contested that advisory opinions participate in the development of international law, except perhaps by those who strictly deny the existence of any and all form of judicial law-making.[27] Advisory opinions notably clear up the ambiguity surrounding

22 See, among many additional sources, Edvard Hambro, 'The Authority of the Advisory Opinions of the International Court of Justice' (1954) 3 *ICQL* 2; Hugh Thirlway, 'Advisory Opinion', *Max Planck Encyclopedia of Public International Law* (OUP 2006); Pierre d'Argent, 'Article 65' in Zimmermann et al (eds), *The Statute of the International Court of Justice: A Commentary* (OUP 2019).

23 See Başak Çalı, 'Authority' in Singh & d'Aspremont (eds), *Concepts for International Law* (Edward Elgar 2019) 40.

24 Thomas B Stoddard, 'Bleeding Heart: Reflections on Using the Law to Make Social Change' (1997) 72 *NYU Law Review* 967. Comp. Gerald Rosenberg's distinction between the 'judicial' and the 'extra-judicial' effects of strategic litigation: Gerald N Rosenberg, *The Hollow Hope: Can Courts Bring About Social Change?* (University of Chicago Press 2008) 10–11.

25 Stoddard (n 24) 6.

26 ibid 7.

27 Karin Oellers-Frahm, 'Lawmaking Through Advisory Opinions?', in von Bogdandy & Venzke (eds), *International Judicial Lawmaking: On Public Authority and Democratic Legitimation in Global Governance* (Springer 2012) 79; Mayr and Mayr-Singer (n 18) 426; Rozemarijn J Roland Holst, 'Taking the Current When It Serves: Prospects and Challenges for an ITLOS Advisory Opinion on Oceans and Climate Change' (2022) *RECIEL* 1.

specific obligations or principles of international law, and do so 'at large,' beyond the context of a specific dispute.[28] Still, this rule-shifting impact may prove inconsequential for the international climate regime, for well-known reasons having to do with the limitations of international law more generally.[29]

Even if they fail to shift rules adequately, advisory proceedings may have culture-shifting effects.[30] They constitute part of 'the large space in which global public consciousness is formed'[31] and, as such, may participate in shaping the international community's values and principles.[32] Seen in this light, storytelling becomes a promising avenue for unveiling what lies in part behind the 'culture-shifting' role of international courts.[33] Doing so is not easy, as is shown by the vagueness of the expressions that commentators use to describe advisory opinions, to which I referred above: we struggle to put into words the not purely legal and yet unanimously recognized effects of what is formally a mere piece of advice issued by an international court. Besides, the ICJ, the IACtHR (in its advisory capacity), and ITLOS arguably work much less

28 Eg relating to climate change, Mariya Gromilova, 'Rescuing the People of Tuvalu: Towards an ICJ Advisory Opinion on the International Legal Obligations to Protect the Environment and Human Rights of Populations Affected by Climate Change' (2015) 10 *Intercultural Human Rights Law Review* 233, 286.

29 Benoit Mayer spells out these limitations in the context of advisory opinions on climate change: Benoit Mayer, 'International Advisory Proceedings on Climate Change' [2023] *Michigan JIL* 41. See also: Daniel Bodansky, 'Advisory Opinions on Climate Change: Some Preliminary Questions' (2023) *RECIEL* 1, 5; and Anne van Aaken, 'Is International Law Conducive To Preventing Looming Disasters?' (2016) 7 *Global Policy* 81. At the domestic level, see notably Elizabeth Fisher, Eloise Scotford & Emily Barritt, 'The Legally Disruptive Nature of Climate Change' (2017) 80 *Modern Law Review* 173 (exploring legal 'disruptions' caused by climate change in a handful of common law jurisdictions); Henry Weaver & Douglas A Kysar, 'Courting Disaster: Climate Change and the Adjudication of Catastrophe' (2017) 93 *Notre Dame Law Review* 295 (studying how 'catastrophic harms disrupt legal formalism' at the hand of case studies drawn from global climate change adjudication).

30 Comp. Laura King, 'Narrative, Nuisance, and Environmental Law' (2014) 29 *Journal of Environmental Law and Litigation* 331, 334. See also the scholarship on 'winning through losing,' which puts forward a similar argument: Gerald Torres, 'Some Observations on the Role of Social Change on the Courts' (2006) *Cornell Law Faculty Publications* 901–902; Douglas NeJaime, 'Winning through Losing' (2010) 96 *Iowa Law Review* 941; Ben Depoorter, 'The Upside of Losing' (2013) 113 *Columbia Law Review* 817.

31 Philippe Sands, 'Climate Change and the Rule of Law: Adjudicating the Future in International Law' (2016) 28 *Journal of Environmental Law* 19, 32.

32 Daniel Bodansky, 'The Role of the International Court of Justice in Addressing Climate Change: Some Preliminary Reflections' (2017) 49 *Arizona State Law Journal* 689, 18–19. See also Roland Holst (n 27) 9.

33 Evidently, legal storytelling does not tell the full tale, and these proceedings 'shape culture' in many other ways.

obviously with stories than other courts such as the European Court of Human Rights, the work of which depends on and develops out of personal life stories told by individual applicants.

These difficulties notwithstanding, the claim of this chapter is that these courts, too, can be studied through a narrative lens, in their capacity both as storytellers and as arenas for others to tell stories. As we are still waiting for two of the three advisory opinions under study in this volume, I propose here to focus on climate change storytelling by participants in the adjudicative process rather than by the courts themselves. Indeed, many actors employed and continue to employ storytelling at all stages of these advisory proceedings. In fact, even if the ICJ, the IACtHR, and ITLOS resolutely opposed the idea of telling climate change stories themselves, these stories would be sure to enter the courtroom through countless other voices—they already did. To conclude this section, let me illustrate this point by means of two examples: the amicus brief submitted by the Avaaz Foundation to the IACtHR, and the opening oral submissions made by several representatives before ITLOS.

My first example is taken from the amicus brief submitted to the IACtHR by the Avaaz Foundation, a non-profit organization that promotes global activism on climate change, among many other causes.[34] This amicus brief consists primarily of a detailed legal analysis spanning about 140 pages, but it also tells a number of personal life stories collected among Avaaz's vast membership. For instance, the brief's executive summary contains the testimony of 'Sol A. from Argentina':

> *Tengo 20 años y mi ansiedad climática es tan grande que desde que tengo 18 ya decidí que me iba a suicidar cuando todo llegue a su punto culminante. Me quitaron mi vida, mi esperanza a un futuro, mis ganas de vivir, pero no me van a quitar mi muerte. Yo quiero ser quien decida cómo morirme, y lo voy a hacer yo misma porque quiero sentir que tengo control sobre, al menos, en una mínima cosa en mi vida.*
>
> I am 20 years old and my climate anxiety is so great that ever since I was 18 I decided that I would commit suicide when everything reaches its

34 *The Environment and Human Rights* (*State Obligations in Relation to the Environment in the Context of the Protection and Guarantee of the Rights to Life and to Personal Integrity – Interpretation and Scope of Articles 4(1) and 5(1) of the American Convention on Human Rights*) Advisory Opinion OC-23/17, Inter-American Court of Human Rights Series A No 23 (15 November 2017) Amicus Brief Submitted to the IACtHR by the Avaaz Foundation, 20 October 2023, available at <https://climatecasechart.com/wp-content/uploads/non-us-case-documents/2023/20231020_18528_na.pdf>.

> climax. They took away my life, my hope for a future, my desire to live, but they are not going to take away my death. I want to be the one who decides how to die, and I'm going to do it myself because I want to feel like I have control over at least one small thing in my life.[35]

We are here far away from the complex balancing of states' rights and obligations under international conventions and thrown in the shoes of a young Argentinian whose perception of the climate crisis is shocking (announcing that they would 'commit suicide when everything reaches its climax') and heart-wrenching ('they took away my life, my hope for a future, my desire to live, …'). Further down, we learn that:

> In preparing this submission, Avaaz collected messages from 100 people from the Americas, including parents, grandparents, educators, and young people, who are feeling the impact of climate change and climate anxiety. Ricardo León V.R.'s words above [echoing Sol A.'s resigned perspective on the inescapability of climate catastrophe] reflect a common sentiment expressed in those messages and exemplify the distress being felt that more action is needed to avert the impending climate crisis which disproportionately affects children and young people. These 100 messages represent just a small portion of the many voices calling for change. Avaaz continues to collect them on a rolling basis at https://secure.avaaz.org/campaign/en/climate_litigation_hub/.[36]

The paragraph above opens the first substantive part of Avaaz's submission, relating to the claim that 'states have an obligation to take action to prevent the disproportionate harm inflicted on children and young people as a result of the climate crisis.' This indicates that Avaaz's campaign of members' testimonies is more than an add-on to the Foundation's legal arguments; it is a constitutive part of Avaaz's contribution to the IACtHR advisory proceeding. By placing at the center stage and recounting in narrative form the lived experiences of those of its members who are most affected by the climate crisis, Avaaz sends a clear message to the IACtHR and the broader legal community about the significance of these experiences and their centrality for the advisory opinion request pending before this Court.[37]

---

35 ibid para. 5.

36 ibid para. 19. The first sentence of this excerpt originally contained the following hyperlink: <https://s3.amazonaws.com/avaazimages.avaaz.org/AVZ+CA+MS+DESIGN+22.pdf>.

37 Comp. the amicus brief submitted jointly by Our Children's Trust and Oxfam International to ITLOS, which does not explicitly contain life stories but begins with a list of 24 children

Another telling illustration of storytelling by participants in the adjudicative process can be found in the first series of oral submissions made to ITLOS on 11 September 2023. Gaston Browne, the Prime Minister of Antigua and Barbuda, opened the oral pleadings of the Commission of Small Island States on Climate Change and International Law (COSIS).[38] Browne's submission set the tone for the following interventions. It laid out the dramatic story of small island states that contributed very little to global warming and yet will suffer, and already do suffer, global warming's most drastic consequences, to the point of (territorial) extinction. Brilliantly, Browne weaved together the story of the long-lasting relationship between the nation he represents and the oceans 'from time immemorial' with the much more recent yet much more tragic story of the coming about of the climate crisis, in the face of which his and other small island nations will be the first to fall 'through no fault of [their] own':

> [This advisory procedure before ITLOS] is the opening chapter in the struggle to change the conduct of the international community by clarifying the obligation of States to protect the marine environment. We are, after all, peoples of the ocean, whether in the Caribbean or the Pacific, in the Atlantic or Indian Oceans, surrounded by the vast expanses of water that have sustained us from time immemorial.

---

and young people in whose voice the brief was purportedly submitted: *Request for an Advisory Opinion submitted by the Commission of Small Island States on Climate Change and International Law* (Advisory Opinion, 21 May 2024) ITLOS Case No 31 (*COSIS Opinion*), Amicus Curiae submitted by Our Children's Trust and Oxfam International, 16 June 2023, available at <https://www.itlos.org/fileadmin/itlos/documents/cases/31/written_statements/4/C31-WS-4-8-Our_Children_s_Trust___Oxfam.pdf>. Avaaz's submission also makes room for the voice of representatives of Indigenous communities such as Raoni Metuktire, Chief of the Kayapo people: '*Minha preocupação não é só com os indígenas, mas com todo o mundo. Porque se eles desmatarem toda a floresta, o tempo vai mudar, o sol vai ficar muito quente, os ventos vão ficar muito fortes. Eu me preocupo com todos, porque é a floresta que segura o mundo. Se acabarem com tudo, não é só* índio *que vai sofrer. Minha preocupação é com o futuro das crianças e jovens que vão crescer neste planeta.*' (English translation: 'My concern is not only with the Indigenous Peoples, but with the whole world. Because if they cut down all the forest, the climate will change, the sun will get too hot, the winds will get too strong. I worry about everyone, because it is the forest that holds the world together. If they put an end to everything, it's not just the Indigenous Peoples who will suffer. My concern is with the future of the children and young people who will grow up on this planet.') (Amicus Brief Submitted to the IACtHR by the Avaaz Foundation, n 34, para. 7)

38 The creation of COSIS to 'construct' the advisory competence of ITLOS raises important issues; see notably Alina Miron, 'COSIS Request for an Advisory Opinion: A Poisoned Apple for the ITLOS?' (2023) 1 *International Journal of Marine and Coastal Law* 1.

In this regard, the COSIS Agreement explicitly acknowledges the fundamental importance of oceans as sinks and reservoirs of greenhouse gasses, and the direct relevance of the marine environment to the adverse effects of climate change on small island States. The ocean is fundamental to the climate system of Earth, so it is befitting that the first in these series of proceedings should be before ITLOS, the guardian of the 1982 UN Convention on the Law of the Sea.

It is befitting no less, because in the past few weeks this summer we have witnessed the highest ocean temperatures on record. Mr President, Members of the Tribunal, we are here today because over a century and a half of anthropogenic greenhouse gas emissions have polluted our precious oceans and devastated the marine environment. Those emissions have fundamentally changed Earth's climate and are posing an existential threat to vulnerable communities worldwide. My country is one of those communities, and we stand in solidarity with all small island and coastal States facing the devastating consequences of climate change. Despite our negligible emissions of greenhouse gases, COSIS members have suffered and continue to suffer the overwhelming burden of climate change's adverse impacts. Indeed, the catastrophic effects of climate change threaten the survival, and in some cases, the very existence of COSIS Member States. Without rapid and ambitious remedial action, climate change may prevent my children and my grandchildren from living on the island of their ancestors, the island that we call home. We cannot remain silent in the face of such injustice. We cannot abandon our peoples to such a cruel fate. [...]

Mr President, for decades, small island States have been stating these truths in international gatherings concerning climate change, including at successive Conferences of the Parties to the UNFCCC. We have talked ourselves hoarse since the 1990s, pointing to the perilous circumstances into which our people and our countries are being plunged. Year after year, we listened as promises to mitigate climate change were made, and year after year, we watched as those promises went unfulfilled. We have patiently listened and waited. We have ardently urged and pleaded, but with little avail.

[...]

Mr President, members of the Tribunal, as I hope my remarks have made clear, the impacts of climate change on the members of COSIS are ongoing, devastating and will continue to worsen in the near future. Small island States may be the first to fall – through no fault of our own – but we will not be the last, for no country on Earth can escape the deadly

> grasp of climate change. The world is teetering dangerously on the precipice of a climate catastrophe. We need your help. We need your guidance. I respectfully request that the honourable members of this Tribunal consider the significance of the advisory opinion, not only for COSIS, but for the protection of our planet and of human civilization. […][39]

This narrative framing was echoed in the speech of Kausea Natano, the Prime Minister of Tuvalu. He, too, emphasized the sharp contrast between the time frame of today's climate emergency and his people's age-old relationship with nature and the oceans: 'Just a few years. That's all we have before the ocean consumes everything my people built across centuries.'[40] Arnold Kiel Loughman, Attorney General of the Republic of Vanuatu, made similar remarks.[41] He also forcefully echoed the David and Goliath-reminiscent story of small island states' far-reaching yet mostly inefficacious attempts to sway major polluters and the broader international community into doing more to prevent the climate crisis, which was also introduced by Gaston Browne above:

> Vanuatu has participated for decades in multilateral climate negotiations with good faith, ambition and the hope that nations would be able to work together to address the single greatest obstacle to the security and well-being of humankind. We have participated vigorously in deliberations of the UNFCCC and at each and every COP. We have raised the alarm at the United Nations and its specialized agencies, and at a wide range of other regional and international fora and institutions. We have listened time and again as major polluters have pledged to address our concerns to do what is necessary to put an end to the nightmare that is unfolding before our eyes, as our islands and our homes are battered by extreme weather events, rising sea levels and myriad of other disasters that are slowly and surely bringing about our demise. We have been patient, but to little avail. We now feel that our good faith has been exploited. Our ambition has been sidelined. Our voices have been ignored and our hope is now hanging by a thread. Time and time again, we have been disappointed by the absence of concrete action at the international level. The debilitating

39 *COSIS Opinion* (n 37) Public Sitting held on 11 September 2023 at 10 a.m., Verbatim Record, ITLOS/PV.23/C31/1/Corr.1, 6–9.

40 ibid 12.

41 'Our government and our people look to this Tribunal with expectant eyes because, for us, time is running out. The ocean is our mother, the source of life. Yet it is being destroyed by the failure of major greenhouse gas emitters to take seriously their obligation to protect and preserve the marine environment.' (ibid 14).

> consequences of the climate crisis are worsening with every second of every day. The spirit of international collaboration has not translated into real and necessary benefits for our nation and its citizens. Already, we are measuring climate change not in degrees or in tons of carbon, but in human lives. Action is required now, and the call for action is not just a matter of lofty ideals; it is a matter of legally binding obligations. Had States taken seriously their obligations, we would not be here today. [...][42]

Perhaps most striking in terms of storytelling was the following intervention, by Naima Te Maile Fifita, acting as counsel to COSIS. Emphasizing the significance of advisory proceedings for the peoples of small island states and the role of the global youth movement in these proceedings, she began on a radically more personal note than one is accustomed to in the Hamburg courtroom:

> Mr President, distinguished members of the Tribunal, it is a great privilege and honour to appear before you as counsel to COSIS, as an indigenous Tuvaluan, as a youth and as a mother to a daughter of the Pacific who opened her eyes to this world just a year ago. As I address this distinguished Tribunal at this historic proceeding, my fears are for the kind of world she will inherit when the land of her ancestors is taken by the rising sea.[43]

Toward the end of this remarkable intervention, which is too long to cite in full in this chapter but well worth a detour, Naime Te Maile Fifita added:

> I am here before you today, Mr President, because of an exchange I had with my grandfather at 12 years of age. I had asked him how he felt about the idea that Tuvalu, his homeland, could soon disappear due to sea level rise. After a moments reflection he responded, 'It will never be gone.' Only five years later, however, he relayed to me with great sadness that one of the islands in Tuvalu where he spent many of his childhood years had completely disappeared under the sea. Climate change is already wreaking havoc on our precious ancestral lands. Mr President, to ensure that my grandfather's declaration holds true, to ensure that Tuvalu never disappears, I endeavour to do my part. In 10 years from now I hope to still be able to take my daughter to the island in Tuvalu after which he named me: Te Maile.

42 ibid 15.

43 ibid 28.

> By delivering a robust advisory opinion, this Tribunal will not only make a historic contribution to the protection and preservation of the marine environment, but also to the continuity of entire civilizations and ancestral connections. This matter is truly a question of life and death. Therefore, I respectfully urge you, Mr President, to consider the profound and timely impact this advisory opinion would have on those vulnerable communities who are deserving of clarity and justice. [...][44]

At the very least, these two examples show how participants in the advisory proceedings on climate change can employ storytelling to buttress their positions and attempt to influence their audience.[45] This brings us to a larger lesson about storytelling: that telling a story necessarily implies an audience.[46] Traditionally, the scholarship on international adjudication has focused on the speakers (the courts and, to a lesser extent, the parties). But the audience, too, merits our attention, for advisory proceedings are an interactive space of 'transaction' between tellers and listeners. Besides, the fact that these two examples are taken from an amicus brief and the verbatim records of oral pleadings indicates that we cannot limit ourselves to official rulings and opinions if we aim to study the narrative dimension of international adjudication. Other forms of communications, such as press releases and annual reports, also deserve scrutiny. I spell out these two lessons in the last two sections of this chapter.

4 Audiences of Legal Storytelling

Legal storytelling is a two-way street—international courts' apparent monologues 'invariably degenerate into dialogues.'[47] The audience of legal stories

---

44 ibid 32–33.

45 Not highlighted in these examples is the blatant omission of events or characters in the stories told; one can think, for instance, of the virtually complete silence surrounding the role and responsibility of Big Oil and other private actors in the oral proceedings before ITLOS.

46 In the present contribution, I use the term 'audience' to refer to the flesh-and-blood readers (or listeners) of the advisory opinions, and thus brush over the distinction between 'narratee,' 'implied reader,' and 'real or actual reader,' which narrative theorists have explored at length. On this distinction, see notably Seymour Benjamin Chatman, *Story and Discourse: Narrative Structure in Fiction and Film* (Cornell University Press 1978) 147–151.

47 Chaïm Perelman & Lucie Olbrechts-Tyteca, *Traité de l'argumentation: La Nouvelle Rhétorique* (Université de Bruxelles 1983) 46 (the original quote is not limited to (international) courts). Comp. James Boyd White, 'Law as Language: Reading Law and Reading

is just as important as the teller.[48] Whether a story is compelling depends in large part on its addressees, and a proficient narrator must understand their audience to weave convincing narratives.[49] This is why Brooks suggests that students of legal storytelling may be especially interested in 'narrative transactions, in questions of narrative transmission and decoding: that is, stories in the situation of their telling and listening, asking not only how these stories are constructed and told, but also how they are listened to, received, reacted to, how they ask to be acted upon and how they in fact become operative.[50]

Simply put, international courts and participants in international adjudication must consider the sensibilities of their audiences. This task is complicated by the fact that there is assuredly no single group of addressees when it comes to an international adjudication context and to a topic as vast and complex as climate change. Having to address successfully different groups, which may have conflicting interests and worldviews, can create significant difficulties in practice and seriously hamper the efficacy of the storytelling.[51]

Literature' (1982) 60 *Texas Law Review* 415, 441 (making the broader point that '[t]he law always assumes a speaker and audience located in the context it defines. This is how it makes a world and makes it real').

48 This section focuses on the audience of legal storytelling. A different but relevant question is that of knowing *on whose behalf* legal stories are told. This interrogation relates to the ethics of legal storytelling, which I do not address in this chapter. For a foundational piece on the subversive and counter-majoritarian potential of legal storytelling, see Richard Delgado, 'Storytelling for Oppositionists and Others: A Plea for Narrative' (1989) 87 *Michigan Law Review* 2411.

49 Andrea Bianchi, 'International Adjudication, Rhetoric and Storytelling' (2018) 9 *Journal of International Dispute Settlement* 28, 45; Jean Salmon, *L'auditoire de la Cour Internationale de Justice: Du bilateral à l'universel* (Europa-Institut der Universität des Saarlandes 1996) 6.

50 Peter Brooks, 'Narrative Transactions—Does the Law Need a Narratology?' (2006) 18 *Yale Journal of Law & the Humanities* 1, 26. Scholars even suggest that 'pleasing the audience' matters in and of itself, rather than as a function of a further goal; see Ingo Venzke's analysis of judicial reasoning as a 'strategy of impression management,' which builds on Lawrence Baum's work in the United States: Ingo Venzke, 'Judicial Authority and Styles of Reasoning: Self-Presentation between Legalism and Deliberation', in Palmer Olsen, Jemielniak & Nielsen (eds), *Establishing Judicial Authority in International Economic Law* (CUP 2016); Lawrence Baum, *Judges and Their Audiences: A Perspective on Judicial Behavior* (Princeton University Press 2006). Even from a traditional perspective, how an advisory opinion is received by its formal addressee (the requesting organ) matters and will determine the impact of the opinion on the development of international law (Oellers-Frahm (n 27) 90).

51 Jean Salmon, 'Who Are the Addressees of the Opinions?', in Boisson de Chazournes & Sands (eds), *International Law, the International Court of Justice, and Nuclear Weapons* (CUP 1999) 35; André Nollkaemper, 'The Court and Its Multiple Constituencies: Three Perspectives on the Kosovo Advisory Opinion', in Milanovic & Wood (eds), *The Law and Politics of the Kosovo Advisory Opinion* (OUP 2015) 219. For instance, see Nienke Grossman's

To tackle this difficulty, we can try and identify the main actors, individual or collective, to which international courts and participants in international adjudication must speak. These addressees range from the individual human being who comes to be exposed to international adjudication all the way up to formal participants in the adjudicatory process, at the forefront of which are states and international organizations. Should also be mentioned non-governmental organizations, national judiciaries, other international adjudicative bodies, and the media broadly speaking.[52] As we can see, the list is virtually endless and contains a multitude of addressees potentially tuning in to advisory proceedings with highly divergent perspectives and expectations.

Jean Salmon's survey of three broad categories of audiences in the context of advisory proceedings helps make sense of this cacophony: (i) the universal audience, composed of the entire community of human beings able to access communications from international courts or participants in the adjudicator process, with a multitude of secondary speakers acting as intermediaries between a court and 'laypeople;'[53] (ii) the specific interlocutor formally addressed by a given procedure—in our context, the actor requesting the opinion; and (iii) the speaker itself.[54]

---

criticism of 'Solomonic' rulings by the ICJ: Nienke Grossman, 'Solomonic Judgments and the Legitimacy of the International Court of Justice', in Follesdal et al (eds), *Legitimacy and International Courts* (CUP 2018). Comp., regarding domestic constitutional courts, Nuno Garoupa & Tom Ginsburg, 'Building Reputation in Constitutional Courts: Political and Judicial Audiences' (2011) 28 *Arizona Journal of International and Comparative Law* 539. Comp. also Peter Brooks' analysis of the United States Supreme Court's attempt to win assent from multiple audiences in its 1966 *Miranda v. Arizona* majority opinion: Brooks (n 2) 21.

52 The IACtHR itself pointed out the important role of national judiciaries in the aftermath of its decisions, including when it exercises its non-contentious jurisdiction: IACtHR, *Gender Identity, Equality, and Non-Discrimination of Same-Sex Couples*, Advisory Opinion of 24 November 2017, para. 26. See, among others, Bodansky (n 29) 6; and Sands (n 31) 15.

53 The use of the term 'communications' to denote the textual outputs of international adjudication may surprise the reader, but it should not. After all, that opinions, judgments, and the like are instances of communication between two or more actors is built into the international legal system. Consider, for instance, the role of Article 67 of the Statute of the ICJ, which provides that the Court shall deliver its opinion in open court after having given notice 'to the Secretary-General and to the representatives of Members of the United Nations, of other states and of international organizations immediately concerned:' as Andreas Paulus notes, 'the public reading of advisory opinions strengthens their international status and enables the Court to address itself to the world' (Andreas Paulus, 'Article 67' in Zimmermann et al (n 22) 7).

54 Salmon (n 49) 11–12. Salmon builds on Perelman & Olbrechts-Tyteca (n 47) 39–40. See also Salmon (n 51).

Leaving aside Salmon's intriguing suggestion that international courts themselves are among their audiences,[55] of particular interest to my efforts in this chapter is the role of intermediary speakers in transmitting and co-constructing the stories told by or at international courts. As any international lawyer knows from personal experience, international adjudication is hardly a topic of everyday conversations. For the content of international proceedings to percolate down into 'popular' knowledge, it needs to be carried over by intermediaries who are both addressees of the communications arising out of international adjudication and secondary speakers of these communications.[56] Among these secondary speakers, legal scholars and the media play a primordial role.[57] Civil society organizations, trade unions, and other interest-communities also matter, especially in their capacity to rely on a vocabulary that makes sense to their constituents.

---

55 See Salmon (n 49) 21. Do international courts speak to themselves? If bizarre at first, this is in fact a plain-word description of (part of) what lies behind the mysterious notion of 'precedence' in international law, especially in the absence of any strict rule of stare decisis (for a precise discussion in the context of the ICJ, see Gleider Hernández, *The International Court of Justice and the Judicial Function* (OUP 2014) chapter VI). International courts will rely on their findings in these three advisory opinions in future cases, not as binding precedent strictly speaking, but as guiding, 'authoritative' statements, departure from which warrants justification—or, as the ICJ puts it, 'while [past] decisions are in no way binding on the Court, it will not depart from its settled jurisprudence unless it finds very particular reasons to do so' (*Application of the Convention on the Prevention and Punishment of the Crime of Genocide* (*Croatia v Serbia*) (Preliminary Objections) [2008] ICJ Rep 412, §53). In practice, this 'self-dialogue' typically takes the form of heavy-handed citations. And this is perhaps even more so because these advisory opinions are precisely advisory, so that the courts' findings will constitute facts-detached, *urbi et orbi* interpretations of international law rather than dispute-specific findings. Hence, the primary 'rippling effect' of advisory opinions may well be on the institutions that rendered the opinions themselves.

56 Comp. the concept of 'intermediary legitimation audience' in Magdalena Bexell, Kristina Jönsson & Nora Stappert, 'Whose Legitimacy Beliefs Count? Targeted Audiences in Global Governance Legitimation Processes' (2021) 24 *Journal of International Relations and Development* 483. Comp. also the chain of audiences analyzed in Marc Busch & Krzysztof Pelc, 'Words Matter: How WTO Rulings Handle Controversy' (2019) 63 *International Studies Quarterly* 464.

57 Venzke (n 50) 261. Incidentally, Lani Guinier pointedly noted that being an effective translator of a court's communications is not 'generally valued in the genre of academic writing,' as opposed to 'academic articles [that] are long, turgid, often inaccessible,' not unlike court communications, which Guinier remarked are drafted by 'Justices who themselves were former law professors, or who seek the praise of the "constitutional law mafia," and [which] may be written more to impress than to inform' (Lani Guinier, 'The Supreme Court 2007—Foreword: Demosprudence Through Dissent' (2008) 122 *Harvard Law Review* 4, 130 (writing about the United States Supreme Court).

This phenomenon is reminiscent of what Torres and Guinier termed 'demosprudence' in the context of the United States, ie, an approach to (American) constitutionalism that 'acknowledg[es] the interpretive function of social movements and other lay actors in developing constitutional jurisprudence.'[58] Arguably, the large influence wielded by intermediary audiences on the eventual impact of advisory proceedings constitutes a 'natural barrier' to unfettered judicial activism.[59] To reinforce the transactional dimension of legal storytelling, we could aim to improve further the opportunity for far-reaching participation in the proceedings.[60] This would permit the courts to receive information broadly from a variety of actors in the form of amicus briefs.[61] In this light, the process matters as much as the output.[62]

5 Storytelling in Other Forms of Court Communications

To study fully storytelling in climate change advisory proceedings, the legal community must forego its habitual focus on 'official' texts—judgments, opinions, orders—and pay equal attention to 'unofficial' documents. Indeed, there seems to be no good reason to look only at the text of the opinions and exclude

58 Gerald Torres & Lani Guinier, 'The Constitutional Imaginary: Just Stories About We the People' (2012) Cornell Law Faculty Publications 1055. See also: Guinier (n 57); Lani Guinier, 'Courting the People: Demosprudence and the Law/Politics Divide', *Essays in Honor of Justice Ruth Bader Ginsburg* (Harvard University Press 2013); Lani Guinier & Gerald Torres, 'Changing the Wind: Notes Toward a Demosprudence of Law and Social Movements' (2014) 123 *Yale Law Journal* 2740.

59 Mayr & Mayr-Singer (n 18) 448.

60 In this context, Daniel Bodansky rightly notes that 'the fact that a majority of the UN General Assembly is needed to request an advisory opinion provides ICJ advisory opinions with a certain degree of process-based legitimacy (arguably dependent in part on the reasons why governments support the request)' (Bodansky (n 29) 7). As a case in point, see the ICJ's recent decision to allow the International Union for Conservation of Nature, an international organization whose membership includes non-state members, to participate in the proceedings pending before it: ICJ, Press Release No 2023/39, 14 June 2023.

61 Oellers-Frahm (n 27) 91–92; Sands (n 31) 26. The obvious danger is another form of cacophony, this time among numerous storytellers. Comp., in the context of international criminal trials, Neha Jain, 'Radical Dissents in International Criminal Trials' (2017) 28 *EJIL* 1163, 1183.

62 Comp., *mutadis mutandis*, Thomas Stoddard's claim that 'the Civil Rights Act of 1964 has had such a powerful cultural impact not just because of what it said, but also because of how it came into being' (Stoddard (n 24) 977).

other forms of communications arising out of these proceedings, such as press releases, annual reports, or speeches.

The role of the media was briefly touched upon above, when discussing the translating responsibility of intermediary audiences of international adjudication. Press releases published by the courts themselves evidently participate in this translation exercise. Most of us, in fact, rely primarily on these press releases to keep abreast of international courts' work. It is unrealistic to expect the vast majority of international adjudication's audiences to read full rulings, given their length and complexity. For example, in a recent maritime delimitation dispute between Nicaragua and Colombia, the ICJ's judgment, which amounted to 119 pages, including separate opinions, was conveyed to the public in a mere 1200-word press release.[63] Given this, it is even more surprising that the legal community pays so little attention to this sort of publication by courts—let alone more novel forms of communication such as social media posts.[64] A narrative approach of the kind espoused in this chapter pushes us to recognize the potentially large power associated with forms of communications that are not technically legal in any recognizable way but that are read widely and thus capable of leaving the biggest imprint on courts' audiences.

Among other forms of communications, 'separate opinions' play an ambiguous role. As noted above, I use this term to refer indiscriminately to all types of opinions and declarations appended to a court's ruling by individual judges.[65] Separate opinions have always been a puzzling category of legal writing for commentators. They are not the mere product of adjudication, like the ruling to which they are attached. But they are not *not* the product of adjudication, in the sense that their drafting and existence are inherently related to the collective judicial activity of the court in question—so much so that they can be said to participate in that collective activity.[66] For the purposes of my analysis,

63 *Question of the Delimitation of the Continental Shelf between Nicaragua and Colombia beyond 200 Nautical Miles from the Nicaraguan Coast (Nicaragua v Colombia)* [2023] available at <https://www.icj-cij.org/sites/default/files/case-related/154/154-20230713-jud-01-00-en.pdf>; ibid, Press Release No 2023/39, 13 July 2023.

64 For notable examples to the contrary, see Jillian Dobson and Sofia Stolk, 'The Prosecutor's Important Announcements: The Communication of Moral Authority at the International Criminal Court' (2020) 16 *Law, Culture and the Humanities* 391; Silvia Steininger, 'Creating Loyalty: Communication Practices in the European and Inter-American Human Rights Regimes' (2022) 11 *Global Constitutionalism* 161.

65 Arguably, collective separate opinions carry much more weight (Salmon (n 49) 22).

66 At the ICJ, see Hernández (n 55) ch IV. See also Hemi Mistry, '"The Different Sets of Ideas at the Back of Our Heads": Dissent and Authority at the International Court of Justice' (2019) 32 *Leiden JIL* 293; and Hemi Mistry, 'A Performative Theory of Judicial Dissent' (2023) 86 *Modern Law Review* 729.

too, separate opinions are puzzling. Through them, individual judges can choose to repeat (and thereby reinforce) the stories told by the majority that supported the opinion adopted by the court. They can also echo stories told by participants in the adjudicatory process or present alternative stories, which diverge from the story adopted by the majority, possibly to the point of being subversive and potentially damaging the storytelling function of the court.[67]

Again, the notion of demosprudence can help us make sense of this ambiguity. Lani Guinier emphasized the importance of 'demosprudence through dissent' in the specific context of the United States Supreme Court.[68] She argued that dissents have a unique potential to spur democratic participation from a broader constituency than merely law experts. Dissenters are active but 'not judicially active': 'rather than commanding the public, demosprudential dissenters call the public—through their representatives or their own marching feet—to act in the name of democracy.'[69]

In the climate change context, majority opinions and separate opinions may well work together and positively reinforce international courts' storytelling function (and prestige), even if the stories they tell diverge. In this case, majority and separate opinions would offer something akin to a multi-perspective account of climate change and the international community's relationship to it, rather than a monological story.[70] Building on the concept of demosprudence, Neha Jain similarly emphasized how 'radical dissents' in international criminal law create 'a civic space for contestation that paradoxically shores up the legitimacy of the international criminal trial.'[71] Separate opinions, even when dissenting, may well bolster the court's role as a storyteller.[72] Nevertheless, discordant storytelling 'comes at a price,' which risks being too high for the ICJ, the IACtHR, and ITLOS to tell efficacious stories.[73]

---

67 For a detailed example of different stories being told in majority and dissenting opinions in the United States context, see Greig E Henderson, *Creating Legal Worlds: Story and Style in a Culture of Argument* (University of Toronto Press 2015) 58–73. For a cursory discussion in the context of the ICJ, see Bianchi (n 49) 34.

68 Guinier (n 57).

69 ibid 129.

70 Bianchi (n 49) 34.

71 Jain (n 61) 1163.

72 This is so especially if we concede that most people's engagement with separate opinions begins and ends with the mere fact of the existence of such opinions. In other words, it seems reasonable to assume a substantial share of the court's audience will not actually read and interpret the content of the separate opinions, but merely note their being attached to the majority opinion (Mistry, 'A Performative Theory of Judicial Dissent' (n 66) 731).

73 Jain (n 61) 1183. For instance, all fourteen judges annexed a separate opinion to the ICJ's *Legality of the Threat or Use of Nuclear Weapons* Opinion; on this, see the creative analysis

6 Concluding Remarks

This chapter shed light on the narrative function of international courts in the context of the advisory proceedings relating to climate change that were brought before the ICJ, the IACtHR, and ITLOS. As these and other climate change litigation initiatives unfold, observers may witness decisive instances of legal storytelling spurred by both the topic under consideration—the immense challenges posed by climate change—and the nature of the proceedings—especially their *urbi et orbi* character. Will international courts succeed in threading the needle, overcoming the many legal obstacles they face, and navigating the political minefield ahead of them? The complications are immense, but so is the narrative potential of these proceedings.

Significant is the question of these proceedings' audiences. They are indubitably difficult to assess and study, ranging from formal participants in the adjudicatory process all the way down to private individuals who are exposed to these proceedings. Still, this chapter argued that this is no cause for setting aside the issue of the audience altogether. Instead, the legal community must integrate this factor into the equation. Only by doing so can we hope to reach a clearer picture of the extra-legal effects of adjudication for the climate.

Relatedly, another important aspect of these proceedings highlighted in this chapter is the role of other forms of court communications, such as press releases, informational videos, and annual reports. Legal storytelling is not limited to the text of a court's ruling, and much of the public's exposure to the work of international courts happens through other media, including by means of intermediary speakers such as newspapers and interest-communities. Instrumentalizing alternative forms of courts communications beyond advisory opinions may prove crucial to unleashing the ICJ, the IACtHR, and ITLOS' narrative potential. Here, separate opinions deserve particular attention because of their ambiguity, as they can function both in support of and in contradiction to the majority opinion's storytelling performance.

History teaches us that advisory opinions can backfire.[74] As the proceedings unfold, commentators and participants in the adjudicative process may still be able to tip the scale in favor of compelling legal storytelling. To do so, they must

---

written by Jean-Pierre Queneudec from the perspective of E.T. (!): Jean-Pierre Queneudec, 'ET and the International Court of Justice: Reflections of an Extra-Terrestrial on the Two Advisory Opinions', in Boisson de Chazournes & Sands (n 51).

74 For example, the above-mentioned *Legality of the Threat or Use of Nuclear Weapons* Opinion disappointed its proponents (Bodansky (n 29) 4). Of course, success is in the eye of the beholder. To some, the ICJ's acknowledgment 'that the environment is not an abstraction but represents the living space, the quality of life and the very health of human beings,

first acknowledge that international courts can and do act as storytellers and as arenas for others to tell stories. I hope to have convinced the reader of the need to explore the space for climate change storytelling in international adjudication. Much remains to be discovered but one thing is already clear: we will not be able to do without climate change stories. We might as well try and reflect on their implications—'storytelling,' it bears repeating, 'is never innocent.'[75]

Acknowledgments

My warm thanks to Nicolas Angelet, Eva Baudichau, Anaïs Brucher, Niels Hoek, Yuliia Khyzhniak, and Johanna Ritter for helpful and enjoyable conversations, and to this volume's two editors, Maria Antonia Tigre and Armando Rocha, for insightful revisions and generous editorial support.

including generations unborn' in para. 29 of this 1996 opinion was as such a resounding success and a stepping stone for future advocacy.

75 Brooks (n 2) 16.

CHAPTER 8

Participation in Climate Change Advisory Proceedings: Bridging the Gap between the Judiciary and the International Community

*Miriam Cohen**

Abstract

Climate change is one of humanity's most pressing issues. Unsurprisingly, international and regional courts have been seised in cases concerning the climate crisis. While parallel proceedings have taken place before international and regional courts, the procedural rules in these Courts are distinct. This can have an impact on the possibility of participation of different actors (ie individuals, NGOs, international organisations, States) in these proceedings, and ultimately, in the inclusion of different perspectives in the outcome of the proceedings. The chapter argues that an inclusive approach to international climate litigation is necessary to meet the challenges posed by climate change. It compares and contrasts the different possibilities of participation within the proceedings before the International Court of Justice (ICJ), the International Tribunal for the Law of the Sea (ITLOS) and the Inter-American Court of Human Rights (IACtHR). It aims to enhance the understanding of the complexities of international climate litigation by emphasizing the question of participation and inclusivity in international climate justice. The chapter discusses the drawbacks and advantages of broad participation in different ongoing advisory proceedings. It ultimately argues that broad participation in advisory proceedings can foster a more inclusive international climate justice and bridge the gap between the international community and the judiciary, as well as garner the legitimacy of advisory opinions and their implementation. The chapter commences with a summary of participatory justice theory and how it relates to the context of climate change advisory proceedings. It then delves into the different rules governing participation in various international and regional jurisdictions. Lastly, it examines participation and inclusivity in international climate change proceedings, highlighting both the advantages and limitations, as well as its contribution to the development of an inclusive climate justice.

* *Université de Montréal*, ORCID ID 0000–0002-5481-5702, email: <miriam.cohen@umontreal.ca>.

 | DOI:10.1163/9789004730618_009

Keywords

climate justice – advisory proceedings – participation – inclusivity – international courts – parallel proceedings

1 Introduction

The rise in international climate litigation has been a subject of interest for numerous scholars, who seek to gain a deeper understanding of its implications. In recent years, there has been a significant increase in the number of lawsuits filed on a global scale, particularly related to climate change issues.[1] Notably, Setzer and Higham point out that 'at least 2,341 cases have been captured in the Sabin Center's climate litigation databases [and that] two-thirds of the total cases (1,157) have been filed since 2015, the year of the Paris Agreement.'[2]

One of the main reasons for the increasing number of climate litigation is the lack of States' action to deal with the climate crisis, which has given rise to civil society engagement in seeking more ambitious climate actions through judicial review.[3] The United Nations Environment Programme (UNEP)'s Global Climate Litigation Report[4] reveals that 'litigation has become a key driver of climate change mitigation and adaptation,' a conclusion shared by the Intergovernmental Panel on Climate Change (IPCC) AR 6 Cycle Report.[5]

Between June 2022 and June 2023, 70% of the climate lawsuits filed in the United States (US) had either non-governmental organizations or individuals as plaintiffs, while outside the US the proportion reaches up to nearly 90%.[6] These numbers refer however to domestic litigation. In the international arena,

1 See: Michael Burger & Maria Antonia Tigre, *Global Climate Litigation Report: 2023 Status Review* (Sabin Center for Climate Change Law, Columbia Law School & United Nations Environment Programme, 2023).
2 Joana Setzer & Catherine Higham, *Global Trends in Climate Change Litigation: 2023 Snapshot* (Grantham Research Institute on Climate Change and the Environment 2023) 13.
3 Maria Antonia Tigre & Armando Rocha, 'Competing Perspectives and Dialogue in Climate Change Advisory Opinions' (2023) 117 *AJIL Unbound* 287, 287.
4 Burger & Tigre (n 1) 74.
5 Martina Angela Caretta et al, 'Water', in Pörtner et al (eds), *Climate Change 2022: Impacts, Adaptation and Vulnerability. Contribution of Working Group II to the Sixth Assessment Report of the Intergovernmental Panel on Climate Change* (CUP 2023) 551, 659.
6 Setzer & Higham (n 2) 18.

legal legitimacy to provoke international tribunals to adjudicate remains in the hands of States or other specific legal bodies due to the nature of international law and the framework within which these tribunals operate. Requests for advisory proceedings have nevertheless recently reached three different international judicial bodies – the Inter-American Court of Human Rights (IACtHR), the International Tribunal for the Law of the Sea (ITLOS), and the International Court of Justice (ICJ).

Despite the notorious climate crisis and the incapability of the international community to fully and timely deliver the necessary measures on mitigation and adaptation, the existing contentious jurisdiction for dispute settlement under the United Nations Framework Convention on Climate Change (UNFCCC) and the Paris Agreement exclusive to State-Parties has never been exercised.[7] As a matter of fact, previous mechanisms of compliance have triggered the denunciation of the Kyoto Protocol.[8] Reluctance against enforcement measures does not apply to civil society which has increasingly contributed to the proliferation of climate litigation.[9] These circumstances raise questions on the access of civil society to these advisory proceedings and the role it would be able to play in the development of international law response against the climate crisis.

Technically, advisory opinions have a strictly consultative function of interpretation and clarification regarding the application of a certain treaty, rule, or obligation provided in international law – that means, non-enforceable on States. However, discussions on their binding nature have always existed[10] and persist until the present day, as interpretations are still stretched to grant advisory opinions further effects.[11] Participation of interested parties other than

7 Pierre-Marie Dupuy & Jorge E. Viñuales, *International Environmental Law* (2nd edn, CUP 2018) 196.

8 Compliance Committee. Canada's withdrawal from the Kyoto Protocol and its effects on Canada's reporting obligations under the Protocol. CC/EB/25/2014/2, 20 August 2014.

9 Pierre-Marie Dupuy & Jorge Viñuales, 'The Challenge of "Proliferation": An Anatomy of the Debate', in Romano et al (eds), *The Oxford Handbook of International Adjudication* (Oxford University Press 2013) 135, 153.

10 On this matter: John Bassett Moore, 'Memorandum – The question of advisory opinions, 18 February 1922', in *Acts and Documents concerning the organisation of the Court. N. 2 Preparation of the Rules of Court (January 30th to March 24th 1922)*, Annex 58a, 383.

11 On this matter, see generally Roberto Ago, '"Biding" Advisory Opinions of the International Court of Justice' (1991) 85 *AJIL* 439; Guillaume Bacot, 'Réflexions sur les clauses qui rendent obligatoires les avis consultatifs de la CPJI et de la CIJ' (1980) *Revue Générale de Droit International Public* 1027. *Rights and Guarantees of Children in the Context of Migration and/or Need of International Protection*. Advisory Opinion OC-21/14, Inter-American

States and international organizations in advisory procedures before international courts has long been at the forefront of debates, with discussions dating back to the 1930s at the former Permanent Court of International Justice.[12] With these requests for advisory opinions, an important question is whether participation of States and other non-State actors, such as international organisations or NGOs, can close the gap between the judiciary and the international community.

Nevertheless, as parallel proceedings relating to diverse aspects of climate change advance before three international and regional courts, it is evident that the rules governing these courts are inherently distinct, and each court may have a unique contribution in clarifying legal questions related to climate change. In this process of elucidating some of the complex issues put to them, the arguments before the courts bear a crucial role. Indeed, a topic such as procedural distinctions can significantly impact the possibility of various actors, including individuals, NGOs, international organizations, and States, to participate in these proceedings. As a result, this procedural divergence can influence the inclusion of diverse perspectives in the outcomes of these legal processes.

This chapter aims to enhance the understanding of the complexities of international climate litigation by emphasizing the question of participation

---

Court of Human Rights Series A No 14 (19 August 2014), § 28: '*While recalling that the advisory function constitutes "a service that the Court is able to provide to all the members of the inter-American system, in order to contribute to compliance with their international commitments" in the area of human rights, the Court considers it critically important to establish with greater precision the rights and guarantees of children in the context of migration—in other words, child migrants and/or in need of international protection, as well as children of migrants. This will lead to the determination of the specific principles and obligations that States must comply with in relation to the human rights of children in order to adopt comprehensive protection measures that are sufficient and pertinent in each situation.*'

12 In the *Case of Consistency of Certain Danzig Legislative Decrees with the Constitution of the Free City*, the Permanent Court of International Justice had to decide whether to conceive access to minority parties of the Danzig Senate, petitioners of the advisory opinion that had reached the Court. Following the rules of the Court, the petitioners could submit written contributions but were later prevented from being heard, a right that was fully granted to the Senate (the challenged party) on the other hand. *Consistency of Certain Danzig Legislative Decrees with the Constitution of the Free City* (Advisory Opinion) PCIJ Rep Series A/B No 65. Further information: Kenneth Keith. 'Advisory Proceedings: International Court of Justice (ICJ)', in *Max Planck Encyclopedia of International Law*, §14, available at: <https://opil.ouplaw.com/display/10.1093/law-mpeipro/e3375.013.3375/law-mpeipro-e3375#law-mpeipro-e3375-bibItem-111> last accessed 10 December 2023.

and inclusivity in international climate justice proceedings. It discusses the drawbacks and advantages of broad participation in advisory proceedings. It argues that participation in advisory proceedings can foster a more inclusive international climate justice and bridge the gap between the broader international community and the judiciary, as well as garner the sociological legitimacy of advisory opinions and their implementation. The chapter starts with a summary of participatory justice theory and how it relates to the context of climate change advisory proceedings (Section 2). It then delves into the different rules governing participation in various international and regional jurisdictions (Section 3). Lastly, the chapter examines participation and inclusivity in international climate change proceedings, highlighting both the advantages and limitations, and its contribution to closing the gap between the judiciary and the international community, through the development of a more inclusive climate justice (Section 4).

2 Participatory Justice Theories and the Challenges of Climate Change Litigation

Understanding participatory justice under international law, and its role in climate justice initiatives, assists in theorising inclusivity and participation in international climate change proceedings. As such, this section discusses participatory justice under international law; it then turns to the discussion of participation in climate change initiatives.

2.1 *Participatory Justice under International Law*

Participatory justice can take various forms, including a right of access to justice, enabling individuals to assert their rights protected by international, transnational, or regional human rights instruments, notably in relation to harm suffered or envisaged affecting their health and/or their environment.[13]

13 Jonas Ebbesson, 'Access to justice in environmental matters in international law: why and how?', in Bétaille (ed), *Le droit d'accès à la justice en matière d'environnement* (Presses de l'Université Toulouse Capitole, 2016) 63.

With regard to the environment,[14] Principle 10 of the 1992 Rio Declaration on Environment and Development[15] (Rio Declaration) establishes the relationship between the three parameters of participatory justice in international law – (1) public participation in decision-making, (2) access to information, and (3) access to justice[16] – which was subsequently confirmed by the 1998 Aarhus Convention on Access to Information, Public Participation in Decision-making and Access to Justice in Environmental Matters.[17]

This right to participatory environmental justice can also be inferred from other international instruments – eg the 2011 Draft Articles on the Prevention of Transboundary Harm,[18] the 2002 Plan of Implementation of the World Summit on Sustainable Development,[19] the 2010 UNEP Guidelines for the Development of National Legislation on Access to Information, Public Participation and Access to Justice in Environmental Matters,[20] and the 2012 'Rio+20' Declaration.[21]

Several regional systems protect this right directly or indirectly, notably through the following binding instruments: European Convention on Human

---

14 For a detailed analysis of the development of the right to public participation in international environmental law, see: Jona Razzaque, 'Information, Public Participation and Access to Justice in Environmental Matters', in Techera et al (eds), *Routledge Handbook of International Environmental Law* (Routledge 2020) 58.

15 Rio Declaration on Environment and Development, Principle 10; Report of the United Nations Conference on Environment and Development (June 3–14, 1982), UN Doc. A/CCONF. 151/26, Vol II, Annex I.

16 For an overview of the development and practice of the rights of access to information, public participation in decision-making and access to justice in environmental matters, since their codification as non-binding principles in Principle X of the Rio Declaration in 2017, see: European Environmental Law Forum. Conference (4th: 2016: Wrocław, Poland), and Uniwersytet Wrocławski. Jerzy & Bar (eds), *Procedural Environmental Rights: Principle X in Theory and Practice*, vol 4 (Intersentia 2017).

17 1998 Aarhus Convention on Access to Information, Public Participation in Decision-making and Access to Justice in Environmental Matters, Economic Commission for Europe Resolution of 21 April 1998, UN Doc ECE/CEP/43 (adopted 25 June 1998, entered into force 30 October 2001) 2161 UNTS 447.

18 'Draft Articles on Prevention of Transboundary Harm from Hazardous Activities', adopted by the International Law Commission at its 53rd session, UN Doc A/RES/56/10 (2001).

19 Plan of Implementation of the World Summit on Sustainable Development; Report of the World Summit on Sustainable Development (August 26-September 4, 2002), A/CONF.199/20, Annex.

20 UNEP Guidelines for the development of national legislation on access to information, public participation and access to justice in environmental matters (Bali), adopted by the Governing Council of the United Nations Environment Programme, decision SS.XI/5, part A of February 26, 2010.

21 UNGA Res 66/228 (11 September 2012) UN Doc A/RES/66/288 ('The Future We Want').

Rights (ECHR),[22] the American Convention on Human Rights (ACHR),[23] the Regional Agreement on Access to Information, Public Participation and Justice in Environmental Matters in Latin America and the Caribbean (the Escazú agreement),[24] the Nordic Environmental Convention,[25] the African Charter on Human and Peoples' Rights (AfCHPR),[26] the North American Agreement on Environmental Cooperation, and the African Convention on the Conservation of Nature and Natural Resources,[27] as well as non-binding instruments such as the 1977 OECD Recommendation on Equal Access and Non-Discrimination in Transboundary Pollution.[28]

These international and regional instruments may provide for different types of participatory justice, depending on the parameters adopted and the procedures chosen, enabling the public to access a national court (to bring an action) or an international court (communication or request for examination or investigation), depending on the scope of application in the case in question.

It should also be noted that, despite differing interpretations of participatory justice within international and regional tribunals and other United Nations (UN) treaty monitoring bodies, a review of case law suggests that public participation (as a human right) is consolidating in international law, since it enables the exercise of its other parameters, namely the rights of access to information and to justice.[29]

---

22 Convention for the Protection of Human Rights and Fundamental Freedoms (adopted 4 November 1950, entered into force 3 September 1953) 213 UNTS 221.

23 American Convention on Human Rights (adopted 22 November 1969, entered into force 18 July 1978) OAS Treaty Series No 36.

24 Regional Agreement on Access to Information, Public Participation and Justice in Environmental Matters in Latin America and the Caribbean (adopted on 4 March 2018, entered into force 22 April 2021) 3388 *UNTS*.

25 Nordic Convention on the Protection of the Environment (adopted 19 February 1974, entered into force 5 October 1976) 1092 UNTS 279.

26 African Charter on Human and Peoples' Rights (adopted 27 June 1981, entered into force 21 October 1982) 1520 *UNTS* 217.

27 African Convention on the Conservation of Nature and Natural Resources (adopted 15 September 1968, entered into force 16 June 1969) 1001 UNTS 4.

28 OECD Recommendation for an Equal Access and Non-Discrimination Regime for Transboundary Pollution (C77/) 28 (Final) (1977) 16 ILM (1977) 977.

29 Leslie-Anne Duvic-Paoli, 'The Status of the Right to Public Participation in International Environmental Law: An Analysis of the Jurisprudence' (2012) 23 *Yearbook of International Environmental Law* 80.

In terms of human rights, since the Optional Protocol to the International Covenant on Economic, Social and Cultural Rights[30] came into force, many have seen it as international recognition of participatory justice, whereby States parties would be called upon to 'renewed attention to adjudicative or quasi-adjudicative review and remedial methods for protecting social rights.'[31] In addition to ensuring the 'adjudication' of economic, social and cultural rights – as a result of the right of access to an individual remedy in the event of potential deprivation of a right, or a State violation of a treaty obligation to protect a right – many believe that such public participation in decision-making on social rights can add value, at both national and international level, given the 'dynamic interaction between the participatory and substantive dimensions of social rights,' whose values of dignity, free choice (freedom and autonomy) and equality are the foundation of a rule of law based on a model of democratic justice.[32]

2.2 *Public Participation in Climate Change Initiatives*

Public participation in environmental process is an important part of environmental and climate change initiatives.[33] As Tigre and Rocha argue, '[t]he dramatic increase in climate litigation over the past decade is a manifestation of climate action democratization in response to the inadequate response from governments and corporations to the climate crisis.'[34] Addressing the complex issue of climate change on a global sphere requires harmonised and inclusive efforts, engaging diverse stakeholders from various sectors. Participatory justice theory, which is characterised by principles of inclusivity, deliberation, and fairness, offers a theoretical framework that can enhance the quality and impact of climate change international proceedings.

Participatory justice theory emphasizes the importance of involving affected parties in decision-making processes that directly impact them. It relies on the idea that all those affected by a conflict should be engaged in finding a

30 Optional Protocol to the International Covenant on Economic, Social and Cultural Rights, UN General Assembly Resolution No A/RES/63/117, 10 December 2008, UN Doc A/63/435. (adopted 10 December 2008, entered into force 5 May 2013) 2922 UNTS 29.

31 Sandra Liebenberg, 'Participatory Justice in Social Rights Adjudication' (2018) 18 *Human Rights Law Review* 623.

32 ibid. See also Nicholas McMurry & Siobhan O'Sullivan, 'A Human Rights-Based Approach to Participation' (2022) 16 *Studies in Social Justice* 554.

33 'Public Participation under Action for Climate Empowerment', United Nations Climate Change, available at: https://unfccc.int/topics/education-and-outreach/workstreams/public-participation.

34 Tigre & Rocha (n 3) 287.

resolution.[35] Drawing on democratic principles, this theory posits that inclusive participation leads to more legitimate and robust outcomes. In the context of climate change, participatory justice theory advocates for the active involvement of communities, Indigenous groups, NGOs, and other stakeholders in shaping policies, strategies, and adaptation/mitigation measures. A similar principle is that of participatory democracy to address climate change.[36]

As will be discussed below, legitimacy is a critical factor in the success of climate change proceedings. By incorporating participatory justice principles, decision-making processes gain credibility and acceptance. It may be posited that participatory approaches in climate change justice initiative may foster increased legitimacy and result in more effective implementation and long-term adherence. While participatory justice often refers to alternative dispute resolution mechanisms, such as arbitration, conciliation, and mediation, it is insightful to dwell on participation in advisory proceedings through the lens of the principles of participatory justice.

While participatory justice theory offers a promising framework for climate change advisory proceedings, challenges and considerations must be addressed. Issues such as power imbalances, representation, and the need for capacity-building are some of the limitations and critiques associated with participatory approaches in the context of climate change.

It is important to emphasise the vital role of participatory justice theory in enhancing the legitimacy and effectiveness of climate change proceedings. Some of the goals of participatory justice calls for a re-evaluation of current decision-making processes and advocates for the adoption of inclusive approaches that empower communities and stakeholders in the global pursuit of climate justice. As the international community continues to grapple with the impacts of climate change, participatory justice theory emerges as a valuable tool for creating more resilient and equitable solutions.

35 Law Commission of Canada, 'Towards Participatory Justice: A Focus on People and Relationships', 2000, available at: https://dalspace.library.dal.ca/bitstream/handle/10222/10291/Participatory%20Justice%20Report%20Pamphlet%20EN.pdf?sequence=1&isAllowed=y.

36 https://www.ucl.ac.uk/global-governance/research/let-people-decide-participatory-democracy-answer-climate-crisis.

3 Inclusivity in International Advisory Proceedings: the Spectrum of Participatory Possibilities

One interesting feature of the parallel international climate change advisory proceedings is the diverging modes of participation allowed in each court and tribunal. In fact, the rules on participation differ depending on the contentious or advisory nature of the proceedings, as well as among courts and tribunals. As discussed below, the IACtHR stands on one side of the spectrum, whose rules allow for broad inclusivity, whereas the ICJ limits participation to States and some international organisations.

Beyond what is allowed by the constitutive treaty of each international or regional institution, striking a balance between allowing broader participation and ensuring procedural fairness and efficiency poses an interesting conundrum. While the IACtHR has experience in dealing with a high number of participation in written and oral submissions in advisory proceedings particularly, the ICJ and the ITLOS have recently seen broader participation compared with their past experience, mostly by States.[37] The following sections describe the legal framework for participation in different international and regional courts and tribunals, with a view to comparing and contrasting the spectrum of participatory possibilities, and how participation in each institution may contribute to bridging the gap between the judiciary and the international community. The focus of the discussion of this framework is on the participation before the three courts that have been seized recently with requests for advisory opinions on climate change: the ICJ, the ITLOS, and the IACtHR.

3.1 *International Court of Justice (ICJ)*

The participation of non-State actors in advisory proceedings before the ICJ is limited to international organizations. Only the UN General Assembly (UNGA), the Security Council, and organs of the UN and specialized agencies that are authorized by the UNGA can request advisory opinions from the ICJ.[38] The Registrar must invite international organizations that are likely to furnish relevant information on the question to submit written statements or to participate in a public hearing.[39] Invited international organizations can also comment on the

---

37 *Allegations of Genocide under the Convention on the Prevention and Punishment of the Crime of Genocide* (*Ukraine v Russian Federation; 32 States intervening*) (Order of 5 June 2023); see also ibid, CR 2023/16.

38 Charter of the United Nations (adopted 26 June 1945, entered into force 24 October 1945) 892 *UNTS* 119, art. 96 (UN Charter), Statute of the International Court of Justice (adopted 26 June 1945, entered into force 24 October 1945) 892 *UNTS* 119, art 65(1) (ICJ Statute).

39 ICJ Statute, art 66(2).

statements made by other parties.[40] Part IV of the Rules of Court on advisory proceedings does not provide further provisions that could allow the participation of non-State actors.[41]

Even though international NGOs are not formally invited to submit written or oral statements in advisory proceedings of the ICJ, they may submit briefs on their own initiative. Practice Direction XII, adopted in 2004, provided formal rules on how to treat such briefs.[42] According to the Practice Direction, these documents are not to be considered as part of the case file, but they can be referred to by States and intergovernmental organizations in the same manner as publications in the public domain.

This willingness by the ICJ to place these briefs 'in a designated location in the Peace Palace', and to inform the parties of their content signals that NGOs can provide relevant information. Having them automatically being part of the public domain also means that the Court can use them as a source of information for their judgments, even if the interested parties do not refer to these briefs themselves.[43]

More recently, as part of the ICJ proceedings on the Obligations of States in respect of Climate Change, the Court authorized for example the International Union for Conservation of Nature and Natural Resources (IUCN) to participate in the proceedings.[44] This was upon IUCN's request per Article 66 of the ICJ Statute, which allows states and international organizations considered likely to be able to furnish information on the question to provide a written or oral statement.[45] What is interesting about allowing IUCN's participation in the proceedings is that IUCN is not just a territorial entity or a 'public international organization' only made up of States. It is actually a hybrid organization that includes States and subnational governments, government agencies, national and international NGOs, and Indigenous people organizations.[46] IUCN was invited to participate in all three advisory proceedings held by the ITLOS,[47]

40 ICJ Statute, art 66(4).

41 Rules of Court of the International Court of Justice (adopted 14 April 1978) ICJ Rep 1983, 131 (ICJ Rules of the Court).

42 Practice Direction No XII, promulgated on 30 July 2004, available at <https://www.icj-cij.org/practice-directions>.

43 Lance Bartholomeusz, 'The *Amicus Curiae* before International Courts and Tribunals' (2005) 5 *Non-State Actors & Int'l Law* 209.

44 International Court of Justice, Press Release No 2023/29, released on June 14 2023.

45 ICJ Statute, art 66.

46 International Union for the Conservation of Nature and Natural Resources, *Members directory*. Members directory | IUCN.

47 See the three advisory proceedings: https://www.itlos.org/en/main/cases/advisory-proceedings/.

which might have been a precedent that influenced the ICJ's decision to invite them as well. At the time of writing, prior to the delivery of the said advisory opinion, 'the highest number of written statements ever … in advisory proceedings before the Court' have been filed: 91 in total – 79 submitted by States (14 European, 13 African, 31 Asia/Pacific region, and 21 from the Americas), and 12 submitted by international organizations; 96 States and 11 international organisations presented oral statements.[48] This unprecedented participation can signal a positive development to bridge the gap between the judiciary and the international community.

3.2 *International Tribunal for the Law of the Sea* (ITLOS)

The procedures relating to the advisory functions of the Seabed Disputes Chamber (SDC) are the same as those for the Tribunal en banc.[49] Advisory opinions are then only open to entities other than States Parties when specifically provided for in the United Nations Convention on the Law of the Sea (UNCLOS)[50] or when an international agreement provides for the request of an advisory opinion.[51]

However, entities other than States Parties can be invited by the Chamber and the Tribunal to intervene throughout the proceedings. International organizations can be identified by the SDC or ITLOS if they are likely to provide relevant information on the question.[52] As such, international organizations have been invited to participate in all three advisory proceedings accepted by the ITLOS. For the 2011 advisory opinion on the *Responsibilities and Obligations of States with respect to Activities in the Area*, the Chamber received written statements from the Interoceanmetal Joint Organization, the IUCN, the International Seabed Authority, and the United Nations Environment Programme (UNEP).[53] The SDC also received a joint statement from Greenpeace International and the World Wildelife Fund for Nature, accompanied by a petition that requested their participation in the advisory proceedings as *amici curiae*.[54]

---

48 International Court of Justice, Press Release No 2024/31, released on 12 April 2024 and Press Release No 2024/81, released on 13 December 2024.

49 United Nations Convention on the Law of the Sea (adopted 10 December 1982, entered into force 16 November 1994) 1833 UNTS 3 UNCLOS, Annex VI (Statute of the International Tribunal for the Law of the Sea), art 40(2) (ITLOS Statute).

50 UNCLOS, art 291(2).

51 ITLOS Statute, art 21; Rules of the International Tribunal for the Law of the Sea, adopted on 1 October 1, 1997, ITLOS/8/Rev.1, art 138(1) (ITLOS Rules).

52 ITLOS Rules, art 133(2).

53 *Responsibilities and Obligations of States Sponsoring Persons and Entities with Respect to Activities in the Area* (*Request for Advisory Opinion Submitted to the Seabed Disputes Chamber* (Advisory Opinion, 1 February 2011) ITLOS Case No 17, §§11 & 16.

54 ibid §13.

Although the States Parties, the Authority, and the intergovernmental organizations that are parties to the case were informed of the statement, it has not been included in the case file, since the two entities are not intergovernmental organizations that were invited by the SDC according to Article 133(2) of the Rules of the ITLOS. The SDC also rejected the request for participation as *amici curiae*.[55]

For the 2015 Request for an Advisory Opinion submitted by the Sub-Regional Fisheries Commission (SRFC) (Case No 21), the Tribunal received written statements from the Forum Fisheries Agency, the International Union for Conservation of Nature and Natural Resources, the Caribbean Regional Fisheries Mechanism, the UN, the Sub-Regional Fisheries Commission, the Food and Agriculture Organisation of the UN, and the Central American Fisheries and Aquaculture Organization.[56] World Wildlife Fund (WWF) International has also submitted a written statement and a request for participation as *amicus curiae*, which was rejected.[57]

On 12 December 2022, the ITLOS received a request for an Advisory Opinion submitted by the Commission of Small Island States on Climate Change and International Law (Case No 31).[58] Through Order No 2022/4, the President of ITLOS listed the intergovernmental organizations that could provide relevant information on the questions and invited them to submit a written statement, namely the UN, UNEP, the UNFCCC Secretariat, the Food and Agriculture Organization of the United Nations, the Intergovernmental Oceanographic Commission of UNESCO, the International Maritime Organization, the IUCN, and the World Meteorological Organization.[59]

As Dolidze puts it, the participation of the IUCN in the Responsibilities and Obligations of Sponsoring States' proceedings (2011) created a precedent for the participation of NGOs in advisory proceedings.[60] The author argues that this specific case plays an important role in the participation of NGOs as *amici curiae* in advisory proceedings before international courts, that such a participation allows their contribution in international lawmaking, and that

55 ibid §14.

56 *Request for an Advisory Opinion submitted by the Sub-Regional Fisheries Commission (SRFC)* (Advisory Opinion, 2 April 2015) ITLOS Case No 15, §17.

57 ibid §23.

58 *Request for Advisory Opinion submitted by the Commission of Small Island States on Climate Change and International Law*, Order No 2022/4 (16 December 2022) available at <https://www.itlos.org/fileadmin/itlos/documents/cases/31/C31_Order_2022-4_16.12.2022_01.pdf>.

59 ibid, annex.

60 Anna Dolidze, 'Advisory Opinion on Responsibility and Liability for International Seabed Mining (ITLOS Case No. 17) and the Future of NGO Participation in the International Legal Process' (2013) 19 *ILSA Journal of Int'l & Comp Law* 379, 381.

participation is particularly relevant in environmental law.[61] In addition, even though ITLOS' Rules of Procedure constrained them to reject NGO *amicus* submissions, they disseminated the WWF and Greenpeace brief among the Parties and displayed it on their website. Dolidze's observation seems to have been reiterated by the ICJ's recent decision to also invite IUCN to their advisory proceeding on the obligations of States regarding climate change.[62]

While these organisations were listed as authorised to present written statements, there were numerous other statements that were submitted by individuals and organisations that were not part of the case file but were nevertheless available on the Court website. The large formal participation in the written proceedings of States (34 in total) and international organisations (9 in total) and the submission of written observations that are publicly available (10 in total, albeit not part of the case file) points to a broad participation in the proceedings, and sheds some light on the links between the international community and the judiciary.

3.3 *Inter-American Court of Human Rights (IACtHR)*

At the IACtHR 'interested parties' can be invited or authorized by the Presidency to submit written opinions on the question.[63] Any person or institution, such as international organizations, NGOs, and academics, can act as *amicus curiae* by submitting a brief to the Tribunal.[64]

In most of the advisory opinions published by the IACtHR, public hearings[65] were held and institutions or individuals participated as *amicus curiae*. For example, in the 2017 advisory opinion on the environment and human rights, interested parties were invited to submit their views according to Article 73(3) of the Rules of Procedure.[66] Written observations were submitted by twenty-four State agencies, national and international associations, NGOs and academic institutions, and nineteen members of the civil society.[67] The President of the Court also called for a public hearing that was held on March 22,

---

61 ibid 382.

62 International Court of Justice, *Press Release No 2023/29* released on June 14, 2023.

63 Rules of Procedure of the Inter-American Court of Human Rights, art 73(3) (IACtHR Rules of Procedure).

64 IACtHR Rules of Procedure, art 44(1).

65 IACtHR Rules of Procedure, art 73(4).

66 *The Environment and Human Rights (State Obligations in Relation to the Environment in the Context of the Protection and Guarantee of the Rights to Life and to Personal Integrity—Interpretation and Scope of Articles 4(1) and 5(1) of the American Convention on Human Rights)* Advisory Opinion OC-23/17, Inter-American Court of Human Rights Series A No 23 (15 November 2017) §5 (Advisory Opinion OC-23/17).

67 ibid §6.

2017, and invited interested parties to present oral comments on the request.[68] The Court ended up examining and considering fifty-two interventions from many different actors.[69] Such a participation of non-State actors in advisory proceedings is a common phenomenon before the IACtHR as it can also be observed in the other advisory opinions published by the Court.

The IACtHR approached environmental procedural rights in its advisory opinion OC-23/17. The Court asserted the right to access to justice as a peremptory norm of international law which 'permits the individual to ensure that environmental standards are enforced and provides a means of redressing any human rights violations that may result from failure to comply with environmental standards and includes remedies and reparation.'[70] In the case of *Baraona Bray v Chile*,[71] the IACtHR later had the opportunity to further develop the interrelations and connections between the exercise of procedural environmental rights with the protection of the environment and the full enjoyment of human rights against the effects of climate change, in synergy with the rationales expressed in the advisory opinion OC-23/17.[72]

Concerning the climate change advisory opinion, which is yet to be delivered at the time of writing, the Court received a record number of 265 written observations from diverse entities. It held 7 days of public hearings, with over 150 participants (3 days in Barbados and 4 days in Brazil). This large and diverse participation (eg, ranging from States, to non-governmental organisations, and individuals) points to a strong connection between the international community and the judiciary, which will be able to benefit from the arguments in the multiple submissions.

4 Participation in International Climate Justice as Access to International Justice: How the Climate Change Advisory Proceedings are Changing the International Adjudication Landscape

The 2017 advisory opinion of the IACtHR on the environment and human rights showcased the relevance of advisory functions for environmental justice. The IACtHR has presented a strong opinion on State responsibility as it

68 ibid §§8–9.

69 ibid §11.

70 ibid §234.

71 *Case of Baraona Bray v Chile* (Preliminary Objections, Merits, Reparations and Costs). Inter-American Court of Human Rights Series C No 481 (24 November 2022) §§100, 114.

72 Gonzalo Aguilar Cavallo, 'La emergencia climática y los derechos humanos' (2023) 27 *Revista de Derecho* 1, 5.

argued that States can have an extraterritorial jurisdiction under certain circumstances and therefore be responsible for human rights violations outside their borders. The Court also interpreted Article 26 of the ACHR as including the protection of a standalone right to a healthy environment.[73] This suggests that advisory opinions can have a strong impact on climate justice. The relevance of advisory opinions, the urgency of acting against climate change, and intergenerational consequences of climate change support a growing access to the advisory functions for climate justice.[74]

However, as stated above, the ICJ advisory proceedings are limited when it comes to non-State actors. The ICJ presents a certain openness to non-state actors by allowing the participation of territorial entities that are involved in the question asked to the court. Furthermore, as discussed, the ICJ adopted Practice Direction XII in 2004, which prevents briefs submitted by *amici curiae* to be considered as part of the case file but allows parties to use these briefs in their written or oral statements, since they are publications in the public domain.[75] However, this openness is not sufficient when it comes to climate justice as a broader non-state actor participation would more broadly represent the interests of the international community on the question. To include a larger scope of non-State actors in advisory opinions of the ICJ, Yael Ronen suggests a non-restrictive interpretation of Article 66 of the Statute of the ICJ.[76]

4.1 *Fostering Access to Justice and Inclusion? Advantages of Broader Participation and Inclusivity in International Climate Change Proceedings*

4.1.1 Quality of Information

The traditional role of *amicus curiae* is to act as a 'friend of the court', providing relevant information when the judges lack knowledge on specific subjects.[77] NGOs can provide a specialist expertise that can prove helpful when the matter

73 See on this point, Angeliki Papantoniou, 'Advisory Opinion on the Environment and Human Rights' (2018) 112 *AJIL* 460.

74 Anxhela Mile, 'Emerging Legal Doctrines in Climate Change Law—Seeking an Advisory Opinion from the International Court of Justice' (2021) 56 *Texas Int'l Law Journal* 59.

75 Armando Rocha, '*Amicus Curiae* before the International Tribunal for the Law of the Sea: The Prospect of an Advisory Opinion on Climate Change and the Law of the Sea' (2022) 6 *Católica Law Review* 87, 99.

76 Yael Ronen, 'Participation of Non-State Actors in ICJ Proceedings' (2012) 11 *The Law & Practice of Int'l Courts & Tribunals* 77, 96.

77 Laura Van den Eynde, 'An Empirical Look at the Amicus Curiae Practice of Human Rights NGOs before the European Court of Human Rights,' (2013) 31(3) *Netherlands Quarterly of Human Rights* 271, 273.

at stake is not familiar to judges. This is particularly important in cases that touch on polarized subjects, such as climate science, because it would provide in certain cases impartial scientific knowledge.[78] In that sense, *amicus curiae* participation, especially from NGOs and academic institutions, helps boost the democratic legitimacy of an advisory opinion.

In some other cases, non-state actors can provide factual information to the court. For example, as part of the ICJ proceedings in the case of the *Aerial Incident of 3 July 1988*, the International Civil Aviation Organization (ICAO) provided factual information to the ICJ about their investigation on the matter and applicable aeronautic legislation.[79]

4.1.2 Bypassing Political Constraints?

Amici curiae can also help to bypass political or diplomatic constraints that would restrain a State that is party to the proceedings from representing the interests of some of its constituents, or from expressing arguments that could be used against it in the future.[80] In that sense, they help represent the 'public interest' in cases where it is not directly presented by one of the parties, thus ensuring the demonstration of a diversity of opinions and allowing for better decision-making by the courts.[81]

4.1.3 Compliance with International Regulations

NGO participation as *amici curiae* can act as a reminder for States that there are watchdogs continuously examining their conduct and verifying that they are complying with their legal obligations.[82] In the case of human rights violations, where NGOs often act as information gatherers and fact-checkers, they are even more essential to the courts because they provide information directly from the 'crime scene', which the State would not have necessarily provided.

NGOs have consistently contributed to the development of international law, particularly in areas like human rights.[83] As climate change impacts and human rights enjoyment are interrelated, the importance of NGOs in the current international climate regime is crucial. Notably, NGOs have adopted

78 Rocha (n 75) 103.

79 ICJ, Observations of the International Civil Aviation Organization, 4 December 1992.

80 Rocha (n 75) 102.

81 Frans Viljoen & Adem Kassie Abebe, '*Amicus Curiae* Participation Before Regional Human Rights Bodies in Africa' (2014) 58 *Journal of African Law* 22, 25.

82 Bartholomeusz (n 43).

83 Steve Charnovitz, 'Nongovernmental Organizations and International Law' (2006) 100 *AJIL* 348, 360.

naming and shaming strategies to denounce the lack of ambitious climate engagements by State-Parties.[84] This role can be exercised either through means of the review mechanisms inherent to the Paris Agreement, such as the nationally determined contributions and the global stock take,[85] or through climate litigation.[86]

In that sense, these 'watchdogs' are particularly important regarding climate change-related human rights violations, because they often occur in lightly populated or remote regions out of the government's monitoring area. NGOs can provide information from a larger area and a more diverse audience than the centralized government's monitoring mechanisms. These violations can also happen directly because of government negligence, in which case NGOs, as impartial *amici curiae*, can provide more trustworthy information than the government would otherwise provide.

4.2 *Drawbacks and Challenges Related to Broader Participation: Where to Draw the Line?*

4.2.1 Overwhelming the Courts and the Selection Problem

The biggest risk identified by some scholars who studied inclusivity in advisory proceedings is the risk of having too many entities applying to be *amici curiae.*[87] Since there are a huge number of NGOs around the world that could provide relevant information to proceedings touching global subjects, like climate change, there is a real threat of overloading international courts with too much information. This would put under threat the courts' capacity to properly read, address, and classify all this information; and since it may be impossible to have each and every NGO who applies represented before courts, it brings the question of how to determine the criteria that should be used to pick which of the *amici* should be selected by courts. It would also be important for courts to ensure that the selected *amici curiae* represent all the different facets of the case (ie, social, economic, cultural or political impacts).[88] Transforming all these factors into a consensus pick could prove to be quite challenging. It is

---

84 Astrid Dannenberg et al, 'Naming and Shaming as a Strategy for Enforcing the Paris Agreement: The Role of Political Institutions and Public Concern' (2023) 40 *PNAS*.

85 Robert Falkner, 'The Paris Agreement and the new logic of international climate politics' (2023) 92 *International Affairs* 1107, 1119.

86 Sharon Yadin, *Fighting Climate Change Through Shaming* (CUP 2023) 10.

87 Rocha (n 75) 104.

88 ibid 104.

therefore relevant for courts to have clearer rules around *amici curiae* to ensure clarity, uniformity, and equality in the selection process.[89]

4.2.2 Transparency Arguments

If the goal of seeking for more inclusivity in *amici curiae* participation in proceedings is in part to improve the public's trust in international courts, there would be a need for more transparency regarding which groups asked to provide briefs, which groups provided one and how they were selected.[90] Nowadays, courts (especially the ICJ) do not always mention when and why their decisions are influenced by an *amicus* brief, while it might in fact provide better transparency and an improved legitimacy for their role.[91] Courts would also have to address the issue of the accessibility of the case's information to potential *amici*, especially regarding the object and facts of the dispute or submission deadlines, which are not always made available online.[92]

4.2.3 Neutrality or Partisanship?

It is not clear if *amici curiae* should be neutral or if they should be advocates of their position. Since *amici curiae* have a lot of different roles in court, it is sometimes hard to determine if they should always behave as independent 'friends of the court', or if they should sometimes be allowed to advocate for one party more than the other. For example, if a human right NGO is invited as *amicus curiae* to an ECtHR proceeding, they may have an interest in defending the victims more than the defendant. Opposingly, an *amicus* who is invited to provide independent facts to the ICJ will be expected to be neutral and impartial.[93] Civil society 'refers to the associations of citizens (outside their families, friends and businesses) entered into voluntarily to advance their interests, ideas and ideologies,'[94] duly acknowledged as having something to contribute to the development of international law, notably concerning environmental issues.[95] It should therefore provide more latitude to *amici curiae* to express their views as they see fit.

89 Luigi Crema, 'Testing *Amici Curiae* in International Law: Rules and Practice' (2012) 22 *Italian Yearbook of Int'l Law* 91.

90 ibid.

91 Bartholomeusz (n 43).

92 Crema (n 89).

93 Bartholomeusz (n 43) 280.

94 UNGA. Fifty-eighth session. Panel of Eminent Persons on United Nations – Civil Society Relations. New York, 11 June 2004, available at <https://digitallibrary.un.org/record/523950/files/A_58_817-EN.pdf>, last accessed on 10 March 2021).

95 Paulo Affonso Leme Machado, *Direito Ambiental Brasileiro* (24th edn, Malheiros 2016) 134.

6 Conclusion

Despite the lack of a binding force, advisory opinions contribute to the development of international law and, with current proceedings, can enhance climate change response.[96] In the context of an issue that is both complex and omnipresent such as climate change, views submitted by participants not only can help connect the judiciary and the international community, but are also likely to provide different perspectives which can contribute to delivering more inclusive climate justice.

Participation in advisory proceedings is expected to influence advisory opinions on climate change. With written observations coming from diverse participants, they may influence how the courts rule on the varied questions posed to them. For example, the ITLOS advisory opinion referred to observations of participants.[97] Similarly, the IACtHR has heard numerous observations from different participants, linking to specific consequences of climate change. The Court might equally be influenced by evidence or arguments submitted by the *amici* submissions. The ICJ, which is potentially the third Court to deliver the opinion, is also likely to be guided by the submissions in its opinion.

As previously mentioned, one of the main issues arising in advisory procedures concerns their legal effects. Despite their clear objective in international law, one cannot deny the potential influence of advisory opinions which renders discussions on their binding nature more limited.[98] For this purpose, the ICJ has concluded that 'a distinction should thus be drawn between the advisory nature of the Court's task and the particular effects that parties to an existing dispute may wish to attribute, in their mutual relations, to an advisory opinion of the Court.'[99]

States' failure to respond to the climate crisis has entailed a massive climate litigation movement led by civil society.[100] As an aftermath, this proliferation in climate litigation may result in the strengthening of transparency and participation through means of the increasing recognition of environmental procedural rights (access to information, access to justice and participation in the

96 Setzer & Higham (n 2) 18.

97 Eg see *Request for an Advisory Opinion Submitted by the Commission of Small Island States on Climate Change and International Law* (Advisory Opinion, 21 May 2024) ITLOS Case No 31, §143.

98 Fourth Annual Report of the Permanent Court of International Justice (June 15th, 1927 – June 15th, 1928). Series E – No 4. Report of the Committee appointed on 2 September 1927, 77.

99 *Difference Relating to Immunity from Legal Process of a Special Rapporteur of the Commission on Human Rights* (Advisory Opinion, 29 April 1999) ICJ Rep 62, §25, 77.

100 Tigre & Rocha (n 3) 287.

decision-making process).[101] A broad participation in these proceedings may also raise the 'buy-in' of the opinions once delivered, and change the dynamics of international climate negotiations.

Procedural environmental rights were first formally conceived in the *Rio Declaration*. Its Principle 10[102] is acknowledged as the most important provision on public participation and served as the theoretical basis for the negotiation of international treaties on the subject, such as the Aarhus Convention and the Escazú Agreement, these treaties establish standards 'against which the compatibility of national standards could be compared and as forecasting the creation of new procedural rights that could be granted to individuals through international law and exercised at the national and possibly international level.'

This chapter has reviewed participation in advisory proceedings before different international and regional courts. Through a discussion of participatory justice theories, and the advantages and drawbacks of inclusivity in international climate proceedings, it argued that increasing participation in advisory proceedings supports inclusivity in international climate justice, the legitimacy of advisory opinions and their implementation. It has also highlighted that through the different advisory proceedings on climate change, large participation fosters a greater connection between the judiciary and the international community. There is hardly a topic that concerns all of humanity as much as the urgency posed by climate change. As international and regional courts grapple with the questions put to them, including the voices of those affected by climate change can enlighten the way and legitimize the processes and the outcomes.

Acknowledgments

The author thanks the Canada Research Chair Program of the Social Sciences and Humanities Research Council of Canada for the research support. The author also expresses gratitude to Janie Renaud, Felix Gagnon, and Enéas Xavier de Oliveira for research assistance.

101 Dupuy & Viñuales (n 9) 153.

102 United Nations General Assembly. Report of the United Nations Conference on Environment and Development. 12 August 1992. A/CONF.151/26 (Vol. I), principle 10: *environmental issues are best handled with participation of all concerned citizens, at the relevant level. At the national level, each individual shall have appropriate access to information concerning the environment that is held by public authorities, including information on hazardous materials and activities in their communities, and the opportunity to participate in decision-making processes. States shall facilitate and encourage public awareness and participation by making information widely available. Effective access to judicial and administrative proceedings, including redress and remedy, shall be provided.*

CHAPTER 9

The Role of States in the Requests for Advisory Opinions

Austyn Campbell, Claire Robertson** and Eran Sthoeger****

Abstract

As the world inches closer to key climate deadlines of 2030 and 2050, countries likely to be severely impacted by the adverse effects of climate change have sought to clarify States' obligations under international law in respect of climate change, using advisory opinion proceedings in various international fora. This chapter considers the critical role of States in advisory opinion proceedings on climate change before international courts and tribunals, including their initiation, litigation, and implementation. In commencing advisory opinion proceedings, smaller States seek to build both pressure and consensus to bring about clarity on key climate issues. That said, all States' submissions have the propensity to shape the development and clarification of international law by directing the court or tribunal to focus on certain issues. However, the representation of States in advisory proceedings is not without challenge. The financial and capacity burdens of participation are often felt far more acutely by less developed countries. It is also often those States that seek to use advisory proceedings to rebalance the asymmetry of the international legal system. Regardless of the findings in climate change advisory proceedings, the engagement of States is integral to ensure such matters are properly litigated before international courts and tribunals.

Keywords

advisory opinions – climate change – International law – International Court of Justice (ICJ) – state obligations – International Tribunal for the Law of the Sea (ITLOS) – Inter American Court of Human Rights (IACtHR).

* Lawyer at Gilbert + Tobin. ORCID ID 0009–0006-9197-6632.

** Lawyer at DLA Piper. ORCID ID 0000–0001-6333-9296.

*** Lawyer and Adjunct Professor at Brooklyn Law School and at Columbia University School of Professional Studies. ORCID ID 0000–0002-6664-8868.

1 Introduction

In the wake of insufficient global action, climate litigation is increasingly being used to further the climate agenda, meet the temperature goals in the Paris Agreement, and limit the adverse effects of climate change on the climate system. While the vast majority of climate-related litigation is filed in domestic courts, the last few years has borne witness to an increase in cases filed in international fora. These include, notably, advisory proceedings before the International Court of Justice (ICJ), the International Tribunal for the Law of the Sea (ITLOS), and the Inter American Court of Human Rights (IACtHR). These proceedings sought to clarify States' obligations in respect of climate change.[1] The first, instituted in December 2022 by the Commission of Small Island States on Climate Change and International Law (COSIS), requested an advisory opinion from ITLOS on the obligations of States Parties to the United Nations Convention on the Law of the Sea (UNCLOS) to protect and preserve the marine environment in relation to climate change caused by anthropogenic greenhouse gas (GHG) emissions.[2] In January 2023, Chile and Colombia jointly requested an advisory opinion from the IACtHR on the scope of States' obligations with respect to climate change in the context of international human rights law.[3] Finally, in March 2023, the United Nations General Assembly (UNGA) requested an advisory opinion from the ICJ on States' obligations under international law to protect the climate system and other parts of the environment from anthropogenic GHG emissions for both present and future generations.[4]

The increase in advisory opinions sought from international courts and tribunals may suggest a desire of States for a 'top-down approach,' whereby

1 For a broader historical context, see Maria Antonia Tigre, 'It is (Finally) Time for an Advisory Opinion on Climate Change: Challenges and Opportunities on a Trio of Initiatives' (2024) 17 *Charleston Law Review* 623.

2 *Request for an Advisory Opinion submitted by the Commission of Small Island States on Climate Change and International Law* (Advisory Opinion, 21 May 2024) ITLOS Case No 31, request submitted on 12 December 2022, available at <https://www.itlos.org/fileadmin/itlos/documents/cases/31/Request_for_Advisory_Opinion_COSIS_12.12.22.pdf> accessed 6 March 2024.

3 Republic of Chile and Republic of Colombia, 'Request for an Advisory Opinion regarding the Climate Emergency and Human Rights' (9 January 2023), English translation <https://climatecasechart.com/wp-content/uploads/non-us-case-documents/2023/20230109_18528_petition-3.pdf> accessed 6 March 2024.

4 UNGA Res 77/276 (29 March 2023) UN Doc A/RES/77/276 ('Request for an Advisory Opinion from the International Court of Justice on the Obligations of States in respect of Climate Change'), <https://www.icj-cij.org/sites/default/files/case-related/187/187-20230412-app-01-00-en.pdf> accessed 6 March 2024.

States' obligations are clarified at the international level to then provide greater certainty or 'teeth' at a domestic level.[5] So what is the role of States in advisory opinion proceedings related to climate change? While such proceedings often permit the participation of international organisations and, in some cases, the private sector, States (as the primary actors in the international legal order) play a crucial role in advisory proceedings. This chapter explores the role of States in initiating, litigating, and implementing climate change advisory opinions, concluding that States' actions are ultimately determinative in the success of the climate change proceedings.

2 Initiating an Advisory Opinion

2.1 *States' Interests in Advisory Opinions*

An increased appreciation of the potentially irreversible damage to the Earth's environment caused by unabated human activity has resulted in greater collective State action, with the support of international organisations, to enhance the legal protection of the environment.[6] While the success of domestic and international climate-related litigation has been, generally speaking, on an upward trajectory, the pursuit of contentious interstate proceedings in international courts and tribunals continues to present many challenges. Historically, States have faced difficulties in articulating the appropriate basis for claims given the adverse effects of climate change are often incremental and, in some cases, occur over generations.[7] Then there are questions of interim measures (often termed a 'band-aid approach'), causation, standing, and consent to jurisdiction. Where matters do proceed, courts and tribunals, by their nature, have a tendency to focus on addressing 'issues after damage has already occurred, instead of focusing on the need for prevention of damage in the first place.'[8]

5 Margaretha Wewerinke-Singh, Julian Aguon, & Julie Hunter, 'Bringing Climate Change before the International Court of Justice: Prospects for Contentious Cases and Advisory Opinions', in Alogna, Bakker & Gauci (eds), *Climate Change Litigation: Global Perspectives* (Brill 2021) 395; André Nollkaemper, 'Conversations Among Courts: Domestic and International Adjudicators', in Romano, Alter & Shany (eds), *The Oxford Handbook of International Adjudication* (OUP 2013) 538.

6 James Crawford, *Brownlie's Principles of Public International Law* (9th edn, OUP 2019) 336.

7 Intergovernmental Panel on Climate Change (IPCC), 'Climate Change 2022: Impacts, Adaptation and Vulnerability. Contribution of Working Group II to the Sixth Assessment Report of the Intergovernmental Panel on Climate Change' (CUP 2022), Technical Summary, [B.1.6], 47 <https://report.ipcc.ch/ar6/wg2/IPCC_AR6_WGII_FullReport.pdf> accessed 6 March 2024.

8 Crawford (n 6) 337.

This requires States to demonstrate material or significant damage as a necessary condition of a claim which is largely at odds with the prevention[9] and precautionary principles[10] – core tenets of international environmental law.

Further, contentious cases before international courts and tribunals take many years to resolve, whereby, upon resolution, the adverse effects being challenged may have already resulted in irreversible damage. And, even when decisions are rendered, they are only binding on the parties to the dispute. As such, advisory opinions have emerged as the preferred tool in the legal arsenal of States to seek clarity on their obligations to protect the environment in the context of climate change. Whilst advisory opinions are not binding, they have the potential to influence States' actions.[11]

There have been several contentious interstate cases concerning environmental harm before international courts and tribunals,[12] yet none have focused on environmental harm resulting from climate change. The lack of contentious cases may suggest that States face too many barriers, whether evidential or otherwise, to bring a viable claim against another State on a specific set of facts. This must be understood in light of States' political realities (being those at domestic, regional and international levels), including, as Coleman contends, the question of the 'willingness of [S]tates to allow a third party to resolve a dispute' being dependent on 'the political nature of the matter.'[13] Advisory opinions may, therefore, offer a helpful avenue to overcome many such hurdles whilst also providing an opportunity to clarify the interpretation and application of States' obligations relating to climate change.

9 *Gabčikovo-Nagymaros Project* (*Hungary v Slovakia*) (Merits) [1997] ICJ Rep 7, §140 (*Gabčikovo-Nagymaros Project*).

10 *Pulp Mills on the River Uruguay* (*Argentina v Uruguay*) [2010] ICJ Rep 14, §164 (*Pulp Mills*); *Responsibilities and Obligations of States Sponsoring Persons and Entities with Respect to Activities in the Area* (*Request for Advisory Opinion Submitted to the Seabed Disputes Chamber* (Advisory Opinion, 1 February 2011) ITLOS Case No 17, 45; Rio Declaration on Environment and Development (3–14 June 1992) UN Doc A/CONF.151/26 (vol. 1) 31 ILM 87, Principle 15.

11 Niccolò Lanzoni, 'The Authority of ICJ Advisory Opinions as Precedents: The Mauritius/Maldives Case' (2022) 2 *Italian Review of Int'l & Comp Law* 297, 298.

12 See, for example, *Gabcíkovo-Nagymaros Project* (n 9); *Pulp Mills* (n 10); *Dispute regarding Navigational and Related Rights* (*Costa Rica v Nicaragua*) [2009] ICJ Rep 213.

13 Andrew Coleman, 'The International Court of Justice and Highly Political Matters' (2007) 4(1) *Melbourne Journal of Int'l Law* 29, 32.

2.2 *Initiating the Climate Change Advisory Opinions*

In practice, the process of initiating advisory proceedings is largely State-led, as can be seen from the recent advisory proceedings on climate change.[14] However, much of the development of international environmental law takes place at the negotiating table rather than in the courtroom – a concerted outcome driven by certain States – with developments reflected in multilateral treaties, protocols, and soft law instruments.[15] In such forums, States with significant financial resources, political power, and, in some cases, substantial fossil fuel interests, often drive the climate agenda and push back against more stringent action on climate change, such as a 'phase out' of fossil fuels. Such was evident at the 28th UNFCCC Conference of the Parties (COP), when COP28 President Sultan Al Jaber gavelled the decision on the Global Stocktake text, dubbed the 'UAE Consensus'.[16] In a statement immediately following the gaveling of the decision, the Alliance of Small Island States (AOSIS) Lead Negotiator, Anne Rasmussen, made the following remarks:

> We did not want to interrupt you, but we are a little confused about what just happened. It seems that you gavelled the decisions, and the small island developing states were not in the room. We were working hard to coordinate the 39 small island developing states that are disproportionally affected by climate change, and so were delayed in coming here. So, we will deliver the statement that we were going to deliver before this text was adopted without us.[17]

While many hailed the UAE Consensus as a historic deal calling for a 'transiti[on] away from fossil fuels in energy systems,' smaller States, including Small

14 See, for example, 'Vanuatu ICJ Initiative' <https://www.vanuatuicj.com/home> accessed 6 March 2024.

15 See, for example, *Request for an Advisory Opinion submitted by the Commission of Small Island States on Climate Change and International Law* (Advisory Opinion, 21 May 2024) ITLOS Case No 31 (*COSIS Opinion*) Written Statement of the United Kingdom, 16 June 2023, §7.

16 Conference of the Parties serving as the meeting of the Parties to the Paris Agreement, 'Report of the Conference of the Parties to the Paris Agreement on its fifth session, held in the United Arab Emirates from 30 November to 13 December 2023' (15 March 2024) UN Doc FCCC/PA/CMA/2023/16, §112.

17 Alliance of Small Island States, 'An Incremental Advance when Exponential Change is Needed: AOSIS Statement at COP28 Closing Plenary' (AOSIS Lead Negotiator, Anne Rasmussen, 13 December 2023) <https://www.aosis.org/cop28-closing-plenary-aosis-statement-on-gst-decision/> accessed 24 January 2024.

Island Developing States (SIDS),[18] considered the deal to fall short, noting there were a 'litany of loopholes,' and that the decision 'does not advance us beyond the status quo.'[19] Some Pacific organisations suggested gaveling the decision without the Pacific Countries in the room was a strategic (and symbolic) move to silence objection from AOSIS.[20] By keeping the topic of climate change at the 'negotiating table,' more powerful States can monopolize discussions, leverage political power, and mitigate dissent.

Despite contributing the least to anthropogenic GHG emissions on average,[21] Least Developed Countries (LDCs) and SIDS are among the most exposed to the adverse effects of climate change. These States face particular economic and governance challenges, which exacerbate existing hurdles to galvanizing the international community on climate action. Challenges such as the tyranny of distance (Nauru and Kiribati are the two most remote countries on Earth) and a necessitated reliance on air and sea transport for the movement of goods and people mean the limited resources of SIDS must be concomitantly deployed to respond to the on-the-ground effects of climate change while undertaking 'an outsized role in international diplomacy.'[22]

Smaller States have often relied on litigation in high-profile international fora as a strategic tool against larger States where there is a power or resource imbalance.[23] Strategic use of litigation can be used to 'gain an advantage through law that is not otherwise possible in the ordinary course of

18 Nicholas Chan, '"Large Ocean States": Sovereignty, Small Islands, and Marine Protected Areas in Global Oceans Governance' (2018) 24 Global Governance 537.

19 Alliance of Small Island States (n 17).

20 Sacha Shaw, 'Pacific Island Countries Blindsided in Climate Conference' *The Diplomat* (13 December 2023) <https://thediplomat.com/2023/12/pacific-island-countries-blindsided-in-climate-conference/> accessed 24 January 2024.

21 Intergovernmental Panel on Climate Change (IPCC), '*Sixth Assessment Report: Synthesis Report: Summary for Policymakers*' (CUP 2023) 5 [A.1.5] <https://www.ipcc.ch/report/ar6/syr/downloads/report/IPCC_AR6_SYR_SPM.pdf> accessed 6 March 2024. This report identifies that LDCs and SIDS have much lower per capita emissions (1.7 tCO2-eq and 4.6 tCO2-eq, respectively) than the global average (6.9 tCO2-eq), excluding CO_2 from land use, land-use change and forestry.

22 Nicholas Chan (n 18) 540.

23 See for example, *Timor Sea Conciliation* (*Timor-Leste v Australia*), Report of the Recommendations of the Compulsory Conciliation Commission between Timor-Leste and Australia on the Timor Sea of 9 May 2018; *Military and Paramilitary Activities in and against Nicaragua* (*Nicaragua v United States of America*) (Merits) [1986] ICJ Rep 14; *In the Matter of South China Sea Arbitration* (*Republic of the Philippines v The People's Republic of China*) PCA Case 2013–19 (2016).

international relations given power imbalances involved.'[24] Advisory opinions in various international fora, therefore, offer smaller States the opportunity to use strategic litigation to leverage outcomes on climate change mitigation and adaptation.

In initiating and participating in international judicial proceedings, States must reflect on the prospects of said participation. Sands opines that there are four distinct but related factors or hurdles to be considered: '[f]*irst*, the question of standing;' '[s]*econd*, the potential role of [the international court / tribunal] in establishing key scientific facts;' '[t]*hird*, their role in identifying the law, and indicating how it might be applied to the facts;' and '*fourth*, their propensity to engage actively with the issues presented to it.'[25] Therefore, smaller States face an uphill battle in challenging the legitimacy of policies pursued by more powerful States.[26]

Smaller States have also recognized that direct challenges to the policies of high-emitting States, through contentious proceedings may result in the impugned State, or a coalition of aligned-States, applying political and financial pressure against the initiating State. As many smaller States are reliant on foreign aid and development assistance, both in terms of financial and human resources, commencing contentious proceedings against States that provide aid could risk its continued flow. Arguably, such a result may have more direct – as well as immediate – implications on the smaller State's population than the anthropogenic GHG emissions of the high-emitting State in question. Whilst not a contentious proceeding, Palau's 2011 attempt to seek an advisory opinion from the ICJ on obligations regarding climate change is a pertinent demonstration of these risks. In that case, it was reported that the United States' threat to cut off certain monetary aid provided to Palau was a determinative factor as to why the request never made it to the floor of the UNGA.[27]

24 Douglas Guilfoyle, 'The Chagos Archipelago before International Tribunals: Strategic Litigation and the Production of Historical Knowledge' (2021) 21(3) *Melbourne Journal of Int'l Law* 1, 2.

25 Philippe Sands, 'Climate Change and the Rule of Law: Adjudicating the Future in International Law' (2016) 28 *Journal of Env'l Law* 19, 27.

26 Douglas Guilfoyle, 'Litigation as Statecraft: Small States and the Law of the Sea' (2023) 1 *BYIL* 16.

27 Rachel Brown, 'The Rising Tide of Climate Change Cases' (2013) 13(2) The Yale Globalist 20 <https://globalist.yale.edu/in-the-magazine/theme/the-rising-tide-of-climate-change-cases/?utm_source=rss&utm_medium=rss&utm_campaign=the-rising-tide-of-climate-change-cases> accessed 29 January 2024; Yale Center for Environmental Law & Policy, 'Climate Change & the International Court of Justice' (2013) *Public Law Research Paper No. 315* <https://papers.ssrn.com/sol3/Delivery.cfm/SSRN_ID2309943_code267610.pdf?abstractid=2309943&mirid=1> accessed 2 February 2024.

In more contemporary proceedings, the request in *Obligations in respect of climate change* (ICJ Advisory Proceedings) was the result of a grassroots campaign. In June 2019, a collective of students from the University of the South Pacific – the Pacific Islands Students Fighting Climate Change – wrote to the heads of States of Pacific Island countries requesting them to seek an advisory opinion from the ICJ on climate change.[28] Vanuatu resolved to place the initiative on the official Pacific Islands Forum agenda, subsequently spearheading the campaign for the advisory opinion from the ICJ. Over a period of two years, Vanuatu led a coalition of 132 nations in ultimately adopting the UNGA Resolution requesting the advisory opinion by consensus.[29] During the plenary session, developed and developing States alike expressed their support for an advisory opinion from the ICJ to clarify obligations under international law in respect to climate change, providing impetus for further climate action.[30]

As a precursor to the 2023 ITLOS proceedings (ITLOS Advisory Proceedings), COSIS, a collective of SIDS formally established on the eve of COP26, sought to bring together likeminded States in pursuit of greater climate action. On 12 December 2022, COSIS formally requested an advisory opinion from ITLOS on States' obligations under UNCLOS to protect and preserve the marine environment from the adverse effects of climate change in the context of anthropogenic GHG emissions. The ITLOS Advisory Proceedings were historic, being the first ever international advisory proceedings on climate change and international law. From 11 to 25 September 2023, the 21 Members of the Tribunal heard oral arguments from 35 States and three international organisations, which included a handful of States outside the 34 States and nine international organisations that filed written statements. The participation at ITLOS was close to the highest historic engagement in advisory proceedings, dwarfed only by the ICJ Advisory Proceedings where 79 written statements were received from 83 States (including from seven LDCs, 18 SIDS, and four that are both LDCs and SIDS),[31] and 12 international organisations, demonstrating the power of advisory proceedings in galvanizing the international community on the issue of climate change.

28 Pacific Islands Students Fighting Climate Change, 'There is a legal solution to climate change: students' (5 July 2020) <https://www.pisfcc.org/news/there-is-a-legal-solution-to-climate-change-students> accessed 29 January 2024.

29 UNGA Res 77/276 (29 March 2023) UN Doc A/RES/77/276 ('Request for an Advisory Opinion from the International Court of Justice on the Obligations of States in respect of Climate Change').

30 UNGA Verbatim Record (29 March 2023) UN Doc A/77/PV.64.

31 Denmark, Finland, Norway, Sweden, and Iceland submitted a joint statement.

2.3 *Drafting the Wording of the Request*

In addition to the crucial role of initiating the advisory opinion itself, States formulate the specific wording of the request, which ultimately shapes the issues for the court or tribunal's consideration. A State initiating an advisory opinion must maximize the appeal to the international community by framing the question/s as underpinned by common interests.[32] For example, in opening oral statements in the ITLOS Advisory Proceedings, COSIS reiterated that climate change was clearly a multilateral issue:[33]

> Small island States may be the first to fall – through no fault of our own – but we will not be the last, for no country on Earth can escape the deadly grasp of climate change.

In multilateralizing the issue of climate change and the marine environment, COSIS engaged with a broad array of States to litigate the matter before ITLOS. However, COSIS' approach was not without criticism. During the written and oral stages, several States raised concerns that a very small number of countries (only two in the first instance) had created an international organization (COSIS) which conferred a power to request advisory opinions focusing on the obligations of States that: (1) were not party to the request; and (2) had no opportunity to be involved in the framing of the request or the decision to make such a request.[34]

In contrast, during the ICJ Advisory Proceedings, States had opportunities to comment on multiple drafts of the request, with the decision to request the advisory opinion from the ICJ receiving support from all UN Member States. The success of UNGA resolution 77/276, therefore, perhaps better highlights the role of States in the climate advisory opinions. *First*, in choosing to pursue an advisory opinion over a contentious case, Vanuatu positioned itself to build consensus amongst States without particular States feeling threatened by the outcome of contentious proceedings. *Second*, in taking the time to build a coalition of States from across the globe, Vanuatu built a strong foundation of States to support the resolution. Arguably, where a request receives global consensus, States may be more willing to adopt and support the ICJ's ultimate

32 Guilfoyle (n 26) 20.

33 'Verbatim Record', *Request for an Advisory Opinion submitted by the Commission of Small Island States on Climate Change and International Law* (International Tribunal for the Law of the Sea, 11 September 2023, ITLOS/PV.23/C31/1/Rev.1) 9.

34 *COSIS Opinion* (n 15) Written Statements of Brazil, France, Guatemala, Indonesia, New Zealand, the United Kingdom.

findings as the process demonstrates States were able to find a 'middle ground,' benefitting both high- and low-emitting States' interests.

3 Litigating an Advisory Opinion

Advisory opinions, whilst not binding, carry significant legal weight and great moral authority: '[a] clear statement by a body such as the ICJ ... may itself contribute to change in attitudes and behaviour.'[35] As such, States can use advisory opinions to 'shape and stabilize normative expectations among the wider set of public and private actors engaged in climate-related work,'[36] contributing to the formation of 'an international public consciousness' on climate change.[37] Advisory proceedings typically include written and oral proceedings,[38] and States play a critical role in shaping how each stage takes place. On top of the substance of each State's position, the role of States in the climate change advisory opinions is best reflected in particular areas, which include: (i) influencing the procedural aspects; (ii) collaboration amongst States to focus the court or tribunal's attention on certain key issues; and (iii) the number and diversity of State representation.

3.1 *Influencing the Procedural Aspects of Advisory Proceedings*

Compared to the substantive elements of an advisory opinion, the importance of the court or tribunal's procedure is often overlooked. An advisory opinion's procedure can influence its success, including how well the subject matter is ventilated: States have already played a central role in shaping the procedure in the climate change advisory opinions before ITLOS and the ICJ.

Looking first to the written stage, in the ITLOS Advisory Proceedings, the Tribunal originally fixed 16 May 2023 as the deadline for States to provide written

35 Sands (n 25) 26.

36 Daniel Bodansky, 'The Role of the International Court of Justice in Addressing Climate Change: Some Preliminary Reflections' (2017) 49 *Arizona State Law Review* 690, 692.

37 Philippe Sands, 'Climate Change and the Rule of Law: Adjudicating the Future in International Law' (Public Lecture at the United Kingdom Supreme Court, London, 17 September 2015) 18 <https://www.supremecourt.uk/docs/professor-sands-lecture-on-climate-change-and-the-rule-of-law.pdf> accessed 29 January 2024.

38 The ICJ has authority to hold, or decline to hold, written and/or oral proceedings. In practice, the ICJ 'has never dispensed with them entirely': *Handbook of the International Court of Justice* (2019) <https://www.icj-cij.org/sites/default/files/documents/handbook-of-the-court-en.pdf> 85, accessed 2 March 2024.

statements.[39] On 15 February 2023, the Tribunal extended the time-limit for the submission of written statements by one month to 16 June 2023.[40] In its Order of 15 February 2023, the Tribunal noted that 'a request for the extension of the time-limit for the submission of written statements has been received.'[41] While the Order did not expressly provide which State (or States) sought the request, the extension suggested that States had influenced the procedural changes. Such influence is even better reflected in the procedure for the written stage of the ICJ Advisory Proceedings.

There, the Court's original Order of 20 April 2023 fixed the deadline for written statements as 20 October 2023, with reply submissions due on 22 January 2024.[42] When, on 30 June 2023, ITLOS set down the oral hearing for the ITLOS Advisory Proceedings to open on 11 September 2023, to take place over a two-week period,[43] States concurrently participating in the ITLOS and ICJ Advisory Proceedings expressed concern that the dates set by ITLOS effectively required them to draft two sets of submissions in parallel. This posed a significant challenge for capacity and resource-constrained States. As such, the Government of Vanuatu coordinated with several States to seek a three-month extension to the deadline for written statements. Fourteen States co-signed Vanuatu's request, with letters separately received by the Court from Chile and COSIS supporting the extension. On 4 August 2023, the ICJ made an order extending the time limit for written statements, with the extension reflecting the amount of additional time requested.[44]

---

39 *COSIS Opinion* (n 15) Order No 2022/4 (16 December 2022) 3, available at <https://www.itlos.org/fileadmin/itlos/documents/cases/31/C31_Order_2022-4_16.12.2022_01.pdf> accessed 7 March 2024.

40 *COSIS Opinion* (n 15) Order No 2023/1 (15 February 2023) 2, available at <https://www.itlos.org/fileadmin/itlos/documents/cases/31/C31_Order_2023-1_15.02.2023_Readable.pdf> accessed 7 March 2024.

41 ibid.

42 ICJ, *Request for an Advisory Opinion of the International Court of Justice on the Obligations of States in respect of Climate Change* (*Obligations in respect of Climate Change Opinion*), Order of 20 April 2023, available at <https://www.icj-cij.org/sites/default/files/case-related/187/187-20230420-ORD-01-00-EN.pdf> accessed 7 March 2024.

43 ITLOS, 'Press Release No 34: Hearing to open on 11 September 2023' (30 June 2023) <https://www.itlos.org/fileadmin/itlos/documents/press_releases_english/PR_341_EN.pdf> accessed 7 March 2024.

44 *Obligations in respect of Climate Change Opinion* (n 42) Order of 4 August 2023, available at <https://www.icj-cij.org/sites/default/files/case-related/187/187-20230804-ord-01-00-en.pdf> accessed 7 March 2024.

The deadline for written statements was extended a second time on 15 December 2023.[45] In the lead up to COP28, international bodies, such as the Melanesian Spearhead Group, the Organisation of African, Caribbean and Pacific States, and The Pacific Community (SPC), wrote to the Court requesting an additional extension of at least four months. These organisations lobbied States at COP28 to write to the ICJ in support of the additional extension request. As a result of these efforts, Kiribati, Nauru, and the African Union wrote to the Court in support of the extension. While the Court only granted an extension of two months,[46] it is clear the requests from States were a determinative factor in the Court's decision to further extend the deadlines.

The significance of coordinated State action was again evidenced on 30 May 2024 where, following another request by 18 States and five international organisations, the ICJ, in an unprecedented fashion, further extended the time-limit for the written comments on the written statements by approximately two months.[47] In pushing for this extension, many States stressed to the Court, among other factors, that: *first*, the ICJ Advisory Proceedings had the largest participation in an advisory opinion in the Court's history, meaning the Court had to consider a broader array of States' circumstances; *second*, the ITLOS Climate Change Opinion would be released on 21 May 2024 leaving little time for States to consider its implications and respond appropriately in their written comments by 24 June 2024; and *third*, *a* number of States participating in the proceedings had significant capacity and resource constraints and therefore the time provided for written comments was insufficient. The granting of each extension highlights the importance of achieving a 'critical mass' of States and international organisations to exert influence on the Court's procedure.[48]

Putting the climate change proceedings to one side, extensions to time limits are not usually a common feature of ICJ advisory proceedings. From the 27 advisory opinions issued to date, the ICJ has only ever made orders extending the timeline for the filing of written submissions on seven occasions.[49] Of

---

45 *Obligations in respect of Climate Change Opinion* (n 42) Order of 15 December 2023, available at <https://www.icj-cij.org/sites/default/files/case-related/187/187-20231215-ord-01-00-en.pdf> accessed 7 March 2024.

46 ibid.

47 *Obligations in respect of Climate Change Opinion* (n 42) Order of 30 May 2024, available at <https://www.icj-cij.org/sites/default/files/case-related/187/187-20240531-ord-01-00-en.pdf> accessed 1 June 2024. The extension was exactly seven weeks and three days from the further extended deadline of 24 June 2024.

48 See Miriam Cohen, Chapter 8 in this book.

49 These seven cases were *Obligations in respect of Climate Change Opinion* (n 42), *Legal Consequences of the Separation of the Chagos Archipelago from Mauritius in 1965* (Advisory

those seven, only three extensions were granted by reason of States writing to the Court requesting an extension,[50] with the extensions granted in *Legality of the Use by a State of Nuclear Weapons in Armed Conflict* in 1993, and the current ICJ Advisory Proceedings being a result of multiple States' requests.

3.2 *Collaboration amongst States to Focus the Court or Tribunal's Attention on Certain Key Issues in the Advisory Proceedings*

In addition to collaboration amongst States on the procedural aspects of an advisory opinion proceeding, collaboration may extend to the substance of the matter. In advisory opinions, States are incentivized to influence the court or tribunal's views and focus on certain issues so as to advance their position and contradict the other States. In the context of the climate change advisory proceedings before ITLOS and the ICJ, collaboration amongst States has been immense. States worked closely together in initiating the advisory opinions and subsequently influencing their procedure. Such collaboration does not cease once the request has been submitted. If anything, States must cooperate and collaborate on an even closer basis in the written and oral phases to ensure a focus on certain issues, with the backing of a State collective.

States' oral submissions play a central role in directing the court or tribunal's attention toward (or away from) specific issues, and identifying areas where States are in consensus or hold opposing views. Unlike the ICJ, where advisory proceedings afforded a second written round to provide comments on other participants' statements, the ITLOS Advisory Proceedings was limited to one written round and one oral round.[51] The oral proceedings thus presented an important opportunity for States to demonstrate alignment on issues or push back on views that States did not wish to see the Tribunal advance. For example, a number of States' oral submissions referenced, with support, the written or oral statements of other States, such as Bangladesh and Comoros in respect

Opinion) [2019] ICJ Rep 95, *Legality of the Use by a State of Nuclear Weapons in Armed Conflict* (Advisory Opinion) [1996] ICJ Rep 66 (*WHO Nuclear Weapons*), *Application for Review of Judgment No 333 of the United Nations Administrative Tribunal* (Advisory Opinion) [1987] ICJ Rep 18, *Application for Review of Judgment No 273 of the United Nations Administrative Tribunal* (Advisory Opinion) [1982] ICJ Rep 325, and *Legal Consequences for States of the Continued Presence of South Africa in Namibia (South West Africa) notwithstanding Security Council Resolution 276 (1970)* (Advisory Opinion) [1971] ICJ Rep 16 (*Namibia Advisory Opinion*).

50 These three cases were *Obligations in respect of Climate Change Opinion* (n 42), *WHO Nuclear Weapons* (n 49), and *Namibia Advisory Opinion* (n 49).

51 *COSIS Opinion* (n 15) Declaration of Judge Kulyk, §2.

to the interpretation of article 192 of UNCLOS.[52] Mozambique made specific reference to the submissions of the United Kingdom in respect of jurisdiction, stating in response that 'these are not compelling reasons for refusing to render this much needed advisory opinion.'[53] Similarly, Belize's submissions expressly challenged the positions several high-emitting States adopted, including Australia and the United Kingdom.[54]

States may also disagree as to what the Tribunal should focus on. During the oral proceedings of the ITLOS Advisory Proceedings, Counsel for the Republic of Mauritius asked the Tribunal to 'confirm in this advisory opinion that sea-level rise, a consequence of pollution that is not permitted by reference to the requirements of Part XII, will not affect existing maritime claims or entitlements.'[55] Timor-Leste, conversely, took a different view:

> Further, as a preliminary point, a small number of participants have raised the issue of the effects of sea-level rise on basepoints and maritime entitlements. Whilst these are very important issues, *Timor-Leste is of the view that these are not at the crux of these proceedings. The focus of these proceedings should, however, be on the environmental issues that are at the core of the questions and which most States have expressed views upon.*[56]

The ITLOS *COSIS Opinion* briefly acknowledged these diverging views:

> Some participants, referring to the mention of sea level rise in the Request, invited the Tribunal to deal with the issue of the relationship between sea level rise and existing maritime claims or entitlements. On the other hand, other participants expressed the view that, while acknowledging the importance of this issue, the present proceedings should focus instead on environmental issues.[57]

52 'Verbatim Record', *COSIS Opinion* (ITLOS, 13 September 2023, ITLOS/PV.23/C31/1/Rev.1), 25–26 (Bangladesh); Verbatim Record, *COSIS Opinion* (ITLOS, 21 September 2023, ITLOS/PV.23/C31/1/Rev.1), 11 (Comoros).

53 'Verbatim Record' *COSIS Opinion* (ITLOS, 18 September 2023, ITLOS/PV.23/C31/11/Rev.1), 8 (Mozambique).

54 ibid, 30–31 (Belize) (emphasis added).

55 ibid 31.

56 'Verbatim Record' *COSIS Opinion* (ITLOS, 20 September 2023, ITLOS/PV.23/C31/14/Rev.1), 7 (Democratic Republic of Timor-Leste) (emphasis added).

57 *COSIS Opinion* (n 15) §149.

Ultimately, the Tribunal concluded:

> … if the Commission had intended to solicit an opinion on the consequences of sea level rise for base points, baselines, claims, rights or entitlements to the maritime zones established under the Convention, or maritime boundaries, and the corresponding obligations, it would have expressly formulated the Request accordingly.[58]

The Tribunal's explicit acknowledgment of specific arguments advanced by States and international organisations demonstrates the role States play in shaping the findings of an advisory opinion. While the wording of COSIS's request put to the Tribunal did much of the heavy lifting in focusing the Tribunal's attention, the wording was sufficiently open to potentially allow the Tribunal to consider and even make findings on the issue of sea-level rise and maritime entitlements. Perhaps if some States had not been so vocal in opposing the Court's consideration of this issue, the Tribunal may have made findings that would be, in the view of some States, unwelcome.

This all demonstrates that advisory opinions can help to create sovereign equality through neutralizing 'any power differences that may exist outside the courtroom.'[59] For example, equal speaking time in the oral rounds levels the playing field and elevates the voices of smaller States:[60] '[n]o matter how powerful a party is outside of the courtroom, inside they "must operate as equals of their adversaries".'[61] Thus, legal argumentation is a means of constraining the powerful. The participation of smaller States in the oral proceedings of the climate change advisory opinions can, therefore, have a significant impact on the direction of the proceedings which allows those States an opportunity to be heard on equal footing.

3.3 *Number and Diversity of State Representation in Advisory Proceedings*

In addition to the content of States' submissions, the number and diversity of States represented in climate change advisory proceedings plays an important

58 ibid, §§149–150.

59 Juliette McIntyre, 'Great Hall, Small States' (Centre for International Law, 10 July 2023) <https://cil.nus.edu.sg/blogs/great-hall-small-states/> accessed 1 February 2024.

60 The authors note there has been criticism regarding the time allocation in the ITLOS Advisory Opinion where COSIS had two full days to present its oral statement, whereas every other State and international organization was permitted 60 minutes to make its oral statements.

61 McIntyre (n 59).

role. Climate change has a global character; virtually all human activities contribute to climate change. Both developed and developing States alike are impacted by the adverse effects of climate change and contribute to such effects (albeit some to a substantially lesser extent). These universal impacts were reflected in the large number of States participating in the ITLOS Advisory Proceedings. In turn, the ICJ Advisory Proceedings saw record participation in the first round of written statements, with 79 written statements received from 83 States,[62] including from seven LDCs, 18 SIDS, and four States that are both LDCs and SIDS. Twelve statements from intergovernmental organisations were received. The 91 written statements received by the ICJ made it the advisory opinion with the greatest State participation in any advisory proceeding in history.[63] The final stage of the ICJ advisory opinion similarly had record participation levels with 88 States and 12 international organisations presenting oral statements.[64]

The subject matter of an advisory opinion drives the level of participation. As set out above, 34 States filed written statements in the ITLOS Advisory Proceedings. Thirty-three States presented oral statements. Almost every State that submitted a written statement also made an oral statement. Historically speaking, this is an anomaly. In past advisory proceedings, greater participation usually occurs in the written rounds with about a third-to-half less dropping off in oral proceedings. The fact that States participated in both rounds of the ITLOS Advisory Proceedings may suggest that States consider the issues to directly affect their interests, requiring their positions to be fully litigated. Alternatively, as some States also used the oral proceedings as an opportunity to respond to other States, whether to agree with their position or offer a different approach, the high participation at the oral proceedings could also be a result of the lack of a second written round.[65]

In addition to the subject matter of advisory opinions influencing participation levels, some States may also face procedural difficulties in participating in advisory opinion proceedings. When it comes to the written phase, ITLOS allows for electronic filing of written pleadings. Conversely, the ICJ's procedure for filing written statements is far more involved and 'traditional.' A State that

62 Denmark, Finland, Norway, Sweden, and Iceland submitted a joint statement.

63 See Miriam Cohen, Chapter 8 in this book.

64 Vanuatu Climate Diplomacy Program, 'Vanuatu's Landmark Climate Change Case Advances with 100 Oral Statements Now Scheduled at the International Court of Justice Hearings' (16 October 2024) <https://mailchi.mp/f08df1162554/vanuatus-landmark-climate-change-case-advances-with-100-oral-statements-scheduled-for-international-court-of-justice-hearings?e=637547bd76&ref=climateinthecourts.com> accessed 4 November 2024, 1.

65 'Verbatim Record' *COSIS Opinion* (ITLOS, 14 September 2023, ITLOS/PV.23/C31/8/Rev.1), 30–31 (Guatemala).

wishes to file a written statement must make an in-person appointment with the ICJ Registry in The Hague.[66] States must provide the Registry with 30 paper copies and a USB containing the Word and PDF versions of the statement by the filing deadline.[67] In addition to these requirements, an original copy of the written statement containing the handwritten signature of a duly authorized official must be filed with the Registry in person.[68] Written comments in response to another State's written submissions must be filed in the same manner.[69] Prior to the filing of written statements in the ICJ Advisory Proceedings, several States wrote to the ICJ seeking dispensation from the requirement to file paper copies in person. It is understood the ICJ Registry rejected this request for some States,[70] however, on an exceptional basis, Nauru was permitted to upload its written submission onto a secure electronic platform.[71] Also on an exceptional basis, the ICJ authorized the late filing of the written statements of Nepal on 27 March 2024, Burkina Faso on 2 April 2024, and The Gambia on 2 April 2024.[72]

As to the oral hearings, both ITLOS and the ICJ still require States to appear in-person. There are many benefits to States appearing in person, however, the oral proceedings can also present challenges, with smaller States potentially barred from participation where they cannot overcome capacity and resource constraints.

4 The Role of States 'Post-Opinion': Lessons from the Past

4.1 *The Non-Binding Status of Advisory Opinions*

Article 59 of the ICJ Statute dictates that parties to a dispute are bound by the decisions of the Court. Advisory opinions, however, contain 'replies' to the

---

66 International Court of Justice, 'Request for Advisory Opinion: Procedure Followed by the International Court of Justice' <https://www.icj-cij.org/sites/default/files/2023-11/advisory-opinion_procedure-followed-by-the-icj_20231121_e.pdf> accessed 22 January 2024, 2.

67 ibid 2–3.

68 ibid 2.

69 ibid 3.

70 This information is based on personal conversations between one of the authors and various States' representatives.

71 Josie-Ann Dongobir, 'Nauru's Written Submission to the ICJ on the Advisory Opinion on Climate Change' (LinkedIn, 25 March 2024) <https://www.linkedin.com/posts/josieanndongobir_icjao-climatechange-nauruadvisoryteam-activity-7177651751641067520-F9q0?utm_source=share&utm_medium=member_desktop> accessed 27 March 2024.

72 *Obligations in respect of Climate Change Opinion* (n 42) 'Press Release 31 of 2024: Filing of written statements' (12 April 2024) <https://www.icj-cij.org/sites/default/files/case-related/187/187-20240412-pre-01-00-en.pdf> accessed 15 April 2024.

questions asked and are not decisions falling under the scope of Article 59.[73] Though advisory opinions are not binding as such, it does not mean they are void of legal significance. Just like judgments, advisory opinions are 'judicial decisions' within the meaning of Article 38 of the ICJ Statute, a subsidiary means for the determination of rules of international law.[74] While advisory opinions are not *formally* binding and do not alter a pre-existing legal situation, advisory opinions contain the Court's analysis of rights and obligations of States under international law:[75]

> As regards the reasoning, this, in both cases, represents the Court's legal conclusions concerning the situation which is being dealt with, and its weight is the same in both cases: there are no two ways of declaring the law.[76]

Considering the reception and reaction to advisory opinions by States and their effect on States' behaviour is a matter for each State to determine,[77] the force of an advisory opinion, by the ICJ or any other international tribunal, is in its persuasive reasoning.[78]

4.3 *The Response and 'Implementation' of Advisory Opinions by Individual States*

As opposed to judgments in contentious cases, advisory proceedings before the ICJ are initiated by a UN organ or agency, and by an international organization such as COSIS in the case of ITLOS. Thus, one can expect States seeking implementation to initiate action within that organ.[79] Yet the content of advisory opinions, such as those concerning climate change, still concerns States' obligations.

The response of States to advisory opinions of the Court has been consistently inconsistent. The Court's opinion in *Reparations for Injuries Suffered in*

73 Eran Sthoeger, 'How do States React to Advisory Opinions? Rejection, Implementation, and what Lies in Between' (2023) *AJIL Unbound* 292.
74 André Gros, 'Concerning the Advisory Role of the International Court of Justice', in Friedmann, Henkin & Lissitzyn (eds), *Transitional Law in a Changing Society: Essays in Honor Of Philip C. Jessup* (Columbia University Press 1972) 315; Sthoeger (n 73).
75 Sthoeger (n 73).
76 André Gros (n 74) 315; Sthoeger (n 73).
77 Daniel Bodansky, 'Advisory Opinions on Climate Change: Some Preliminary Questions' (2023) 32 *RECIEL* 185, 190; Sthoeger (n 73).
78 Bodansky (n 77) 5.
79 For more on this see Sthoeger (n 73).

the Service of the United Nations,[80] which, while being of general significance with respect to the international legal personality of the United Nations, was delivered against the backdrop of the assassination of mediator Count Folke Bernadotte. The Court opined that the United Nations could bring an international claim against the responsible *de jure* or *de facto* government. Israel later paid the United Nations compensation, and the Secretary-General considered the matter settled.[81]

In more recent examples, Israel rejected the *Construction of the Wall* advisory opinion.[82] The Supreme Court of Israel considered the opinion shortly after it was delivered, noting the non-binding nature of the opinion and stating that, as the 'highest judicial body in international law,' the 'ICJ's interpretation of international law should be given its full appropriate weight.'[83] However, the Supreme Court ultimately rejected the advisory opinion and the Court's conclusion as to the legality of the wall as a whole, and decided it had no implications on the Supreme Court's established methodology of examining the legality of each segment of the wall separately.[84]

In its immediate response to the *Chagos* opinion, the United Kingdom reaffirmed its position on its sovereignty over the Archipelago, and its commitment to the obligations identified by the Tribunal in the binding award in the *Chagos Arbitration*, mainly to return the Archipelago to Mauritius once it is no longer needed for defense purposes.[85] The United Kingdom further stressed the non-binding nature of the advisory opinion and that the status of the Archipelago 'as a United Kingdom territory' is 'essential' for the US naval base, Diego Garcia.[86] An unsuccessful attempt to rely on the opinion was made

80 *Reparations for Injuries Suffered in the Service of the United Nations* (Advisory Opinion) [1949] ICJ Rep 174.

81 Letter from the Minister for Foreign Affairs of the Government of Israel to the Secretary-General Concerning a Claim for Damage Caused to the United Nations by the Assassination of Count Folke Bernadotte and a reply thereto from the Secretary -General (14 June 1950, S/1506) <https://www.un.org/unispal/document/auto-insert-178849/> accessed 8 March 2023; Sthoeger (n 73).

82 See, for example, *Alian v Prime Minister* [2005] HCJ 4825/04, Israel Supreme Court (Statement of Response) [552] referring to *Beit Sourik Village Council v Government of Israel* [2004] HCJ 2056/04, Israel Supreme Court, 30 May 2004.

83 *Mara'abe v Prime Minister of Israel* [2009] HCJ 7957/04, Israel Supreme Court, 15 September 2005, §56.

84 ibid, §74.

85 Philippa Webb, 'The United Kingdom and the Chagos Archipelago Advisory Opinion: Engagement and Resistance' (2021) 21(3) *Melbourne Journal of Int'l Law* 1, Part. V.

86 UNGA Verbatim Record (22 May 2019) UN Doc A/73/PV.83, 11 (Statement of United Kingdom); ibid 12–16.

before the English Court of Appeal, where the court held that the opinion 'is not a judgment in the traditional sense of determining a dispute as between parties where the judgment has binding effect.'[87]

Mauritius responded to *Chagos* through various UN forums.[88] Perhaps most notable, however, is its initiation of contentious proceedings against the Maldives to delimit the maritime boundary between Maldives and the Chagos Archipelago. The two States agreed to constitute a nine-member Special Chamber of ITLOS, which issued its judgment on Maldives' preliminary objections on 28 January 2021.[89] The Special Chamber rejected Maldives' arguments that the United Kingdom was an indispensable third party to the proceedings and that a sovereignty dispute continued to persist between Mauritius and the United Kingdom. The Special Chamber held that the *Chagos* advisory opinion, while not binding, was 'authoritative' and made 'determinations' with 'legal effect and clear implications for the legal status of the Chagos Archipelago' such that 'Mauritius can be regarded as the coastal State in respect of the Chagos Archipelago for the purpose of the delimitation of a maritime boundary even before the process of the decolonization of Mauritius is completed.'[90]

Despite no change in the United Kingdom's official position, Mauritius and the United Kingdom announced, on 3 November 2022, the start of negotiations 'on the exercise of sovereignty' over the Archipelago (with an intention to conclude the talks by early 2023). The States noted their intention 'to secure an agreement on the basis of international law to resolve all outstanding issues,' taking into account 'relevant legal proceedings'.[91] On 3 October 2024, after two years of negotiations, Mauritius and the United Kingdom jointly announced that they have reached agreement, 'subject to the finalisation of a treaty', settling all outstanding issues. According to the announcement, the two States agreed that Mauritius 'is sovereign over the Chagos Archipelago, including Diego Garcia' and that the United Kingdom will exercise sovereign rights with

87 *R (Hoareau) v Secretary of State for Foreign and Commonwealth Affairs* [2020] EWCA Civ 1010, §116.

88 See Sthoeger (n 73).

89 *Dispute concerning Delimitation of the Maritime Boundary between Mauritius and Maldives in the Indian Ocean (Mauritius/Maldives) (Preliminary Objections)* (Judgment, 28 January 2021) ITLOS Case No 28.

90 ibid, §§246–250.

91 James Cleverly (Secretary of State for Foreign, Commonwealth and Development Affairs), 'Statement on the British Indian Ocean Territory Chagos Archipelago' (House of Commons, London, 3 November 2022) <https://questions-statements.parliament.uk/written-statements/detail/2022-11-03/hcws354> accessed 11 March 2024.

respect to Diego Garcia for an initial period of 99 years.[92] The States jointly proclaimed the deal as:

> … a demonstration of our enduring commitment to the peaceful resolution of disputes and the rule of law.[93]

When it comes to advisory opinions with more general application, such as those concerning climate change, the effects are harder to ascertain, as implementation may be easier to assess in situations requiring action from a limited number of States.[94] The role advisory opinions play in States' decision-making is particularly hard to predict when they are but one element in a wider global political context.[95]

The ICJ's 1948 advisory opinion in *Conditions for Admission*, for example, found that admissions should be considered solely on the basis of the criteria of Article 4 of the UN Charter.[96] Yet, some Member States continued to use admission to the United Nations as a political tool which resulted in another request for an advisory opinion from the UNGA, asking if it could admit new members without a Security Council recommendation, thus bypassing the political impasse in the latter. The Court answered in the negative, and admissions continued to be influenced by political considerations, in contradiction to the first opinion of the Court.[97]

With respect to the *Nuclear Weapons* opinion, the Opinion received a lukewarm reception from the UNGA, representing, perhaps, a certain disappointment with the Court's conclusions, with the voting on it reflecting the pre-existing divide on the topic.[98] While the 2017 Treaty on the Prohibition of

---

92 Foreign, Commonwealth and Development Office, '*UK* and Mauritius joint statement, 3 October 2024' (3 October 2024) <https://www.gov.uk/government/news/joint-statement-between-uk-and-mauritius-3-october-2024> accessed 31 October 2024 (Chagos Statement).

93 ibid.

94 Sthoeger (n 73).

95 See Lea Klingst-Main & Sophie Marjanac, Chapter 11 in this book.

96 *Conditions of Admission of a State to Membership in the United Nations (Article 4 of the Charter)* (Advisory Opinion) [1948] ICJ Rep 57.

97 *Competence of the General Assembly for the Admission of a State to the United Nations* (Advisory Opinion) [1950] ICJ Rep 4.

98 UNGA Res 51/45(M) (10 December 1996) UN Doc A/RES/51/45(M) ('Advisory Opinion of the International Court of Justice on the Legality of the Threat or Use of Nuclear Weapons').

Nuclear Weapons (TPNW)[99] – which correlates to the opinion of the Court that States must eventually negotiate a nuclear weapon free world – represented a significant development, the 70 State-parties do not include any of the nuclear States, thus the principle divide on this issue is ultimately as it was. However, given the Court also concluded that the use of nuclear weapons cannot be said to be illegal in all circumstances,[100] the continued existence of nuclear weapons can be said to be in accordance with the Court's opinion.

5 Concluding Remarks

Alongside the judicial bodies rendering advisory opinions, States are the most important actors in these processes. While the idea to request an opinion may not always originate with States, it *must* garner significant State interest and support, individually or through the competent bodies. States have an indispensable role: they draft and mold the requests; participate in the legal proceedings and influence them in form and substance; and ultimately are key actors in their implementation. They are thus critical to the success of the process before, during, and in its aftermath.

As climate change is a global issue requiring the collective action of all States, advisory opinions have emerged as the preferred tool of States thus far, given their ability to multilateralize issues. The advisory opinions on climate change before ITLOS, the ICJ, and the IACtHR, both collectively and separately, demonstrate the unique role that States, particularly smaller States facing a marked asymmetry of power,[101] have in pushing for greater climate action.[102] They demonstrate how the international legal system can be an equalizer, affording all States the same opportunities to press matters of global concern. However, while the processes themselves may be 'equal' for all States, there remain challenges to equitable access, including for individuals and non-government organisations.[103]

Advisory opinions may be initiated with a view of securing greater political and legal action on climate change. Arguably, States which seek advisory

99 *Treaty on the Prohibition of Nuclear Weapons* (adopted 7 July 2017, entered into force 22 January 2021) 3379 UNTS 1.

100 *Legality of the Threat or Use of Nuclear Weapons* (Advisory Opinion) [1996] ICJ Rep 266.

101 Tom Long, *A Small State's Guide to Influence in World Politics* (OUP 2022).

102 Scholarship on the political and legal positioning of 'smaller States' is often predicated on observations about their vulnerability: 'that smallness (variously defined) begets a precarious vulnerable position (variously defined) in world politics' Chan (n 18) 540.

103 ICJ Statute, art 66.

opinions are unlikely to expect the relevant court or tribunal's reply to automatically produce a change of behavior. Rather, 'it is usually hoped that a successful judicial or arbitral outcome will provide a standard around which other States may rally in order to place diplomatic pressure on a malefactor.'[104] As lawyers, we may be more attuned to focusing on an immediate victory or failure in court, rather than considering the litigation's success in promoting wider objectives, or contributing to a 'broader symbolic legacy' capable of driving legal and political change.[105] However, advisory opinions which clarify State obligations in respect of climate change may form part of a longer-term strategy, creating political leverage to advance policy objectives or change norms.[106]

Widespread State representation in advisory opinions enriches the court or tribunal's understanding of the complex issues at hand, bringing legitimacy and greater weight to an advisory opinion. Broad participation shapes an opinion as an authoritative statement, which may then increase State acceptance of its legal pronouncements. The more States are heard, the more accepting they may be, even if not in complete agreement with the opinion. In this way, advocates can play a critical role in shaping States' submissions which, in turn, guide the tribunal or court's focus. From legal representatives to diplomats and civil society activists, States' advocates exert pressure and influence at all levels. That said, a healthy skepticism of the extent to which advocates impact legal change, particularly in respect of climate change, is warranted. As the late Professor Boyle opined, ultimately advocates before international institutions represent States and 'of course have to do what the client wants.'[107]

More can be done to encourage wider State participation. Doing away with the administrative burdens of filing in-person with the ICJ Registry is but one initiative capable of making the Court's procedural requirements facilitative, rather than prohibitive, of State participation. Allowing States to file

104 Douglas Guilfoyle, (n 24) 3; Benedict Kingsbury, 'International Courts: Uneven Jurisdiction in Global Order', in Crawford & Koskenniemi (eds), *The Cambridge Companion to International Law* (CUP 2012) 203, 217–218.

105 Frédéric Mégret, 'Immunities of Foreign Officials for international Crimes; The Dilemmas of Strategic Litigation' (2023) *Journal of Human Rights Litigation* 66, 1.1 <https://doi.org/10.1093/jhuman/huac067> accessed 6 February 2023.

106 Guilfoyle, (n 26) 4; see also Michael A Becker, 'Lawfare: Law as a Weapon of War. By Orde F Kittrie' (2017) BYIL 199, 201; Ben Batros & Tessa Khan, 'Thinking Strategically about Climate Change', in Rodríguez Garavito (ed), *Litigating the Climate Emergency: How Human Rights. Courts, and Legal Mobilization Can Bolster Climate Action* (CUP 2021) 104.

107 Alan Boyle, 'Remarks by Alan Boyle' (2015) 109 *Proceedings of the Annual Meeting (American Society of International Law)* 198, 199.

submissions electronically provides several benefits, including that States can maximize the time spent refining submissions without the need to factor in travel and printing time. At a minimum, a State could make a written statement even if unable to participate at the oral stage. Current procedural requirements may, therefore, skew the diversity of representation and views presented before the ICJ in future opinions. Where a whole section of the global community is largely absent from the ICJ's considerations due to barriers to participation, those States may ultimately be less inclined to accept the findings.

States' reactions are largely dependent on the content of the opinions themselves and their correlation with their pre-opinion views.[108] A possible eventuality is that the opinions do not affect the behavior of States in a discernible way, as in the *Conditions for Admission* advisory opinion, with States continuing to engage on climate change through the political processes of the COP as before, even where the opinions identify applicable legal obligations external to the climate change regime. In this way, States often refer to the non-binding nature of advisory opinions when dismissing their application, as in the case of the *Construction of a Wall* and *Chagos*. Some States may, therefore, reject any opinion which identifies obligations beyond those agreed in climate change treaties.[109]

With that in mind, there is the possibility of the opinions clarifying an existing duty to negotiate a new effective climate change treaty which meets the necessary action called for by the IPCC. Should that occur, States may push for a new treaty under the UNFCCC regime that updates and amends the obligations of States contained in the Paris Agreement. On the other hand, if some States take the view that the opinions rely on an unfounded interpretation of existing law, those may harden their positions during negotiations to avoid any language that allows for further expansive interpretations of the law.[110] Ultimately, if the climate change opinions are ignored by a majority (or powerful minority) of States, further opinions may follow which consider the legal consequences of States failing to adjust their behavior.

Some have opined that the value of these advisory opinions will be first and foremost in support of domestic litigation.[111] Conversely, they may serve as a basis for some States to resort to legal action in the form of contentious cases

---

108 For various options of possible replies, see, for example, Bodansky (n 77).

109 Benoit Mayer, 'International Advisory Proceedings on Climate Change' (2023) 44 *Michigan Journal of Int'l Law* 41; Malgosia Fitzmaurice & Agnes Viktoria Rydberg, 'Using International Law to Address the Effects of Climate Change: A Matter for the International Court of Justice?' (2021) 4 *Yearbook of International Disaster Law* 281, 303.

110 ibid 7.

111 ibid 6; Nollkaemper (n 5) 38; Fitzmaurice & Rydberg (n 110) 302.

against other States. With respect to interstate litigation, it is noteworthy that States have chosen conciliation as the default mechanism to address climate change disputes arising under the UNFCCC and the Paris Agreement.[112] That said, the mechanism for such conciliation has yet to be established. Only the Netherlands has accepted the jurisdiction of the ICJ under these agreements, and Solomon Islands and Tuvalu have accepted binding arbitration.[113]

Putting aside the question of whether interstate litigation is politically astute, the availability of forums with jurisdiction over interstate disputes concerning climate change must be considered. The availability of the ICJ's jurisdiction under the 'optional clause' is ultimately limited.[114] A potentially more available venue, given the ITLOS' *COSIS Opinion*, is under UNCLOS.[115] This follows the Tribunal's opinion that States' actions concerning the reduction of GHGs are also obligations under UNCLOS, and that the Paris Agreement is not *lex specialis* to UNCLOS and 'should be applied in such a way as not to frustrate the very goal of the Convention.'[116]

Notably, whether before the ICJ or under UNCLOS, interstate litigation is not a straightforward matter. Respondents are likely to raise a host of issues to counter such cases – both on jurisdiction and their merits – such as on jurisdiction *ratione loci*, standing, third-party rights, or causality between their actions and specific climate events.[117]

Of course, the various *legal* options explored above are not exclusive of the *political* effects and ramifications of the advisory opinions. Such ramifications too are ultimately dependent, among other things, on the actions States take in response to the various opinions, for example through the UNGA. Eventually,

112 United Nations Framework Convention on Climate Change (adopted 9 May 1992, entered into force 21 March 1994) 1771 UNTS 107, art 14; Paris Agreement (adopted 12 December 2015, entered into force 4 November 2016) 3156 UNTS 79, art 24.

113 'Declarations by the Parties' (*United Nations Climate Change*) <https://unfccc.int/process-and-meetings/the-convention/status-of-ratification/declarations-by-parties> accessed 11 March 2024; Paris Agreement (n 113).

114 Only 74 States have accepted the optional jurisdiction of the Court, some of which include conditions that would exclude such proceedings. For more see Nataša Nedeski, Tom Sparks & Gleider Hernández, 'The World Is Burning, Urgently and Irreparably – A Plea for Interim Protection against Climatic Change at the ICJ' (2023) 22(2) *The Law and Practice of Int'l Courts and Tribunals* 301.

115 Alan Boyle, 'Protecting the Marine Environment from Climate Change: The LOSC Part XII Regime', in Elise Johansen, Signe Veierud Busch & Ingvild Ulrikke Jakobsen (eds), *The Law of the Sea and Climate Change: Solutions and Constraints* (CUP 2021) 81, 97–99.

116 *COSIS Opinion* (n 15) §224.

117 See also Bodansky (n 77) 6; Maike Meguro, 'Litigating Climate Change through International Law: Obligations Strategy and Rights Strategy' (2020) 33 *Leiden Journal of Int'l Law* 933; Boyle (n 115) 99–101.

this can create further political and legal pressure to take effective action on the issue at hand, even for States which reject or ignore the opinions.[118] The climate change advisory opinion proceedings before ITLOS, the ICJ, and the IACtHR, may therefore pressure States to take action that, in effect, brings about the reduction of global emissions, which is really where the success of these proceedings should ultimately be measured.

118 Sthoeger (n 73).

CHAPTER 10

The Role of Civil Society in the Climate Change Advisory Proceedings

Harjeevan S. Narulla and Rohan A. Nanthakumar***

Abstract

This chapter examines the influential role of civil society in the climate change advisory proceedings before the International Court of Justice (ICJ), International Tribunal for the Law of the Sea (ITLOS), and Inter-American Court of Human Rights (IACtHR). While these proceedings primarily engage states and intergovernmental organisations, civil society actors, including NGOs, youth groups, Indigenous communities, and transnational advocacy networks, have been essential catalysts and contributors. The chapter first analyses procedural limitations at each tribunal and contrasts the relatively restrictive policies of the ICJ and ITLOS with the IACtHR's inclusive approach. Despite procedural constraints, civil society has effectively engaged in advisory proceedings, employing strategies like amicus curiae submissions, coordinated campaigns, and knowledge-sharing initiatives. We highlight five key ways civil society shapes these proceedings: (1) catalysing the advisory requests, (2) contributing substantive input despite procedural limitations, (3) educating and coordinating participants, (4) promoting advisory opinions' implementation, and (5) leveraging advisory opinions to support broader climate litigation. These actions underscore civil society's pivotal role in advancing climate justice within international law, amplifying diverse voices, and enhancing climate litigation's impact beyond the immediate advisory context.

Keywords

civil society – advisory proceedings – strategic climate litigation – human rights and climate change – international law – climate justice – rules of procedure

* Barrister, Doughty Street Chambers; Honorary Research Associate, University of Oxford's Sustainable Law Programme; Visiting Senior Fellow, Grantham Research Institute on Climate Change and the Environment at the London School of Economics, ORCID ID: 0009–0007-6730-5561, email: h.narulla@doughtystreet.co.uk.

** Consulting Counsel (International Law), Blue Ocean Law; Research Fellow (Centre for Comparative Constitutional Studies), University of Melbourne; ORCID ID: 0009–0002-5353-9993, email: rohan@blueoceanlaw.com.

 | DOI:10.1163/9789004730618_011

1 Introduction

The advisory opinions on climate change before the International Court of Justice (ICJ), the International Tribunal for the Law of the Sea (ITLOS) and the Inter-American Court of Human Rights (IACtHR) are historic proceedings of great significance to the climate litigation community. Part of the reason for this significance is the involvement and focus on the obligations of States in relation to climate change. This draws attention to the actions and arguments made by States and intergovernmental organisations in these proceedings, which naturally diverts focus away from civil society actors. Our task in this chapter is to turn the focus back upon civil society actors, and to attempt to understand their complex and shifting role in this unique set of proceedings. This chapter proceeds in two substantive sections.

The first section will 'zoom in,' by analysing the precise practice and procedure of the ICJ, ITLOS, and the IACtHR, in turn, to identify the ways in which civil society is permitted to engage in advisory proceedings in general. The avenues for formal participation will be shown to be narrow and limited, with the exception of the IACtHR. The second section will 'zoom out' to provide observations on how civil society has, in practice, been effective users of the advisory procedures in the context of the climate change advisory proceedings, despite these procedures not being designed for their use. Five observations are advanced: (1) civil society is highly active in climate litigation; (2) civil society has played an essential and strategic role in catalysing the climate change advisory proceedings; (3) despite technical and procedural constraints to its formal participation, civil society has actively contributed to the climate change advisory proceedings, directly and indirectly, by employing various means and strategies; (4) civil society has an important role in championing and supporting the implementation of advisory opinions after they have been furnished; and (5) civil society will use advisory opinions in their broader climate litigation strategies and efforts and, in so doing, can extend the reach of the advisory opinions beyond its most obvious and immediate impacts (namely, to clarify existing international law for States).

For our purposes, we consider 'civil society' to at least encompass environmental non-governmental organisations (NGOS), climate change activists and lawyers, scholars and academic or other research institutions. We would also include philanthropic funders,[1] and re-granters,[2] within the scope of civil

1 Such as, eg, the Gates Foundation or Open Society Foundation.

2 Such as, eg, the Foundation for International Law and the Environment (FILE).

society.[3] It would be remiss of us not to also emphasise specific cohorts or groups which contribute so significantly to climate litigation, in particular, 'the Youth' and Indigenous peoples and communities, as a core part of civil society. Indeed, as will be discussed below, the Youth can be credited with instigating the campaign for an ICJ advisory opinion in the first place.[4] And local and Indigenous peoples have been credited with catalysing the phenomenon of 'climate litigation' to begin with,[5] together with other approaches to ecological and environmental protection.[6] We also include Transnational Advocacy Networks (TANs) in our conception of civil society.[7] TANs are formed by numerous

3 The role of funders and re-granters is crucial, but under-studied. For a recent relevant treatment of these actors in climate litigation scholarship, see Jolene Lin & Jacqueline Peel, *Litigating Climate Change in the Global South* (OUP, 2024) 148, 179–180.

4 Children and young people have also been plaintiffs in significant climate litigation efforts, at domestic and international levels: see eg Committee on the Rights of the Child, *Decision adopted by the Committee on the Rights of the Child under the Optional Protocol to the Convention on the Rights of the Child, concerning Communication Nos. 104–107/2019: Chiara Sacchi et al v Argentina, Brazil, France, and Germany* (CRC/C/88/D/104/2019, CRC/C/88/D/105/2019, CRC/C/88/D/106/2019, CRC/C/88/D/107/2019), 11 November 2021; *Held v. Montana* CDV-2020-307, Montana First Judicial District Court, WL 1997864, decision of 14 August 2023 (USA); *Minister for the Environment v Sharma* [2022] FCAFC 35 (Australia).

5 The petition brought by the Inuit people to the Inter-American Commission of Human Rights (IACHR), seeking to compel the United States of America (USA) to join the Kyoto Protocol, is regarded by some as the first instance of climate litigation. In that petition, the Inuit people argued that the US's emissions amounted to a breach of human rights accorded to the Inuit people as it led to the loss of permafrost, and consequently, the loss of the ways of life of the Inuit people, given its adverse effects on housing, communication, safety, and food gathering. See Lin & Peel (n 3) 193. ('[w]hile the IACHR's response was disappointing, this petition can be viewed as the birth of the movement of seeking legal protection of rights accorded by international treaties in domestic and international courts.')

6 Lin & Peel (n 3) 189–193. There are several examples of Indigenous peoples who have used litigation to complement other efforts (including protest and advocacy) to protect their lands from environmentally destructive economic activities such as oil drilling and illegal logging. See eg *Mayagna (Sumo) Awas Tingni Community v. Nicaragua*, Merits, Reparations and Costs, Judgment of 31 August 2001, Inter-American Court of Human Rights 2001 Series C, No. 79; *Maniwa v Malijiwi* [2014] PGNC 25 (Papua New Guinea); *The Maya Leaders Alliance v The Attorney General of Belize* [2015] CCJ 15 (AJ), CCJ Appeal No BZCV2014/ 002, BZ Civil Appeal No 27 of 2010, 30 October 2015 (Belize). Note further, that the recognition of legal personhood of natural entities such as rivers is attributable in part to the efforts of Indigenous peoples: eg Whanganui River in NZ: Te Awa Tupua (Whanganui River Claims Settlement) Act 2016 (New Zealand); Atrato river in Colombia's Chocó region: *Atrato River Decision* T- 622/ 16 of November 10, 2016 (Sentencia T- 622/ 16 de Noviembre 10, 2016) (Colombia).

7 Keck and Sikkink define TANs as networks of activists, distinguishable largely by the centrality of principled ideas, causes, and norms in motivating their formation: Margaret E Keck & Kathryn Sikkink, *Activists Beyond Borders: Advocacy Networks in International Politics* (2nd edn, Cornell University Press 1998) 1.

civil society actors working in concert to achieve a particular systemic outcome.[8] As Lin and Peel explain in the context of the Global South, it is through transnational networks that there can be learning and sharing of information resources and legal strategies, norm diffusion, and flows of financial, legal and material support for climate litigation.[9]

As a final matter of introduction, we make two caveats. First, we are writing in our capacity as legal practitioners. We are intentionally descriptive and observational. While we draw on some scholarship, we do not offer an account of the role of civil society in the climate change advisory proceedings from the perspective of the social or political sciences. We warmly encourage others to engage in sustained scholarly work on this topic from those perspectives. Second, the authors have been and are currently active as counsel and legal advisers in each of the climate change advisory proceedings, as well as in other climate litigation. We have written this piece exclusively in our personal capacities; any views expressed and errors made are entirely our own and are not attributable to any States, organisations, or individuals we are affiliated with or otherwise represent. We acknowledge that any observations we make and conclusions we draw may necessarily be informed by our direct experiences in the field and that this may enhance, in some respects, but also limit in others, the overall authority of this piece.

2 The Technical Explanation: Procedural Rules for Civil Society Organisations at the ICJ, ITLOS and the IACtHR

To properly consider the role of civil society in the advisory opinions before the ICJ, ITLOS and the IACtHR, it is necessary to explore the procedural rules for each Court, and whether they permit formal or informal civil society participation in the proceedings. This section analyses the practice and procedure of the ICJ, ITLOS and the IACtHR in turn, to identify the ways in which civil society is permitted to engage in advisory proceedings in general. With this grounding, we will explore in Part C how civil society has operated in practice across the advisory proceedings.

8 TANs in the climate space include, eg, Climate Action Network (CAN) or the Fossil Fuel Non-Proliferation Treaty Initiative (FFNPT Initiative).

9 Lin & Peel (n 3) 148.

2.1 *Rules of Procedure for Civil Society Participation at the ICJ*

The practice and procedure of the ICJ is governed by the Charter of the United Nations,[10] the Statute of the International Court of Justice,[11] the Rules of the Court,[12] and non-binding Practice Directions. The procedure of the Court differs between contentious and advisory proceedings. Compared with contentious cases, the procedure for advisory proceedings is relatively flexible. Unlike other international courts and tribunals, such as the International Criminal Court (ICC), IACtHR, and the European Court of Human Rights (ECtHR), the ICJ has a limited formal role for NGOs and other forms of public participation by civil society.

Article 34(1) of the ICJ Statute makes clear that 'only States may be parties in cases before the Court.' Article 34(2) creates a role for public international organisations in contentious proceedings, stating that the Court 'may request of public international organisations information relevant to cases before it, and shall receive such information presented by such organisations on their own initiative.' In the context of advisory opinion proceedings, Article 66(2) of the ICJ Statute similarly provides for participation by States and 'international organisations:'

> The Registrar shall also, by means of a special and direct communication, notify *any state entitled to appear before the Court or international organization* considered by the Court, or, should it not be sitting, by the President, *as likely to be able to furnish information on the question*, that the Court will be prepared to receive, within a time-limit to be fixed by the President, written statements, or to hear, at a public sitting to be held for the purpose, oral statements relating to the question. (Emphasis added).

Therefore, unlike contentious cases, in advisory proceedings the Court must first invite participation from designated international organisations to prepare written statements. In practice, these are generally intergovernmental organisations, with some scope for inviting other international organisations of different kinds. In practice, an international organisation will often first request to participate in the advisory proceeding and the Court will authorise

---

10 Charter of the United Nations, signed 26 June 1945, 1 UNTS XVI (entered into force 24 October 1945).

11 Statute of the International Court of Justice, signed 26 June 1945, [1945] UKTS 67 (entered into force 24 October 1945).

12 Rules of Court of the International Court of Justice (adopted 14 April 1978) ICJ Rep 1983, 131.

them to do so. This approach has been maintained in the current ICJ proceedings, where, at the time of writing, the Court has (on request) invited and authorised the following 13 organisations to participate, none of which are civil society organisations: the International Union for the Conservation of Nature (IUCN),[13] the Commission of Small Island States on Climate Change and International Law (COSIS),[14] the European Union,[15] the African Union,[16] the Organisation of Petroleum Exporting Countries (OPEC),[17] the Organisation of African, Caribbean and Pacific States,[18] the Melanesian Spearhead Group,[19] the Forum Fisheries Agency,[20] the Pacific Community,[21] the Pacific Islands Forum,[22] the Alliance of Small Island States[23] the Parties to the Nauru Agreement Office,[24] and the World Health Organisation.[25]

The Court's previous practice in relation to NGO and public participation has been to limit its scope, with isolated exceptions. For example, the Court has previously consented to receiving an *amicus curiae* brief from the International League for the Rights of Man in the 1950 *International Status of South-West Africa* advisory opinion.[26] In the current advisory opinion proceedings on the right to strike, the Court has invited six non-state organisations with consultative status at the International Labour Organisation to participate in

13 International Court of Justice, *Obligations of States in respect of Climate Change (Request for Advisory Opinion)*, Press Release of 25 April 2023, General List No 187.

14 International Court of Justice, *Obligations of States in respect of Climate Change (Request for Advisory Opinion)*, Press Release of 22 June 2023, General List No 187.

15 International Court of Justice, *Obligations of States in respect of Climate Change (Request for Advisory Opinion)*, Press Release of 23 June 2023, General List No 187.

16 International Court of Justice, *Obligations of States in respect of Climate Change (Request for Advisory Opinion)*, Press Release of 18 July 2023, General List No 187.

17 International Court of Justice, *Obligations of States in respect of Climate Change (Request for Advisory Opinion)*, Press Release of 1 September 2023, General List No 187.

18 International Court of Justice, *Obligations of States in respect of Climate Change (Request for Advisory Opinion)*, Press Release of 20 September 2023, General List No 187.

19 ibid.

20 ibid.

21 International Court of Justice, *Obligations of States in respect of Climate Change (Request for Advisory Opinion)*, Press Release of 24 November 2023, General List No 187.

22 International Court of Justice, *Obligations of States in respect of Climate Change (Request for Advisory Opinion)*, Press Release of 20 December 2023, General List No 187.

23 ibid.

24 International Court of Justice, *Obligations of States in respect of Climate Change (Request for Advisory Opinion)*, Press Release of 4 March 2024, General List No 187.

25 International Court of Justice, *Obligations of States in respect of Climate Change (Request for Advisory Opinion)*, Press Release of 26 March 2024, General List No 187.

26 Lance Bartholomeusz, "The Amicus Curiae Before the International Courts and Tribunals" (2005) 5 *Non-State Actors and International Law* 216, p. 231.

the proceedings.[27] The Court is careful to note that such an approach is '*in light of the tripartite structure of the International Labour Organisation, which is comprised of representatives of Governments, employers and workers*,' and therefore a case-specific aberration.[28] The Court has also previously requested an *amicus* brief from Palestine, that is, neither a State nor international organisation at the relevant time.[29] However, based on the Court's approach to the case to date, it is unlikely that a similar request would be made of an NGO or other civil society group in the present ICJ proceedings on climate change. The Court has adopted a similarly stringent approach in contentious proceedings by regularly rejecting previous petitions by NGOs to participate by way of *amicus curiae* briefs.[30]

In addition to the procedural barriers to formal civil society participation, there have been isolated judicial statements from the Court directly challenging the role played by NGOs and civil society in international law. For example, in the 1996 *Legality of the Threat or Use of Nuclear Weapons* advisory opinion, Judge Guillaume critiqued the influence of the International Association of Lawyers against Nuclear Arms in successfully lobbying States to request an advisory opinion through the UN General Assembly.[31] Nonetheless, following reforms to the European Convention on Human Rights to allow *amicus* participation in 1998, the ICJ adopted Practice Direction XII in 2004 to regulate the submission of *amici curiae* in advisory opinion proceedings. The relevant provisions of the Practice Direction are as follows:

1. Where an *international non-governmental organization* submits a *written statement and/or document* in an advisory opinion case on its own initiative, such statement and/or document *is not to be considered as part of the case file*.
2. Such statements and/or documents *shall be treated as publications readily available* and may accordingly be referred to by States and intergovernmental organizations presenting written and oral statements in the case in the same manner as publications in the public domain.

---

27 International Court of Justice, *Right to Strike under ILO Convention No. 87* (*Request for Advisory Opinion*) Order 16 November 2023, General List No 191.

28 ibid.

29 Anna Dolidze, 'Advisory Opinion on Responsibility and Liability for International Seabed Mining (ITLOS Case No. 17) and the Future of NGO Participation in the International Legal Process' (2013) 19(2) *ILSA Journal of International and Comparative Law* 379, 393.

30 ibid.

31 *Legality of the Threat or Use of Nuclear Weapons* (Advisory Opinion) [1996] ICJ Rep 226, Separate Opinion of Judge Guillaume, 65–66.

3. Written statements and/or documents submitted by international non-governmental organizations *will be placed in a designated location in the Peace Palace*. All States as well as intergovernmental organizations presenting written or oral statements under Article 66 of the Statute will be informed as to the location where statements and/or documents submitted by international non-governmental organizations may be consulted. (Emphasis added).[32]

The Practice Direction is clear in establishing that any *amicus curiae* will not form part of the case file. However, 'international non-governmental organisations' are still able to submit 'written statement[s] and/or document[s]' on their own initiative. The status of those statements and documents is akin to public documents, described as 'publications readily available.' They therefore may be referenced by States and participating intergovernmental organisations in their written or oral submissions. The physical copies of any statements or documents provided by NGOs will be placed in the Peace Palace, with States and intergovernmental organisations notified as to their location.

This peripheral formal role for civil society stands in contrast to other courts such as the ICC, the IACtHR and the ECtHR, and may indicate an intention from the Court to circumscribe the substantive influence that civil society has over legal proceedings before the Court. Nonetheless, the current ICJ proceedings on climate change have seen wide participation from civil society organisations that have taken the opportunity to submit *amicus curiae* briefs, presumably with the knowledge that such documents would not form part of the case file, or even be publicly acknowledged by the ICJ. A list of civil society submissions is captured on the Sabin Centre for Climate Change Law's Climate Litigation Database, and includes joint or individual *amici curiae* from over 20 civil society organisations.[33] It remains to be seen what doctrinal influence, if any, these submissions will have in the context of complex proceedings where 91 States and international organisations filed initial written statements,[34] followed by 62 of those same States and international organisations filing a

32 International Court of Justice, *Practice Direction XII*, adopted 30 July 2004, accessed at: <https://www.icj-cij.org/practice-directions#fn1>.

33 Sabin Centre for Climate Change Law, *Request for an advisory opinion on the obligations of States with respect to climate change* (2024) accessed at: <https://climatecasechart.com/non-us-case/request-for-an-advisory-opinion-on-the-obligations-of-states-with-respect-to-climate-change/>.

34 International Court of Justice, *Obligations of States in respect of Climate Change (Request for Advisory Opinion)*, Press Release of 12 April 2024, General List No 187.

second round of written comments.[35] Based on the ITLOS advisory opinion and past ICJ advisory opinions, it may also be difficult to ascertain if civil society submissions have had any bearing on the final opinion once it is released, given that both ITLOS and the ICJ do not generally identify arguments made by particular parties in their advisory opinions. A close textual analysis of the opinion, cross-referenced against arguments set out in *amici curiae* and in State and international organisation written submissions will be required to make any empirical claims about the doctrinal impact of civil society submissions. While such an analysis is possible in relation to the recently released ITLOS advisory opinion, it is well beyond the scope of this chapter. We will instead consider the Tribunal's practice and procedure relating to civil society involvement, which largely mirrors the ICJ's regime, before concluding this Part with an analysis of the IACtHR's substantively different approach.

2.2 *Rules of Procedure for Civil Society Participation at the ITLOS*

The rules of procedure that apply to ITLOS are set out in the UN Convention on the Law of the Sea (UNCLOS),[36] the Statute of the Tribunal,[37] and the Rules of the Tribunal.[38] ITLOS has a very similar procedure to the ICJ, in limiting formal participation rights to States and intergovernmental organisations. This is set out in Article 133 of the Rules of the Tribunal:

1. The Registrar shall forthwith give notice of the request for an advisory opinion to all States Parties.
2. The Chamber, or its President if the Chamber is not sitting, shall identify the intergovernmental organizations which are likely to be able to furnish information on the question. The Registrar shall give notice of the request to such organizations.
3. States Parties and the organizations referred to in paragraph 2 shall be invited to present written statements on the question within a time-limit fixed by the Chamber or its President if the Chamber is not sitting. Such

35 International Court of Justice, *Obligations of States in respect of Climate Change (Request for Advisory Opinion)*, Press Release of 16 August 2024, General List No 187.

36 United Nations Convention on the Law of the Sea (adopted 10 December 1982, entered into force 16 November 1994) 1833 UNTS 3.

37 Statute of the International Tribunal for the Law of the Sea (10 December 1982) UN Doc A/CONF.62/122, Annex VI.

38 International Tribunal for the Law of the Sea, 'Rules of the Tribunal' (adopted 28 October 1997, amended 25 September 2020).

statements shall be communicated to States Parties and organizations which have made written statements.[39]

A notable difference between the ITLOS and ICJ rules is that Article 133(2) of the ITLOS rules refers specifically to 'intergovernmental organizations,' whereas the ICJ Rules at Article 66(2) refer to 'international organizations.' As we have set out above, this means that in limited circumstances the ICJ has adopted a slightly more flexible approach to involvement of non-state actors who are not intergovernmental organisations. ITLOS has no similar procedural history, based presumably on its unambiguous procedural language, and also its comparative dearth of advisory opinions proceedings, having had only three – the current proceedings before the Tribunal on climate change; the 2013 proceedings on illegal, unreported, and unregulated fishing requested by the Sub-Regional Fisheries Commission;[40] and the 2011 advisory opinion submitted to the Seabed Disputes Chamber, on the responsibilities and obligations of States with respect to activities in the Area.[41] In the 2013 advisory opinion, the Tribunal adopted a more inclusive approach to *amicus curiae* submissions than the ICJ, by noting submissions from Greenpeace International (GPI) and World Wildlife Fund for Nature (WWF), communicating those submissions to the States and intergovernmental organisations participating in the case, uploading them to the Tribunal's website for the case, and allowing them to submit *amici* for both written stages of the proceedings.[42] They did however deny the request of WWF and GPI to make oral submissions in the case. As Dolidze notes, by approaching civil society in this way, 'the Tribunal allowed the NGOs to achieve the aims which would have been attained with their official participation in the case.'[43]

In the present proceedings before the Tribunal, it was clear that other members of civil society had taken note of the Tribunal's practice in 2013, with 10 civil society written statements submitted to the Tribunal on behalf of 13 civil

39 ibid, art 133.

40 *Request for an Advisory Opinion submitted by the Sub-Regional Fisheries Commission* (Advisory Opinion of 2 April 2015), Case No 21, ITLOS Reports 2015, 4 (*SRFC Opinion*).

41 *Responsibilities and obligations of States with respect to activities in the Area* (*Request for Advisory Opinion submitted to the Seabed Disputes Chamber*), Advisory Opinion, Case No 17, ITLOS Reports 2011, p. 10.

42 *SRFC Opinion* (n 40) see §§13, 15, 23, and 27.

43 Dolidze (n 30) 381.

society actors.[44] The Tribunal did not modify its procedure from 2013, again uploading written statements to the Tribunal's website, communicating the submissions to parties in the case, and denying the civil society actors the opportunity to make oral submissions. The increase in participation from civil society can presumably be attributed to those organisations seeing value in this level of engagement, which is greater than that afforded under the ICJ rules of procedure. However, both ITLOS and the ICJ stand in stark contrast to the IACtHR, which has the most inclusive and expansive procedure in relation to engagement with civil society organisations.

2.3 *Rules of Procedure for Civil Society Participation at the IACtHR*

The IACtHR's rules of procedure are set out in the American Convention on Human Rights (ACHR),[45] the IACtHR Statute,[46] and the Rules of Procedure of the Inter-American Court.[47] As with the ICJ, the procedure for advisory opinions is relatively flexible, with the rules for contentious cases applied by analogy in advisory proceedings where the Court finds them applicable.[48] The Court retains wide discretion to determine when contentious procedures may be compatible.[49] Advisory proceedings generally have a written and an oral

44 See the case page on the ITLO website: https://www.itlos.org/en/main/cases/list-of-cases/request-for-an-advisory-opinion-submitted-by-the-commission-of-small-island-states-on-climate-change-and-international-law-request-for-advisory-opinion-submitted-to-the-tribunal/ (visited on 3 October 2024). The civil society actors who contributed to the ITLOS proceeding included the following: United Nations Special Rapporteurs on Human Rights & Climate Change, Toxics & Human Rights and Human Rights & the Environment; High Seas Alliance; ClientEarth; Opportunity Green; Center for International Environmental Law (CIEL) and Greenpeace International; Advisory Committee on Protection of the Sea (ACOPS); World Wide Fund for Nature (WWF); Our Children's Trust and Oxfam International; Observatory for Marine and Coastal Governance; and One Ocean Hub.

45 American Convention on Human Rights (adopted 22 November 1969, entered into force 18 July 1978) 1144 UNTS 123.

46 See also Statute of the Inter-American Court of Human Rights, Adopted by the General Assembly of the OAS at its ninth regular session, held in La Paz, Bolivia, October 1979 (Resolution No 448).

47 Rules of Procedure of the Inter-American Court of Human Rights, entered into force 1 January 2010, approved by the Court during its LXXXV Regular Period of Sessions, held from November 16 to November 28, 2009, reprinted in Basic Documents Pertaining to Human Rights in the Inter-American System (updated to June 1010), OEA/Ser.L/V/I.4 rev. 13, 30 June 2010, at 185.

48 IACtHR Rules of Procedure, art 74.

49 *Proposed Amendments to the Naturalization Provisions of the Constitution of Costa Rica*, IACtHR Advisory Opinion OC-4/84 of 19 January 1984, Ser.A, No 4, §17.

phase, although the Court may decide to dispense with the oral phase.[50] Unlike the ICJ and ITLOS, the IACtHR has very broad standing provisions as set out in Article 73 of the IACtHR Rules of Procedure. Civil society and non-State and non-intergovernmental actors play an important role in all stages of the proceedings. When the Court receives a request for an advisory opinion, the Court must transmit the request to all OAS Member States, the OAS Secretary General and Permanent Council, the Inter-American Commission and OAS organs who may be implicated in the substance of the case.[51] The Court also publishes a request on its website and puts out press releases, so as to ensure that civil society and other relevant actors are well aware of the proceedings.

During the written proceedings, the President is authorised to invite any 'interested party' to submit a written brief on the relevant issues. There is no requirement, as there is before the ICJ, that interested parties are 'likely able to furnish information on the question.'[52] Instead, where the Presidency exercises its discretion to include interested parties, the right to participate is essentially without qualification: 'The Presidency may invite or authorize any interested party to submit a written opinion on the issues covered by the request.'[53] The only exception to the general right to participate is if a State is seeking an advisory opinion on the compatibility of its laws under Article 64(2), in which case the President must first consult with the State concerned before inviting participation from interested parties.[54]

The expansive approach to interested parties is consistent across advisory and contentious proceedings, with Article 44 of the Rules of Procedure allowing for the submission of *amicus curiae* briefs in contentious cases. The Court's Rules of Procedure define *amicus curiae* as being a:

> person or institution who is unrelated to the case and to the proceeding and submits to the Court reasoned arguments on the facts contained in the presentation of the case or legal considerations on the subject-matter of the proceeding by means of a document or argument presented at a hearing.[55]

---

50 IACtHR Rules of Procedure, art 74(4): 'At the conclusion of the written proceedings, the Court shall decide whether oral proceedings should take place and shall establish the date for a hearing, unless it delegates the latter task to the Presidency.'

51 IACtHR Rules of Procedure, art 73(1).

52 ICJ Statute, art 66(2).

53 IACtHR Rules of Procedure, art 73(3).

54 ibid.

55 IACtHR Rules of Procedure, art 2(3).

This inclusive approach also extends to oral proceedings. Over time the Court has evolved its practice to hear oral arguments from interested parties, based on a rule used in the context of contentious proceedings, stating that the Court 'may hear as an alleged victim, witness, expert witness, or in any other capacity, any person whose evidence, statement, testimony or opinion it deems to be relevant.'[56] In recent advisory proceedings, the Court's practice has consisted of inviting all parties that have submitted written comments to present oral arguments.[57] That approach was followed in the current advisory proceedings on climate change, with the Court receiving a record number of written submissions from over 300 parties.[58]

All of these parties were invited to make oral submissions at three sets of hearings, held in Barbados, a small island developing State, and in Brasilia and Manaus, Brazil, where the intent seemed to be proximity to the Amazon region as a means of signifying the Court's appreciation of the significance of these proceedings for key ecosystems and Indigenous communities. Many interested parties accepted the opportunity to make oral submissions, which appeared to be grouped according to areas of thematic focus. Most English-speaking, Global North civil society actors were invited to make oral submissions in Barbados,[59] while the remaining parties appeared at the hearings in Brasilia and Manaus. From our observations, this gave each set of proceedings a distinct character, which altered to some extent the role played by civil society. In Barbados, the high concentration of climate legal professionals, invariably but not exclusively from the Global North, meant a more legalistic and technical set of exchanges between the Court and interested parties. This stood in clear contrast to the tenor and substance of oral submissions made in Manaus, where Indigenous groups, Afro-descendant groups, and individuals and organisations representing other vulnerable communities provided oral submissions akin to witness

56 ibid, art 58(a) (emphasis added).

57 See for example *The Right to Information on Consular Assistance Within the Framework of the Guarantees of Legal Due Process.* Advisory Opinion OC-16/99, Inter-American Court of Human Rights Series A No 16 (1 October 1999) §8*; International Responsibility for the Promulgation and Enforcement of Laws in Violation of the Convention* (*Arts. 1 and 2 of the American Convention on Human Rights*), Advisory Opinion OC-14/94, Inter-American Court of Human Rights Series A No 14 (9 December 1994) §20.

58 Inter-American Court of Human Rights, *Observations on the Request for Advisory Opinion* (2024), accessed at: https://www.corteidh.or.cr/observaciones_oc_new.cfm?nId_oc=2634 (visited on 3 October 2024).

59 Inter-American Court of Human Rights, *Observations on the Request for Advisory Opinion* (2024), accessed at: https://www.corteidh.or.cr/tablas/166POS-Barbados/index.html. (visited on 3 October 2024).

testimony, focusing on the impacts of climate change on their lives. Apparent thematic grouping of interested parties allowed the Court to focus on discrete topics in each session. For example, during the hearings in Manaus on 29 May 2024, the Court heard from the International Organisation for Migration the Office of the United Nations High Commissioner for Refugees, Open Society Justice Initiative, and the Legal Clinic on Cross-border Human Mobility, which allowed a detailed and focused inquiry into the topic of climate migration and displacement.[60] While it is unclear to what extent interested parties collaborated in preparation for these oral hearings, the Court's approach to case management certainly allowed for civil society alignment and cross-fertilisation through the mechanism of the hearing itself. In this way, the Court's proactive approach to civil society seemed to complement the diversity and depth of expertise across the many interested parties participating in the proceedings. This stands in contrast to civil society engagement before ITLOS and the ICJ, but, as we explore in the next Part, that is not necessarily an impediment to their effective utilisation of those proceedings to pursue their goals.

3 A More Holistic Account: Observations from the Field

The earlier section demonstrated the formal role of civil society in advisory proceedings, particularly from a technical and procedural vantage point. Of course, the story does not end there. The authors contend that the role of civil society in the advisory opinion (AO) proceedings takes on great significance if one is to 'zoom out' and adopt a more holistic view. The bigger picture reveals that civil society has been an effective user of the AO procedures despite these procedures not being designed for their use. We advance five observations to illuminate that bigger picture.

3.1 *Civil Society is Highly Active in the Field of Climate Litigation*

Climate litigation started with – and is sustained by – the efforts of civil society. Different actors take on different functions and perform different tasks in the field. These actors are often operating synergistically. They are responsible for bringing the lion's share of climate litigation. As Lin and Peel note, such

60 Inter-American Court of Human Rights, *Observations on the Request for Advisory Opinion* (2024), accessed at: https://www.corteidh.or.cr/observaciones_oc_new.cfm?nId_oc=2634 (visited on 3 October 2024).

environmental NGOs have filed (either on their own or as part of a coalition) about 70% of the climate litigation cases in the Global South.[61]

The roles played by civil society actors are many and varied. Some are focused on devising litigation strategies and then investigating and building up cases to sue governments and corporate polluters as parties to the litigation in their own name and right (either separately or in concert with others). Some act on behalf of litigants they have retained as clients, including on pro bono bases. Some may depart from traditional public interest lawyering methods and approach climate litigation as 'movement lawyers.'[62] Some do not bring litigation directly, but seek to intervene in proceedings as friends of the court or *amicus curiae*. Some do not engage in climate litigation 'on the record,' but give support to those who are engaged in such litigation, ranging from advocacy and strategy, legal research, funding and communications. Beyond this, many actors in civil society play an important role in reporting on climate litigation and updating the general public on developments in climate litigation. Many civil society actors can engage in any or all of these strategies at any given time, choosing the most appropriate strategy for the specific circumstances of a given case or desired policy objective.[63]

61 Lin & Peel (n 3) 149.

62 As to 'movement lawyering': see https://www.movementlawlab.org/about/movement-lawyering, visited on 3 October 2024 ('Movement lawyers work in deep collaboration with social movements, leveraging every legal hook possible to build the collective power needed to transform our political and economic systems towards human dignity, multiracial democracy, and ecological harmony.') The authors note that some practitioners regard the term '*movement lawyering*' as simply a modern term to describe an existing and deeply established approach to strategic litigation carried out for decades by public interest lawyers working in the fields of civil liberties, human rights and environmental law.

63 For example, take ClientEarth, whose many functions are detailed by Lin and Peel in these terms (p. 189): 'ClientEarth is well-known in the Global North for bringing some of the most ground- breaking climate lawsuits against governments and companies. ClientEarth describes itself as 'a charity that uses the power of the law to protect people and the planet … we work on laws throughout their lifetime, from the earliest stages to implementation. And when those laws are broken, we go to court to enforce them. ClientEarth's work in the Global North has a strong focus on litigation alongside other legal interventions. In contrast, ClientEarth's work in the Global South focuses on the earlier phases of the lifecycle of the law. This includes stakeholder engagement to support effective implementation of climate change laws, and training lawyers, public prosecutors, and judges. In some instances, ClientEarth lawyers provide legal support to local communities and lawyers in their climate litigation efforts.'

3.2 *Civil Society Has Played a Role in Catalysing the Climate Change Advisory Proceedings*

Civil society has long played a role in the development of international law,[64] including by seeking to persuade governments or international agencies to seek authoritative judgments.[65] As Becker has observed in the context of ICJ proceedings, although the Statute of the ICJ provides that only States may appear as parties before the Court, 'other types of actors (non-governmental organizations, corporations, international organizations) can play a key role in persuading States to initiate ICJ proceedings, whether in the form of a contentious case or by supporting an advisory opinion request.'[66] As Becker puts it, civil society can 'play a critical role in creating the conditions that make it feasible to pursue justice at the ICJ, including by shaping how States define their interests and by promoting "the rule of law from below".'[67]

This has occurred in previous requests for advisory opinions. In the 1990s, a coalition of NGOs led a campaign to have the ICJ furnish an advisory opinion on the question of the legality of nuclear weapons.[68] While two judges expressed concerns about the role of civil society lurking behind the advisory opinion request,[69] most members of the Court raised no concerns over the role of civil society. Civil society has also catalysed the circumstances under which contentious cases are brought.[70]

---

64 See, eg, Arnold Pronto, 'Some Thoughts on the Making of International Law' (2008) 19 *EJIL* 601, 603.

65 Michael A Becker, 'Pay No Attention to that Man behind the Curtain: The Role of Civil Society and Other Actors in Decisions to Litigate at the International Court of Justice', in *Max Planck Yearbook of United Nations Law* (Brill 2023) 91 (citing, see S Charnovitz, Two Centuries of Participation: NGOs and International Governance' (1997) 18 *Michigan JIL* 183, 272–273).

66 ibid, 90 [abstract].

67 ibid, 107.

68 *Legality of the Threat or Use of Nuclear Weapons* (Advisory Opinion) [1996] ICJ Rep 226.

69 Judge Guillaume noted the intensive work of advocacy groups to secure the resolution and 'to induce States hostile to nuclear weapons' to appear in the proceedings. Judge Guillaume considered that the Court might 'pierc[e] the veil' and find the request inadmissible because it came from 'powerful pressure groups' rather than the UN General Assembly itself: *Legality of the Threat or Use of Nuclear Weapons* (n 69) Separate Opinion of Judge Guillaume, 287–288. Judge Oda considered that the campaign, as led by NGOs, was an improper attempt to short-circuit the political process of negotiation on the subject matter and that civil society involvement had contributed to the very inadequacy of the question put to the Court, which 'did not reflect a meaningful consensus:' *Legality of the Threat or Use of Nuclear Weapons* (n 69) Separate Opinion of Judge Oda, 341.

70 Becker (n 65) 99. For instance, this happened in the Whaling Case. Becker recalls the story in the following terms: '[T]he International Fund for Animal Welfare (IFAW) played

Civil society catalysed the ICJ climate change advisory proceedings. A group of law students from the University of the South Pacific are credited with instigating the campaign for an advisory opinion, which was embraced by the Republic of Vanuatu, who then spearheaded the diplomatic campaign for a UNGA resolution requesting an advisory opinion from the Court.[71]

The story is well-known and set out elsewhere.[72] However, it is worth recounting again for the explicit purpose of singling out and appreciating the role that was played by civil society. In a short piece on the role of advocates in the conception of advisory opinion requests,[73] Wewerinke-Singh, Viñuales and Aguon – colleagues, who have together been advising the Republic of Vanuatu in relation to an ICJ climate change advisory opinion from its inception – recount the early phases of work. This recount offers a helpful vignette of the important, catalysing role, that civil society plays. For instance, they recall that:

> It all began on the Vanuatu campus of the University of the South Pacific, where students from twelve Pacific Island countries (Cook Islands, Fiji, Kiribati, Marshall Islands, Nauru, Niue, Samoa, Solomon Islands, Tokelau, Tonga, Tuvalu, and Vanuatu) were tasked with identifying legal strategies for addressing climate change. This group acted as the initial advocates. They conceived the ambitious idea of seeking an advisory opinion from

a more direct role in laying the foundation for ICJ litigation. After Japan launched a new 'scientific whaling' program in 2005 involving higher catch limits, IFAW convened a series of high- level expert panels to study potential legal strategies to challenge Japan's actions, including an ICJ case. The effort to draw upon professional expertise (rather than IFAW simply proposing that Australia take Japan to the ICJ) gave the idea enhanced credibility. IFAW also found itself in the right place at the right time. Japanese whaling became an issue in the 2007 Australian election as the opposition Labor Party made a pledge to pursue litigation if elected. When the Labor Party then prevailed, Australia, after some delay, took the weighty decision in 2010 to bring the case against Japan, a close ally and trading partner.'

71 V Volvovici, 'Pacific Islands Students Target UN Court as Key Weapon to Fight Climate Change' (16 September 2022) Reuters, available at: https://www.reuters.com/world/asia-pacific/pacific-islands-students-target-un-court-key-weapon-fight-climate-change-2022-09-16/ (visited 3 October 2024). An alliance of over 1,500 civil society organizations also pledged support for the campaign. Climate Action Network International, 'Thousands of Civil Society Organisations Call on Countries to Support Vanuatu Climate Justice Initiative' (5 May 2022), available at: https://climatenetwork.org/2022/05/05/thousands-of-civil-society-organisations-call-on-countries-to-support-vanuatu-climate-justice-initiative/ (last visited 3 October 2024).

72 Margaretha Wewerinke-Singh, Jorge E. Viñuales & Julian Aguon, 'The Role of Advocates in the Conception of Advisory Opinion Requests' (2023) 117 *AJIL Unbound* 277–281.

73 ibid.

the ICJ on climate change and human rights. They formed an organization, the Pacific Islands Students Fighting Climate Change, and embarked on a campaign to rally support for the idea, emphasizing 'the obligations of States to protect the rights of present and future generations from the adverse effects of climate change.'

A second track of advocacy emerged when the government of Vanuatu decided to embrace the students' idea and launched a diplomatic campaign toward its realization. In navigating the legal complexities of the diplomatic process, Vanuatu sought the counsel of Blue Ocean Law, a boutique international law firm from Guam known for its grassroots orientation and commitment to advancing the rights of Indigenous peoples.

Guided by the vision of the Pacific Island youth and Vanuatu leaders, the diverse team at Blue Ocean Law – comprised of both in-house and external counsel – added a third track of advocacy, crafting a legal strategy aimed at generating the legal change that could begin to deliver on the hitherto elusive promise of climate justice for the peoples of the Pacific and the world at large.

While these tracks of advocacy were distinct, the various advocates involved made efforts to ensure that they were mutually reinforcing. The government of Vanuatu and its legal team liaised with the youth leaders to turn their demands into a carefully crafted legal strategy capable of securing the necessary support of UN members while retaining the integrity of the legal question being asked of the ICJ. Dozens of public events featuring youth leaders, Vanuatu officials and members of the legal team, along with other speakers, were held to communicate the various dimensions of the initiative to different audiences.

The youth leaders themselves campaigned with vigor and sophistication, as illustrated by the 'climate justice flotilla' sailing past UN headquarters in September 2022. The *vaka*, or traditional canoe, symbolized the journey from the Pacific to the United Nations, its arrival coinciding with Vanuatu's first official announcement of the initiative at the General Assembly. Banners with 'Our Survival Is Our Human Right,' 'Vote Yes for Climate Justice,' and 'AO Let's Go' bolstered the visibility and appeal of the campaign at this critical juncture.

There are at least four intersection points with civil society. The first is at the very outset, with the idea emerging from the collective imagination and dedication of a group of law students from the University of South Pacific. The second is at the commencement of the formal campaign, spearheaded by Vanuatu, where counsel affiliated with Blue Ocean Law were retained to work with the Republic of Vanuatu in devising a legal strategy for ushering a request for an ICJ advisory opinion through the UNGA. The third intersection is the broader advocacy and campaigning work undertaken by the Youth, which seek to enhance awareness-raising and consensus-building. A fourth intersection point came later, at the various stages of consultation around the negotiation and drafting of the legal question to be referred to the Court, which involved working with youth leaders and grassroots movements.[74] Overall, these efforts helped to create the political and social conditions under which a request for a climate change advisory opinion could be made by the UNGA, by consensus, to the ICJ.

3.3 *Civil Society Has Actively Contributed to the Climate Change Advisory Proceedings, Directly and Indirectly, by Employing Various Means and Strategies*

In the context of the climate change advisory proceedings, we have observed various techniques and strategies being deployed by civil society actors, both separately and in concert. We discuss these below.

3.3.1 Making Submissions, as Party or *Amicus Curiae*

We have observed civil society make submissions across each of the three advisory proceedings on climate change, in different ways. The high watermark is the IACtHR advisory opinion proceeding, which attracted civil society submissions from more than 300 organisations, as noted above. These submissions came from a large suite of civil society actors, including local communities and Indigenous peoples, NGOs, individuals with academic or organisational affiliations, academic institutions, individuals in their private capacities, and even an energy company. These submissions are official and on the case file.[75] A large proportion of these civil society actors also made oral submissions at the public hearings in Barbados and Brazil.

Civil society actors also made submissions to both ITLOS and the ICJ in their respective advisory opinion processes, as we set out above. For these proceedings, the written statements submitted by civil society actors are not included as part of the case file. In the ITLOS context, the Tribunal's Registry still added

74 ibid, 278–279.

75 Inter-American Court of Human Rights, *Observations on the Request for Advisory Opinion* (2024), accessed at: https://www.corteidh.or.cr/observaciones_oc_new.cfm?nId_oc=2634 (visited on 3 October 2024).

civil society submissions to the online case page of the website, consistently with past practice of the Tribunal in an earlier 2013 advisory proceeding.[76]

Whether on the case file or not, civil society submissions play an important role in advisory opinion proceedings. They helpfully add to the suite of materials made available to the Court and to the parties in advance of the hearing. As Judge MacGregor of the IACtHR has recognised in his separate opinion furnished in *Lhaka Honhat*,[77] the active participation of civil society in the procedures and proceedings of the Court, including the *amicus curiae* mechanism, is 'one of the fundamental pillars' of the Court's work and ultimately 'strengthens the multidimensional dialogue in favour of inter-American public order in the region.'[78] Although civil society submissions are less formally authoritative than State and international organisations' submissions, 'they allow the Court to benefit from greater insight regarding domestic and international law and, by drawing on valuable contributions from civil society, [the Court] can gain a panoramic view of the implications of its decision.'[79]

Consistent with these remarks, the authors have observed – in the context of the climate change advisory proceedings – the unique and important contribution that civil society submissions can make. Civil society submissions can be broad and bold. Civil society actors have different stakeholders to States and intergovernmental organisations and this means they may be less constrained (or have different types of constraints) on what they can or cannot say. Of crucial importance, civil society submissions can more readily adopt diverse and distinctive perspectives and inject new and fresh voices into the proceeding. They can act as a bridge between courts and particular people and groups who are affected by and thus have an interest in the advisory proceeding, and who possess knowledge and perspectives that would be of assistance to the Court, but who – by reason of procedural rules and technical constraints – may have no (or limited) formal avenues to intervene in the proceedings. In the context of the climate change advisory opinions, this would encompass groups such as Indigenous peoples and young people, who have contributed least to climate change and are disproportionately affected by its impacts; and who bring distinctive and important perspectives that may be of assistance to a court or tribunal in the exercise of its advisory jurisdiction. In our view, the contributions

76 *Request for an Advisory Opinion submitted by the Sub-Regional Fisheries Commission* (Advisory Opinion of 2 April 2015), Case No 21, ITLOS Reports 2015, 4.

77 *Case of Indigenous Communities of the Lhaka Honhat (Our Land) Association v Argentina* (Merits, Reparations and Costs). Inter-American Court of Human Rights Series C No 400 (6 February 2020) §§70–82.

78 ibid, §79.

79 ibid, §79.

of such cohorts have been profound and powerful.[80] The quality of any advisory opinion process on climate change would be diminished if these critical perspectives were entirely absent. Civil society performs a helpful function in bridging the gap and finding pathways for these important contributions.

3.3.2 Building Knowledge in Participants to Advisory Opinion Processes and Creating Opportunities for Productive Coordination

Civil society actors are often subject-matter experts. A key function they perform is to impart knowledge on participants to advisory opinion processes who do not necessarily possess specialised knowledge or require some further building of capacity. One way in which civil society does this is by developing and sharing briefing materials. Other ways include facilitating opportunities for knowledge production, information-sharing and coordination. Such strategies have been employed in the context of the climate change advisory proceedings. There have been many resources developed and shared by numerous civil society actors in connection with each of the climate change advisory proceedings.[81] *Amicus curiae* submissions can also be understood as a type of

80 By way of example, the UN Special Rapporteur on the human right to a clean, healthy & sustainable environment said in a Tweet dated 27 March 2024: '[t]he Greenpeace International submission to the International Court of Justice for its advisory opinion on the climate crisis is one of the most powerful legal documents that I have ever read, weaving stories and law into an unorthodox but compelling brief.' Available at: https://twitter.com/Greenpeace/status/1773377611726512135 (visited on 3 October 2024).

81 For example: (1) the Pacific Islands Students Fighting Climate Change released a '*Youth Climate Justice Handbook*', which sought to provide key briefing materials and information for an advisory opinion on climate change and human rights, from the perspective of the youth. The Youth Climate Justice Handbook comprised of three parts: (a) Summary for Policymakers, designed to assist policymakers' decisions regarding whether, and how, their governments should contribute to the ICJ climate advisory proceedings; (b) Legal Memorandum, containing legal analysis on the questions asked of the ICJ in UNGA Resolution 77/276; and (c) a Status Report on the principles of international human rights law relevant to climate change: see https://www.pisfcc.org/handbook (visited on 3 October 2024). (2) The Institute for Governance & Sustainable Development prepared several background documents on scientific and legal considerations at the nexus of climate change and human rights to support the efforts of civil society in submitting arguments to the IACtHR in connection with its advisory opinion on *The Climate Emergency and Human Rights*. These briefing materials included a climate science brief; a compendium of climate change and human rights jurisprudence; a collection and summary of secondary sources on climate change and human rights; perspectives on 'fair share' for the purposes of CBDR-RC; analysis of legal remedies to address climate change and protect human rights; and background note on the need for fast near-term climate mitigation to slow feedbacks and tipping points; ad a primer on cutting methane as the best strategy for slowing warming in the decade leading up to 2030:

shared resource, regardless of their status as being formally included in the case file or not. This is particularly true in the unique scenario of three parallel sets of advisory proceedings on climate change with substantial doctrinal overlap, where publicly released submissions by civil society can also be used as a resource to inform written and oral submissions being made before the other courts. It is also reasonable to assume that the vast collective corpus of publicly available legal submissions made before the IACtHR in particular, but also ITLOS and the ICJ, will inform and catalyse future climate litigation at the international, regional and domestic level. The simultaneous public production of such varied legal analyses on almost all dimensions of climate litigation is unprecedented and will be an important resource for the climate litigation and research community for years to come.

Moreover, in our capacities as counsel and legal advisers to various players across the climate change advisory proceedings, we have been involved in events organised by civil society actors which were directed towards sharing knowledge and experience and supporting coordination efforts amongst like-minded participants. This was in part to strengthen common positions and ensure they are put in mutually reinforcing ways; to better understand areas of divergence; and workshop approaches and responses to any contrary arguments or positions. Such opportunities took various forms, be it online or in-person, and in both open and closed environments. These opportunities are particularly important as they help to improve the quality of argumentation in the advisory opinion process, before arguments are put to the relevant court or tribunal.

3.3.3 Campaigning

A byproduct of litigation is that it can pave the way for other campaigning, advocacy and awareness-raising pursuits. And the reverse is also true: such pursuits can identify legal issues on which litigation strategies can be

---

see https://www.igsd.org/contributions-to-the-inter-american-court-of-human-rights-advisory/ (visited on 3 October 2024). (3) ClientEarth published a legal analysis on the legal issues raised by the request for an ITLOS advisory opinion in March 2023, ahead of the deadline for Written Statements in June 2023 and the hearing in September 2023: see https://www.clientearth.org/media/c1spsafh/itlosao_legal-briefing_final.pdf (viewed 3 October 2024). (4) CIEL, ClientEarth, the Pacific Islands Students Fighting Climate Change, and World Youth for Climate Justice published a joint legal memorandum following the release of the ITLOS Advisory Opinion, identifying key matters which they jointly consider '*could – and should – be taken into consideration*' for the purposes of the ICJ AO process: see https://www.ciel.org/reports/legal-memorandum-advisory-opinion-on-climate-change-itlos/ (visited on 3 October 2024).

developed and implemented. In the context of climate change, the synergies are well-understood and many civil society actors operate at the intersection point. From the perspective of the climate change advisory proceedings, two observations can be made. First, some civil society actors have leveraged the opportunity presented by the climate change advisory opinions to advance related campaigns. One illustration of this is provided by the attention given to fossil fuels. For example, the Fossil Fuel Non-Proliferation Treaty Initiative – a TAN dedicated to a global campaign calling for a multilateral process to phase out fossil fuel production and use – advanced an argument in the IACtHR AO proceeding that sought to develop the critical link between fossil fuel production, the climate crisis and existing obligations under human rights law.[82] Second, as we have already mentioned, the ICJ advisory opinion process itself emerged out of a campaigning effort which commenced with students from the University of South Pacific, and increased momentum from the efforts of other civil society actors,[83] which ran parallel and complementary to the diplomatic campaign spearheaded by Vanuatu.

3.3.4 Reporting and Public Education

Civil society reports on and provides an educative function in relation to the climate change advisory proceedings (and other developments in climate litigation). This includes publishing explanations of the advisory opinions,[84] publishing summaries of submissions made to the advisory proceedings,[85]

82 *Request for an advisory opinion on the Climate Emergency and Human Rights submitted to the Inter-American Court of Human Rights by the Republic of Colombia and the Republic of Chile*, Amicus Brief of the Fossil Fuel Non-Proliferation Treaty Initiative, available at: https://corteidh.or.cr/sitios/observaciones/OC-32/8_fossil_fuel.pdf (visited on 3 October 2024).

83 For example, Greenpeace's vessel – the Rainbow Warrior – did a tour around various island nations as part of their campaign for an ICJ advisory opinion: see Kate O'Callaghan, 'Groundbreaking Climate Campaign sets sail for International Court of Justice' (Greenpeace News, 29 March 2023), available at https://www.greenpeace.org.au/news/groundbreaking-climate-campaign-sets-sail-for-international-court-of-justice/ (visited on 3 October 2024).

84 Client Earth put out explainers on each of the three climate change advisory opinions: see https://www.clientearth.org/campaigns/international-court-actions/ (visited on 3 October 2024).

85 For example, CIEL has set out on its website key arguments ventilated within the ITLOS process: see https://www.ciel.org/at-historic-itlos-hearings-states-stake-out-positions-on-climate-duties-and-ocean-protection/ (visited on 3 October 2024); and supplied links and summaries of key amicus briefs submitted to the ICJ and the Inter-American Court of Human Rights in relation to their respective climate change advisory processes: see https://www.ciel.org/issue/amicus-briefs/ (visited on 3 October 2024).

providing updates in real-time on the proceedings as they are being carried out,[86] and publishing analyses and commentaries on the advisory opinions once they have been furnished.[87] These contributions are important; by shining a spotlight on the procedure and increasing the general knowledge and awareness of the public, these efforts help to set a culture of expectation and accountability around the advisory procedures, which promotes bona fide engagement with the advisory procedure by its participants and safeguards against abuse of process and bad faith.

3.4 *Civil Society Has an Important Role in Supporting the Implementation of Advisory Opinions*

Civil society plays a critical role in promoting the outcomes of the advisory opinions and in pursuing efforts to ensure their implementation. Civil society organisations may pursue other avenues, both political and legal – including further litigation – as a means of implementing an advisory opinion.

For instance, it has been observed that the judgments of the IACtHR constitute a 'crucial tool' for those in the human rights community when pushing for state compliance on the international plane and challenging laws and practices before domestic courts. In this way, the decision of the court plays a salient role in 'empowering domestic actors to advocate legal or policy changes in order to improve the living conditions for people in the region.'[88] This rings true when tracking the influence of the 2017 advisory opinion of the IACtHR on the relationship between human rights and the environment, in which the court articulated an autonomous right to a healthy environment and a vision of extraterritoriality for human rights obligations under the American

86 For example, on 29 March 2023, Greenpeace tweeted: '*BREAKING The UN just unanimously passed a resolution calling for an advisory opinion from the highest court in the world on climate change and human rights*': available at https://x.com/Greenpeace/status/1641102618217914370 (visited on 3 October 2024). Greenpeace gave live updates to the IACtHR AO hearings in April, see https://x.com/Greenpeace/status/1783189301775204415 (visited on 3 October 2024).

87 See, eg, CIEL, ClientEarth, the Pacific Islands Students Fighting Climate Change and World Youth for Climate Justice published a joint legal memorandum following the release of the ITLOS Advisory Opinion, identifying key matters which they jointly consider '*could – and should – be taken into consideration*' for the purposes of the ICJ AO process: see https://www.ciel.org/reports/legal-memorandum-advisory-opinion-on-climate-change-itlos/ (visited on 3 October 2024).

88 Lisa Mardikian, 'The Right to a Healthy Environment before the IACtHR' (2023) 72 *ICLQ* 945, 952.

Convention.[89] This 2017 advisory opinion has been relied upon routinely in climate litigation brought by civil society at the international, regional and national levels respectively.[90]

In the context of the climate change advisory proceedings, at the time of writing, only the ITLOS advisory opinion has been handed down. Civil society has championed that advisory opinion, both for the purpose of trying to ensure further gains (and avoid backsliding) in the upcoming ICJ advisory opinion proceedings, but also for the purpose of transposing the guidance provided by ITLOS to improve prospects in other contentious climate litigation efforts at the local, regional and global levels. They have done so in numerous forms, from blog posts,[91] through to academic discussion papers,[92] and joint legal briefings.[93]

---

89 *The Environment and Human Rights* (*State Obligations in Relation to the Environment in the Context of the Protection and Guarantee of the Rights to Life and to Personal Integrity – Interpretation and Scope of Articles 4(1) and 5(1) of the American Convention on Human Rights*) Advisory Opinion OC-23/17, Inter-American Court of Human Rights Series A No 23 (15 November 2017).

90 See, eg, Committee on the Rights of the Child, *Decision adopted by the Committee on the Rights of the Child under the Optional Protocol to the Convention on the Rights of the Child, concerning Communication Nos 104–107/2019: Chiara Sacchi et al v Argentina, Brazil, France, and Germany* (CRC/C/88/D/104/2019, CRC/C/88/D/105/2019, CRC/C/88/D/106/2019, CRC/C/88/D/107/2019), 11 November 2021, §§10.5, 10.7, 10.12; UN Human Rights Committee, *Views adopted by the Committee under article 5 (4) of the Optional Protocol, concerning communication No 3624/2019: Daniel Billy et al v Australia,* CCPR/C/135/D/3624/2019, 22 September 2022, para. 3.4; *Verein Klimaseniorinnen Schweiz and Others v Switzerland* (App No 53600/20) ECtHR [GC] 9 April 2024, §225; *Duarte Agostinho and Others v Portugal and 32 Other States* (App No 39371/20) ECtHR [GC] 9 April 2024, §§59, 63; *Ranjitsinh v Union of India* (2024) INSC 280, §32 (India); *Waratah Coal Pty Ltd v Youth Verdict Ltd & Ors* (*No 6*) [2022] QLC 21, §1431 (Australia).

91 See, eg, Dr Constantinos Yiallourides, Professor Surya Deva, "A Commentary on ITLOS' Advisory Opinion on Climate Change (24 May 2024) *British Institute of International and Comparative Law Blog*, available here: https://www.biicl.org/blog/77/a-commentary-on-itlos-advisory-opinion-on-climate-change?cookiesset=1&ts=1728009659.

92 See, eg, Margarett Young, Jacqueline Peel, Ellycia Harrould-Kolieb & Janine Felson, 'ITLOS' Climate Opinion: What's its significance?' (July 2024) *Melbourne Climate Futures* (Discussion Paper), available at: https://www.unimelb.edu.au/__data/assets/pdf_file/0010/4999627/MCF-Discussion-Paper_ITLOS-opinion_v.2.pdf.

93 See, eg, CIEL, ClientEarth, Pacific Islands Students Fighting Climate Change, World's Youth for Climate Change, *Legal Memorandum: Advisory Opinion on Climate Change Delivered by the International Tribunal for the Law of the Sea: Relevance for the International Court of Justice Climate Advisory Proceedings* (July 2024), available at: https://www.clientearth.org/media/wfhekdoq/final_-legal-memorandum_-relevance-of-itlos-climate-ao-for-the-icj-ao-2.pdf (viewed 3 October 2024).

3.5 *Civil Society's Use of the Advisory Procedures Has Improved the Prospects for Climate Litigation*

Some may assume that, at first blush, an advisory opinion does not assist the efforts of climate litigation at the domestic level. An advisory opinion seeks to clarify the state of existing law, *for States*, so they can manage their relations and conduct with *other States* within a framework of cooperation. Yet, we observe that civil society actors are using the advisory procedure – a procedure that is not designed for their use – to improve prospects of climate litigation efforts at local, domestic and transnational levels.

To explain this further, it is helpful to draw on and adapt a concept developed by Lin and Peel to describe multi-scalar activities carried out by civil society in the context of TANs.[94] Drawing on Keck and Sikkink,[95] Lin and Peel describe a process by which domestic NGOs bypass their state and seek support from international allies to bring pressure to bear on the State from outside their system. International actors in turn pressure key state actors, corporations and intergovernmental bodies, providing key legitimacy and impetus to the efforts of domestic NGOs.[96]

Adapted to our context, the various actors engaging collaboratively in climate litigation efforts – at local, regional and global levels – can be viewed as a TAN. Given that most strategic litigation is brought by civil society actors and that these same actors have had a hand in catalysing the climate change advisory opinion processes, we can see that these actors are operating in a multi-scalar capacity. Civil society has therefore used the advisory processes as an opportunity to engage international courts and tribunals in their advisory capacities, bypassing domestic courts and other dispute settlement mechanisms at local and transnational levels, so as to induce international and external pressure on domestic courts and other actors.

By engaging with ITLOS, the IACtHR and the ICJ respectively, these civil society actors are hoping that favourable advisory opinions will make contentious climate litigation become more reasonable and enjoy increased prospects of success. This relies on the Courts clarifying the state of law in such a way as to alleviate some of the prevailing difficulties in climate litigation at present, thereby ushering in a new and better era of climate litigation.

At the time of writing, we are only partway through this multi-scalar process. Based on the ITLOS advisory opinion, there are already opportunities for civil society to leverage in their contentious climate litigation efforts. For

94 Lin & Peel (n 3) 153–154.
95 Keck & Sikkink (n 7) 20.
96 Lin & Peel (n 3) 153–154.

example, ITLOS advised that the UN climate regime is not *lex specialis*. While the Paris Agreement is relevant, State obligations under the Convention are distinct and are not satisfied simply by complying with obligations and commitments under Paris.[97] This is significant for the efforts of civil society in pursuing climate litigation in a contentious arena where domestic courts can be reticent to enter the fray on the polycentric issues of policy which are raised by climate change, particularly in circumstances where States have entered into a framework of cooperation on these issues at the international level through the UNFCCC Conference of the Parties (COP) process. The understanding of that regime as not *lex specialis*, but as applying concurrently with UNCLOS, is helpful in that it shows how climate change is not a discrete area to be substantively regulated by a single instrument or regime. This reduces the legitimacy risks associated with 'cutting across' the COP-negotiation processes. Once it is accepted that the COP process is but one mechanism by which States can cooperate around climate change, which does not have a feature of exclusivity (or primacy), it becomes much more palatable for a court to apply the applicable law to quell disputes that arise in the context of climate change and its impacts.

Further, the ITLOS advisory opinion clarified that the standard of conduct applicable to relevant obligations under the Convention is 'stringent' due diligence.[98] All necessary measures must be taken to discharge that standard, where necessary measures must be determined objectively, considering the best available science, relevant international rules and standards, and State capabilities.[99] Moreover, the standard of due diligence is especially stringent in the context of transboundary harm.[100] As part of exercising due diligence in taking necessary measures to protect and preserve the marine environment, States must ensure non-state actors (eg fossil fuel companies) under their jurisdiction or control comply with such measures.[101] Civil society has therefore secured the benefit of the first judicial pronouncement of a burdensome due diligence standard in the context of climate change, involving a requirement that corporate emitting conduct must be regulated. These are positions which are familiar to numerous civil society actors engaged in or working on climate litigation, but now – with the clarifications of ITLOS (and possibly also

97 *Request for an Advisory Opinion Submitted by the Commission of Small Island States on Climate Change and International Law* (Advisory Opinion, 21 May 2024) ITLOS Case No 31, §§222–224.

98 ibid §§241–243, 256, 258, 398–400.

99 ibid §§207–229, 243.

100 ibid §§256, 258.

101 ibid §396.

the IACtHR and the ICJ) – these arguments will land with more force in future climate litigation.

The full gamut of opportunities (and risks) this multi-scalar approach will bring to future climate litigation efforts remains to be seen. We expect the IACtHR to provide a helpful clarification of the role of human rights law in this regard; and the International Court of Justice to deliver a careful and nuanced articulation of existing international law obligations across the whole corpus of international law for states who have, by their GHG emissions over time, contributed to causing significant harm to the climate system and other parts of the environment. With this, the authors are hopeful that the advisory opinions will bring about a recalibration of how climate litigation (and climate law generally) is handled and will yield more ambitious climate action as a result. Of immediate relevance, such a recalibration would empower civil society to pull more levers in their climate litigation strategies moving forward.

4 Conclusion

Civil society has played a significant role in catalysing, supporting and participating in the climate change advisory proceedings before the IACtHR, ITLOS and the ICJ. With the exception of the IACtHR, which has adapted its procedure over time to recognise civil society as a 'fundamental pillar' of the Court's work,[102] civil society actors have traditionally had a limited formal role before ITLOS and the ICJ. This lack of a formal role has not been an impediment to comparatively high levels of civil society participation by way of *amici curiae* before ITLOS and the ICJ, notwithstanding the fact that such submissions do not form part of the case file. Many of the same civil society actors have been active across the three advisory opinions, which goes some way to explaining this level of engagement despite natural questions about its strategic utility for resource-constrained public interest organisations.

Despite these restrictions, this chapter has sketched a bigger picture in which civil society can be seen in practice as effective and highly strategic users of advisory procedures. We have explored the way in which civil society has been active in climate litigation at the domestic, regional and now international level; its role as a key catalyst for the advisory opinions, particularly in the proceedings before the ICJ; the manner in which civil society has creatively used the advisory opinion processes to directly and indirectly influence the

102 *Case of Indigenous Communities of the Lhaka Honhat (Our Land) Association v Argentina* (n 78) Separate Opinion of Judge Ferrer Mac-Gregor Poisot, §79.

proceedings and build capacity; civil society's key role as a champion supporting the implementation of advisory opinions after they are handed down; and finally have offered some reflections on the manner in which civil society is likely to leverage the advisory opinions to further their domestic, regional and international litigation strategies.

As practitioners in the field, we consider that civil society has enhanced the quality of the advisory proceedings and improved prospects for more meaningful climate action. This is perhaps unsurprising; the various actors within civil society are highly motivated, perform myriad functions, and have sophisticated strategies which all coalesce around a shared goal to address the climate crisis. Any court that is confronted with a case concerning climate change would in our view be well assisted by the work carried out by civil society in the climate litigation field.

SECTION 3

The Lasting Impact of Advisory Opinions

CHAPTER 11

The Downstream Impact of Advisory Opinions in the Case Law of Other International Bodies and Domestic Litigation

Lea Main-Klingst and Sophie Marjanac***

Abstract

This chapter discusses the downstream impact of advisory opinions in litigation around the world, first by considering both the legal and political impact of previous advisory opinions. It then looks at the overlapping themes in the three advisory opinions on climate change, before analysing the potential impact of these climate advisory opinions on international and regional bodies, as well as domestic courts. Here it considers the differences in monist and dualist systems. Finally, in demonstrating the impact and utility of advisory opinions, the chapter takes the findings in ITLOS' 2024 climate advisory opinion on environmental impact assessments and demonstrates how these may impact global law and policy in respect of GHG emissions, specifically by taking a look at recent case law from around the world.

Keywords

impact of advisory opinions – climate litigation themes – cross-fertilisation – monist – dualist – ITLOS and EIAS

1 Introduction

Late 2022 and early 2023 marked a significant time for the development of international law in relation to the climate crisis. In December 2022, the

* ClientEarth, LMain-Klingst@clientearth.org, <https://orcid.org/0009-0005-8370-5843>. The opinions expressed in this publication are those of the author. They do not purport to reflect the opinions or views of ClientEarth. Please note that the author was part of the representation in some of the international cases discussed in this article.

** Polluter Pays Project, sophie@polluterpaysproject.org.

Commission of Small Island States on International Law and Climate Change (COSIS) submitted a request for an advisory opinion on the Law of the Sea and climate change to the International Tribunal for the Law of the Seas (ITLOS). In January 2023, Colombia and Chile submitted a request for an advisory opinion on human rights and the climate emergency to the Inter-American Court of Human Rights (IACtHR). Finally, in March 2023 the UN General Assembly (UNGA) passed a resolution by consensus, asking the International Court of Justice (ICJ) to opine on State obligations to prevent and provide redress for climate harms.[1]

While each of these requests was initiated in a unique manner (the first, by a collective of States who formed a new inter-governmental organisation with the express authority to request advisory opinions; the second at the request of two State signatories to a regional human rights treaty; and the third after a global campaign for a UNGA Resolution, led by Pacific university students and the Republic of Vanuatu), each took place against a backdrop of growing calls on governments to effectively respond to the climate crisis in light of perceived (diplomatic) failures. These movements grew despite the conclusion of the 2015 Paris Agreement and the corresponding annual Conferences of the Parties (COPs) to the United Nations Framework Convention on Climate Change (UNFCCC) rapidly becoming the most well attended UN conferences each year.[2] The political support for these advisory opinions from the UNGA and initiating States shows that there is an acknowledgement among a majority of States, particularly small island and other climate vulnerable States, that general international law (with relevant human rights and marine protection obligations) has an important role to play in responding to what the UN Secretary General has called 'an existential threat to the world as we know it.'[3]

With this almost simultaneous emergence of three climate advisory opinions, discussion has arisen around their scope, effect and application, especially

1 For an overview of the three requests, see Maria Antonia Tigre, 'It Is (Finally) Time for and Advisory Opinion on Climate Change: Challenges and Opportunities on a Trio of Initiatives' (2024) 17 *Charleston Law Review* 623.

2 UNFCCC, 'Observer organizations at COP 28' <https://unfccc.int/process-and-meetings/parties-non-party-stakeholders/non-party-stakeholders/overview/observer-organizations/observer-organizations-at-cop-28#COP-28-Notifications-to-observers> accessed 13 August 2024.

3 United Nations, 'Climate Crisis Past Point of No Return, Secretary General Says, Listing Global Threats at General Assembly Consultation on 'Our Common Agenda' Report' (*United Nations*, 10 March 2022) <https://press.un.org/en/2022/sgsm21173.doc.htm> accessed 13 August 2024.

as advisory opinions by the ICJ and ITLOS do not have legally binding force unless expressly provided for. Nonetheless, their relevance and importance are widely acknowledged. Given the unique nature of climate change as a universal challenge and 'common concern of mankind,'[4] these advisory opinions may prove to be an important tool in advancing global climate action.

The ITLOS delivered the first of the three climate advisory opinions on the obligations of the States on 21 May 2024, which, among other things, emphasises the central role of emissions reductions as part of the State obligation to protect and preserve the marine environment. From this ground-breaking finding alone, it can be seen that this advisory opinion, and the two still to follow, will have legal implications across the globe, including through influence, interpretation and application in other courts at national, regional, and international level. These effects are likely to be context-specific, although we attempt to outline some of those possible impacts in this Chapter.

Due to climate change being of a quintessentially international character and its intersection with and implications for other legal regimes, in particular, those protecting human rights, as well as the contemporaneous nature of the three advisory opinions, their reach and influence is likely to be greater than previous advisory opinions. This holds particularly true, as the law has, in the past decade, just started to grapple with the implications of climate change for existing legal frameworks, with a particularly high degree of cross-pollination and influence across jurisdictions. These three international courts are being given, and in the case of the ITLOS have made use of, an opportunity to offer the legal clarity necessary to break the political deadlock and to allow courts and decision-makers around the world to start to draw on a cohesive body of norms to adjudicate future disputes as between States and the individuals under their protection, as well as, crucially, to elucidate the legal consequences/obligations vis-a-vis those States who may well soon face devastating losses, or even disappear beneath the waves. As the impacts of climate change worsen, international, national, and regional courts, decision-makers, States, and individuals around the world will look to these advisory opinions for guidance on a range of emerging issues. And finally, it is notable that despite some populist backlash against international institutions, international courts and tribunals have been experiencing an uptick in requests for advisory opinions and dispute settlement, underlining that they remain the seminal interpretants of international norms. As this chapter suggests, the impact of these advisory

4 United Nations Framework Convention on Climate Change (adopted 9 May 1992, entry into force 21 March 1994) 1771 UNTS 107, Preamble (UNFCCC).

opinions will therefore extend far beyond the limits of their 'enforceability' or 'binding character' and will be analysed, relied upon, cited and no doubt both celebrated and challenged around the world for years to come.

2 Preliminary Remarks on Advisory Opinions

As explained by Galvão Teles and Guerreiro Teixeira in Chapter 2, an advisory opinion (AO) is a consultative process resulting in a legal pronouncement that expounds the law and is not the settlement of a dispute. In relation to the three advisory opinions on climate change, judicial decision-makers have been asked to clarify what obligations arise for States under different international legal frameworks, customary law and general principles of law – all predating broad awareness of and international agreement to act on climate change – and therefore not explicitly providing for considerations of climate change.

The terminology of 'not legally binding' is frequently used in relation to advisory opinions, including by those wishing to undermine their importance. It is true that as a matter of law, advisory opinions by the ICJ and ITLOS are not legally binding. Nonetheless, such advisory opinions are authoritative statements on the law in question, contributing to the development and concretisation of (general) international and customary law and thereby play an essential role in shaping and advancing the international legal order. They carry significant normative force, with some authors suggesting that advisory opinions formulate 'shared or community expectations.'[5] The legal clarity provided through advisory opinions must also be understood as a contribution towards preventing future disputes.[6] In contrast, the IACtHR has clarified that, in applying the American Convention on Human Rights (ACHR), domestic judges and courts have to 'take into account not only the treaty, but also the interpretation thereof made by the [IACtHR], which is the ultimate interpreter of the [ACHR],'[7] as '[b]oth the non-contentious and the contentious

5 Karin Oellers-Frahm, 'Lawmaking Through Advisory Opinions?' (2011) 12(5) *German LJ* 1033, 1055.

6 Laurence Boisson de Chazournes, 'Advisory Opinions and the Furtherance of the Common Interest of Mankind', in Chazournes, Romano & Mackenzie (eds), *International Organizations and International Dispute Settlement – Trends and Prospects* (Transnational Publishers 2002).

7 *Almonacid-Arellano et al v Chile* (Preliminary Objections, Merits, Reparations and Costs) Inter-American Court of Human Rights Series C No 154 (26 September 2006) §124.

jurisdiction undeniably share the same goal of the Inter-American human rights system,'[8] this being the protection of fundamental rights.[9]

Advisory opinion requests are phrased as questions, emphasising the role of the court in clarifying and interpreting issues of law and frequently also seek clarification on the 'legal consequences' of acts, omissions or violations, as in the current climate change advisory opinion pending before the ICJ.

2.1 *Legal and Political Impact of Previous Advisory Opinions*

Against this background, it is worth looking at the legal and political impacts of previous advisory opinions and the insights these might offer. As has been shown in previous chapters, ICJ advisory opinions have provided conclusive statements on customary international law, interpreted and clarified treaty provisions, made pronouncements on the law in the absence of a generally agreed rule,[10] and were also essential to furthering and supporting public discourse.

For example, the ICJ's *Nuclear Weapons Advisory Opinion* influenced subsequent treaty discussions on the interpretation of the Nuclear Non-Proliferation Treaty.[11] It also played a role in the public discourse around campaigns to ban the use of nuclear weapons and the development of international environmental law principles. This language of non-proliferation has since been mirrored in the Fossil Fuel Non-Proliferation Treaty Initiative, which seeks to create a negotiating mandate for a treaty aimed at halting the expansion of fossil fuels, ensuring an equitable phase-out and a just energy transition.[12]

Advisory opinions of the ICJ have also led to the creation of new UN bodies, as a means to give effect to the opinion and act as a supervisory body,[13] and

---

8 *Gender Identity, and Equality and Non-Discrimination of Same-Sex Couples*, Advisory Opinion OC-24/17, Inter-American Court of Human Rights Series A No 24 (24 November 2017) §26.

9 Maria Antonia Tigre, Natalia Urzola & Juan Sebastián Castellanos, 'A Request for an Advisory Opinion at the Inter-American Court of Human Rights: Initial Reactions' (*Climate Law – A Sabin Center Blog*, 17 February 2023).<https://blogs.law.columbia.edu/climatechange/2023/02/17/a-request-for-an-advisory-opinion-at-the-inter-american-court-of-human-rights-initial-reactions/> accessed 13 August 2024>.

10 *Reservations to the Convention on Genocide* (Advisory Opinion, 28 May 1951) ICJ Rep 15.

11 United Nations Office for Disarmament Affairs, 'Treaty on the Non-Proliferation of Nuclear Weapons (NPT)' <https://disarmament.unoda.org/wmd/nuclear/npt/> accessed 13 August 2024.

12 Fossil Fuel Treaty < https://fossilfueltreaty.org/> accessed 14 March 2024.

13 Christof Heyns & Magnus Killander, 'South West Africa/Namibia (Advisory Opinions and Judgments)', *Max Planck Encyclopaedia of International Law* (March 2007) <https://opil-ouplaw-com.peacepalace.idm.oclc.org/display/10.1093/law:epil/9780199231690/law-9780199231690-e209> accessed 13 August 2024; *Legal Consequences for States of the*

have spelled out guidance for UN member States and the UNGA on the implementation of the advisory opinions. In situations of non-compliance, UNGA resolutions that reinforced the findings of ICJ opinions have been adopted and frequently called on UN Member States 'to comply with their legal obligations as mentioned in the advisory opinion.'[14]

ICJ advisory opinions have also guided action at the EU level. In at least two decisions, the Court of Justice of the European Union (CJEU) accepted and relied on the ICJ's determinations and findings made in advisory opinions, which necessarily informed subsequent EU action.[15]

Important considerations and determinations on the effect and role of advisory opinions can also be found in the jurisprudence of ITLOS. In a contentious case before a Special Chamber of ITLOS, the Chamber was called upon to determine the legal effect of the previous ICJ advisory opinion on the Chagos Archipelago.[16] The legal status of the archipelago had been at the centre of these advisory opinion proceedings,[17] where the ICJ had determined that the decolonisation process of Mauritius had not been lawfully completed; that the continued presence and administration of the UK of the archipelago was therefore unlawful and had to be brought to an end.

In the subsequent maritime delimitation proceedings before the ITLOS Special Chamber, the Maldives raised preliminary objections submitting that the United Kingdom was an indispensable third party to these proceedings, as, according to the Maldives, a territorial sovereignty dispute existed between the UK and Mauritius over the Chagos Archipelago, in respect to which Mauritius now sought to delimit its maritime entitlements. Mauritius rebutted that the

---

Continued Presence of South Africa in Namibia (South West Africa) notwithstanding Security Council Resolution 276 (1970) (Advisory Opinion, 21 June 1971) ICJ Rep 16.

14 See for example UNGA Res No ES-10/15, which acknowledged the advisory opinion, 'demanded' that Israel 'comply with its obligations as mentioned in the advisory opinion' and called on UN Member States 'to comply with their legal obligations as mentioned in the advisory opinion.' UNGA Res No ES-10/15 (10 July 2004) UN Doc A/RES/ES-10/15 ('Advisory Opinion of the International Court of Justice on the Legal Consequences of the Construction of a Wall in the Occupied Palestinian Territory, including in and around East Jerusalem').

15 Case C-104/16P *Council of the European Union v Front Polisario* [2016] ECLI:EU:C:2016:973, §§88–89; Case C-363/18 *Organisation juive européenne and Vignoble Psagot Ltd v Ministre de l'Economie et des Finances* [2019] OJ C10/13.

16 *Dispute concerning Delimitation of the Maritime Boundary between Mauritius and Maldives in the Indian Ocean (Mauritius v Maldives) (Preliminary Objections)* (Judgment, 28 January 2021) ITLOS Case No 28, §236.

17 *Legal Consequences of the Separation of the Chagos Archipelago from Mauritius in 1965* (Advisory Opinion) [2019] ICJ Rep 95.

findings in the ICJ's advisory opinion disposed of the issue of sovereignty, 'the conclusions of which carry legal consequences for all UN Member States and international institutions.'[18]

In its determination, the Special Chamber found that: 'judicial determinations made in advisory opinions carry no less weight and authority than those in judgments because they are made with the same rigour and scrutiny by the "principal judicial organ" of the United Nations with competence in matters of international law.'[19] The Special Chamber took note of rulings of the CJEU (as mentioned above), which, while not considering an advisory opinion by the ICJ to be binding, attached 'due importance' to its legal and factual findings.[20] The Special Chamber adopted the view that determinations made in an ICJ advisory opinion could not be disregarded because of their non-binding nature. Instead, the Special Chamber considered these determinations to have legal effect.[21] Ultimately, the Tribunal thus reiterated the findings of the ICJ in relation to the legal status of the Chagos Archipelago, holding that Mauritius' sovereignty was established and no sovereignty issue between Mauritius and the UK existed, as: '[t]he determinations made by the ICJ with respect to the issues of the decolonization of Mauritius in the Chagos advisory opinion have legal effect and clear implications for the legal status of the Chagos Archipelago.' Mauritius' sovereignty over the Archipelago could 'be inferred from the ICJ's determinations.'[22]

In October 2024, the governments of the Republic of Mauritius and the United Kingdom publicly announced that they had reached an agreement which recognised Mauritius sovereignty over the archipelago, meaning that the islands would be returned to Mauritius.

In its jurisprudence, the IACtHR frequently cites the work of other international courts, including the advisory opinions of the ICJ and ITLOS. Out of three courts considered in this chapter, the IACtHR enjoys the broadest advisory jurisdiction.[23] At the same time, it allows for the broadest participation in

---

18 *Mauritius v Maldives* (Preliminary Objections) (n 16) §142.
19 ibid, §203.
20 ibid, §204.
21 ibid, §205.
22 ibid, §246.
23 Lucas C Lima, 'Should I stay or should I go? The effects of denunciation of the American Convention and the Inter-American Court of Human Rights' Advisory Opinion 26/2020', 30 April 2021, *in QIL – Questions of International Law*, <https://www.qil-qdi.org/should-i-stay-or-should-i-go-the-effects-of-denunciation-of-the-american-convention-and-the-inter-american-court-of-human-rights-advisory-opinion-26-2020/#_ftn1> accessed 18 July 2024.

its advisory proceedings,[24] including from civil society actors, as well as States, or intergovernmental organisations located outside the region. This perhaps also explains why advisory opinions of the IACtHR enjoy reach and consideration far beyond the Inter-American system. This holds particularly true when looking at its 2017 advisory opinion on human rights and the environment.[25] Finally, consistent adherence to advisory opinions by States and other international actors may, over time, contribute to the formation, strengthening, and/or establishing of customary international law.[26]

Taken together, this illustrates that member States of the UN and/or the States bound by the international agreement in question, while not being legally bound by the advisory opinions themselves, are bound by the legal obligations that arise from general international law as well as the treaties, agreements or conventions invoked, interpreted and determined in advisory proceedings. In other words, they are bound by the obligations upon which an advisory opinion relies and an advisory opinion can have 'simply elucidated and confirmed their obligations.'[27] This chapter will, therefore, briefly consider the thematic overlaps between the three different advisory opinions before examining their possible impact in and on other (inter)national legal fora and proceedings.

3 Overlapping Themes in the Three Climate Advisory Opinions and the Risk of Fragmentation

Due to the timeline of the three climate advisory opinions – with ITLOS having rendered its AO and the IACtHR having concluded its hearings in May 2024

24 See Miriam Cohen, Chapter 8 in this book.

25 *The Environment and Human Rights* (*State Obligations in Relation to the Environment in the Context of the Protection and Guarantee of the Rights to Life and to Personal Integrity – Interpretation and Scope of Articles 4(1) and 5(1) of the American Convention on Human Rights*) Advisory Opinion OC-23/17, Inter-American Court of Human Rights Series A No 23 (15 November 2017). (OC-23/17).

26 Teresa F Mayr & Jelka Mayer-Singer, 'Keep the Wheels Spinning: The Contributions of Advisory Opinions of the International Court of Justice to the Development of International Law' (2016) 76 *ZaöRV* 425.

27 John Dugard, 'Advisory Opinions and the Secretary-General with Special Reference to the 2004 Advisory Opinion on the Wall', in Kohen & Boisson de Chazournes (eds), *International Law and the Quest for its Implementation | Le droit international et la quête de sa mise en oeuvre – Liber Amicorum Vera Gowlland-Debbas* (Brill 2010) 399, 410.

– and the questions put to the ICJ being the broadest in terms of scope and applicable law, this section will start out with taking a look at the questions before the ICJ. WE identify thematic overlaps between the three advisory opinions and the possible impact of developments before the IACtHR and ITLOS on the ICJ advisory proceedings and in domestic litigation.

The questions before the ICJ seek clarification on the international legal obligations that exist on States to protect the climate system from GHG emissions, and what legal consequences arise where the acts or omissions of States have caused significant harm, with a particular view to vulnerable groups and States. While the question also enumerates a number of international agreements and general principles of international law, the list is not phrased in an exhaustive manner and therefore seeks clarification on the international legal regime as a whole. Nonetheless, debates around applicable law are bound to arise as States will or are likely seeking to limit the number of sources from which obligations in relation to climate change arise. However, this has already been addressed by ITLOS in its May 2024 advisory opinion, where it determined that separate sets of obligations pertaining to climate change could arise under separate international legal instruments (in this case, UNCLOS and the Paris Agreement), as these different international legal instruments have and pursue different core aims.[28]

The international legal instruments listed in the question to the ICJ include numerous human rights treaties and conventions. The rights and freedoms protected therein are often mirrored in and/or similar to the human rights protected by the ACHR and, therefore, soon to be interpreted by the IACtHR in its climate advisory opinion. The IACtHR will likely confirm the applicability of the ACHR to climate harms – in line with developments before UN treaty bodies and the ECtHR.[29] Notably, one dissenting opinion before the ITLOS criticised the majority's approach for failing to take into account human rights.[30]

Further to this, in particular the first and sixth questions before the IACtHR are not dissimilar to the questions asked of the ICJ, as they directly raise the issue of the common but differentiated responsibilities and respective capabilities (CBDR-RC) principle and burden-sharing necessary to achieve the temperature limit of the Paris Agreement.[31] The responses to these questions,

28 *Request for an Advisory Opinion submitted by the Commission of Small Island States on Climate Change and International Law* (Advisory Opinion, 21 May 2024) ITLOS Case No 31, §§223–224 (*COSIS Opinion*).

29 *Verein KlimaSeniorinnen Schweiz and Others v Switzerland* (App No 53600/20) ECtHR [GC] 9 April 2024.

30 *COSIS Opinion* (n 28) 'Declaration of Judge Pawlak', §1.

31 The full text of the three separate requests for advisory opinions is included in Annex I.

together with the other four that relate to State duties to protect human rights by the ACHR, will be widely cited and referred to in Latin American jurisprudence, and are likely to also influence international bodies, domestic courts, and human rights bodies across the world. In the oral proceedings before the IACtHR, many of the participants noted the relevance of CBDR-RC, which garnered interest and questions from the judges regarding its practical implications. Clarification on these points from either the IACtHR or the ICJ may therefore offer necessary guidance and assistance to other international, regional, or domestic courts and human rights bodies.

For example, considerations on States' shares in reducing global emissions have already found their way into national jurisprudence. While not explicitly reflecting considerations on CBDR-RC or equity, the finite 'carbon budget' approach adopted, for example, in the Dutch *Urgenda*[32] and the German *Neubauer*[33] cases demonstrates how national courts have tackled the question of apportioning responsibility and the obligation to reduce emissions.

Another important overarching theme is the role of scientific evidence in informing the obligations of States and the potential of these three advisory opinions to make clear findings related to the facts and science of climate change, and in particular, the harms caused by the deterioration of the environment as a result of rising GHG emissions. As mentioned, findings on CBDR-RC and exactly what level of historic and current emissions constitute 'significant harm to the climate system' could be relevant to judges around the world. Findings on scientific evidence of climate harms, the cumulative nature of GHGs, inertia in the climate system, the need for urgent action, the threat of tipping points, the definition of significant impacts, as well as necessary mitigation action such as fossil fuel phase-out, high-risk mitigation methods such as carbon capture and storage or the concept of offsetting, could have global implications.

In its advisory opinion, ITLOS clarified that State measures must be informed by the best available science providing that the margin of appreciation afforded to States is to be objectively assessed and, therefore, amongst other factors, bounded by the scientific evidence. The Tribunal considered all this relevant to the standard of due diligence required of States and determined that, on the basis of the scientific evidence that clearly established the high risk of serious and irreversible harm, is 'stringent.'[34]

---

32 *Urgenda Foundation v Kingdom of the Netherlands* (Supreme Court of the Netherlands, Judgment of 29 December 2019) ECLI:NL:HR:2019:2007.

33 *Neubauer et al v Germany* (Federal Constitutional Court of Germany, Judgment of 24 March 2021) 1 BvR 2656/18, 1 BvR 78/20, 1 BvR 96/20 & 1 BvR 288/20.

34 COSIS *Opinion* (n 28) §§396–399.

In international law, due diligence is understood as a duty of conduct on States, described as 'a threshold, indicating the degree of commitment required of the State in relation to certain primary obligations.'[35] This threshold is understood as one of 'responsible government,' taking all reasonable and necessary steps to comply with its obligations. The exact content of the due diligence duty varies, as it is informed by applicable rules, practices, and norms of international law relevant to the context and the provision(s) from which it emerges.[36] It has been addressed in previous advisory opinions, such as ITLOS' Seabed Disputes Chamber 2011 AO, which found that: '[t]he content of "due diligence" obligations may not easily be described in precise terms. Among the factors that make such a description difficult is the fact that "due diligence" is a variable concept. *It may change over time as measures considered sufficiently diligent at a certain moment may become not diligent enough in light, for instance, of new scientific* (...)) *knowledge.*'[37] (emphasis added). This was reaffirmed in ITLOS' May 2024 advisory opinion on climate change.[38]

In its frequently cited 2017 advisory opinion on the environment, the IACtHR determined that protection of human rights required that States act diligently, which included adherence to the precautionary principle where 'plausible indications' existed that an activity could cause severe and irreparable harm to the environment, requiring States to take effective measures to address them.[39] According to the IACtHR, the duty to act with due diligence corresponds 'to the State obligation to ensure the free and full exercise of the rights recognized in the [ACHR] to all persons subject to their jurisdiction, according to which States must take all appropriate measures to protect and preserve the rights recognized in the Convention.'[40] By acknowledging that a high level of due diligence may be required of States in light of the severe risks

---

35 Serena Forlati, 'L'objet des différentes obligations primaires de diligence: Prévention, cessation, répression?', in *Le standard de due diligence et la responsabilité internationale* (*Journée de* étude *franco-italienne du Mans*) (Pédone 2018) 40.

36 Timo Koivurova & Krittika Singh, 'Due Diligence', *Max Planck Encyclopedia of Public International Law* (online edn, August 2022); Irini Papanicolopulu, 'Due Diligence in the Law of the Sea', in Krieger et al (eds), *Due Diligence in the International Legal Order* (Oxford University Press 2020); Lavanya Rajamani, 'Due Diligence in Climate Change Law', in Krieger, Peters & Kreuzer (eds), *Due Diligence in the International Legal Order* (OUP 2021) 163.

37 *Responsibilities and Obligations of States Sponsoring Persons and Entities with Respect to Activities in the Area* (*Request for Advisory Opinion Submitted to the Seabed Disputes Chamber* (Advisory Opinion, 1 February 2011) ITLOS Case No 17, §117.

38 *COSIS Opinion* (n 28) §239.

39 OC-23/17 (n 25) §§125, 180.

40 Ibid.

associated with climate change, the ITLOS AO has provided important findings for the other two courts to consider.

Returning to Question 2 of the ICJ AO: After the initial assessment on 'significant harm,' the second question is then divided into two parts, addressing the legal consequences of causing significant harm with respect to (i) States and, in particular, vulnerable small island developing States; and (ii) peoples and individuals of present **and** future generations (emphasis added).[41] Although the first sub-section refers to intra-State obligations and duties, the second section is very broad and the answer may have implications for the duties of States to peoples and individuals (including future generations) both within *and* outside their territories. The ICJ's response to this question, therefore, has the potential to influence human rights law at all levels, globally.

The risk of fragmentation, that is, different and potentially contradicting outcomes, has been raised given the thematic overlap briefly outlined above – and is further explained by Susan Ann Samuel and Alejandro Carrillo Bañuelos in Chapter 4 of this book. This may be resolved to some extent due to the timing of the publication of the opinions. At the same time, the rules of treaty interpretation are important in this context. The ITLOS advisory opinion referred to the Vienna Convention on the Law of Treaties as part of the applicable law, which provides that their interpretation of international legal instruments should be taken together with other relevant rules of international law.[42] Article 237 of UNCLOS itself provides that the provisions under Part XII on the protection and preservation of the marine environment are also to be understood in light of other, related, commitments. UNCLOS thereby expressly provides that other applicable rules of international law and specific obligations arising from other international agreements are relevant to the content of the State obligations under Part XII UNCLOS – as then analysed throughout the advisory opinion.

Similarly, Article 29 of the ACHR provides that the Convention should not be interpreted in a manner that excludes or limits the effects of other international acts. Its advisory opinion OC-10/89 confirmed the findings of the ICJ's *South West Africa* advisory opinion, namely that: 'an international instrument must be interpreted and applied within the overall framework of the judicial system in force at the time of the interpretation.'[43] In subsequent case law, the IACtHR has relied on other international instruments to inform obligations

---

41 See the request in Annex I.

42 Vienna Convention on the Law of Treaties (entered into force 27 January 1980) 1155 UNTS 331 (VCLT), art 31; *COSIS Opinion* (n 28) §§128ff.

43 *Interpretation of the American Declaration of the Rights and Duties of Man Within the Framework of Article 64 of the American Convention on Human Rights*, Advisory Opinion OC-10/89, Inter-American Court of Human Rights Series A No 10 (14 July 1989) §37.

under the Inter-American system, as well as the Vienna Convention on the Law of Treaties (VCLT) to affirm that: 'human rights treaties are live instruments, whose interpretation must go hand in hand with evolving times and current living conditions.'[44] The IACtHR has also made findings that are of particular importance to the considerations in this chapter. Namely, it determined that due to the indivisible nature of human rights and environmental protection, the principles, rights, and obligations of international environmental law 'make a decisive contribution to establishing the scope of the obligations under the [ACHR].'[45] This approach to harmonisation of international law pursued by the different international courts should therefore contribute to limiting fragmentation. It is against this background that we offer the following analysis.

4 Analysis and Potential Impact of the Climate Advisory Opinions in Litigation

4.1 *Influence and Utility for International and Regional Human Rights Decision-Making Bodies*

4.1.1 Human Rights Treaty Bodies

The human rights treaty bodies (HRTB), established under each of the UN's major international human rights treaties, often have both an adjudicative function that receives and issues views on individual communications about alleged violations of treaty obligations, as well as conducting regular cycles of 'periodic review' of State compliance with treaty obligations. These 'compliance committees' established under each treaty also often draft guidance for States on compliance with rights protected by each treaty called 'General Comments.'

HRTBs are likely to rely heavily on the guidance provided by the AOs, although they tend to cite external sources to varying degrees, particularly in decisions related to individual communications. For example, in *Sacchi et al v Argentina et al*,[46] the Committee on the Rights of the Child (CRC) relied on other UN sources, OC-23/17, and ECtHR jurisprudence. In *Billy et al v Australia*,[47]

44 *Case of the 'Mapiripán Massacre' v Colombia* (Merits, Reparations and Costs Judgment) Inter-American Court of Human Rights Series C No 134 (15 September 2005) §106, fn 185.

45 OC-23/17 (n 25) §55.

46 UN Committee on the Rights of the Child 'Decision adopted under the Optional Protocol, concerning Communication No 108/2019' (23 September 2021) UN Doc CRC/C/88/D/108/2019 (*Sacchi Decision*).

47 UN Human Rights Committee 'Views adopted under article 5 (4) of the Optional Protocol, concerning Communication No 3624/2019' (18 September 2023) UN Doc CCPR/C/135/D/3624/2019.

the Human Rights Committee (HRC) relied on its own previous case law and General Comments. General Comments of the HRC take a range of sources into account, including decisions of regional human rights courts and advisory opinions.[48] Considering the overlapping human rights considerations in the different advisory opinions, we are of the view that the trio of climate advisory opinions are likely to be referred to in future General Comments made by HRTBs, as well as individual communications where the theme of climate change arises. In *Sacchi*, the CRC was called upon to assess whether the respondent States, amongst the world's largest emitters of GHGs, were breaching their obligations under the Convention on the Rights of the Child by (amongst others) failing to prevent foreseeable domestic and extraterritorial human rights violations resulting from climate change.[49] Here the CRC looked to the IACtHR's advisory opinion on the environment for clarifications on the scope of extraterritorial jurisdiction, reaffirming and adopting the test established therein.[50] Similarly, considerations on CBDR-RC and the scientific evidence were relevant in informing the Committee's decision.[51] Determinations in the three climate AOs are, therefore, likely to be reflected in the jurisprudence of HRTBs. Further, given that General Comments influence the approach of HRTBs to the process of periodic review under each treaty (and could also influence the Human Rights Council's Universal Periodic Review), the influence of the advisory opinions is likely to permeate throughout the international human rights system.

4.1.2 Regional Human Rights Courts and Tribunals

There is clearly healthy cross-fertilisation between each of the regional human rights courts, although evidence suggests this can be asymmetrical, with judges citing and adopting concepts from other courts in an ad hoc, un-systematic fashion.[52] A minority of judges on the ICJ have also adopted the thinking and decisions of the regional human rights courts, most notably Judge Antônio

48 UN Human Rights Committee, 'General Comment No 36 (2018) on article 6 of the International Covenant on Civil and Political Rights, on the right to life' (30 October 2018) UN Doc CCPR/C/GC/36, fns. 191, 265.

49 *Sacchi Decision* (n 46) §3.3.

50 ibid §10.5.

51 ibid §10.10.

52 Erik Voeten, 'Borrowing and Nonborrowing among International Courts' (2010) 39(2) *The Journal of Legal Studies* <https://www.jstor.org/stable/10.1086/652460> accessed 14 August 2024.

Augusto Cançado Trindade.[53] The ECtHR has regularly referred to the case law of the IACtHR,[54] although there is some evidence to suggest that this depends on the political context.[55]

Each of the IACtHR, the ECtHR, and the African Court of Human and Peoples' Rights (ACtHPR) have previously also cited advisory opinions of the ICJ, although there is variation in the frequency of these references. The ECtHR has cited the ICJ's advisory opinions in varying contexts,[56] together with advisory opinions of the IACtHR.[57] As the newest of the human rights regional courts,

---

53 Mia Swart, 'A Move away from Solitude: Judge Cançado Trinidade's Contributions to a More Representative International Law' (*Third World Approaches to International Law Review*, 22 September 2023) <https://twailr.com/a-move-away-from-solitude-judge-cancado-trindades-contributions-to-a-more-representative-international-law/> accessed 14 August 2024.

54 *Mamatkulov and Askarov v Turkey* (App No 46827/99) ECtHR 4 February 2005, cited rules of procedure of IACtHR (§§43–44) and refers to IACtHR system (§49); *Ergin v Turkey (No 6)* (App No 47533/99) ECtHR 4 May 2006, cited case law of IACtHR (§25); *Kurt v Turkey* (App No 24276/94) ECtHR 25 May 1998, cited case law of IACtHR (§67); *X v Poland* (App No 20741/10) ECtHR 16 September 2021, cited case law of IACtHR (§45); *Lexa v Slovakia* (App No 54334/00) ECtHR 23 September 2008, cited case law of IACtHR (§§97–98).

55 Voeten (n 52) 563.

56 *Vasiliauskas v Lithuania* (App No 35343/05) ECtHR 20 October 2015, cited the ICJ's *Advisory Opinion on the Reservations to the Convention on the Prevention and Punishment of the Crime of Genocide* to support the notion that the principles underlying the Genocide Convention were principles which were recognised by civilised nations as binding on States even without any conventional obligation, and to find that the crime of genocide was clearly recognised as a crime under international law in 1953 (see §§80 and 167); *Chiragov and Others v Armenia* (App No 13216/05) ECtHR 16 June 2015, cited the ICJ's *Kosovo Advisory Opinion* in relation to the relevance of the right to self-determination of peoples (eg §§13–14) and on the difference between UNSC resolutions and treaties (1104); *Cyprus v Turkey* (App No 25781/94) ECtHR 10 May 2001, cited the ICJ's Advisory on the *Legal Consequences for States of the Continued Presence of South Africa in Namibia* in relation to the availability of domestic remedies; *Kononov v Latvia* (App No 36376/04) ECtHR 24 July 2008, a dissenting opinion cited the ICJ's Advisory Opinion on the *Legal Consequences of the Construction of a Wall in the Occupied Palestinian Territory* in relation to the relationship between HR law and IHL, and cited the *Namibia Advisory Opinion* in relation to the interpretation of international legal instruments; *Georgia v Russia (II)* (App No 38263/08) ECtHR 21 January 2021, cited the ICJ's Advisory Opinion on *Legality of the Threat or Use of Nuclear Weapons* and on *Legal Consequences of the Construction of a Wall in the Occupied Palestinian Territory* (§§89–90); *Al-Dulimi and Montana Management Inc v Switzerland* (App No 5809/08) ECtHR 21 June 2016, cited the ICJ's *Namibia* Advisory Opinion regarding States' obligations to comply with UNSC resolutions (§42).

57 *Palomo* Sánchez and Others v Spain (App Nos 28955/06, 28957/06, 28959/06 & 28964/06) ECtHR 12 September 2011, cited IACtHR *Advisory Opinion OC-5/85* in relation to 'the fundamental nature of freedom of expression for the existence of a democratic society, stressing among other things that freedom of expression was a sine qua non for the

the ACtHPR has been more cautious, with literature suggesting that only one dissenting judgement has so far referenced the ICJ, citing to its Advisory Opinion on *Reparations for Injuries suffered in Service to the UN*.[58]

Due to recent developments before the ECtHR in relation to climate change (namely with the delivery of the rulings in *Verein KlimaSeniorinnen* and *Duarte Agostinho*), the following paragraphs will focus on this regional court alone.

In a 1998 judgment, the ECtHR considered that the context in which the ICJ operates was distinct from the ECtHR:

> … The subject matter of a dispute may relate to any area of international law … unlike the Convention institutions, the role of the International Court is not exclusively limited to direct supervisory functions in respect of a law-making treaty such as the Convention. Such a fundamental difference in the role and purpose of the respective tribunals, coupled with the existence of a practice of unconditional acceptance under Articles 25 and 46, provides a compelling basis for distinguishing Convention practice from that of the International Court.[59]

In a 2005 decision, the ECtHR referred to the practice of the ICJ, the UN HRC, the UN Committee against Torture, and the IACtHR in its consideration of an application for interim measures. The ECtHR clarified that although all these bodies operated: 'under different treaty provisions to those of the Court, have

---

development of trade unions' (§§26 & 56); *Savickis and Others v Latvia* (App No 49279/11) ECtHR 9 June 2022, cited IACtHR *Advisory Opinion OC-4/84* (§74) and other IACtHR case law; *Humpert and Others v Germany* (Apps Nos 59433/18, 59477/18, 59481/18 & 59494/18) ECtHR 14 December 2023, cited IACtHR *Advisory Opinion OC-27/21* (para. 62) and other IACtHR case law; *Ramadan v Malta* (App No 76136/12) ECtHR 21 June 2016, cited IACtHR *Advisory Opinion OC-4/84* and other IACtHR case law; *Marguš v Croatia* (App No 4455/10) ECtHR 27 May 2014, cited case law of IACtHR eg §138: 'The Court also notes the jurisprudence of the Inter-American Court of Human Rights, notably the above-cited cases of Barrios Altos, Gomes Lund et al., Gelman and The Massacres of El Mozote and Nearby Places, where that court took a firmer stance and, relying on its previous findings, as well as those of the Inter-American Commission on Human Rights, the organs of the United Nations and other universal and regional organs for the protection of human rights, found that no amnesties were acceptable in connection with grave breaches of fundamental human rights'; *Petropavlovskis v Latvia* (App No 44230/06) ECtHR 13 January 2015, cited IACtHR *Advisory Opinion OC-4/84*, and other case law.

58 *Femi Falana vs The African Union*, Case No 001/2011 (AfrCtHPR, 26 June 2012) Dissenting Opinion of Sophia Akuffo, Bernard Ngoepe & Elsie Thompson cited the ICJ's *Advisory Opinion on Reparation for Injuries Suffered in the Service of the United Nations* at 18.1.1.

59 *Loizidou v Turkey* (App No 15318/89) ECtHR [GC] 28 July 1998, §§84–85, as discussed in Ian Brownlie, *The Rule of Law in International Affairs* (Kluwer 1998) 76.

confirmed in their reasoning in recent decisions that the preservation of the asserted rights of the parties in the face of the risk of irreparable damage represents an essential objective of interim measures in international law,'[60] thereby drawing on the case law of international legal bodies.

Finally, in *Hassan v UK*, the ECtHR considered that 'the Convention cannot be interpreted in a vacuum and should so far as possible be interpreted in harmony with other rules of international law of which it forms part.'[61] It made findings consistent with ICJ case law and referenced advisory opinion determinations.[62] As stated at the outset, it is our submission that due to the unique character of climate change, and the still limited jurisprudence at the international level, cross-pollination is to be expected. The same may be said about the ECtHR's April 2024 climate change decisions.

In the *KlimaSeniorinnen* ruling, the ECtHR took note of the three climate advisory opinions as part of its overview of relevant international materials and developments.[63] Much of the ECtHR's findings relied on scientific evidence to illustrate the harmful effects of climate change on the full enjoyment and realisation of human rights. In its consideration of whether the State had taken sufficient measures to comply with its obligations under the European Convention on Human Rights (ECHR), the Court also provided for an objective assessment, bounding the margin of appreciation, amongst other factors, with considerations of the best available science. The ECtHR's decision in *KlimaSeniorinnen* was handed down just a few weeks before the ITLOS advisory opinion. One ITLOS judge criticised the ITLOS opinion in his separate declaration for failing to consider recent developments, including the ECtHR's decision. He noted the importance of that decision in dismissing 'the relatively popular argument that courts cannot rule on the protection of persons affected by climate change within the framework of international human rights law.'[64] Further, he considered such developments essential and not occurring in isolation, which underlines the importance of cross-pollination of these different developments.

In its simultaneous decision of *Duarte Agostinho and Others v Portugal and Others*, the ECtHR took note of the developments in IACtHR AO 23/17, General Comments of HRTBs, and the *Sacchi* decision. This underlines the premise of the chapter that the overlap in legal themes and issues relevant to the adjudication of climate change and the important clarifications provided for in the

60 ibid, §124.

61 *Hassan v UK* (App No 29750/09) ECtHR 16 September 2014, §77.

62 ibid, §82.

63 *Verein KlimaSeniorinnen* (n 29) §§187–188, 227.

64 *COSIS Opinion* (n 28) Declaration of Judge Pawlak, §3.

three climate advisory opinions will likely have an important role to play in the climate litigation that may follow – including, but not exclusive of, litigation before human rights bodies. Of course, decisions of the ECtHR have effects outside the Council of Europe. In particular, the tests of States' margin of appreciation and the principle of proportionality when balanced against the need to protect Convention rights, as detailed by the ECtHR, are likely to be directly influenced by any statements made by the ICJ on the theme of due diligence and legal consequences for excessive or 'significant' GHG emissions.

4.2 *Influence and Utility for Domestic Courts*

4.2.1 Monist and Dualist Systems

One of the key factors in determining the influence of the three advisory opinions in national legal systems will also be whether a State adopts a monist or dualist approach to international law. Monist systems may incorporate international law directly into the body of domestic law, whereas dualist systems require explicit ratification or other positive parliamentary action, or reference in domestic statute. The terms monist and dualist are not binary. Still, they are useful in describing the spectrum of approaches and attitudes of domestic courts to the incorporation of international norms and principles into domestic decision making.

In more monist States, domestic courts may consider advisory opinions as persuasive authority when deciding cases that directly involve international or domestic legal issues, including the three climate advisory opinions, and may also refer to the advisory opinions as guidance on interpreting and applying international norms, as relevant to domestic norms. For example, in the 2015 *Urgenda* decision of the Hague District Court, the UNFCCC and decisions made under it, such as the Kyoto Protocol, the Paris Agreement, and principles of general international law were taken into account in setting the threshold for the Dutch State's duty of care under domestic tort law (and later under human rights law by the Court of Appeal and Supreme Court). The Hague Court said:

> [4.42] From an international law perspective, the State is bound to UN Climate Change Convention, the Kyoto Protocol (with the associated Doha Amendment as soon as it enters into force) and the 'no harm' principle … The court – and the Parties – states first and foremost that the stipulations included in the convention, the protocol and the 'no harm' principle do not have a binding force towards citizens (private individuals and legal persons). Urgenda therefore cannot directly rely on this principle, the convention and the protocol …
>
> [4.43] This does not affect the fact that a state can be supposed to want to meet its international law obligations. From this it follows that an

> international law standard – a statutory provision or an unwritten legal standard – may not be explained or applied in a manner which would mean that the state in question has violated an international law obligation, unless no other interpretation or application is possible. This is a generally acknowledged rule in the legal system. This means that when applying and interpreting national law open standards and concepts, including social proprietary, reasonableness and propriety, the general interest or certain legal principles, the court takes account of such international law obligations. This way, these obligations have a 'reflex effect' in national law. [sic][65]

Alternately, the High Court of Australia has been generally recognised as adopting a dualist, ambivalent approach to international law,[66] with the high-water mark for an 'incorporation' approach over a 'transformative' approach occurring in the 1990s.[67] Nevertheless, many Australian federal and state statutes (particularly those related to human rights) both ratify and incorporate or refer to international treaties and conventions. Thus, Australian courts and tribunals do regularly consider and interpret international law, including advisory opinions, in various contexts.[68]

This is shown in a recent decision of a regional court in the State of Queensland. Under local land management legislation, the Queensland Land Court was required to assess whether a proposed new coal mine ought to proceed, taking into account its potential impacts on the local environment and human rights protected by the *Human Rights Act 2019* (Qld). The decision-maker found that the mine should not proceed, given the risks from climate change to present and future generations, and cited various sources of international law, as well as decisions of the ECtHR, in reaching her conclusions.[69] Accordingly,

65 *Urgenda v The Netherlands*, The Hague District Court (24 June 2015) ECLI:NL:RBDHA:2015:7196.

66 Alice de Jonge, 'Australia', in Shelton (ed), *International Law and Domestic Legal Systems: Incorporation, Transformation, and Persuasion* (OUP 2011) 23.

67 Hilary Charlesworth, 'International Law and the High Court' PrecedentAULA 38 (2005) <https://classic.austlii.edu.au/au/journals/PrecedentAULA/2005/38.pdf > accessed 15 August 2024.

68 Rosemary Grey et al' Cases before Australian Courts and Tribunals concerning Questions of Public International Law 2022' (2022) 41(1) *Australian Year Book of International Law Online* <https://brill.com/view/journals/auso/41/1/article-p377_16.xml?language=en&ebody=article%20details> accessed 15 August 2024.

69 *Waratah Coal Pty Ltd v Youth Verdict Ltd, The Bimblebox Alliance Inc, John and Susan Brinnand & Chief Executive, Department of Environment and Science*, [2020] QLC 33; [2021] QLC 4; [2021] QLC 36; [2022] QLC 3; [2022] QLC 4, Queensland Land Court Judgment of 25 November 2022.

one can see how the advisory opinions and their influence may permeate in local legal contexts, despite a dualist system, and a lack of express ratification or adoption by national legislatures.

In the United States (US), a jurisdiction that has also typically been seen as antithetical to the incorporation of international law into domestic decision-making, there are also statutory routes into national law. For example, the Alien Tort Statute,[70] establishes the right of foreigners to sue in the US for violations of 'the law of nations.' Significantly, the territorial scope of the statute was dramatically cut down by the US Supreme Court decision in *Kiobel v Royal Dutch Petroleum Co.*[71] Nonetheless, findings on climate science and key elements of State obligations in respect of science could even influence courts in the US, currently grappling with a series of constitutional and civil rights claims from young people seeking to protect the due process right to 'a climate system capable of sustaining human life.'[72]

Arguments regarding the United Kingdom (UK)'s alleged non-compliance with the obligations of the Paris Agreement were dismissed in cases challenging the expansion of Heathrow Airport[73] and a decision by the UK's export credit agency (UKEF) to provide finance for an liquified natural gas (LNG) project in Mozambique.[74] In the latter case, the Court of Appeal found that although the UK's international obligations under the Paris Agreement were taken into account in UKEF's decision-making process, as an unincorporated treaty it:

> does not give rise to domestic legal obligations ... it is actually an application of the constitutional law principle of dualism: the court cannot and should not second guess the executive's decision-making in the international law arena where there is no domestic legal precedent or guidance. The standard for judicial review may be, and is in this case, less intense where the issue is one that is not properly within the province of the domestic court.'[75]

70 28 USC 1350. The district courts shall have original jurisdiction of any civil action by an alien for a tort only, committed in violation of the law of nations or a treaty of the USA.

71 *Kiobel v Royal Dutch Petroleum Co*, 569 U.S. 108 (2013).

72 See Legal Actions at <https://www.ourchildrenstrust.org/>.

73 [2020] UKSC 52.

74 *R (Friends of the Earth Limited) v The Secretary of State for International Trade/UK Export Finance* [2023] EWCA Civ 14, §40.

75 ibid, §40.

Nonetheless, despite direct recognition of the dualist constitutional principle, the Court *did* consider the provisions of the Paris Agreement a relevant factor to be taken into account, in applying common law principles of judicial review, deciding that the Executive's decision to provide finance for the project was compliant with the Paris Agreement and not *ultra vires*.[76] This decision shows that even where domestic courts do not consider international law enforceable in domestic courts, the substance, meaning, and effect of international law may still influence a range of decisions on the subject at the national level, under typical administrative law principles. Given the range of issues and economic sectors touched by climate change, from national energy policy to infrastructure financing decisions, to transport and agricultural policy, the scope for impact of the coming advisory opinions from the ICJ, in particular, to influence domestic courts, is potentially very wide.

This demonstrates that the monist/dualist approach does not fully determine how the forthcoming advisory opinions will be relevant to questions related to climate change in national contexts, and that the long arm of their influence could indeed stretch further than expected.

4.2.2 National Climate Change Litigation, Including 'Framework Cases' against States

There is a particularly strong case that the advisory opinions will influence national litigation against States for inadequate climate policy under statutory, constitutional and/or human rights laws. When examining national level action in relation to climate change, research from the Grantham School at the London School of Economics has discerned a clear trend toward the adoption of domestic climate change framework laws, now operational in 60 countries around the world.[77] This legislation frequently establishes long-term emission reduction objectives and goals, enshrines NDCs under the Paris Agreement, and makes various other commitments at the national level. The trend for passing such legislation is matched by the increasing global trend of climate change litigation, of many types.[78]

Where States have national framework laws, developments at the international level can clarify, for example, whether State policies have been designed ambitiously enough and in line with a State's international obligations. The ITLOS, ICJ, and IACtHR advisory opinions will assist in the application of

76 ibid, §55.

77 Joana Setzer & Catherine Higham, Global *Trends in Climate Change Litigation: 2023 Snapshot* (Grantham Research Institute on Climate Change and the Environment 2023) 13.

78 ibid.

principles such as due diligence, reliance on the best available science, best efforts and highest possible ambition under the Paris Agreement. They may also clarify the interpretation of national statutory provisions referring to these principles, such as those in the Climate Change Response Act 2002 of New Zealand,[79] for example. Any clarifications from these international courts on the content of due diligence and on the criteria States ought to adopt when designing climate policy, even at a high level, will greatly influence the national level adjudication of disputes under national framework laws.[80]

Where States do not have national framework laws, but have adopted international human rights obligations into domestic law (such as in Australia) the advisory opinions will provide guidance on the way that human rights obligations require States to take climate action, and the manner in which human rights courts can assess the adequacy of action. They are likely to be influential in the decision making of the ECtHR and at the national level, for example, in a national case on foot against the State of Poland.[81] This case seeks stricter emission reduction targets for the State of Poland based on alleged violations of Polish personal rights (which protect the rights to life, property, and health) under the Polish Civil Code. The Polish courts are likely to be impacted by the advisory opinions, if not directly, then indirectly, through ECtHR law and subsequent European Union law.[82] In a clear illustration of cross-jurisdictional fertilisation in human rights claims, in a framework climate case brought by the association *Klimaatzaak* against the Belgian State and Governments of Wallonia and Flanders, the Brussels Court of Appeal examined the complex relationship between national, European Union, and ECHR law and found that:

> The Court also considers that the clear and precise nature of norms such as Articles 2 and 8 of the ECHR should not be assessed *in abstracto*, by examining the text alone, but by taking into account both the

79 Climate Change Response Act 2002, Public Act 2002 No 40, Date of assent: 18 November 2002.

80 For criteria that could/ought be taken into account as part of national due diligence, see Sophie Marjanac & Sam Hunter Jones, 'Staying within Atmospheric and Judicial Limits: Core Principles for Assessing whether State Action on Climate Change Complies with Human Rights' in Rodriguez-Garavito (ed) *Litigating the Climate Emergency* (CUP 2022) 157–176.

81 Sophie Marjanac & Janusz Buszkowski, 'The Polish Climate Case – Legal Briefing' (*ClientEarth*, June 2021) <https://www.clientearth.org/media/ilnjfico/clientearth-legal-briefing-on-polish-climate-case.pdf> accessed 15 August 2024.

82 ibid.

> interpretation given to it by its authorized interpreters (notably the European Court of Human Rights) and the context (national but not exclusively) in which the provision finds application. On the national level, the question is to determine whether the 'reception structures' of the Belgian legal system allow the judge to give effect to the norm concerned 'without profound normative modification' …
>
> Indeed, as indicated above, the ECHR is a living instrument that must be interpreted in the light of current conditions, which may involve taking into account non-binding sources of law …, or even factual elements such as scientific studies on which there is unanimous agreement, or political consensus at international, European or national level. This is particularly true in a matter as complex as global warming: it is impossible to determine whether the public authority knew or ought to have known of the existence of a risk, and whether it took sufficient measures to mitigate that risk, without referring to knowledge of experts in the field. In this sense, the fact can inform the law, without, as the Walloon Region fears, creating or abolishing it. Only such an approach can guarantee the effectiveness of the rights enshrined in the ECHR. To deprive these rights of any direct effect in all circumstances, in their 'positive obligations' aspect, would be tantamount to preventing their holders from gaining access to the courts and would run counter to the 'effectiveness' aspect of the subsidiarity principle referred to above.[83]

The Court then went on to assess the national policy context and found that the three Belgian governments had not done enough with respect to emission reductions, ordering that they must reduce national emissions by 55% by 2030.

In contrast, the above 'harmonised' approach has not been followed by the courts of the UK in recent years, which have rejected several climate cases brought on similar grounds by both individuals and non-governmental organisations. In the *Plan B Earth* case,[84] the claimants also alleged a violation of their Article 2 and 8 ECHR rights through the UK's inadequate emissions reduction target, together with various direct breaches of the Paris Agreement. The High Court of England and Wales found that insofar as the claimants relied on the UK's alleged non-compliance with the Agreement,

83 *VZW Klimaatzaak v Kingdom of Belgium, the Walloon Region, the Flemish Region, and the Brussels-Capital Region*, Process No 2021/AR/15gs, 2022/AR/737 & 2022/AR/891, Judgment of the Court of Appeals of 30 November 2023, §152.

84 *R (Plan B Earth & Others) v The Prime Minister & Others* [2021] EWHC 3469 (Admin).

> [u]nincorporated treaties such as the Paris Agreement do not form part of domestic law, and domestic courts cannot determine whether the UK has violated its obligations under an international treaty … The problem is that the Claimants are using compliance with the Paris Temperature Limit as a test for compliance with Article 2 (and Article 8). The effect is that the Court is being asked to enforce the Paris Agreement, contrary to the guidance in SC.[85]

It should be noted that the UK government agreed to adopt a net zero by 2050 target before the above decision was made.[86]

4.2.3 The ITLOS and Environmental Impact Assessment

Most of the previous subsections in this part have focused on how findings from the ICJ and the IACtHR could influence domestic systems, particularly related to human rights and other public law principles. However, the advisory opinion of the ITLOS has already made a significant contribution to the development of international environmental law, related to pollution of the marine environment. The detailed and clear guidance issued by the Tribunal is likely to have global implications on the law governing environmental impact assessments (EIAS) in respect of GHG emissions at both the international and national levels and is accordingly also relevant to business conduct and operations.

The ITLOS advisory opinion concluded that Article 194(1) UNCLOS requires States to 'take all necessary measures to prevent, reduce and control' the emissions of GHGS into the atmosphere, taking into account the best available science, and adopting a precautionary approach.[87] They found that States should apply a 'stringent' due diligence standard, taking into account 'scientific and technical information, relevant international rules and standards, the risk of harm and the urgency involved.'[88] The Tribunal's interpretation of the obligations under Article 194(2) is 'even more stringent'[89] requiring States to 'take all measures necessary' to control emissions of GHGS from activities within their jurisdiction or under their control, including both 'damages that actually occurred but also damage that is likely to occur.'[90]

85 Relying on *R (SC) v SSWP* [2021] UKSC 26, [2021] 3 WLR 428 per Lord Reed at 77, 84 and 91. See §§25 and 53 of the judgement.

86 *The Climate Change Act 2008* (2050 Target Amendment) Order 2019.

87 *COSIS Opinion* (n 28) §§212–213.

88 ibid, §239.

89 ibid, §258.

90 ibid, §248.

Applying these findings to the detailed procedural obligations to adopt laws and regulations to prevent, reduce and control pollution of the marine environment from land-based sources (Article 207) and from or through the atmosphere (Article 212),[91] as well as the obligation to monitor the risks or effects of pollution (Article 204), to publish reports (Article 205) and to assess the potential effects of activities (Article 206), the ITLOS found that 'the obligation to conduct environmental impact assessments is crucial to ensure that activities do not harm the marine environment' and that 'the duty of due diligence would not be considered to have been fulfilled if an environmental impact assessment was not undertaken for activities at risk of affecting the environment' (consistent with international law and other findings of the ICJ).[92]

Applying these principles to GHGs, they then found that the articles of UNCLOS 'impose specific obligations on State Parties to … conduct environmental impact assessments as a means to address marine pollution from anthropogenic GHG emissions,' from all land and sea-based sources. Most importantly, they also found that the cumulative impacts of GHG emissions from a particular project or activity must be taken into account and 'evaluated in interaction with other activities.'[93]

EIAs are the most commonly used, and globally accepted, environmental planning and management tools.[94] However there is wide variation across States in the integration of climate change into EIA processes.[95] The findings of the ITLOS clarify and crystalise the obligation of States to pass laws requiring EIAs for all land and sea-based activities that lead to GHG emissions above a certain threshold, and for the effects of those emissions to be assessed on a cumulative basis.

The ITLOS also issued a clear repudiation of the 'drop in the ocean argument' often deployed by developers and proponents of fossil fuel projects,

---

91 The Tribunal found that jurisdiction or control applies to activities undertaken by public or private actors on the States' territory, but also within its exclusive economic zone and continental shelf, or on-board ships carrying their flag.

92 ibid, §§354, 356.

93 ibid, §365: 'In the context of pollution of the marine environment from anthropogenic GHG emissions, planned activities may not be environmentally significant when taken in isolation whereas they may produce significant effects if evaluated in interaction with other activities.'

94 UNEP, 'Assessing Environmental Impacts: A Global Review of Legislation' (3 January 2018) <https://www.unep.org/resources/assessment/assessing-environmental-impacts-global-review-legislation> accessed 15 August 2024.

95 Rose Mayembe et al, 'Integrating climate change in Environmental Impact Assessment: A review of requirements across 19 EIA regimes' (2023) 869 *The Science of the Total Environment.*

who claim that the effects of a single project on global climate change are not significant enough to justify assessment, refusal of permission, or additional measures to control fossil fuel extraction or single point source of GHGs.[96] This has been a particularly controversial legal issue in environmental law in many jurisdictions. For example, in Australia, which has a rich jurisprudence on the assessment of cumulative impacts,[97] a state-level court adopted a carbon budget approach[98] to cumulative GHG in *Gloucester Resources Limited v Minister for Planning,* relating to the approval of a new coal mine.[99] In that case, the court accepted expert scientific evidence that:

> … global [GHG] emissions are made up of millions, and probably hundreds of millions, of individual emissions around the globe. All emissions are important because cumulatively they constitute the global total of [GHG] emissions, which are destabilising the global climate system at a rapid rate. Just as many emitters are contributing to the problem, so many emission reduction activities are required to solve the problem.[100]

However, in another case decided on 16 May 2024, the Federal Court of Australia was asked to interpret the national legislative regime for protecting 'matters

96 Brian J Preston, 'Contemporary issues in Environmental Impact Assessment – Are Climate Impacts Impacts? Climate Science in the EIA and Judicial Review' *Climate Impact Seminar* (27 February 2020) <https://lec.nsw.gov.au/documents/speeches-and-papers/Preston_CJ_-_Contemporary_Issues_in_Environmental_Impact_Assessment_27.02.20.pdf> accessed 15 August 2024.

97 *Tarkine National Coalition Inc v Minister for the Environment and Others* [2015] FCAFC 89.

98 Per the decision at 441, the carbon budget approach is 'A commonly used approach to determine whether the NDCs of the parties to the Paris Agreement cumulatively will be sufficient to meet the long term temperature goal of keeping the global temperature rise to between 1.5°C and 2°C is the carbon budget approach. The carbon budget approach is based on the well-proven relationship between the cumulative anthropogenic emissions of GHGs and the increase in global average surface temperature.' The carbon budget approach 'is a conceptually simple, yet scientifically robust, approach to estimating the level of [GHG] emission reductions required to meet a desired temperature target,' such as the Paris Agreement targets of 1.5°C or 2°C (Steffen report [38]). The approach is based on the approximately linear relationship between the cumulative amount of CO_2 emitted from all human sources since the beginning of industrialisation (often taken as 1870) and the increase in global average surface temperature (Figure 2 in IPCC (2013) Summary for Policy-Makers, cited in Steffen report, [39]). Once the carbon budget has been spent (emitted), emissions need to become 'net zero' to avoid exceeding the temperature target.

99 Preston (n 96).

100 *Gloucester Resources Limited v Minister for Planning and Environment (No 2)* [2018] NSWLEC 1200.

of national environmental significance,' and found that the decision-maker need not take the climate change effects of coal and gas projects into account, because it accepted that if the project did not proceed, the market would respond by increasing supply of fuel from other sources, which would mean that the emissions from the project would be replaced by emissions from other projects.

This is known as the 'market substitution' argument, which allowed the decision-maker to conclude that the effects of the project would not be 'a substantial cause of adverse impacts on the environment' in light of global emissions in other parts of the world. In that case, the judges commented that:

> Notwithstanding [the] conclusions on the grounds of appeal, the arguments on this appeal do underscore the ill-suitedness of the present legislative scheme of the EPBC Act to the assessment of environmental threats such as climate change and global warming and their impacts on [matters of national environmental significance] in Australia ... This proceeding, and the merits decision-making underlying it, might be said to raise the question whether the legislative scheme is fit for purpose in this respect.[101]

The Court's extraordinary *obiter dicta* arguably suggests that Australia's legislative approach would not meet the 'stringent' due diligence standard set out by the ITLOS, which as explained, must be targeted to contribute to the global reduction of GHGS, and must incorporate the precautionary approach.

The extent of indirect or downstream impacts from a project subject to an EIA is another controversial question in national law that is directly addressed by the ITLOS AO. In a UK case decided on 20 June 2024, the Supreme Court of England and Wales found by 3 to 2 votes that the EU's EIA Directive[102] and UK's implementing regulations did require the GHG emissions from the burning of the oil product to be included and considered in the public EIA process for a proposed new onshore oil drilling facility in southern England.[103]

---

101 *Environment Council of Central Queensland Inc v Minister for the Environment and Water* [2024] FCAFC 56 (16 May 2024).

102 Directive 2011/92/EU of the European Parliament and of the Council of 13 December 2011 on the assessment of the effects of certain public and private projects on the environment, implemented through Town and Country Planning (Environmental Impact Assessment) Regulations 2017 (SI 2017/571).

103 *R (on the application of Finch on behalf of the Weald Action Group) (Appellant) v Surrey County Council and others (Respondents)* [2024] UKSC 20.

The court concluded that, as it was common ground that all the oil from the project would be eventually refined and combusted, there was a causal link between the project and those emissions, which would have an 'inevitable' significant effect on the environment.[104] The court concurred with another recent decision of the Oslo District Court,[105] following the conclusions of the Norwegian Supreme Court, which decided the same issue of interpretation of the EIA Directive, finding that:

> combustion emissions from petroleum extraction are such a significant and particularly characteristic consequence of these kinds of projects that they must clearly be considered indirect climate effects within the meaning of the EIA Directive. The whole purpose of petroleum extraction is to make geologically stored carbon available in the form of oil or gas. [GHG] emissions from the carbon are thus both an inevitable and intentional effect from the project. … If combustion emissions are not included, this will mean that the provisions of the EIA Directive on the assessment of indirect climate impacts from petroleum operations will in practice have no real content.[106]

Overall, and finally, one of the key challenges discussed by scholars[107] in respect of EIAs for GHGs is the ultimate failure of legislative schemes to require decision-makers to impose sufficient controls on the extraction of fossil fuel products[108] and the subsequent failure of these regimes to regulate and sufficiently reduce overall emissions. Arguably, the ITLOS Advisory Opinion means that EIA laws and regulations that do not include cumulative and indirect or downstream (also known as scope 3) assessments and subsequent directions to decision-makers to control or reduce those emissions from all fossil fuel projects, are insufficient and may 'fail to meet this new and higher stringent' standards that must now be part of each State's international legal obligations to protect the marine environment under UNCLOS. States that fail to meet this new and higher threshold may be found to have breached their international

---

104 ibid, 79–82.

105 *Nature & Youth Norway & Ors v The State represented by the Ministry of Petroleum and Energy*, HR-2020-2472-P (Case No 20–051052SIV-HRET).

106 *Greenpeace Nordic v The State of Norway (represented by the Ministry of Petroleum and Energy)*, Case No 23–099330TVI-TOSL/05, 53–54.

107 Lindsay Luke & Bram Noble, 'Consideration and influence of climate change in environmental assessment: an analysis of British Columbia's liquid natural gas sector' (2018) 37(5) Impact Assessment and Project Appraisal 37(5).

108 According to Preston (n 98), such EIAs can become 'tick the box' exercises.

legal duties to other States, and could potentially face international responsibility (with the relevant consequences at the international level), such as under the dispute resolution provisions of UNCLOS. In monist systems, it could also be argued that, at the national level, an administrative resolution (such as an environmental permit) could be challenged as unlawful for being in violation of an international legal obligation that is directly applicable in the legal order and, therefore, binding on a public authority in the decision-making process. The above demonstrates the importance of the ITLOS advisory opinion for the law of EIAs and their assessment of climate change impacts. Time will tell how this opinion is used by creative litigants seeking to improve climate protection laws and regulations.

5 Conclusion

Advisory opinions rendered by international courts and tribunals can have downstream impacts on the case law of other international bodies and in domestic litigation. While advisory opinions of ITLOS and the ICJ do not have binding legal effect, it is evident that they carry significant persuasive weight and influence. Downstream impacts can include treaty interpretation, development of customary international law, coherence of international law, and guidance for domestic/national courts, including sub-national courts. The impact and role of advisory opinions will be strengthened through the findings of other courts, tribunals, and judicial bodies, be it at the international, regional, or national level. Finally, a certain level of divergence is to be expected and, we say, likely unavoidable. While fragmentation is, of course, an undesirable outcome, a healthy level of divergence and ambiguity may be a good thing, to allow courts to build on each other's findings, and strengthen legal protection, while at the same time allowing for context-specific flexibility.

Acknowledgments

The authors would like to thank Emma O'Brien and Francesco Maletto for their input and assistance.

CHAPTER 12

The Impact on Domestic Law of Climate Change-Related Advisory Opinions: the Experience of the IACtHR and the ITLOS

Gastón Medici-Colombo and Armando Rocha***

Abstract

As advisory opinions clarify States' obligations under international law, it is natural that domestic measures aimed at complying with such obligations need to be re-assessed in light of those advisory opinions, regardless of their non-binding character. This chapter looks to the stance taken by the IACtHR itself on the domestic impact of its opinions and to the case law of domestic courts on this matter, although mindful that States may have changed, or need to change, their domestic laws after, and consequential to, an IACtHR's opinion. In the analysis of the advisory opinions of the ITLOS, this chapter looks very briefly at the adoption of domestic legislation after the rendering of its opinions. This chapter does not assess the experience related to the ICJ's opinions.

Keywords

advisory opinions – compliance – control of conventionality – enforcement – execution – implementation – Inter-American Court of Human Rights – International Tribunal for the Law of the Sea

* *Universitat de Barcelona* and *Centre d'Estudis de Dret Ambiental de Tarragona*, ORCID No 0000–0003-4259-2828.

** *Universidade Católica Portuguesa*, School of Law, Católica Research Centre for the Future of Law, ORCID No 0000–0002-8181-1512.

 | DOI:10.1163/9789004730618_013

1 Introduction

The question underlying this chapter is, 'What happens to a State's domestic law after an international court or tribunal renders an advisory opinion?' It is an odd question at first sight, since international courts and tribunals work within the international legal order (not domestic legal orders), and since advisory opinions do not settle any dispute and, thus, do not require any change in the existing international law. In fact, the purpose of an advisory opinion is to *clarify* the law. However, as authoritativeness stems from the way a court or a tribunal is perceived by society (and not from the nature or bindingness of a judgment or opinion), opinions rendered by international courts and tribunals can contribute to the development of international law in the same manner as a binding judgment.[1] This happens because treaties such as the American Convention on Human Rights (ACHR),[2] the United Nations Convention on the Law of the Sea (UNCLOS),[3] the United Nations Framework Convention on Climate Change (UNFCCC),[4] or the Paris Agreement[5] are not an 'end-game,' using Wessel's nomenclature,[6] but rather require a certain evolutionary reading to withstand the passage of time. What this ultimately implies is that an evolutive reading of States' international obligations may require adjustments at the level of States' domestic legal orders.

This helps explain the upsurge in requests for opinions on States' obligations in relation to climate change before the International Tribunal for the Law of the Sea (ITLOS), the Inter-American Court of Human Rights (IACtHR), and the International Court of Justice (ICJ). These requests seek clarification of States' obligations to mitigate and adapt to climate change under a varied set of rules and principles of international law and ultimately seek to press States to adopt climate policies within their domestic legal order.

Clarifying States' obligations, of course, impacts the fabric of international law. These advisory opinions, once rendered, are likely to be used by applicants

1 Eg Samantha Besson, 'Legal Philosophical Issues of International Adjudication', in Romano, Alter & Shany (eds), *The Oxford Handbook of International Adjudication* (OUP, 2015) 413; Armin von Bogdandy & Ingo Venzke, 'Beyond Dispute: International Institutions as Law-makers' (2011) 12 *German Law Journal* 979; Alan Boyle & Christine Chinkin, *The Making of International Law* (OUP, 2007) 268.

2 Adopted 22 November 1969, entered into force 18 July 1978, OASTS No 36, 1144 UNTS 123.

3 Adopted 10 December 1982, entered into force 16 November 1994, 1833 UNTS 3.

4 Adopted 9 May 1992, entered into force 21 March 1994, 1771 UNTS 107.

5 Adopted 12 December 2015, entered into force 4 November 2016, 3156 UNTS 79.

6 Jared Wessel, 'Relational Contract Theory and Treaty Interpretation: End-Game Treaties v. Dynamic Obligations' (2004) 60 *NYU Annual Survey of American Law* 149.

resorting to other courts (international or domestic) and inform the views adopted by these courts.[7] However, this chapter assesses the impact of the advisory opinions on domestic law – ie, on the processes that are adopted at the domestic level subsequently to an opinion (eg, a change in policies, practices, or laws and regulations), as a means to comply with a State's international obligations as clarified thereunder. Compliance, therefore, cannot be assessed with regards to the opinion itself, since advisory opinions do not require any specific tangible State action, but rather with respect to the obligation set out in an international law rule. Complying with these obligations (eg obligations set out in the ACHR, the UNCLOS, the UNFCCC, or the Paris Agreement) requires more than a mere internalization of these treaties. Because the relation between international and domestic law is *not* one of 'two nations; between whom there is no intercourse and no sympathy,'[8] compliance with these treaties requires the adoption of sectorial policies or legislative measures aligning a State's domestic regulatory framework with its international obligations (as clarified over time by international courts and tribunals).[9]

Nonetheless, contrary to the internalization of treaties, the execution of a judgment, or the use of an opinion as an authority by a domestic court, the impact of advisory opinions on domestic law is often, if not always, informal, implied, and unacknowledged – and thus less palpable or detectable.[10] It may be the case, for instance, that a State thought the opinion did not require any change of its domestic law, or that its non-binding nature was an opportunity to preserve the full discretion of a State's constitutional organs. From a methodological angle, the main challenge of this chapter, therefore, is to *find* and *interpret* evidence of State (in)action subsequent to the rendering of an opinion by an international court or tribunal.

In line with Shany,[11] one could look for cases where there is a shift or change in States' behavior subsequent to the rendering of an opinion, even if the link is not openly assumed. However, it is more likely to find indirect signs of such impact on the case law of apex courts, which may be more explicit in their reasoning. Accordingly, in the analysis of the effects of the advisory opinions of the IACtHR, this chapter looks – firstly – to the stance taken by the IACtHR itself

7 See Lea Main-Klingst & Sophie Marjanac (Chapter 11 of this book).

8 Disraeli, *Sybil, or the Two Nations*: 1845 (Routledge 1930) 76.

9 Eg *Request for an Advisory Opinion submitted by the Commission of Small Island States on Climate Change and International Law* (Advisory Opinion, 21 May 2024) ITLOS Case No 31, §§265–80 (*COSIS Opinion*).

10 See, more generally, Natalie Klein & Jack McNally, *Compliance with Decisions of the Dispute Settlement Bodies of the UN Convention on the Law of the Sea* (Brill 2023) 22–23.

11 Yuval Shany, 'Assessing the Effectiveness of International Courts: A Goal-Based Approach' (2012) 106 *AJIL* 225.

on the matter and – secondly – to the case law of domestic courts, although mindful that States may have changed, or need to change, their domestic laws after, and consequential to, an IACtHR's opinion (Section 2). In the analysis of the advisory opinions of the ITLOS, this chapter looks very briefly at the adoption of domestic legislation after the rendering of its opinions, since the International Seabed Authority acts as a public repository of national laws and regulations related to deep seabed mining (Section 3). This chapter does not assess the experience related to the ICJ's opinions. Section 4 concludes.

2 The Domestic Law Impact of the Advisory Opinions Rendered by the IACtHR

Article 64 of the ACHR establishes the advisory jurisdiction of the IACtHR, which can take the form of an interpretative[12] or a compatibility consultation.[13] Other courts and tribunals also have an advisory jurisdiction, but the rules on standing, subject-matter jurisdiction, and participatory opportunities make the IACtHR's advisory competence unique.

On the one hand, all Member States of the OAS can submit a request for an interpretative or compatibility consultation,[14] even if they are not parties to the ACHR or have not accepted the IACtHR's contentious jurisdiction. This makes the advisory jurisdiction a mechanism of the entire inter-American human rights system (IAHRS), rather than of the more restricted ACHR regime.[15] On the other hand, requests for an opinion may refer to the 'interpretation of [the ACHR] or of other treaties concerning the protection of human rights in the American States.'[16] Therefore, requests are not limited to the interpretation of the ACHR, but rather include

> any provision dealing with the protection of human rights set forth in any international treaty applicable in the American States, regardless of whether it be bilateral or multilateral, whatever be the principal

12 ACHR, art 64(1).

13 ACHR, art 64(2).

14 Moreover, the organs listed in current Chapter VIII of the Charter of the OAS can also request an interpretative consultation to the IACtHR.

15 *'Other Treaties' Subject to the Consultative Jurisdiction of the Court (art. 64 American Convention on Human Rights)*, Advisory Opinion OC-1/82, Inter-American Court of Human Rights Series A No 1 (24 September 1982) §19.

16 ACHR, art 64(1).

> purpose of such a treaty, and whether or not non-Member States of the inter-American system are or have the right to become parties thereto.[17]

This means that the list of treaties that can potentially be brought to the IACtHR's attention, under an advisory proceeding, is broad and non-restrictive, expressing a systemic understanding of human rights' (universal) protection.[18]

In this context, one concern of the IACtHR is the sociological legitimacy of its advisory opinions. To secure such a perception of legitimacy and authoritativeness, the IACtHR provides very broad participatory opportunities in these proceedings.[19] This includes the participation of all Organisation of American States (OAS) Member States – who have a legal right to submit their written observations and participate in public hearings organized as part of the proceedings, not as parties but rather to protect their 'legitimate interests.'[20] Furthermore, the Presidency of the IACtHR may invite any interested (natural or legal) person to participate in the proceedings. Unsurprisingly, civil society has been using this opportunity very liberally. In the advisory proceedings regarding the climate emergency and human rights, there was a record number of participants, ranging from States (including Vanuatu, which is not a Member State of the OAS) to international bodies, organs, or organizations, and passing by infra-State entities and more than 200 briefs from civil society (ie local communities, individuals, NGOs, or academic centers).[21]

The ACHR remains silent regarding the effects of advisory opinions on the consulting States or the rest of State Parties. This silence has given place to divisive debates regarding the bindingness of the opinions among commentators, as well as judges and regulators throughout the region, when deciding if or how to apply them to domestic issues. These debates have even caught the attention of a broader public (ie the media) when interpretations rendered in the opinions were seen as controversial by a government or a group. The

---

17 *'Other Treaties'* (n 15) 12 first resolutive paragraph; and §21.

18 *Institution of Asylum and its Recognition as a Human Right in the Inter-American System of Protection (interpretation and scope of Articles 5, 22(7) and 22(8), in relation to Article 1(1) of the American Convention on Human Rights)*. Advisory Opinion OC-25/18, Inter-American Court of Human Rights Series A No 25 (30 May 2018) §15.

19 *Restrictions to the Death Penalty (Arts. 4.2 and 4.4 American Convention on Human Rights)*. Advisory Opinion OC-3/83, Inter-American Court of Human Rights Series A No 3 (8 September 1983) §22.

20 ibid §24.

21 IACtHR, 'Observations on the Request for an Advisory Opinion', available here: <https://www.corteidh.or.cr/observaciones_oc_new.cfm?nId_oc=2634&lang=es&lang_oc=es>, accessed 26 July 2024. See also Miriam Cohen (Chapter 8), Harjeevan Narulla & Rohan Nanthakumar (Chapter 10) in this book.

impact of the opinion OC-24/17 on gender identity and equality and non-discrimination with regard to same-sex couples[22] on the legal, social and political agenda of Costa Rica and other ACHR States is a clear example.[23]

The IACtHR pronounced a few times on the effects of its opinions. In its first-ever advisory ruling (1982), it affirmed that opinions 'lack the same binding force that attaches to decisions in contentious cases.'[24] In 1997, it clarified, however, that opinions have 'undeniable legal effects.'[25] In 2014, the IACtHR expressed again about the opinion's effects, explaining them as connected to the 'conventionality control' doctrine, and consequently distinguishing between effects on ACHR States and other OAS States.[26] This explanation dispelled doubts regarding the IACtHR's understanding of its opinions' effects, but it did not fully overcome debates, not among commentators or among judges and regulators.

2.1 *The Effects of the Advisory Opinions on the Legal Order of* ACHR *State Parties*

As mentioned, in its opinion OC-21/14, the IACtHR explained the advisory opinions' effects as connected to the so-called 'conventionality control' doctrine. Indeed, the IACtHR explained those effects as a further development of its flagship doctrine. This means that, to properly understand the scope of the opinions' effects, we must revisit (at least briefly) the IACtHR's gradual construction of its doctrine.

---

22 *Gender Identity, and Equality and Non-Discrimination with respect to Same-Sex Couples. State Obligations in relation to Change of Name, Gender Identity, and Rights deriving from a Relationship between Same-Sex Couples (Interpretation and Scope of Articles 1(1), 3, 7, 11(2), 13, 17, 18 and 24, in relation to Article 1 of the American Convention on Human Rights)*. Advisory Opinion OC-24/17 of Nov 24, 2017. Series A No 24.

23 Luis Manuel Madrigal, 'Por qué la opinión de la Corte IDH es vinculante para Costa Rica y no violenta su soberanía' (elmundo.cr, 9 January 2018), available here: <https://elmundo.cr/costa-rica/la-opinion-la-corte-idh-vinculante-costa-rica-no-violenta-soberania/>, accessed 26 July 2024; David Bolaños Acuña, 'Las Ideas de Fabricio Alvarado Sobre la Corte IDH, Puestas a Prueba (*Semanario Universidad*, 3 February 2018), available here: <https://semanariouniversidad.com/pais/ideas-fabricio-alvarado-sobre-corte-idh-puestas-a-prueba/>, accessed 6 May 2019.

24 *'Other Treaties'* (n 15) §51.

25 *Reports of the Inter-American Commission on Human Rights (Art. 51 American Convention on Human Rights)*. Advisory Opinion OC-15/97, Inter-American Court of Human Rights Series A No 15 (14 November 1997) §26.

26 *Rights and Guarantees of Children in the Context of Migration and/or Need of International Protection*. Advisory Opinion OC-21/14, Inter-American Court of Human Rights Series A No 14 (19 August 2014).

Based on Articles 1 and 2 of the ACHR, the conventionality control doctrine was introduced by the IACtHR in the case *Almonacid Arellano et al v Chile*, where the IACtHR stated that

> … when a State has ratified an international treaty such as the [ACHR], its judges, as part of the State, are also bound by such Convention. This forces them to see that all the effects of the provisions embodied in the [ACHR] are not adversely affected by the enforcement of laws which are contrary to its purpose and that have not had any legal effects since their inception. In other words, the Judiciary must exercise a sort of *'conventionality control'* between the domestic legal provisions which are applied to specific cases and the [ACHR]. To perform this task, *the Judiciary has to take into account not only the treaty, but also the interpretation thereof made by the [IACtHR], which is the ultimate interpreter of the* [ACHR].[27]

Accordingly, the IACtHR established a mandate for domestic judges to conduct a conformity control between the domestic law and the ACHR, considering not only its wording but also the interpretations thereof made by the IACtHR. The IACtHR insisted on this doctrine in the *Case of the Dismissed Congressional Employees*, adding that judges must carry out this control even *ex officio*, although always 'in the context of their respective spheres of competence and the corresponding regulations.'[28] Furthermore, in the case *Cabrera García and Montiel Flores v. Mexico*, the IACtHR clarified that all States' organs (not only judicial ones) must ensure compliance with the ACHR[29] and, in *Gelman v Uruguay* the conventionality control was explicitly defined as a function and task of any public authority – any institution, organ or authority – , and not only the judicial branch.[30]

A further development of the conventionality control was the expansion, both in normative and hermeneutic terms, of the legal substance against which

27 *Almonacid-Arellano et al v Chile* (Preliminary Objections, Merits, Reparations and Costs Judgment). Inter-American Court of Human Rights Series C No 154 (26 September 2006), §124 (emphasis added).

28 *Case of the Dismissed Congressional Employees* (*Aguado Alfaro et al*) *v Peru* (Preliminary Objections, Merits, Reparations and Costs). Inter-American Court of Human Rights Series C No 158 (4 November 2006), §128.

29 *Case of Cabrera García and Montiel Flores v Mexico* (Preliminary Objection, Merits, Reparations and Costs). Inter-American Court of Human Rights Series C No 220 (26 November 2010), §225.

30 *Case of Gelman v Uruguay* (Merits and Reparations). Inter-American Court of Human Rights IACtHR Series C No 221 (24 February 2011), §239.

domestic law shall be contrasted (*material controlante*). On the one side, the IACtHR began to refer not only to the ACHR but also to 'other instruments of similar nature, that comprise the *corpus juris* arising from the human rights conventions to which the State is a party.'[31] On the other side, the IACtHR started to reflect on what kind of interpretations shall integrate this controlling substance: only interpretations delivered in cases in which the State executing the conformity control was a party or also interpretations delivered in other cases (*inter-partes* or *erga omnes* effect)?; and only interpretations made in judgments or also interpretations made in another kind of resolutions and orders? Regarding the first question, the IACtHR observed that, while judgments produce *res judicata* effects on the State parties to the case, they produce *res interpretata* effects on the rest of the ACHR States (*erga omnes*).[32] Regarding the second, in what matters here, the answer was unanimously provided by the IACtHR in its opinion OC-21/14:

> … the different organs of the State must carry out the corresponding control of conformity with the [ACHR], *based also on the considerations of the Court in exercise of its non-contentious or advisory jurisdiction*, which undeniably shares with its contentious jurisdiction the goal of the inter-American human rights system, which is 'the protection of the fundamental rights of the human being'.[33]

With this extract, which would be continuously repeated in the following advisory rulings, the IACtHR clarified its understanding of the opinions' effects on the States parties to the ACHR. These effects are those of the *res interpretata* (*erga omnes*) and deploy their strength in the exercise of the conventionality control that all the domestic authorities must conduct, by testing the conformity of national orders (norms, acts, omissions, etc) with the human rights *corpus juris*.[34] In other words, interpretations rendered in advisory opinions

31 *Case of the Dismissed Congressional Employees* (n 28) Separate Opinion of Judge Sergio García Ramírez, §2; *Case of the Massacres of the Río Negro v Guatemala* (Preliminary Objection, Merits, Reparations and Costs). Inter-American Court of Human Rights Series C No 250 (4 September 2012), §262; *Case of Gudiel* Álvarez *et al* (*"Diario Militar"*) *v Guatemala. Merits, Reparations and Costs.* Inter-American Court of Human Rights Series C No 253 (20 November 2012), §330.

32 *Case of Gelman v Uruguay. Monitoring Compliance with Judgment.* Order of the Inter-American Court of Human Rights of Mar 20, 2013, §69.

33 *Rights and Guarantees of Children in the Context of Migration* (n 26) §31 (emphasis added).

34 Sergio García Ramírez, 'The Relationship between Inter-American Jurisdiction and States (National Systems): Some Pertinent Questions' (2015) 5 *Notre Dame Journal of Int'l &*

integrate the legal substance to be used by the authorities of all ACHR States when conducting the conformity control, regardless of whether the State has participated in the advisory proceedings.

This is the stance of the IACtHR on the bindingness of the advisory opinions so far.[35] Opinions are not legally binding if 'binding' means that they produce effects comparable to those of judgments on the State that is party to the case (*res judicata*).[36] However, they can be considered as legally binding or quasi-binding[37] if 'binding' means that they must be followed as part of the controlling legal substance in the exercise of conventionality control. A different question is whether, with this stance, the IACtHR has overreached its authority and/or is illegitimately interpreting the ACHR and/or altering the correct functioning of the IAHRS and whether this could be acceptable or not for the States.[38]

An additional aspect is how domestic courts perceive the advisory opinions' effects. In this regard, the practice of domestic courts is determined by the interplay between the IAHRS and the constitutional order of each country. Even though the practice of courts is all but consistent or constant, there

---

Comp Law 115, 136; Eleanor Benz, *The Advisory Function of the Inter-American Court of Human Rights* (Nomos 2023) 388.

35 This stance is aligned with part of the relevant doctrine. See Victor Manuel Rodriguez Rescia, *La Ejecución de Sentencias de la Corte Interamericana de Derechos Humanos* (1st edn, IJSA 1997) 61; Faúndez Ledesma, *El Sistema Interamericano de Protección de los Derechos Humanos: Aspectos institucionales y procesales* (3rd edn, Instituto Interamericano de Derechos Humanos 2004); Pedro Nikken, 'La función consultiva de la Corte Interamericana de Derechos Humanos' (1999) *Biblioteca Jurídica Virtual del Instituto de Investigaciones Jurídicas de la UNAM* 161, 176; Sergio García Ramírez, 'El control judicial interno de convencionalidad' (2011) 28 *Revista del Instituto de Ciencias Jurídicas de Puebla* 123, 138; Augusto Guevara Palacios, *Los Dictámenes Consultivos de la Corte Interamericana de Derechos Humanos: Interpretación Constitucional y Convencional* (JB Bosch Editor 2012).

36 Eduardo Vio Grossi, 'La naturaleza no vinculante de las opiniones consultivas de la Corte interamericana de derechos humanos' (2018) 2(2) *Revista Jurídica Digital UANDES* 200.

37 Jorge Contesse, 'The Rule of Advice in International Human Rights Law' (2021) 115(3) *AJIL* 367, 369.

38 On this note, see eg Ariel Dulitzky, 'An Inter-American Constitutional Court? The Invention of the Conventionality Control by the Inter-American Court of Human Rights' (2015) 50(1) *Texas Int'l Law Journal* 45; Álvaro Paúl Díaz, 'Los enfoques acotados del control de convencionalidad: Las únicas versiones aceptables de esta doctrina' (2019) 87(246) *Revista de Derecho* 49; Karlos Castilla Juárez, '¿Control interno o difuso de convencionalidad? Una mejor idea: la garantía de tratados' (2012) XIII *Anuario Mexicano de Derecho Internacional* 51; Laurence Burgorgue-Larsen, 'Conventionality Control: Inter-American Court of Human Rights (IACtHR)' (*Max Planck Encyclopedias of International Law*, December 2018) <https://opil.ouplaw.com/display/10.1093/law-mpeipro/e3634.013.3634/law-mpeipro-e3634> accessed 25 April 2024.

seems to be a discrete majority among high courts of ACHR States in favor of a binding or quasi-binding nature of the IACtHR' case law, including its advisory opinions. A study published in 2012 by Guevara Palacios[39] concluded that this view was common to apex courts of Argentina,[40] Bolivia,[41] Colombia,[42] Costa Rica,[43] and the Dominican Republic.[44] The same recognition took place later on in Ecuador.[45] On the contrary, supreme courts in Venezuela[46] and Guatemala[47] have specifically rejected the opinions' binding effect. Worth mentioning are the stances of high courts in Peru and Mexico. While the Constitutional Court of Peru initially aligned itself with the view of a binding nature of opinions,[48] a 2020 decision related to the OC-24/17 showed that the majority within the Court does not favor this view anymore.[49] In a similar vein, somehow altering a previous stance on the matter,[50] the Mexican Supreme Court decided in a very recent resolution that IACtHR's opinions are not binding for Mexican domestic judges although having 'legal relevance' and 'high interpretative authoritativeness.'[51] Standards contained in those opinions can become binding if used by the IACtHR or the Supreme Court in their judgments.[52] Finally, high courts in Brazil, Chile, and Uruguay have left the issue unsettled.[53]

---

39 Guevara Palacios (n 35).

40 Supreme Court of Argentina, Judgment in *Mazzeo, Julio Lilo y otros*, Recurso de casación e inconstitucionalidad. M. 2333. XLII. y otros, 13 Jul 2007, §20.

41 Plurinational Constitutional Court of Bolivia, 2003–06127-12-RAC, Judgment No 0491/2003-R, 15 Apr 2003.

42 Constitutional Court of Colombia, Judgment No T-1319/01, 7 Dec 2001, although the same court held in 2014 that the IACtHR jurisprudence is of interpretative relevance, but not necessarily binding, unless certain criteria are fulfilled, such as that it is uniform and reiterated, Benz (n 34) 375, mentioning Judgments No. C-500/14, 16 Jul 2014 and No C-327/16, 22 Jun 2016.

43 Constitutional Chamber of the Supreme Court of Justice of Costa Rica, Judgment No 2313–95, 9 May 1995.

44 Supreme Court of the Dominican Republic, Resolution No 1920–2003, 13 Nov 2013.

45 Constitutional Court of Ecuador, judgment 184–18-SEP-CC, 29 May 2018, § 58; judgment 10–18-CN/19, 12 Jun 2019, § 81; and judgment 11–18-CN/19, 12 Jun 2019, §§ 23–39.

46 Supreme Tribunal of Venezuela (Constitutional Chamber), 01–0415, Judgment 1942, 15 Jul 2003.

47 Guevara Palacios (n 35) 455, mentioning a judgment of 18 Nov 2009.

48 Constitutional Court of Peru, Judgment No 5854–2005–PA/TC, 8 Nov 2005; and No 2798–04–HC/TC, 9 Dec 2009.

49 Benz (n 34) 383–385, mentioning Judgment No 676/2020, 3 Nov 2020.

50 Supreme Court of Mexico, Contradicción de Tesis 293/2011, 03 Sep 2013; and Tesis jurisprudencial 21/2014 (10a.), 30 Apr 2014.

51 Supreme Court of Mexico, Contradicción de criterios 175/2022, 17 Jun 2024.

52 ibid.

53 Burgorgue-Larsen (n 38).

Unlike judgments, the IACtHR does not monitor compliance with the standards delivered in advisory opinions, and thus, measuring their actual impact in domestic law is a complex task.[54] Changes or rejection of changes in regulations or governmental practices as a response to opinions can be very subtle, undeclared, or go unnoticed. However, with regard to more divisive issues, the chances to record their impact increase. That was the case of the OC-24/17 on non-discrimination against LGBTIQ+ People, which triggered in Costa Rica and Ecuador successful lawsuits and regulatory adjustments in favor of the rights of this community, in particular, the same-sex couples' marriage and the name change of trans people.[55] The question regarding the bindingness of advisory opinions recurrently emerged in social and judicial arenas of both countries (and beyond) after the OC-24/17, with high courts supporting their binding effects.[56]

2.2 *The Effects of Advisory Opinions on OAS States Not Parties to the ACHR*

Authorities of OAS Members that are not parties to the ACHR are also affected by advisory opinions, but in a distinctive manner, since they are not under the mandate of the conventionality control. In its opinion, OC-21/14, the IACtHR mentioned:

> … the interpretation given to a provision of the Convention through an advisory opinion provides all the organs of the Member States of the OAS, including those that are not parties to the Convention but that have undertaken to respect human rights under the Charter of the OAS (…), with a source that, by its very nature, also contributes … to achieving the effective respect and guarantee of human rights.
>
> Given the broad scope of the Court's advisory function (…) everything indicated in this Advisory Opinion also has legal relevance for all the OAS Member States that have adopted the American Declaration, irrespective of whether they have ratified the [ACHR] … [57]

---

54 Pablo Saavedra Alessandri, 'A Broader Look At the Transformative Impact of the Inter-American Court of Human Rights' Decision', Von Bogdandy et al (ed) *The Impact of the Inter-American Human Rights System: Transformation on the Ground* (OUP 2024) 537, 549.

55 ibid 550–556.

56 Constitutional Court of Ecuador (n 45); Constitutional Chamber of the Supreme Court of Justice of Costa Rica, Judgment No 12782-2018, 8 Aug 2018.

57 *Rights and Guarantees of Children in the Context of Migration* (n 26) §§31–2.

According to IACtHR, opinions provide domestic authorities of these States with legally *relevant* sources and interpretative guides. That relevance is explained by the authoritativeness of the IACtHR – particularly strong when interpreting inter-American treaties (eg the OAS Charter[58] or the American Declaration of the Rights and Duties of Man[59]) – but also by the legitimacy of its advisory jurisdiction that extends to all OAS Member States, and not only ACHR Parties. This is confirmed by the practice of some States, such as Canada or the United States (US), which participate in advisory proceedings in accordance with the rules of procedure.[60]

2.3 *The Foreseeable Impact of the Advisory Opinion on Climate Emergency in Domestic Law*

On 9 January 2023, Chile and Colombia submitted an interpretative consultation to the IACtHR, with the main purpose of clarifying '… the scope of State obligations … in order to respond to the climate emergency within the framework of international human rights law …'[61] A wide range of questions were raised on, for instance, obligations of prevention and guarantee of human rights, differentiated obligations in relation to vulnerable groups and communities, procedural obligations and shared and differentiated responsibilities.

When rendering the opinion, the IACtHR is not constrained by the number or literal wording of the questions and can answer only some or rephrase them in order to provide better assistance in the protection of human rights. As we

58 Charter of the Organization of American States (adopted 39 April 1948, entered into force 13 December 1951) 119 UNTS 3.

59 American Declaration of the Rights and Duties of Man, adopted by the Ninth International Conference of American States, Bogotá, Colombia, 2 May 1948.

60 Eg the USA participated in *Interpretation of the American Declaration of the Rights and Duties of Man Within the Framework of Article 64 of the American Convention on Human Rights*, Advisory Opinion OC-10/89, Inter-American Court of Human Rights Series A No 1 (14 July 1989), and *Denunciation of the American Convention on Human Rights and the Charter of the Organization of American States and the Consequences for State Human Rights Obligations (Interpretation and Scope of Articles 1, 2, 27, 29, 30, 31, 32, 33 a 65 and 78 of the American Convention on Human Rights and 3(l), 17, 45, 53, 106 and 143 of the Charter of the Organization of American States)*. Advisory Opinion OC-26/20, Inter-American Court of Human Rights Series A No 26 (9 November 2020). Canada participated in *Juridical Condition and Rights of Undocumented Migrants*. Advisory Opinion OC-18/03, Inter-American Court of Human Rights Series A No 18 (17 September 2003).

61 Chile and Colombia, 'Request for an advisory opinion on the Climate Emergency and Human Rights submitted to the Inter-American Court of Human Rights by the Republic of Colombia and the Republic of Chile' (9 Jan 2023), available here: <https://www.corteidh.or.cr/docs/opiniones/soc_1_2023_en.pdf>, accessed 15 Mar 2024.

write this chapter,[62] the approach to be taken by the IACtHR can only be a matter of speculation. That being said, a consistent, commendable, and probable approach for the IACtHR to be taken is to answer the request by applying to the climate issue the 'environmental obligational framework' that it has been developing, mainly from the OC-23/17[63] onwards, and that was recently employed in the case *Inhabitants from La Oroya v Peru*.[64]

In applying this framework, the IACtHR could explain, for instance, how the *duty to regulate* must apply to climate mitigation and adaptation. If inspired by the recent European Court of Human Rights' (ECtHR) case law,[65] the IACtHR, while interpreting the Paris Agreement, may refer to the duty to establish and quantify clear and ambitious national limits to GHG emissions, perhaps through a carbon budget method.[66] Or maybe the IACtHR could observe that a failure to comply with the established GHG limits can imply, on its own, a human rights violation that needs to be avoided by instituting solid and transparent monitoring (and enforcement) mechanisms applicable to every economic sector, as part of the *duty to supervise and monitor*.[67] Although the European and the Inter-American human rights systems are very different, it is likely that both courts will get to a close and coherent interpretative result.[68] A further example of the application of the 'environmental obligational

---

62 On 31 July 2024.

63 *Environment and Human Rights* (*State Obligations in relation to the Environment in the context of the Protection and Guarantee of the Rights to Life and to Personal Integrity – Interpretation and Scope of Articles 4(1) and 5(1) of the American Convention on Human Rights*). Advisory Opinion OC-23/17, Inter-American Court of Human Rights Series A No 23 (15 November 2017); see Maria Antonia Tigre & Natalia Urzola, 'The 2017 Inter-American Court's Advisory Opinion: Changing the Paradigm for International Environmental Law in the Anthropocene' (2021) 12(1) *Journal of Human Rights and the Environment* 24.

64 *Case Inhabitants from La Oroya v Peru* (Merits, Reparations and Costs). Inter-American Court of Human Rights Series C No 511 (27 November 2023). See an illustration of the framework in the Concurring Vote of Judges Ricardo C. Pérez Manrique, Eduardo Ferrer Mac-Gregor Poisot and Rodrigo Mudrovitsch, §33.

65 *Verein KlimaSeniorinnen Schweiz and Others v Switzerland* (App no 53600/20) ECtHR [GC] 9 Apr 2024.

66 ibid §§570–572. See Chris Hilson, 'The ECtHR's Klimaseniorinnen Judgment: The Meaning of Carbon Budget within a Wide Margin of Appreciation' (2024) *Climate Law – A Sabin Center Blog*, available here: <https://blogs.law.columbia.edu/climatechange/2024/04/11/the-ecthrs-klimaseniorinnen-judgment-the-meaning-of-carbon-budget-within-a-wide-margin-of-appreciation/>

67 *Environment and Human Rights* (n 63) 60.

68 Armando Rocha & Rômulo Sampaio, 'Climate Change before the European and the Inter-American Courts of Human Rights. Comparing Possible Avenues before Human Rights Bodies' (2023) 32 *RECIEL* 279.

framework' to the climate emergency context would be the development of the *duty to require and approve environmental impact assessments*.[69] The IACtHR should clarify if and how GHG emissions (and climate impacts) must be considered in the assessments and, perhaps, to what extent the discretion of authorities consenting to carbon-intensive activities is restricted. Additionally, the IACtHR, interpreting the Escazú Agreement,[70] could develop the right to *access to justice* by requiring States to guarantee particularly broad standing criteria in climate cases, especially when vulnerable groups are involved.[71]

The IACtHR's interpretations in the future opinion will have to be applied by the domestic authorities – executive, legislative, and judicial – when exercising the control of conventionality. Even though these examples may be qualified as the low-hanging fruit among possible interpretations of States' obligations in the context of climate change, they still imply considerable efforts for many countries of the region that have not developed a strong and clear climate regulatory framework yet. This is the main impact of the advisory opinion: to ask States to assess their national policies in light of the IACtHR's findings and align their national regulatory framework accordingly. In this sense, depending on how far and detailed the opinion will be, it can have a significant disruptive impact on some State Parties to the ACHR. This impact will be reinforced with the use of the opinion in climate litigation cases before national courts.

Some final aspects to be considered when thinking about the foreseeable impact of the opinion on climate emergency in domestic orders are those of the procedural implementation of the quasi-binding interpretations through the doctrine of conventionality. First, contrary to judgments, interpretations rendered in opinions are facts-detached and, thus, of general character. This implies that, in the process of application of the created standard (binomial norm-interpretation) to a concrete case, a margin of appreciation exists for national authorities. This margin will be broader or thinner depending on how clear, precise, and unconditional the standard is. Second, as mentioned, the IACtHR has affirmed that the conventionality control must be exercised 'in the context of [the] respective spheres of competence and corresponding procedural regulations.'[72] There is an ongoing debate regarding what this

69 *Environment and Human Rights* (n 63) 61.

70 Regional Agreement on Access to Information, Public Participation and Justice in Environmental Matters in Latin America and the Caribbean [*Escazú Agreement*] (adopted 4 March 2018, entered into force 22 April 2021) 3388 UNTS.

71 Gastón Medici-Colombo & Thays Ricarte, 'The Escazú Agreement Contribution to Environmental Justice in Latin America: An Exploratory Empirical Inquiry through the Lens of Climate Litigation' (2024) 16(1) *Journal of Human Rights Practice* 160.

72 *Case of the Dismissed Congressional Employees* (n 28).

means or should mean, and inconsistencies in the IACtHR's case law have been noted.[73] An acceptable view is that of Judge Ferrer Mac-Gregor Poisot, who explained that this should not be interpreted as a restriction to exercise the control but as a way to 'calibrate' its intensity according to the competence of each entity.[74] For instance, domestic courts entitled to exercise a diffuse constitutional control are apt to declare domestic laws void an unconventional, while other entities not entitled to exercise that kind of control should limit themselves, for instance, not to apply the unconventional norm or merely to note the possible unconventionality.[75] Additionally, even for those entities that have broad competences to carry out a strong conventionality control, there are certain rules or good practices to be followed. One of them is that conventionality control must always be applied in the least disruptive manner for the domestic order. For instance, interpretations of domestic provisions in conformity with the conventional order would always be preferred over non-application or derogation of the former.[76] Third and final observation, provisions or interpretations that are more favorable to human rights (from domestic or international law rules) always prevail in accordance with the *pro homine* principle, which is a cardinal principle of the IAHRS.[77] In this sense, Guevara Palacios argues that domestic courts can only detach from interpretations in advisory opinions due to justice reasons and the application of cardinal principles of the IAHRS – *pro homine, progressivity, or non-discrimination* – , and as long as they do so expressly and giving reasons for it.[78]

3 The Domestic Law Impact of the Advisory Opinions Rendered by the ITLOS

Whereas the purpose of human rights treaties is to secure the observance of human rights in jural relations of domestic law, most law of the sea rules are aimed at governing jural relations between States, ie valid at the level of international law. This explains why, contrary to the domestic law impact of rulings

73 Álvaro Paúl, 'The Emergence of a More Conventional Reading of the Conventionality Control Doctrine' (2019) 49 *Revue Générale de Droit* 275.

74 *Case of Cabrera García and Montiel Flores v Mexico* (n 29) Concurring Opinion of Ad Hoc Judge Eduardo Ferrer Mac-Gregor Poisot §§34–41.

75 ibid §35.

76 Néstor Pedro Sagüés, 'Las opiniones consultivas de la Corte Interamericana, en el control de convencionalidad' (2015) 20 *Pensamiento Constitucional* 275, 276, 277.

77 ACHR, art 29.

78 Guevara Palacios (n 35) 465.

and opinions of the IACtHR, the potential impact of the opinions of the ITLOS on domestic litigation is shorter. This also explains why, in the case of the IACtHR, resorting to the case law of domestic courts helps to assess the domestic law impact of its opinions, whereas, in the case of the opinions rendered by the ITLOS, one can look to the adoption of new laws, or the amendment or repeal of existing laws, after (and perhaps consequential to) the rendering of such opinions. The UNCLOS does not clarify the impact of advisory opinions on domestic law – and the ITLOS has not yet been in a position of needing to clarify this impact. As such, this part of the chapter is naturally shorter, as the evidence available is almost non-existent.

So far, the ITLOS has rendered three advisory opinions. The first referred to the deep seabed mining, and namely the responsibilities and obligations of sponsoring States in relation to activities in the Area.[79] The second referred to flag and coastal States' obligations in relation to fishing activities.[80] The third referred to States' obligations under the UNCLOS to mitigate and adapt to climate change.[81] The purpose of this chapter is precisely to assess what the impact of this third opinion on domestic laws can be, considering that the cornerstone of this opinion refers to States' obligation to adopt a proper national regulatory framework aimed at reducing GHG emissions.[82] To that end, this section assesses the very short evidence existing on the domestic impact of the other advisory opinions.

As mentioned before, from a methodology angle, the main difficulty of assessing the impact of advisory opinions in the domestic legal order of States is the lack of data where such impact is openly acknowledged by State authorities. Or, alternatively, data regarding cases where such impact is openly rejected. A good example is the *Sub-Regional Fisheries Commission* (*SRFC*) advisory opinion: despite the core importance of this opinion to the requesting organization and its Member States, there is no tangible evidence that can suggest whether the findings espoused in this opinion were incorporated or rejected by those Member States.

A better example is the impact of the 2011 opinion on the *Responsibilities and Obligations of States Sponsoring Persons and Entities with respect to Activities in the Area*. The International Seabed Authority – which is responsible for

79 *Responsibilities and Obligations of States Sponsoring Persons and Entities with respect to Activities in the Area* [Advisory Opinion, 1 Feb 2011] ITLOS Case No 17 (*Responsibilities and Obligations of Sponsoring States Opinion*).

80 *Request for an Advisory Opinion submitted by the Sub-Regional Fisheries Commission* (*SRFC*) [Advisory Opinion, 2 Apr 2015] ITLOS Case No 21.

81 *COSIS Opinion* (n 9).

82 ibid §§265–280.

'organiz[ing] and control[ling] activities in the Area, particularly with a view to administering the resources of the Area'[83] – asked States 'to provide information on, or texts of, relevant national laws, regulations and administrative measures.'[84] Furthermore, it created an open national legislation database.[85] According to the data of this latter, some States adopted domestic acts regarding the exploration for and exploitation of deep seabed minerals, namely Belgium,[86] Cook Islands,[87] Federated States of Micronesia,[88] Fiji,[89] Kiribati,[90] Nauru,[91] Singapore,[92] Tonga,[93] Tuvalu,[94] and the United Kingdom.[95] Others reported to the International Seabed Authority that they had prior legislation or that they were reviewing their own laws and regulations, whilst the majority of States did not reply to the International Seabed Authority.

This could suggest that the ITLOS' advisory opinion was inconsequential in terms of domestic law impact, but the fact is that those States that adopted new laws on the exploration for or exploitation of deep seabed minerals beyond national spatial jurisdiction, or that amended prior legislation, showed an impressive alignment in terms with the findings of the ITLOS in that advisory opinion – even though they do not mention it explicitly. Looking at the timelines, it is unlikely that a national act adopted after the ITLOS' advisory opinion was not to some extent influenced by this opinion, but the lack of an

83 UNCLOS, art 157(1).
84 Doc No ISBA/17/C/20, §3.
85 Available here: <https://www.isa.org.jm/national-legislation-database/>
86 Law No 2013/11348, of Aug 17, 2013, available here: <https://www.isa.org.jm/wp-content/uploads/2022/05/Belgium-2-Aug.pdf>
87 Seabed Minerals Act (Act No 5 of 2019), available here: <https://static1.squarespace.com/static/5cca30fab2cf793ec6d94096/t/5d3f683993ea3f0001b7379c/1564436729995/Seabed+Minerals+Act+2019>
88 Seabed Resources Act (Public Law No 20–102), available here: <https://www.cfsm.gov.fm/ifile/20%20congress/LAWS/PUBLIC_LAW_20-102.pdf>
89 International Seabed Mineral Management Decree (Decree No 21 of 2013), available here: <https://www.isa.org.jm/wp-content/uploads/2022/05/Fiji2013.pdf>
90 Seabed Minerals Act (Act No 1 of 2017), available here: <https://faolex.fao.org/docs/pdf/kir177489.pdf>
91 International Seabed Minerals Act (Act No 26 of 2015), available here: <https://www.isa.org.jm/wp-content/uploads/2022/05/Nauru_ISM.pdf>
92 Act No 6 of 2015, available here: <https://www.isa.org.jm/wp-content/uploads/2022/05/Singapore.pdf>
93 Seabed Minerals Act (Act No 10 of 2014), available here: <https://www.isa.org.jm/wp-content/uploads/2022/05/Tonga-2014.pdf>
94 Seabed Minerals Act (Act No 14 of 2014), available here: <https://www.isa.org.jm/wp-content/uploads/2022/05/Tuvalu-2014.pdf>
95 Deep Sea Mining Act of 1981, as amended by the Deep Sea Mining Act of 2014, available here: <https://faolex.fao.org/docs/pdf/uk150471.pdf>

explicit, open, and formal acknowledgment does not allow any safe conclusion in this regard.

Furthermore, the *notes verbales* sent by other States Parties display a certain States' aspiration, although implied, to comply with all international rules and standards, such as those clarified in the ITLOS' advisory opinion, perhaps because the topic itself (the exploration for and exploitation of resources in the international seabed Area) is primarily regulated by the UNCLOS. With regards to other States Parties, it is not possible to interpret their silence.

Although the *COSIS Opinion* aims to assist the requesting body only,[96] it is likely to impact the climate policies of all States, since the opinion is an authoritative pronouncement from a law of the sea specialized court that unveils what States' obligations to mitigate climate change under the UNCLOS are.[97] Although international courts cannot replace States, they are 'purveyors of legitimacy' that 'help us understand what needs to be done, or what is being done inadequately or not at all.'[98] In this sense, an opinion rendered by the ITLOS that clarifies what State action needs to be adopted pursuant to the UNCLOS is likely to pressure all States to adopt more stringent mitigation policies. Moreover, the *COSIS Opinion* can be used, domestically, as a justification for the adoption of more politically divisive measures,[99] since States can shield themselves in the court pronouncement in order to adopt more ambitious mitigation efforts (and thus outsource guilt to the ITLOS).[100] Accordingly, one can expect that the *COSIS Opinion*, together with the opinions eventually rendered by the IACtHR and the ICJ, may be openly and formally invoked in domestic decision-making processes prior to the adoption of climate change-related policies, laws, and regulations, as well as in judicial processes before domestic courts.

4 Conclusion

As advisory opinions seek to clarify the existing States' obligations under international law, they can impact States' domestic laws. That can result from the

96 *COSIS Opinion* (n 9) §§107–108.

97 See Guerreiro Teixeira & Galvão Teles (Chapter 2 in this book).

98 Philippe Sands, 'Climate Change and the Rule of Law: Adjudicating the Future in International Law' (2016) 28 *Journal of Environmental Law* 19, 24.

99 Armando Rocha, 'Suing States: The Role of Courts in Promoting States' Responsibility for Climate Change', in Garcia & Cortês (eds), *Blue Planet Law – The Ecology of our Economic and Technological World* (Springer, 2023) 99, 101–102.

100 ibid 102.

simple fact that complying with an international obligation requires the adoption of specific legislation and policies at the level of domestic law.

This impact is clearer in the case of advisory opinions of the IACtHR clarifying human rights obligations owed by States to individuals under their jurisdictions and legal order. To that end, States may bear negative and positive obligations to put in place and maintain a proper regulatory framework aimed at securing the protection of such human rights and freedoms. More subtle, but equally real, are the impacts on domestic orders of advisory opinions that clarify obligations in State-to-State jural relations that involve the adoption of domestic norms. A good example is the advisory opinion rendered by the ITLOS regarding States' obligations to mitigate and adapt to climate change under the UNCLOS. As the ITLOS referred in this opinion, to perform the obligations listed in Part XII of the UNCLOS, namely those related to the prevention, reduction, and control of GHG emissions, and those aimed at preserving and restoring the marine environment, require more of the adoption of a national legislative framework.[101]

Nonetheless, when adopting a national legislative act, States do not openly or expressly acknowledge the upstream influence of an advisory opinion from an international court. The influence, therefore, is often visible – but also implied, informal, and unacknowledged. A good case study is the ITLOS' advisory opinion on the responsibilities and obligations of sponsoring States with respect to the activities in the Area. As this is an activity primarily regulated by the UNCLOS, it is just natural that domestic laws will be adopted in line with, or at least aware of, the ITLOS' advisory opinion. Few States have flagged to the International Seabed Authority the adoption of new laws, or the amendment of existing laws, subsequent to the rendering of that opinion, but all of these latter States aligned their national legislation with the findings of the ITLOS, although they do not acknowledge it openly. The same can be said with regard to the ACHR and the opinions of the IACtHR, which hold a *res interpretata* effect. This means that States also need to align their domestic laws with the findings of the IACtHR. However, with regard to these opinions, adjustments to (or rejection to amend) regulations or governmental practices as a response to them can go unnoticed, making the measurement of their actual impact a very complex task. Still, and particularly in politically charged issues, because domestic courts have a mandate to control the conventionality of national statutory norms, it is easier to find signs of such impact, namely when a domestic

101 ibid §§265–280.

court renders a national rule incompatible with the ACHR as interpreted by the IACtHR in one of its opinions.

Being climate change a 'politically charged issue' suggests that the trio of advisory opinions requested to the ITLOS, the IACtHR, and the ICJ will be invoked more frequently, openly, and formally before courts, but also by political bodies who may be reluctant to adopt more ambitious climate policies as a result of their sensitivity among the electorate. As such, it is unclear to what extent these opinions will shape States' domestic legislation, but it seems fair to assume that they will be used as a catalyst for the adoption of policies and legislation at the domestic level.

CHAPTER 13

Finding the 'Rosetta Stone'? Concluding Remarks on the Role of Advisory Opinions in International Law in the Context of the Climate Crisis

*Armando Rocha** *and Maria Antonia Tigre***

Abstract

As a conclusion, this chapter provides a quick overview of the main findings of the book, presented not chapter by chapter, but rather in a topical manner. First, the chapter looks to the message of hope for concerned States, civil society movements, and individuals, who were able to conduct parallel initiatives that ended up with the submission of three requests for advisory opinions before three of the major international courts and tribunals. Second, the chapter assesses the expected impact of advisory opinions on climate change, namely in international and domestic lawmaking and judicial proceedings. These impacts prove that advisory opinions are taken seriously, as can be noticed in the recent agreement between the United Kingdom, Mauritius, and the United States of America concerning the sovereignty over the Chagos archipelago. Third, and finally, the chapter analyses the critical areas for future research so that these advisory opinions are a first but decisive step for future judicial development of international law – ie, how the advisory opinions may be used as a 'Rosetta Stone' to clarify and develop international climate law.

Keywords

civil society movements – concerned individuals – concerned states – future research agenda – impact on domestic law – impact on international negotiations – impact on litigation

* *Universidade Católica Portuguesa*, School of Law, Católica Research Centre for the Future of Law, https://orcid.org/0000-0002-8181-1512, email: armandorocha@ucp.pt

** *Sabin Center for Climate Change Law*, Columbia Law School, https://orcid.org/0000-0003-4308-1958, email: mb4913@columbia.edu.

 | DOI:10.1163/9789004730618_014

1 Introduction

International law is a system of hope – hope that States comply with the rules and principles they consented to despite the lack of enforcement mechanisms as sophisticated as within domestic legal systems. The trio of requests for an advisory opinion on climate change embody this idea of hope that States are concerned with the international rule of law and, therefore, that judicial clarification or development of the international law on climate change has the potential to compel recalcitrant States to enhance their mitigation and adaptation laws and policies. Hope, therefore, was a major guiding force behind the trio of requests for an advisory opinion. Ultimately, hope that – by emphasizing the clarity and bindingness of the obligations stemming from the United Nations Framework Agreement on Climate Change (UNFCCC),[1] the Paris Agreement,[2] and other international law rules and principles relevant in the context of climate change – the International Tribunal for the Law of the Sea (ITLOS), the Inter-American Court of Human Rights (IACtHR), and the International Court of justice (ICJ), will also emphasize that international law is *law*, being the stabilization of expectations its central function in our societies (eg under the UNFCCC or the Paris Agreement) despite past frustration.[3]

Hope is an intangible and immaterial value that is hardly protected by any legal system – and much less by international law, where no centralized sovereign or law enforcer exists. However, the experience also shows that States are concerned with the rule of law, be it a genuine concern or only a concern with securing a predictable set of rules applicable to all States. The *Chagos* Advisory Opinion[4] is a prime example of how hope and a concern with the international rule of law can be a guiding force in international law processes. Although Mauritius was deprived of a judicial mechanism to question the continued administration of Chagos by the United Kingdom, it could form a coalition vote in the UN General Assembly (UNGA) to secure the approval of a request for an advisory opinion.[5] This was similar to the coalition vote under the Vanuatu initiative for requesting an advisory opinion from the ICJ on States' obligations regarding climate change. In 2019, the advisory opinion

1 United Nations Framework Convention on Climate Change (adopted 9 May 1992, entry into force 21 March 1994) 1771 UNTS 107.

2 Paris Agreement (adopted 12 December 2015, entry into force 4 November 2016) 3156 UNTS 79.

3 Nikas Luhmann, *Law as a Social System* (Klaus E Ziegert tr, OUP 2004) 142 ff.

4 *Legal Consequences of the Separation of the Chagos Archipelago from Mauritius in 1965* (Advisory Opinion) [2019] ICJ Rep 95.

5 UNGA Res 71/292 (22 June 2017) UN Doc A/RES/71/292.

rendered by the ICJ concluded that the separation of the Chagos archipelago from Mauritius in 1964 (ie, before the independence of Mauritius) was contrary to States' international obligations' on decolonization,[6] and thus that 'the United Kingdom is under an obligation to bring an end to its administration of the Chagos archipelago as rapidly as possible.'[7] In this light, what incentive did the United Kingdom have to return sovereignty over the Chagos archipelago to Mauritius as a result of a *non-binding* advisory opinion? This question can only be answered by the United Kingdom authorities. Still, it should not pass unnoticed that, on 3 October 2024, the United Kingdom, Mauritius, and the United States of America (which holds a military base in Chagos) announced an agreement to return Chagos to Mauritius' sovereignty.[8]

The *Chagos* opinion brings hope to those awaiting the advisory opinions on climate change. Given recent developments, it seems likely that the IACtHR and the ICJ will adopt a similar approach to ITLOS in the *COSIS Opinion*[9] – a stance that is both cautious and bold. Upon the release of all three advisory opinions, the international community will gain a sort of 'Rosetta Stone' for climate law: a foundational guide to decipher the core principles of international climate law, including (but not limited to) obligations under the UNFCCC and the Paris Agreement, and to clarify the responsibilities of states in addressing climate change.

In Chapter 3, Alice Ollino and Irini Papanicolopulu provide an in-depth analysis of the findings in the ITLOS' *COSIS Opinion*, alongside anticipated insights from the IACtHR and ICJ. Here, in this conclusion, our focus shifts to what lies ahead: the broader message that emerges from the pursuit of these three advisory opinions on climate change and what future directions may be envisioned.

2 A Message of Hope for Concerned States, Civil Society Movements, and Individuals

In Chapter 4, Melissa Stewart explains how the prospects for State-to-State litigation under Article 14 of the UNFCCC and Article 24 of the Paris Agreement

6 ibid §§177–180.
7 ibid §§177–180.
8 See 'Joint statement between the governments of the Republic of Mauritius and the United Kingdom of Great Britain and Northern Ireland concerning the Chagos Archipelago, including Diego Garcia' (3 October 2024) available at <https://www.gov.uk/government/news/joint-statement-between-uk-an-mauritius-3-october-2024> last accessed 8 November 2024.
9 *Request for an Advisory Opinion submitted by the Commission of Small Island States on Climate Change and International Law* (Advisory Opinion, 21 May 2024) ITLOS Case No 31 (*COSIS Opinion*).

are very short. The dispute settlement system established therein, requiring express State consent to the jurisdiction of the ICJ or the arbitral tribunal, is a protective design flaw and a design choice that prevents States from engaging in judicial disputes referring to the interpretation or enforcement of these treaties. Thus, States' obligations regarding climate change seem to be a non-contractible behavior, in the sense that they seem unable to be challenged by other States or verified by a court.

Nonetheless, Stewart, but also Austyn Campbell, Claire Robertson, and Eran Sthoeger in Chapter 9, explain how all design systems have their glitches. Therefore, the fact that the ICJ or the arbitral tribunal do not hold contentious jurisdiction under Articles 14 of the UNFCCC or 24 of the Paris Agreement does not mean that States do not bear international obligations in respect of climate change or that these obligations are immune from any kind of international judicial oversight. In fact, the fragmentation of international law (from a regime and institutional angle) is an opportunity to find new avenues for bringing climate change into the international judiciary's docket. Therefore, one message of hope from this process of requesting advisory opinions on climate change is that creativity and ingeniousness are a powerful tool available to concerned States, civil society movements, and individuals: they can help find glitches in the system and discover new *fora* and new legal arguments to be used before international courts and tribunals.

One cannot ignore that States may fear retaliation or damaging diplomatic relations or that they can be captured by entrenched economic interests (including a genuine concern with economic growth and the well-being of their citizens). Nonetheless, the trio of requests for advisory opinions on climate change shows the opposite. Some States are keen to pursue climate justice by taking the initiative of requesting an advisory opinion (IACtHR), or by creating an international organization as a platform to request such an opinion (ITLOS), or at least by investing and taking the lead in mobilizing other States to request an opinion (ICJ). Moreover, although States are concerned with economic interests that may appear incompatible with reducing greenhouse gas (GHG) emissions, they are also risk-averse as economic agents. Therefore, clarity on the existing law and the resulting obligations is also their core concern. This, hand in hand with a concern for reputation, helps explain why the UNGA request for an advisory opinion from the ICJ was approved by consensus after a formal endorsement by a large number of States.

Even though understanding the reasons behind a State's climate agenda is a complex task, one major factor contributing to the lack or insufficiency of States' climate action is that climate change is one example of a non-cooperative or Nash equilibrium. In such a case, unless States can interfere with other States' policies to cope with GHG emissions and their negative externalities, they have no incentive to change their domestic climate laws and policies.[10] From their standpoint, the core question is, 'why should States adopt measures that affect their citizens' economic growth and well-being if other States keep emitting GHG and no international court or tribunal holds jurisdiction to assess their behavior'? Other answers could be given, but the message from the trio of requests for an advisory opinion, as well as from the European Court of Human Rights' (ECtHR) ruling in the *Verein KlimaSeniorinnen* case,[11] is that international law and international courts and tribunals may be leveraged successfully to pressure States to reduce GHG emissions from their territory or jurisdiction. According to ITLOS and the ECtHR, even the manner in which these (due diligence) obligations are performed domestically is also a matter of international law.[12] This proves that States' obligations regarding climate change are *legal* obligations subject to judicial scrutiny (although limited).

For concerned States, the next step is probably not before courts but rather in climate negotiations. For instance, the message in the *COSIS Opinion* that '[i]n the context of marine pollution from anthropogenic GHG emissions, States with greater means and capabilities must do more to reduce such emissions than States with less means and capabilities'[13] must be consequential. Therefore, it is expected that developing States wish to bring the common but differentiated responsibilities and respective capabilities (CBDR-RC) principle into climate negotiations. This same principle applies to all topics addressed in the trio of advisory opinions. While advisory opinions can clarify the foundational legal framework and delineate States' obligations regarding climate change, international cooperation among States remains essential to reduce GHG emissions effectively.[14] The tool for securing such cooperation and reconciling States' interests is precisely the negotiation of international treaties, namely at the Conferences of the Parties (COPs) to the UNFCCC and the Paris Agreement.

In this context, the trio of advisory opinions on climate change may be the catalyst needed to bring States to the negotiating table. As mentioned before, climate change is an example of a negative externality that creates a Nash equilibrium. This implies that a State is only encouraged to reduce GHG emissions

10 Eric A Posner & Alan O Sykes, *Economic Foundations of International Law* (Harvard University Press 2013) 19.

11 *Verein KlimaSeniorinnen Schweiz and Others v Switzerland* (App No 53600/20) ECtHR [GC] 9 April 2024.

12 ibid §§538 & 550; *COSIS Opinion* (n 9) §§234 ff.

13 *COSIS Opinion* (n 9) §227.

14 ibid §§294–321.

from its territory or jurisdiction (with all the resulting economic implications) if others do the same. If the major international courts and tribunals (including the ECtHR and, eventually, the African Court on Human and Peoples' Rights (AfCtHPR) find that States have an obligation to mitigate and adapt to climate change, namely by reducing GHG emissions and cooperating at the regional and global level, this may be a symbolic encouragement for recalcitrant States.

In this sense, getting the major international courts and tribunals (regional and international, specialized or with a generic subject matter jurisdiction) is a tale of success from the angle of small island and other developing States that broke the glass ceiling. This success, however, is also shared with concerned individuals and civil society. The role of grassroots movements in the trio of climate change advisory opinion requests is explained by Cohen (Chapter 8), Narulla and Nanthakumar (Chapter 10), and analyzed in detail by Maria Antonia Tigre.[15] From the standpoint of these concerned individuals and civil society movements, the message of hope is quite clear: they were able to assist and influence the requesting States (before the IACtHR), organs (before the ICJ), and organizations (before the IACtHR) in all stages, including the shaping and writing of the questions asked to these courts and tribunals. Furthermore, individuals (in their private capacity) and associations (representative of civil society movements) have never been so participative in submitting *amicus curiae* briefs or assisting states and international organizations in their written submissions. Therefore, the narrative espoused before these international courts and tribunals (or the 'story' narrated to them, as De Spiegeleir refers to in Chapter 7) was also crafted by individuals and civil society movements.

The conclusion seems obvious: the trio of requests for an opinion on climate change was probably only possible because of the role of such grassroots movements. As such, it is worth studying in more detail how these concerned civil society movements can be agents of change at the international level, namely through this more informal activity at the fringes of international law. If one can hint at future developments, it is legitimate to assume that these civil society movements will keep working on other initiatives (before courts or at different levels) to pressure States into adopting more stringent mitigation policies and that similar initiatives will be adopted with respect to other environmental causes. In this regard, assisting the initiative before the AfrCtHPR – where the lack of resources is abundant – would be the most laudable initiative from civil society movements. The initiative before the AfrCtHPR is explained in Chapter 6 by Lupin and Nekura, who also refer to

15 Maria Antonia Tigre, 'It is (Finally) Time for an Advisory Opinion on Climate Change: Challenges and Opportunities on a Trio of Initiatives' (2024) 17 *Charleston Law Review* 623.

the pivotal role of civil society movements and the need for knowledge and human and financial resources to assist the initiative.

3 The Impact on Domestic and International Processes

The advisory opinions rendered by ITLOS, the IACtHR, and the ICJ are apt to clarify and develop the international law on climate change. Their findings constitute what before we called the 'Rosetta Stone': a code that can assist States in reading the UNFCCC, the Paris Agreement, and other rules and principles of international law relevant to the climate context. Clarifying the existing States' obligations regarding climate change has a profound impact on processes of international law and domestic law, including lawmaking and judicial litigation.

In Section 2, we mentioned that some States are expected to use the advisory opinions in diplomatic negotiations. At least, it is fair to assume that those who took the lead in the processes that resulted in the requests for advisory opinions will use their findings during the COPs to the UNFCCC and the Paris Agreement. But more than that, because of the institutional authoritativeness of ITLOS, the IACtHR, and the ICJ as knowledgeable and third-party interpreters of the UNFCCC, the Paris Agreement, and other rules and principles of international law related to climate change (as explained by Galvão Telles and Guerreiro Teixeira in Chapter 2), their findings are expected to serve as a guide in enhancing States' obligations and the institutional governance of climate change, as well as a protective talisman against setbacks in climate negotiations. One cannot ignore the role of State consent in the creation of rules and principles of international law. Still, unless there are compelling reasons for States to rule out the findings of ITLOS, the IACtHR, and the ICJ, it would be strange if States concerned with the international rule of law would not take into account the findings of those courts. Furthermore, since climate change results from the concentration of GHG in the atmosphere (ie a common pool shared by all States), 'prevent[ing] dangerous anthropogenic interference with the climate system,'[16] and '[h]olding the increase in the global average temperature to well below 2°C above pre-industrial levels and pursuing efforts to limit the temperature increase to 1.5°C above pre-industrial levels,'[17] requires coordination of State action under international law. Negotiating and signing

16 UNFCCC, art 2.

17 Paris Agreement, art 2(1)(a).

international treaties is the tool for coordinating States' efforts at the international level.

However, the bulk of the mitigation effort is to be pursued at the level of domestic law and policies. Unsurprisingly, this was highlighted by ITLOS and the ECtHR, who pointed to States' primary obligation to adopt and effectively implement a regulatory framework at the domestic level aimed at reducing GHG emissions from their territory or jurisdiction.[18] Their findings expressly suggested that such a regulatory framework is needed to target private operators whose economic activity is responsible for GHG emissions. Moreover, their findings implied that the topic of liability for climate change-related harm in general, and corporate liability specifically, need greater development. The next frontier in climate change responsibility and liability lies precisely in how domestic laws regulate corporate accountability. In addition, climate mitigation and adaptation are always country-driven, in the sense that the value-based choices and trade-offs require multisectorial, micro-decision making that only the domestic authorities can perform. As a result, an expected impact of the advisory opinions on climate change is on the decision-making processes that implement, at the domestic level, States' climate obligations. Médici-Colombo and Rocha, in Chapter 12, include prior examples of domestic implementation of advisory opinions rendered by ITLOS and the IACtHR. The authors found that since advisory opinions are non-binding and do not require a specific State action or execution process, implementing advisory opinions at the domestic level is often unacknowledged and varies according to the regime of international law in question. The message of hope, however, is that practice hints that States are willing to incorporate the findings developed in advisory opinions in their domestic statutory norms. As such, the advisory opinions on climate change can provide at least a sense of direction for domestic lawmakers.

Finally, perhaps the most apparent impact of the trio of advisory opinions on climate change is on litigation before domestic or international courts and tribunals, as explained by Main-Klingst and Marjanac in Chapter 11. In fact, a common obstacle in climate litigation is identifying a sufficiently characterized legal obligation to reduce GHG emissions. To that end, the obvious starting points are the UNFCCC and the Paris Agreement. Still, their provisions do not seem as detailed as necessary to invoke a *detailed* legal obligation to reduce GHG emissions before a court. This happens concerning domestic and international courts alike.

18 *COSIS Opinion* (n 9) §§265–280; *Verein KlimaSeniorinnen* (n 11) §§544–554.

Nonetheless, a clarification and development of these obligations (including what they imply in terms of States' behavior) means these opinions can be used before courts as an authority to substantiate a climate change-related claim. This is especially important in face of Article 4 of the Paris Agreement, which looks to States' self-differentiation as the *Grundnorm* of the international law on climate change. In this context, the findings of international courts and tribunals, hand in hand with their authority as knowledgeable bodies, can be used in order to challenge a State's climate (in)action.

4 Where Next? A Roadmap for Future Research

The main purpose of this edited volume is to pave the way for future research on the trio of advisory opinions on climate change – together with the ECtHR's ruling in the *Verein KlimaSeniorinnen* case and an eventual opinion rendered by the AfrCtHPR. The opinions are likely to unlock a rich research agenda, as the chapters in this book have highlighted. The *COSIS opinion*, for instance, still needs to be fully explored and analyzed in its complexities. Similarly, once the advisory opinions from the ICJ and the IACtHR are rendered (which is expected to take place in 2025), it will take time for scholars and practitioners to digest and assess their implications.

Looking ahead, a research agenda on climate change advisory opinions should aim to provide a comprehensive analysis of these decisions while also delving into specific aspects in greater detail. The first step will be to offer broad analyses of the advisory opinions of ITLOS, ICJ, and IACtHR. Being a 'Rosetta Stone' means that these advisory opinions will serve as foundational texts for the international law on climate change. Accordingly, although one cannot expect a detailed clarification of what States' obligations are in a facts-detached advisory opinion, still the role of scholarship is to unveil the implications of these advisory opinions and, namely, how they can be used to reveal more detailed States' obligations under international law in addressing climate change.

Beyond this general analysis, other specific doctrinal aspects within these opinions will require in-depth study. In this conclusion chapter, we do not aim to exhaust this matter, but would like to point out the topics that, in our view, deserve in-depth research, following the advisory opinions.

The obligation to mitigate climate change. The first topic needing research is the obligation, at the level of primary norms, to mitigate climate change. Research focuses on the wording of Article 4 of the Paris Agreement, plus other rules and principles stemming from the UNFCCC and general environmental law. Even an optimistic reading of such instruments has to come to terms with their shortcomings, including the centrality of self-differentiation and the careful writing of verbal formulations that question their legal bindingness. However, the COSIS *Opinion* and the *Verein KlimaSeniorinnen* ruling already indicated other sources of an obligation to mitigate climate change. Together with the IACtHR's and the ICJ's opinions, these pronouncements from international courts and tribunals suggest that (i) such obligation has multiple sources, (ii) entailing that delimiting the exact content of the legal obligation to mitigate climate change implies looking at the requirements flowing from all sources. A joint reading of the multiple sources probably unveils a more detailed legal obligation.

Due diligence obligations. Another critical area for academic research is the advisory opinions' treatment of due diligence obligations, particularly how they define States' *ex ante facto* responsibility to prevent climate harm. As a topic, due diligence obligations have been largely studied in the context of environmental law, and it probably represents the most solid breakthroughs of ITLOS and ICJ in the last decade. Due diligence obligations have also gained the attention of scholarship. Nonetheless, while the ECtHR in *Verein KlimaSeniorinnen* censored a State's complete lack of mitigation measures as an infringement of a due diligence obligation, it remains to be seen how comfortable courts are with assessing and censoring that State's insufficiency of climate measures. The first judgment is absolute and binary, but the insufficiency of measures and the balance with other State policies requires from courts a greater refinement of thought and implies a particular interference with domestic policies. Strict guidelines on how to perform this assessment in the context of climate change require scholars' attention.

Reparations. Even though States have created mechanisms under the umbrella of loss and damage, the topic of reparations is politically explosive. This helps to explain why the subject of reparations for climate harm is understudied. Furthermore, from a technical angle, studying reparations for climate change-related harm implies relating State and non-State actors' responsibility for climate change and how claims under different international law regimes and formulated by different subjects relate to each other.

Vulnerabilities. Scholars should also consider how the advisory opinions safeguard vulnerable groups, including women, children, and Indigenous populations, and how they approach intergenerational equity to protect future generations. The COSIS *Opinion* devoted large sections to the needs of developing States as a whole but did not discuss other sources of vulnerability, while the ECtHR mentioned in the *Verein KlimaSeniorinnen* ruling that '[t]he Court is also aware that the damaging effects of climate change raise an issue of intergenerational burden-sharing … and impact most heavily on various vulnerable groups in society, who need special care and protection from the authorities.'[19] It is still unclear what the findings of the IACtHR and the ICJ will be on this matter, but one cannot ignore that the law is about one's protection in a situation of vulnerability. Whatever their findings, the advisory opinions on climate change will certainly pressure in-depth studies on how the law aims to protect the most vulnerable against climate change-related risks and hazards.

Competition and coordination. Another critical area of future study is a comparative analysis of the advisory opinions from ITLOS, the ICJ, and the IACtHR, hand in hand with the rulings from the ECtHR and other judicial and para-judicial bodies of international law. In fact, in contrast with domestic law, there is no horizontal or vertical integration among courts in international law. This explains the potential for contradiction between the findings of different courts and tribunals, as well as their need to find informal means of dialogue and cooperation to avoid conflicting views on States' obligations to mitigate and adapt to climate change. The trio of requests for advisory opinions on climate change is a prime example of how international courts and tribunals may be encouraged to compete to render the first, best, or most authoritative advisory opinion. Interdisciplinary studies can shed light on how judges work and thus help create room for a coherent development of the international law on climate change.

The chapters presented in this book open the door to many of these questions, but they also highlight the significant scholarly research that remains to be conducted. Whether through expanding discussions on how States and advocacy groups have engaged with the advisory process or through detailed doctrinal analysis of the decisions themselves, this book sets the stage for more comprehensive and specialized academic inquiry. Ultimately, the extent to which these advisory opinions shape the future of climate litigation, both internationally and domestically, will be a focal point of legal and academic analysis in the years to come. The greatest message of hope resulting from the advisory opinions is perhaps this one: opening the door for future research means that there is a road to be paved, which will ultimately guide our societies into a carbon-neutral future.

---

19 *Verein KlimaSeniorinnen* (n 11) §410.

APPENDIX 1

Questions Posed in the Advisory Opinion Requests

A. International Tribunal on the Law of the Seas

12 December 2022

Excellency,

We have the honour to inform you, in our capacity as the Co-Chairs of the Commission of Small Island States on Climate Change and International Law (the "Commission"), representing the Commission pursuant to Article 3(3) of the Agreement for the Establishment of the Commission (the "Agreement"), that we hereby submit a request for an advisory opinion from the International Tribunal for the Law of the Sea (the "Tribunal") on the legal questions set out below.

On 31 October 2021, the Agreement established the Commission as an international organization with Antigua and Barbuda and Tuvalu as the original signatories. It was duly registered with the Secretariat of the United Nations in accordance with Article 102 of the Charter of the United Nations, and a Certificate of Registration was issued on 3 February 2022. Pursuant to Article 3(1) of the Agreement, Membership in the Commission is open to all Members of the Alliance of Small Island States. Thus far, instruments of accession have been deposited by the Republic of Palau,* Niue, the Republic of Vanuatu, and Saint Lucia.

Article 21 of the Statute of the Tribunal provides:

The jurisdiction of the Tribunal comprises all disputes and all applications submitted to it in accordance with this Convention and all matters specifically provided for in any other agreement which confers jurisdiction on the Tribunal.

Article 138 of the Rules of the Tribunal provides that the Tribunal may give an advisory opinion "on a legal question if an international agreement related to the purposes of the Convention specifically provides for the submission to the Tribunal of a request for such an opinion." Article 138 further provides that such a request for an advisory opinion "shall be transmitted to the Tribunal by whatever body is authorized by or in accordance with the agreement to make the request to the Tribunal" (emphases added).

In this respect, Article 2(2) of the Agreement provides (emphasis added):

Having regard to the fundamental importance of oceans as sinks and reservoirs of greenhouse gases and the direct relevance of the marine environment to the adverse effects of climate change on Small Island States, the Commission shall be authorized to request advisory opinions from the International Tribunal for the Law of the Sea ("ITLOS") on any legal question within the scope of the 1982 United Nations

Convention on the Law of the Sea, consistent with Article 21 of the ITLOS Statute and Article 138 of its Rules. On these bases, and pursuant to a unanimous Decision of its Members in accordance with Article 3(5) of the Agreement, the Commission decided at a duly constituted meeting on 26 August 2022 to refer the following legal questions to the Tribunal for an advisory opinion:

What are the specific obligations of State Parties to the United Nations Convention on the Law of the Sea (the "UNCLOS"), including under Part XJI:

a. to prevent, reduce and control pollution of the marine environment in relation to the deleterious effects that result or are likely to result from climate change, including through ocean warming and sea level rise, and ocean acidification, which are caused by anthropogenic greenhouse gas emissions into the atmosphere?
b. to protect and preserve the marine environment in relation to climate change impacts, including ocean warming and sea level rise, and ocean acidification?

B Inter-American Court of Human Rights

January 9, 2023

Request for an Advisory Opinion on Climate Emergency and Human Rights to the Inter-American Court of Human Rights from the Republic of Colombia and the Republic of Chile.

I. Introduction

The Republic of Colombia and the Republic of Chile (hereinafter "Colombia" and "Chile" or "the petitioners") submit this request for an advisory opinion to the Inter-American Court of Human Rights (hereinafter, IACHR Court or the Court) with the purpose of clarifying the scope of State obligations, in their individual and collective dimension, to respond to the climate emergency within the framework of international human rights law, taking into account the differentiated effects that such emergency has on the people of different regions and population groups, nature and h uman survival on our planet.

Both countries face the daily challenge of dealing with the consequences of climate emergencies, including the proliferation of droughts, floods, landslides and fires, among others. These phenomena highlight the need to respond urgently and based on the principles of equity, justice, cooperation and sustainability with a human rights approach.

These environmental impacts extend throughout the Americans and the world, generating significant impacts on people's rights and putting future generations at risk. However, the effects of climate change are not being experienced uniformly throughout the international community. In fact, they are already being felt in the most vulnerable communities given their geography, climatic and socioeconomic conditions and infrastructure, including several countries in the Americas region. Severely, these effects are not being experienced in proportion to the contribution of these countries and communities to climate change.

The Republics of Colombia and Chile are aware of the relevance of the human right to a healthy environment and its close link to a series of substantive and procedural rights that affect the life, survival and development of present, and future generations protected under the American Convention on Human Rights (hereinafter 'American Convention" or ACHR) and numerous inter-American and universal human rights and environmental treaties.[1] In this sense, human rights not only provide a necessary perspective to evaluate.

The project also provides fundamental tools for seeking timely, fair, equitable and sustainable solutions to the emergency.

For this reason, the States of Colombia and Chile consider it necessary to advance in determining the scope of the obligations set forth in the American Convention and inter-American treaties, in what is relevant to address the situations generated by the climate emergency,[2] its causes and consequences. This, in order to promote measures to guarantee rights and public policies necessary to respond to this phenomenon in an urgent, equitable, fair and sustainable manner.

Consequently, with the purpose of advancing and accelerating the responses to the climate emergency from each of the States, in a collective manner -regionally and globally-, a series of questions are formulated to this Tribunal, which allow guiding towards solutions based on human rights, with an intersectional perspective.

---

1 For example, I/A Court H.R. Environment and Human Rights (State obligations in relation to the environment in the framework of the protection and guarantee of the rights to life and personal integrity – interpretation and scope of Articles 4(1) and 5(1), in relation to Articles 1(1) and 2 of the American Convention on Human rights). Advisory Opinion OC-23/17 of November 15, 2017. Series A No. 23., (hereinafter "OC- 23/17. Environment and human rights").

2 United Nations (UN). Framework Convention on Climate Change; UN. Paris Agreement, part of the United Nations Framework Convention on Climate Change; UN – Economic Commission for Latin America and the Caribbean (ECLAC). Regional Agreement on Access to Information, Public Participation and Access to justice in Environmental Matters in Latin America and the Caribbean (Escazú Agreement); Convention on Access to Information, Public Participation in Decision-making and Access to Justice in Environmental Matters (Aarhus Convention), among others.

II. The Climate Emergency and Its Consequences from a Human Rights Perspective

We are facing a climate emergency with devastating potential for life on earth.[3] The scientific and political consensus, evidenced in the *Intergovernmental Panel on Climate Change* (IPCC) *Special Report on Global Warming of 1.5°C*, indicates that global warming, if it continues to increase at the current rate, could reach 1.5°C between 2030 and 2052.[4] For some experts, this would pose a serious threat to human survival[5]

Furthermore, according to the IPCC, climate change has already begun to generate adverse impacts around the world, including loss of ecosystems, reduced food security, increased migration and displacement, human rights impacts and increased inequality.[6] If we do not limit global warming to a maximum increase of 1.5°C as established in the Paris Agreement,[7] these adverse effects will worsen and humanity will approach a point of no return that will result in irreversible damage, including loss and damage, especially in scenarios of insufficient climate action. The course of our common history as humanity depends on taking immediate action to address this challenge at the global level.

As Michelle Bachelet emphasized in her last speech as United Nations High Commissioner for Human Rights: "*As we speak here, the world continues to face an increasingly serious crisis – worsening conflicts, deepening inequalities and climate change that threatens our very existence*".[8] For its part, in its February 2022 report, the IPCC has estimated that the increase in temperature and extreme weather generated by human

3 More than 11,200 scientists from 153 countries declared in 2019 that humanity faces a climate emergency. *See* Ripple et al, World Scientists' Warning of a Climate Emergency, BioScience, Volume 70, Issue 1, January 2020, pp. 8–12.

4 IPCC, *Summary for Policymakers of the IPCC Special Report on the Impacts of 1.5°C* Global Warming Relative to Levels, 2018, p. 6.

5 Allen M. et al. (2018) SUMMARY FOR POLICY MAKERS, *in* IPCC (2018) Global Warming of 1.5°C.

6 ("*Human activities are estimated to have caused global warming of about 1.0°C* relative to pre-industrial levels, with a likely range of 0.8°C to 1.2°C. Global warming is likely to reach 1.5°C between 2030 and 2052 if it continues to increase at the current rate (high confidence level)."

7 UN. Paris Agreement, December 12, 2015.

8 UN, Speech by Michelle Bachelet, United Nations High Commissioner for Human Rights at the Level Event on the occasion of the 50th session of the Human Rights Council, June 15, 2022.

action is causing irreversible impacts uch faster than our capacity to adapt to these changes.[9]

The adverse impacts of global warming have effects around the world.[10] However, as already mentioned, certain countries and communities face particularly severe consequences. Thus, the climate emergency has a devastating and differentiated impact on certain geographical regions and groups in vulnerable situations, such as children, indigenous peoples, peasant communities, among others, which may worsen if there is no significant reduction in emissions accompanied by urgent adaptation measures.[11] This will be exacerbated if we exceed the thresholds established by the scientific community.[12]

For the Americans region, the IPCC Fifth Assessment Report indicates that limited water resources as a result of glacial retreat in the Andes and altered regional precipitation cycles could greatly affect the population.[13] Likewise, a rise in sea level and increase in surface water temperature will have an impact on coastal communities,

9 IPCC, "Summary for Policy Makers", in Impact Adaptation, and Vulnerability, Working Group II contribution to the Sixth Assessment Report of the IPCC, February 2022.

10 Xu Y., Ramanathan V., & Victor D. G. (2018) *Global warming will happen faster than we think,* Comment, Nature. 564 (7734): 30–32, 30–31. See also: Arias P. A., *et al.* (2021) *Technical Summary,* in Climate Change 2021: The Physical Science Basis.

11 Inter-American Development Bank (IDB). Climate change poses significant threats to all Caribbean states, despite the minimal contribution of these countries to global greenhouse gas (GHG) emissions.

12 Intergovernmental Panel on Climate Change, Summary for Policymakers of the IPCC Special Report on the Impacts of 1.5°C Global Warming Relative to Levels, 2018, p. 6.

13 Marengo J.A. *et al.* (2014) Central and South America, In: *Climate Change 2014 Impacts, Adaptation and Vulnerability. Part B: Regional Aspects.* Contribution of Working Group II to the Fifth Assessment Report of the Intergovernmental Panel on Climate Change at 1520 – 1521 ("In early stages of glacial retreat, the associated flow tends to increase due to accelerated glacier melting, but after the peak flow as the glacial water reservoir empties, runoff has to decrease … Glacial retreat may exacerbate current water-related vulnerability by decreasing the water regulation capacity of mountains, making water supply for various purposes, as well as ecosystem integrity, more costly and less reliable.")'; *see also id.* At 1543 ("Current vulnerability in terms of water supply in semi-arid areas and in the tropical Andes is expected to increase further due to climate change. This would be exacerbated by glacial retreat, decreased precipitation and increased evapotranspiration demand as expected in the semi-arid regions of Central and South America. These scenarios would affect water supply for large cities, small communities, food production and hydropower generation").

the water supply and economies throughout the region.[14] This may disproportionately affect coastal and island nations in the Caribbean Basin.[15]

The Andes region is among the most sensitive areas in the world to migration and displacement associated with climate change.[16] In Colombia, an increase of more than 1.5°C will result in an increase in the intensity and frequency of extreme temperatures, storms, floods, landslides and heat waves.[17] The Amazon rainforest, one of the world's largest reservoirs of biodiversity, is threatened.[18] Indeed, the Amazon is home to 40% of the world's remaining tropical rainforest and 25% of the world's terrestrial

14 Marengo J.A. *et al.* (2014) Central and South America, In: *Climate Change 2014 Impacts, Adaptation and Vulnerability. Part B: Regional Aspects.* Contribution of Working Group II to the Fifth Assessment Report of the Intergovernmental Panel on Climate Change at 1524–1525 ("The coastal states of [Latin America] and the Carribbean have a human population of more than 610 million, three-quarters of whom live within 200km of the coast (Guarderas et al., 2008). For example, a study of seven countries in the region of (El Salvador, Nicaragua, Costa Rica, Panama, Colombia, Venezuela, Ecuador), Lacambra and Zahedi (2011) concluded that more than 30% of the population lives in coastal areas directly expired to climatic events. Since the probability of flooding increases with an increase in sea level, a higher probability of flooding could be expected in sites showing >40% change, over the past 60 years, in the 100-year total sea level (excluding hurricanes) … If extreme ocean surface temperatures continue, projections using SRES scenarios (A1Fl, 3°C sensation, and A1B with 2°C and 4.5°C sensation) indicate that Mesoamerican coral rees are likely to collapse by mid-century (between 2040 and 2070), causing significant economic losses (Vergara, 2009).")

15 Marengo J.A. *et al.* (2014) Central and South America, In: *Climate Change 2014 Impacts, Adaptation and Vulnerability. Part B: Regional Aspects.* Contribution of Working Group II to the Fifth Assessment Office of the High Representative for the Least Developed Countries and Small Island Developing States at 6 ("As recognized in the Programme of Action for the Sustainable Development of Small Island Developing States, adopted in 1994, [Small Island Development States (SIDS)] are particularly vulnerable to global climate change. Their climate is influenced by ocean-atmospheric interactions, such as trade winds, El niño, monsoons and tropical cyclones. With populations, arable land and infrastructure tending to be concentrated in the coastal zone, any rise in sea level will have significant and profound effects on settlements, living conditions and island economies. These climatic characteristics, combined with their particular socio-economic situation, make SIDS, of which 9 are LDCs, some of the most vulnerable countries in the world to climate change. Moreover, the fact that SIDS combined have a population of about 65 million people contributing less than 1 percent of GHG emissions indicates that they will suffer disproportionately from the damaging impacts of climate change and some will become uninhabitable).")

16 IPCC, "Chapter 12. Central and South America", in *Impact Adaptation, and Vulnerability, Working Group II contribution to the Sixth Assessment Report of the IPCC*, February 2022, p. 1691.

17 *Ibid.*, p. 1701.

18 *Ibid.*, p. 1691.

biodiversity.[19] Moreover, if the trend of Amazon deforestation continues and surpasses the tipping point that allows deforestation of the biome, there will be devastating impacts on rainfall regulation.[20] In addition, this change would not only have devastating effects for not only in out region but globally insofar as it could contribute to the extreme global warming effect (*hothouse earth*).[21]

Among other impacts, it is estimated that in the Andean region there will be an increase of between 100–200% of people affected by floods, a greater transmission of diseases such as malaria, dengue and chikungunya, the negative impact of up to 35% of the region's fauna and flora, the reduction of harvests due to increasingly frequent droughts, the reduction of agriculture dut to the rise in temperature and the reduction of fishing due to the acidification of the ocean.[22] This, according to the IPCC, is undoubtedly a cause that will increase global human mobility, as there is already evidence that this is happening. This displacement will have differentiated impacts on the most vulnerable populations, including coastal populations and island dwellers, indigenous peoples, Afro-descendant communities, peasants, among others.[23]

In addition, the adverse effects of climate change will be felt more strongly in those sectors of the population that are already in situations of vulnerability,[24] due to factors such as the impact of coastal or rural areas, poverty, gender, age, belonging to indigenous peoples, race or ethnicity, national origin, migrant status, among others.[25] For example, the United Nations Rapporteur on Migration, in a report of July of this year, has highlighted that 80% of the people displaced due to climate-related phenomena

---

19 ECLAC. Bogotá Office-Natural Heritage, Biodiversity and Protected Areas Fund (Colombia).

20 Lenton T. M., Rockstrom J., Gaffney O., Rahmstorf X., Richardson K., Steffen W., & Schellnhuber H. J. (2019) *Climate tipping points – too risky to bet against,* Comment, Nature 575(7783): 592–595. See also: Wunderling N., Donges J.F., Kuths J, & Winkelmann R. (2021) *interacting tipping elements increase risk of climate domino effects under global warming.* Earth Syst. Dyn. 12(2): 601–619; Klose A. K., Wunderling N., Winkelmann R., & Donges J. F. (2021) *What do we mean, 'tipping cascade',* Environ. Res. Lett. 16(12): 125011, 1–12,1; Rocha J. C., Peterson G., Bodin ö., & Levin S. (2018) *Cascading regime shifts within and across scales,* Science 362(6421): 1379–1383, 1383 (English only).

21 See: Steffen, Will, et al., *Trajectories of the Earth System in the Anthropocene.* Harvard University, July 6, 2018.

22 *Ibid.*, pp. 1693–1703.

23 Inter-American Commission on Human rights (IACHR). *Climate Emergency, Scope and Inter-American Human Rights Obligations*, Resolution 3/2021, December 31,2021, p. 26.

24 World Health Organization (WHO), "Evolution of WHO Air Quality Guidelines: Past, Present and Future." Copenhagen, Denmark: WHO Regional Office for Europe (2017), p. 2, available (in English).

25 UN – General Assembly, Human Rights Council, *Human rights and climate change,* A/HRC/RES/41/21, Resolution adopted by the Human Rights Council on 12 July 2019, pp. 2–3.

are women and girls.[26] Likewise, the adverse effects of climate change are exacerbating migration with differentiated impacts for indigenous peoples and Afro-descendant communities. This confirms the need to adopt an intersectional approach to this issue.

Thus, there is a close link between the climate emergency and the impact on human rights.[27] At the same time, human rights law can help to accelerate responses to the climate emergency by promoting policies to ensure that the obligations of various key actors to respect and guarantee human rights are fulfilled. Discussing this issue in front of a regional Court also allows to address not only national or regional obligations, but also those linked to international cooperation and shared but differentiated obligations from a human rights perspective.

III. The Need for Inter-American Standards to Accelerate Climate Emergency Response

In the face of the climate emergency and its impacts, it is necessary to take urgent mitigation and adaptation measures to address the crisis. While the measures required may vary in nature, human rights obligations can provide fundamental guidance to accelerate responses in a fair, equitable and sustainable manner.

In 2017, the Inter-American Court issued an Advisory Opinion at the request of the Republic of Colombia, to address the link between the environment and human rights. In that Opinion, the Court recognizes the right to a healthy environment as an autonomous and individual right, refers to the adverse effects of climate change[28] and mentions the obligations of States to avoid transboundary environmental damage that could affect the human rights of persons outside their territory.[29] This opinion was fundamental to broaden the understanding of the interrelationship between the environment and human rights and the regional and national policies linked to the guarantee of these rights.

---

26 UN – General Assembly. *Report of the Special Rapporteur on the human rights of migrants,* Seventy-seventh session, 19 July 2022, para. 47.

27 See, for example, Stockholm Declaration on the Human Environment, adopted at the United Nations Conference on the Human environment, Stockhold, 5–16 June 1972, UN Doc./CONF.48/14/Rev.1, proclamation 1 ("Both aspects of the human memo, the natural and the man-made, are essential to human well-being and to the enjoyment of fundamental human rights, including the right to life itself"); and UN General Assembly, Res. 45/94 of December 14, 1990, UN Doc. A/RES/45/94, art.1 ("everyone has the right to live in an environment adequate to his health and well-being").

28 IACHR Court. OC-23/17. Environment and Human rights, paras. 47, 96, 126.

29 *Ibid.,* para. 101.

However, it is necessary to further clarify the basis and scope of the human rights affected by the climate emergency, as well as the State's obligations to address them, individually and collectively, by urgently addressing their causes and consequences and taking into account considerations of equity, justice, precaution and sustainability.

In this sense, the termination of the scope of human rights obligations in the face of the climate emergency will serve to specific the meaning, opportunity and the scope of the obligations of the national State, of subnational entities (cities, regions or departments), of the responsibility towards non-State actors and transnational, regional and global obligations in the matter.

Likewise, international human rights law takes into account, as an unavoidable yardstick, the life, survival and protection of the rights of individuals, peoples and communities.[30] To this extent, it encourages the adoption of measures that take into account current generations in their diversity, the differentiated geographic impacts and the rights of future generations.

Moreover, international human rights and environmental treaties have an important collective dimension of guaranteeing rights. They also provide elements of human rights and the protection of nature in the interpretation of the scope of the shared but differentiated responsibilities of the States as a whole in the face of the climate emergency.[31] This requires differentiating the contribution to climate change derived from their emissions, the differentiated impacts of the latter on their subsistence, considering the protection of fundamental biomes to respond to the crisis (as is the case of the Amazon biome). Shared but differentiated responsibilities must also be examined in terms of the need to avoid, minimize and address the damages and losses generated by global warming and the climate emergency, and the need to generate mechanisms and practices that allow for reparation and adaptation at the national, regional, sub-regional and global levels in a fair, equitable and sustainable manner.

In this sense, the interpretations of the Inter-American Court of various instruments of the Inter-American system can provide important guidelines that link the obligations arising from various international normative frameworks, including those on climate change. These can guide the measures to be adopted to guarantee human rights, including the right to a healthy environment, the right to survival of peoples, the right to life, etc.

30 *Ibid.*, paras. 109 and 114.

31 The preamble of the Paris Agreement states, in this regard: "Recognizing that climate change is a problem of all humanity and that, in taking action to address it, Parties should respect, promote and take into account their respective obligations relating to human rights, the right to health, the rights of indigenous peoples, local communities, migrants, children, persons with disabilities and persons in vulnerable situations and the right to development, as well as gender equality, the empowerment of women and intergenerational equity".

In the international context, relevant litigation and strategies have been promoted to determine state obligations in the face of climate emergencies. For example, Vanuatu has consolidated a coalition for countries in the Pacific and Caribbean to request an advisory opinion from the International Court of justice, which focuses mainly on the issue of damages and loss and state obligations in multilateral agreements relevant to the effects of climate change.[32] Likewise, the European Court of Human Rights has numerous cases pending related to climate change,[33] three of which have been declared admissible and will soon be heard by the Grand Chamber,[34] and in a similar vein, the United Nations Human Rights Committee recently adopted a decision in an individual petition in which it condemned Australia for failing to protect the human rights to enjoyment of one's culture, privacy and family of the indigenous Torres Islands community for failing to adopt adequate measures to protect them from the adverse impacts of climate change.[35]

In our continent, the advisory opinions of the Inter-American Court have provided States with important parameters to ensure the guarantee of human rights throughout the nearly five decades of operation of the Inter-American Court.[36] Among others, the Opinions have examined issues such as states of emergency, freedom of expression, equality, healthy environment,[37] among others. These guidelines have been relevant

32 Climate change has led to extreme weather in Vanuatu, such as Cyclone Harold in 2020, which resulted in the loss of entire communities, lives and a third of the country's Gross Domestic Product in a single dat. *See* Vanuatu ICJ Initiative.

33 Columbia University, Columbia Law School, Sabin Center for Climate Change, Global Climate Change litigation database.

34 European Court of Human Rights, Cláudia Duarte Agostinho and others v. Portugal and 33 other States, Application No. 3937/20; Caréme v. France, Case No. 7189/21, and Verin Klimaseniorinnen Schweiz and others v. Switzerland, Application no. 53600/20.

35 UN – Human Rights Committee, Daniel Billy et al. v. Australia, CCPR/C/135/D/3642/2019, 22 September 2022.

36 IACHR Court. Rules of Procedure. On Advisory Opinions. Article 70. Interpretation of the Convention 1. Requests for advisory opinions provided for in Article 64(1) of the Convention shall state precisely the specific questions on which the opinion of the Court is sought. Requests for an advisory opinion formulated by a member state or by the Commission shall also indicate the provisions the interpretation of which is sought, the considerations giving rise to the request, and the name and address of the Agent or Delegates. 3. If the initiative for the advisory opinion comes from an OAS organ other than the Commission, the request shall specify, in addition to what is mentioned in the previous paragraph, the manner in which the consultation refers to its sphere of competence.

37 IACHR Court. Judicial Guarantees in States of Emergency (Arts. 27.2, 25 and 8 American Convention on Human Rights). Advisory Opinion OC-9/87 of October 6, 1987. Series A No. 9; I/A Court H.R.. Compulsory Membership in an Association of Journalists (Arts. 13 and 29 American Convention on Human Rights). Advisory Opinion OC-5/85 of November 13, 1985. Series A No. 5; I/A Court H.R.. Gender identity, and equality and non-discrimination of same-sex couples. State obligations in relation to the change of name, gender, identity,

to clarify the scope of international human rights obligations, in a context in which numerous constitutions and jurisprudential lines of the national high courts include with constitutional rank the human rights obligations derived from human rights treaties.

Therefore, a possible expert opinion of the Inter-American Court will allow both the requesting countries and the rest of the countries in the region to have a guide for the development of policies and programs at the local, national and international levels in accordance with the commitments acquired under the American Convention and other human rights and environmental treaties for a better approach to the climate crisis, taking into account the obligations of prevention, guarantee and protection.

IV. *Questions for the* IACHR *Court*

A. *On the State Obligations Derived from the Duties of Prevention and Guarantee of Human Rights Related to the Climate Emergency*

Taking into account the State's obligations to prevent and guarantee the right to a healthy environment[38] and the scientific consensus expressed in the reports of the Intergovernmental Panel on Climate Change (IPCC)[39] on the seriousness of the climate emergency and the urgency and duty to respond adequately to its consequences, as well as to mitigate its pace and scale:

1. What is the scope of the duty of States to prevent climate phenomena generated by global warming, including extreme events and slow onset events, in accordance with inter-American treaty obligations in light of the Paris Agreement and the scientific consensus that encourages not to increase global temperature beyond 1.5°C[40]?

---

and the rights derived from a bond between same-sex couples (interpretation and scope of Article 1(1), 3, 7, 11(2), 13, 17, 18 and 24, in relation to Article 1 of the American Convention on Human Rights). Advisory Opinion OC-24/17 of November 24, 2017. Series A No. 24.

38 According to the Court's case law and doctrine, protected by the American Convention, Article 11 of the Protocol of San Salvador and Article 1 of the Regional Agreement on Access to Information, Public Participation and Justice in Environmental Matters in Latin America and the Caribbean (Escazú Agreement).

39 See, *inter alia*: Intergovernmental Panel on Climate Change (IPCC), *Impact Adaptation, and Vulnerability, Working Group II contribution to the Sixth Assessment Report of the IPCC*, February 2022; Intergovernmental Panel on Climate Change, *Summary for policy makers in IPCC Special Report on the impacts of global warming of 1.50C above pre-industrial levels*, 2018.

40 United Nations. Paris Agreement, December 12, 2015; Intergovernmental Panel on Climate Change, *Summary for policy makers in IPCC Special Report on the impacts of global warming of 1.50C above pre-industrial levels*, 2018, p. 6.

2. In particular, what measures should States take to minimize the impact of the damages caused by the climate emergency, in light of the obligations established in the American Convention? In this regard, what differentiated measures should be taken with respect to populations in situations of vulnerability or intersectional considerations?
   A. What considerations should a State take to implement its obligation to (i) regulate; (ii) monitor and oversee; (iii) require and approve social and environmental impact studies; (iv) establish a contingency plan; and (v) mitigate activities within its jurisdiction that aggravate or may aggravate the climate emergency?
   B. What principles should inspire mitigation, adaptation and response actions to the losses and damages generated by the climate emergency in the affected communities?

B. *On the State Obligations to Preserve the Right to Survival in the Face of Climate Emergency in the Light of Science and Human Rights*

Taking into account the right to access to information and the obligations on active production of information and transparency, as set forth in Article 13[41] and derived from the obligations under articles 4.1 and 5.1 of the American Convention,[42] in light of Articles 5 and 6 of the Regional Agreement on Access to Information, Participation and Access to Justice in Environmental Matters in Latin America and the Caribbean (Escazú Agreement)[43]:

1. What is the scope that States should give to their conventional obligations in the face of the climate emergency, in terms of:
   i. environmental information for all people and communities, including those linked to the climate emergency;
   ii. climate mitigation and adaptation measures to be adopted to address the climate emergency and the impacts of such measures, including specific just transition policies for groups and individuals particularly vulnerable to global warming;
   iii. responses to prevent, minimize and address economic and non-economic losses and damages associated with the adverse effects of climate change;
   iv. the production of information and access to information on greenhouse gas emission levels, air pollution, deforestation and short-lived

41 IACtHR. OC-23/17. The Environment and Human Rights, para. 221 and ff.

42 See, *inter alia*: IACtHR. OC-23/17. The Environment and Human Rights, paras. 54 and 55.

43 ECLAC, Regional Agreement on Access to Information, Public Participation and Justice in Environmental Matters in Latin America and the Caribbean (Escazú Agreement), 2018.

climate forcers, analysis of sectors or activities contributing to emissions or others; and

v. the determination of impacts on people, such as human mobility – migration and forced displacement-, effects on health and life, loss of non-economic assets, etc.?

2. To what extent does access to environmental information constitute a right whose protection is necessary to guarantee the rights to life, property, health, participation and access to justice, among other rights negatively affected by climate change, in accordance with the state obligations protected under the American Convention?

C. *On the Differential Obligations of States with Respect to the Rights of Children and New Generations in the Face of Climate Emergencies*

In consideration of Article 19 of the American Convention,[44] *in light of the corpus iuris* of international human rights law, including Article 12 of the Convention on the Rights of the Child[45] and recognizing the consensus of the scientific community that identifies children as the group most vulnerable in the long term to the imminent and anticipated risks to life and well-being from the climate emergency[46]:

---

44 ACHR. "Article 19. Rights of the Child. Every minor child has the right to the measures of protection required by his condition as a minor on the part of his family, society, and the State."

45 Convention on the Rights of the Child (CRC). Article 12. 1. States Parties shall assure to the child who is capable of forming his or her own views the right to express those views freely in all matters affecting the child, the views of the child being given due weight in accordance with the age and maturity of the child. 2. For this purpose, the child shall in particular be provided the opportunity to be heard in any judicial and administrative proceedings affecting the child, either directly, or through a representative or an appropriate body, in a manner consistent with the procedural rules of national law.

46 Smith K. and Woodward A. (2018), *Human health: impacts, adaptation, and co-benefits*, Intergovernmental Panel on Climate Change, p. 717: "Children, young people, and the elderly are at increased risk of climate related injury and illness (Perera, 2008). For example, adverse effects of malaria, diarrhea, and undernutrition are presently concentrated among children, for reasons of physiological susceptibility. ... Maternal antibodies acquired in utero provide some protection against dengue fever in the first year of life, but if infection does occur in infants, it is more likely to provoke the severe hemorrhagic form of illness. Children are generally at greater risk when food supplies are restricted: households with children tend to have lower than average incomes, and food insecurity is associated with a range of adverse health outcomes among young children" (citations omitted). See also, Canadian Ministry of Health (2008) *Human Health in A Changing Climate*, p. 20. "Infants and children are especially vulnerable to environmental degradation because of their inability to protect themselves, relatively high intake of water, air and certain foods, rapid growth and development, immature physiology and metabolism, and potential for high cumulative exposures over their lifetime."

1. What is the nature and scope of a State Party's obligation to adopt timely and effective measures in the face of a climate emergency to ensure the protection of children's rights derived from its obligations under Articles 1, 4, 5, 11 and 19 of the American Convention?
2. What is the nature and extent of a State Party's obligation to provide children with meaningful and effective means to freely and fully express their views, including the opportunity to initiate or otherwise participate in, any judicial or administrative proceedings concerning the prevention of climate change that constitutes a threat to their lives?

D. *On the State's Obligations Arising from Consultation and Judicial Procedures in the Event of a Climate Emergency*

In consideration of Articles 8 and 25 of the American Convention,[47] and taking into account hat scientific observation has indicated that there is a limit to the amount of greenhouse gases that can continue to be emitted before reaching dangerous climate change with no return, and that this imit could be reached in this decade[48]:

1. What is the nature and extent of a State Party's obligation with respect to the provision of judicial remedies effective to provide adequate and timely protection and redress for the impact on their rights due to the climate emergency?

---

47 IACtHR. OC-23/17. The Environment and Human Rights paras. 233 to 241.

48 Xu Y., Ramanathan V., & Victor D. G. (2018) *Global warming will happen faster than we think*, Comment, Nature 564(7734): pp. 30 and 31. "But the latest IPCC special report underplays another alarming fact: global warming is accelerating. Three trends – rising emissions, declining air pollution and natural climate cycles – will combine over the next 20 years to make climate change faster and more furious than anticipated. In our view, there's a good chance that we could breach the 1.5°C level by 2030, not by 2040 as projected in the special report (see 'Accelerated warming'). The climate-modelling community has not grappled enough with the rapid changes that policymakers care most about, preferring to focus on longer-term trends and equilibria." Since publication of the Comment by Xu, Ramanathan and Victor, the IPCC has updated its estimate of when the 1.5°C level could be breached: see, Arias P. A., *et al.* (2021) *Technical Summary*, in Climate Change 2021: The Physical Science Basis, *Contribution of Working Group I to the Sixth Assessment Report of the Intergovernmental Panel on Climate Change*, Masson-Delmotte V., *et al.* (eds.), TS-9. "Timing of crossing 1.5°C global warming: Slightly different approaches are used in SR1.5 and in this Report. SR1.5 assessed a likely range of 2030 to 2052 for reaching a global warming level of 1.5°C (for a 30-year period), assuming a continued, constant rate of warming. In AR6, combining the larger estimate of global warming to date and the assessed climate response to all considered scenarios, the central estimate of crossing 1.5°C of global warming (for a 20-year period) occurs in the early 2030s, in the early part of the likely range assessed in SR1.5, assuming no major volcanic eruption. (Section TS.1.3, Cross-Section Box TS.1."

2. To what extent should the consultation obligation take into account the consequences on the climate emergency of an activity or projections of the emergency?

E. *On the Conventional Obligations of Protection and Prevention for Environmental and Territorial Defenders, as Well as Women, Indigenous Peoples and Afro-Descendant Communities in the Context of the Climate Emergency*

In accordance with the obligations arising from Articles 1.1 and 2 of the American Convention[49] and in the light of Article 9 of the Escazú Agreement[50]:

1. What measures and policies should States adopt in order to facilitate the work of environmental defenders?
2. What specific considerations should be taken into account to guarantee the right to defend the healthy environment and territory of women human rights defenders in the context of the climate emergency?
3. What specific considerations should be taken into account to guarantee the right to defend the healthy environment and territory in view of intersectional factors and differentiated impacts, among others, on indigenous peoples, peasant communities and Afro-descendants in the face of the climate emergency?

---

49 ACHR. Article 1. Obligation to Respect Rights. 1. The States Parties to this Convention undertake to respect the rights and freedoms recognized herein and to ensure to all persons subject to their jurisdiction the free and full exercise of those rights and freedoms, without any discrimination for reasons of race, color, sex, language, religion, political or other opinion, national or social origin, economic status, birth, or any other social condition. Article 2. Domestic Legal Effects. Where the exercise of any of the rights or freedoms referred to in Article 1 is not already ensured by legislative or other provisions, the States Parties undertake to adopt, in accordance with their constitutional processes and the provisions of this Convention, such legislative or other measures as may be necessary to give effect to those rights or freedoms.

50 Escazú Agreement. Article 9. Human Rights defenders in environmental matters. (1) Each Party shall guarantee a safe and enabling environment for persons, groups and organizations that promote and defend human rights in environmental matters, so that they are able to act free from threat, restriction and insecurity. (2) Each Party shall take adequate and effective measures to recognize, protect and promote all the rights of human rights defenders in environmental matters, including their right to life, personal integrity, freedom of opinion and expression, peaceful assembly and association, and free movement, as well as their ability to exercise their access rights, taking into account its international obligations in the field of human rights, its constitutional principles and the basic concepts of its legal system. (3) Each Party shall also take appropriate, effective and timely measures to prevent, investigate and punish attacks, threats or intimidations that human rights defenders in environmental matters may suffer while exercising the rights set out in the present Agreement.

4. In the face of the climate emergency, what information should the State produce and public in order to determine the capacity to investigate various crimes committed against human rights defenders, including reports of threats, kidnappings, homicides, forced displacement, gender-based violence, discrimination, etc.?
5. What due diligence measures should States consider to ensure that attacks and threats against environmental defenders in the context of the climate emergency do not go unpunished?

F. *On the Shared and Differentiated Obligations and Responsibilities in Terms of the Rights of States in the Face of the Climate Emergency*

Bearing in mind that the climate emergency affects the entire world, and there are obligations to cooperate and also to make reparations arising from the American Convention as well as from other international treaties[51]:

1. What considerations and principles should States and international organizations take into account, collectively and regionally, to analyze shared but differentiated responsibilities in the face of climate change from a human rights and intersectionality perspective?
2. How should States act both individually and collectively to guarantee the right to reparation for damages generated by their actions or omissions in the face of the climate emergency, taking into account considerations of equity, justice and sustainability?

Taking into account the climate crisis is having a greater impact on some regions and populations, including the Caribbean, island and coastal countries and territories of our region and their inhabitants[52]:

1. How should the obligations of cooperation between States be interpreted?

---

51 ACHR. Article 26. Progressive Development. The States Parties undertake to adopt measures, both internally and through international cooperation, especially those of an economic and technical nature, with a view to achieving progressively, by legislation or other appropriate means and subject to available resources, the full realization of the rights implicit in the economic, social, educational, scientific, and cultural standards; Protocol of San Salvador, Articles 1, 12 and 14; Stockholm Declaration and action plan for the human environment, Principle 24; Rio Declaration on the Environment and Development, adopted at the United Nations Conference on Environment and Development, Río de Janeiro, June 14, 1992, UN Doc. A/CONF.I51/26/Rev.1 (Vol. 1), Principles 7 and 19.

52 See, for example, Inter-American Development Bank (IDB). Climate change poses a serious threat to all Caribbean nations despite their low contribution to global greenhouse gas (GHG) emissions, and UN News: The Caribbean is 'ground zero' for the global climate emergency: UN Secretary-General, July 3, 2022.

2. What obligations and principles should guide the actions of States in order to ensure the right to life and survival of the most affected regions and populations in the various countries and in the region?

Considering that one of the impacts of the climate emergency is to aggravate the factors that lead to human mobility – migration and forced displacement of people[53]:

3. What obligations and principles should guide the individual and coordinate actions to be taken by States in the region to address non-voluntary human mobility exacerbated by the climate emergency?

C International Court of Justice

Algeria, Andorra, Angola, Antigua and Barbuda, Australia, Austria, Azerbaijan, Bahamas, Bangladesh, Barbados, Belgium, Belize, Bulgaria, Cabo Verde, Canada, Chile, Colombia, Costa Rica, Croatia, Cyprus, Czechia, Denmark, Djibouti, Dominican Republic, Eritrea, Estonia, Fiji, Finland, France, Gabon, Gambia, Georgia, Germany, Ghana, Greece, Guinea-Bissau, Guyana, Hungary, Iceland, Ireland, Italy, Jamaica, Kiribati, Latvia, Lebanon, Libya, Liechtenstein, Lithuania, Luxembourg, Madagascar, Maldives, Malta, Marshall Islands, Mauritania, Mauritius, Mexico, Micronesia (Federated States of), Monaco, Montenegro, Morocco, Mozambique, Myanmar, Namibia, Nauru, Nepal, Netherlands, New Zealand, North Macedonia, Norway, Palau, Panama, Papua New Guinea, Portugal, Republic of Moldova, Romania, Rwanda, Saint Kitts and Nevis, Saint Lucia, Saint Vincent and the Grenadines, Samoa, Serbia, Seychelles, Sierra Leone, Singapore, Slovakia, Slovenia, Solomon Islands, Spain, Sri Lanka, Suriname, Sweden, Switzerland, Timor-Leste, Togo, Tonga, Trinidad and Tobago, Tunisia, Tuvalu, Uganda, Ukraine, United Kingdom of Great Britain and Northern Ireland, United Republic of Tanzania, Vanuatu, Viet Nam and State of Palestine:*draft resolution

Request for an Advisory Opinion of the International Court of Justice on the Obligations of States in Respect of Climate Change

The General Assembly,

Recognizing that climate change is an unprecedented challenge of civilizational proportions and that the well-being of present and future generations of humankind depends on our immediate and urgent response to it,

53 IACtHR. OC-23/17. The Environment and Human Rights para. 182.

Recalling its resolution 77/165 of 14 December 2022 and all its other resolutions and decisions relating to the protection of the global climate for present and future generations of humankind, and its resolution 76/300 of 28 July 2022 on the human right to a clean, healthy and sustainable environment,

Recalling also its resolution 70/1 of 25 September 2015 entitled "Transforming our world: the 2030 Agenda for Sustainable Development",

Recalling further Human Rights Council resolution 50/9 of 7 July 2022[54] and all previous resolutions of the Council on human rights and climate change, and Council resolution 48/13 of 8 October 2021,[55] as well as the need to ensure gender equality and empowerment of women,

Emphasizing the importance of the Charter of the United Nations, the Universal Declaration of Human Rights,[56] the International Covenant on Civil and Political Rights,[57] the International Covenant on Economic, Social and Cultural Rights,[58] the Convention on the Rights of the Child,[59] the United Nations Convention on the Law of the Sea,[60] the Vienna Convention for the Protection of the Ozone Layer,[61] the Montreal Protocol on Substances that Deplete the Ozone Layer,[62] the Convention on Biological Diversity[63] and the United Nations Convention to Combat Desertification in Those Countries Experiencing Serious Drought and/or Desertification, Particularly in Africa,[64] among other instruments, and of the relevant principles and relevant obligations of customary international law, including those reflected in the Declaration of the United Nations Conference on the Human Environment[65] and the Rio Declaration on Environment and Development,[66] to the conduct of States over time in relation to activities that contribute to climate change and its adverse effects,

---

54 See Official Records of the General Assembly, Seventy-seventh Session, Supplement No. 53(A/77/53), chap. VIII, sect. A.

55 Ibid., Seventy-sixth Session, Supplement No. 53A (A/76/53/Add.1), chap. II.

56 Resolution 217 A (III).

57 Resolution 2200 A (XXI), annex.

58 Ibid.

59 United Nations, Treaty Series, vol. 1577, No. 27531.

60 Ibid., vol. 1833, No. 31363.

61 Ibid., vol. 1513, No. 26164.

62 Ibid., vol. 1522, No. 26369.

63 Ibid., vol. 1760, No. 30619.

64 Ibid., vol. 1954, No. 33480.

65 Report of the United Nations Conference on the Human Environment, Stockholm, 5 –16 June 1972 (A/CONF.48/14/Rev.1), part one, chap. I.

66 Report of the United Nations Conference on Environment and Development, Rio de Janeiro, 3-14 June 1992, vol. I, Resolutions Adopted by the Conference (United Nations publication, Sales No. E.93.I.8 and corrigendum), resolution 1, annex I.

Recalling the United Nations Framework Convention on Climate Change,[67] the Kyoto Protocol[68] and the Paris Agreement,[69] as expressions of the determination to address decisively the threat posed by climate change, urging all parties to fully implement them, and noting with concern the significant gap both between the aggregate effect of States' current nationally determined contributions and the emission reductions required to hold the increase in the global average temperature to well below 2 degrees Celsius above pre-industrial levels and to pursue efforts to limit the temperature increase to 1.5 degrees Celsius above pre-industrial levels, and between current levels of adaptation and levels needed to respond to the adverse effects of climate change,

Recalling also that the United Nations Framework Convention on Climate Change and the Paris Agreement will be implemented to reflect equity and the principle of common but differentiated responsibilities and respective capabilities, in the light of different national circumstances,

Noting with profound alarm that emissions of greenhouse gases continue to rise despite the fact that all countries, in particular developing countries, are vulnerable to the adverse effects of climate change and that those that are particularly vulnerable to the adverse effects of climate change and have significant capacity constraints, such as the least developed countries and small island developing States, are already experiencing an increase in such effects, including persistent drought and extreme weather events, land loss and degradation, sea level rise, coastal erosion, ocean acidification and the retreat of mountain glaciers, leading to displacement of affected persons and further threatening food security, water availability and livelihoods, as well as efforts to eradicate poverty in all its forms and dimensions and achieve sustainable development,

Noting with utmost concern the scientific consensus, expressed, inter alia, in the reports of the Intergovernmental Panel on Climate Change, including that anthropogenic emissions of greenhouses gases are unequivocally the dominant cause of the global warming observed since the mid-20th century, that human-induced climate change, including more frequent and intense extreme events, has caused widespread adverse impacts and related losses and damages to nature and people, beyond natural climate variability, and that across sectors and regions the most vulnerable people and systems are observed to be disproportionately affected,

Acknowledging that, as temperatures rise, impacts from climate and weather extremes, as well as slow-onset events, will pose an ever-greater social, cultural, economic and environmental threat,

---

67 United Nations, Treaty Series, vol. 1771, No. 30822.

68 Ibid., vol. 2303, No. 30822.

69 See FCCC/CP/2015/10/Add.1, decision 1/CP.21, annex.

Emphasizing the urgency of scaling up action and support, including finance, capacity-building and technology transfer, to enhance adaptive capacity and to implement collaborative approaches for effectively responding to the adverse effects of climate change, as well as for averting, minimizing and addressing loss and damage associated with those effects in developing countries that are particularly vulnerable to these effects,

Expressing serious concern that the goal of developed countries to mobilize jointly USD 100 billion per year by 2020 in the context of meaningful mitigation actions and transparency on implementation has not yet been met, and urging developed countries to meet the goal,

Decides, in accordance with Article 96 of the Charter of the United Nations, to request the International Court of Justice, pursuant to Article 65 of the Statute of the Court, to render an advisory opinion on the following question:

> Having particular regard to the Charter of the United Nations, the International Covenant on Civil and Political Rights, the International Covenant on Economic, Social and Cultural Rights, the United Nations Framework Convention on Climate Change, the Paris Agreement, the United Nations Convention on the Law of the Sea, the duty of due diligence, the rights recognized in the Universal Declaration of Human Rights, the principle of prevention of significant harm to the environment and the duty to protect and preserve the marine environment,
>
> a. What are the obligations of States under international law to ensure the protection of the climate system and other parts of the environment from anthropogenic emissions of greenhouse gases for States and for present and future generations;
>
> b. What are the legal consequences under these obligations for States where they, by their acts and omissions, have caused significant harm to the climate system and other parts of the environment, with respect to:
>
>   i. States, including, in particular, small island developing States, which due to their geographical circumstances and level of development, are injured or specially affected by or are particularly vulnerable to the adverse effects of climate change?
>
>   ii. Peoples and individuals of the present and future generations affected by the adverse effects of climate change?

APPENDIX 2

Table of International Instruments and National Legislation

1 International Treaties

Covenant of the League of Nations (adopted 28 June 1919, entered into force 1 October 1920) League of Nations Official Journal (February 1920) 3

1945 Charter of the United Nations (adopted 26 June 1945, entered into force 24 October 1945) 892 UNTS 119

1945 Statute of the International Court of Justice (adopted 26 June 1945, entered into force 24 October 1945) 892 UNTS 119

1948 Charter of the Organization of American States (adopted 39 April 1948, entered into force 13 December 1951) 119 UNTS 3

1950 Convention for the Protection of Human Rights and Fundamental Freedoms (adopted 4 November 1950, entered into force 3 September 1953) 213 UNTS 221 (*European Convention on Human Rights*)

1966 International Covenant on Civil and Political Rights (adopted 16 December 1966, entered into force 23 March 1976, 999 UNTS 171

1966 International Covenant on Economic, Social and Cultural Rights (adopted 16 December 1966, entered into force 3 January 1976) 993 UNTS 3

1969 African Convention on the Conservation of Nature and Natural Resources (adopted 15 September 1968, entered into force 16 June 1969) 1001 UNTS 4

1969 Vienna Convention on the Law of Treaties (adopted 23 May 1969, entered into force 27 January 1980, 1155 UNTS 331

1969 American Convention on Human Rights (adopted 22 November 1969, entered into force 18 July 1978) OAS Treaty Series No 36

1974 Nordic Convention on the Protection of the Environment (adopted 19 February 1974, entered into force 5 October 1976) 1092 UNTS 279

1979 Statute of the Inter-American Court of Human Rights (adopted 1 October 1979, entered into force 1 January 1980) OAS Resolution No 448

1981 African Charter on Human and Peoples' Rights (adopted 27 June 1981, entered into force 21 October 1986) 1520 UNTS 217

1982 United Nations Convention on the Law of the Sea (adopted 10 December 1982, entered into force 16 November 1994) 1833 UNTS 3

1985 Vienna Convention for the Protection of the Ozone Layer (adopted 22 March 1985, entered into force 22 September 1988) 1513 UNTS 293

DOI:10.1163/9789004730618_016

1987 Montreal Protocol on Substances that Deplete the Ozone Layer (adopted 16 September 1987, entered into force 1 January 1989) 1522 UNTS 3

1988 Additional Protocol to the American Convention on Human Rights in the Area of Economic, Social, and Cultural Rights (adopted 17 November 1988, entered into force 16 November 1999) OAS Treaty Series No 69 (*San Salvador Protocol*)

1990 African Charter on the Rights and Welfare of the Child (adopted 11 July 1990, entered into force 25 November 1999) CAB/LEG/24.9/49

1991 ECOWAS Protocol on the Community Court of Justice (adopted 6 July 1991, established on 30 January 2001) Doc A/P.l/7/91, *Official Journal of the ECOWAS*, vol 19 (July 1996) 4

1992 United Nations Framework Convention on Climate Change (adopted 9 May 1992, entry into force 21 March 1994) 1771 UNTS 107

1997 Kyoto Protocol to the UNFCCC (adopted 11 December 1997, entry into force 16 February 2005) 2303 UNTS 162

1998 Protocol on the Establishment of an African Court on Human and Peoples' Rights (adopted 9 June 1998, entered into force 25 January 2004) AU Doc OAU/LEG/EXP/AFCHPR/PROT (III)

1998 Aarhus Convention on Access to Information, Public Participation in Decision-making and Access to Justice in Environmental Matters, Economic Commission for Europe Resolution of 21 April 1998, UN Doc ECE/CEP/43 (adopted 25 June 1998, entered into force 30 October 2001) 2161 UNTS 447

1999 Treaty for the Establishment of the East African Community (adopted 30 November 1999, entered into force 7 July 2000) 2144 UNTS 255 (*EAC Treaty*)

2003 Protocol to the African Charter on Human and People's Rights on the Rights of Women in Africa (adopted 1 July 2003, entered into force 25 November 2005) 3268 UNTS 1

2008 Optional Protocol to the International Covenant on Economic, Social and Cultural Rights, UN General Assembly Resolution No A/RES/63/117, 10 December 2008, UN Doc A/63/435 (adopted 10 December 2008, entered into force 5 May 2013) 2922 UNTS 29

2009 African Union Convention for the Protection and Assistance of Internally Displaced Persons (adopted 23 October 2009, entered into force 6 December 2012) 3014 UNTS 3

2013 Protocol 16 to the ECHR (adopted 2 October 2013, entered into force 1 August 2018) ETS No 214

2015 Paris Agreement (adopted 12 December 2015, entry into force 4 November 2016) 3156 UNTS 79

2016 Protocol to the African Charter on the Rights of Older Persons (adopted 31 January 2016, not yet in force)

2017 Treaty on the Prohibition of Nuclear Weapons (adopted 7 July 2017, entered into force 22 January 2021) 3379 UNTS 1

2018 Protocol to the African Charter on the Rights of Persons with Disabilities (adopted 29 January 2018, not yet in force)

2018 Regional Agreement on Access to Information, Public Participation and Justice in Environmental Matters in Latin America and the Caribbean (adopted on 4 March 2018, entered into force 22 April 2021) 3388 UNTS (*Escazú Agreement*)

2021 Agreement for the Establishment of the Commission of Small Island States on Climate Change and International Law (adopted and entered into force 31 October 2021) 3444 UNTS (*COSIS Agreement*)

2 International Non-Binding Instruments

1948 American Declaration of the Rights and Duties of Man (adopted at the 9th International Conference of American States held in Bogotá, Colombia, on 2 May 1948)

1977 OECD Recommendation for an Equal Access and Non-Discrimination Regime for Transboundary Pollution (C77/) 28 (Final) (1977) 16 ILM (1977) 977

1992 Rio Declaration on Environment and Development (3–14 June 1992) UN Doc A/CONF.151/26 (vol. 1) 31 ILM 87

2002 Plan of Implementation of the World Summit on Sustainable Development; Report of the World Summit on Sustainable Development (August 26-September 4, 2002), Doc No A/CONF.199/20

2009 Nairobi Declaration on the African Process for Combating Climate Change (adopted at the African Ministerial Conference on the Environment, on 29 May 2009)

2009 African Commission of Human and Peoples' Rights Resolution on Climate Change and Human Rights and the Need to Study Its Impact in Africa (25 November 2009) ACHPR/Res153 (XLVI) 09

2010 UNEP Guidelines for the development of national legislation on access to information, public participation and access to justice in environmental matters (Bali), adopted by the Governing Council of the United Nations Environment Programme, Decision No SS.XI/5, part A of February 26, 2010

2014 African Commission on Human and Peoples' Rights '271: Resolution on Climate Change in Africa', adopted at the 55th ordinary session of the African Commission on Human and Peoples' Rights held in Luanda, Angola (28 April–12 May 2014)

2018 'State Reporting Guidelines and Principles on Articles 21 and 24 of the African Charter relating to Extractive Industries, Human Rights and the Environment' adopted at the 62nd Ordinary Session of the African Commission on Human and Peoples' Rights (25 April–9 May 2018)

3 Rules of Procedure

Rules of Court of the International Court of Justice (adopted 14 April 1978) ICJ Rep 1983, 131

Rules of the International Tribunal for the Law of the Sea (adopted on 1 October 1997) ITLOS/8/Rev.1

Rules of Procedure of the Inter-American Court of Human Rights (adopted 16 November 2009)

Rules of Court of the African Court on Human and Peoples' Rights (adopted 1 September 2020)

4 UN General Assembly Resolutions

UNGA Res 171(II) (1947) UN Doc A/519 ('Need for greater use by the United Nations and its organs of the International Court of Justice')

UNGA Res 625 (XXV) (24 October 1970) ('Declaration on Principles of International Law Concerning Friendly Relations and Cooperation among States in Accordance with the Charter of the United Nations')

UNGA Res 43/53 (6 December 1988) UN Doc A/43/755 ('Protection of Global Climate for Present and Future Generations of Mankind')

UNGA Res 51/45(M) (10 December 1996) UN Doc A/RES/51/45(M) ('Advisory Opinion of the International Court of Justice on the Legality of the Threat or Use of Nuclear Weapons')

UNGA Res No ES-10/15 (10 July 2004) UN Doc A/RES/ES-10/15 ('Advisory Opinion of the International Court of Justice on the Legal Consequences of the Construction of a Wall in the Occupied Palestinian Territory, including in and around East Jerusalem')

UNGA Res 66/228 (11 September 2012) UN Doc A/RES/66/288 ('The Future We Want')

UNGA Res 71/292 (22 June 2017) UN Doc A/RES/71/292 ('Request for an Advisory Opinion of the International Court of Justice on the Legal Consequences of the Separation of the Chagos Archipelago from Mauritius in 1965')

UNGA Resolution 73/295 (22 May 2019) UN Doc A/RES/73/295 ('Advisory opinion of the International Court of Justice on the Legal Consequences of the Separation of the Chagos Archipelago from Mauritius in 1965')

UNGA Res 77/276 (29 March 2023) UN Doc A/RES/77/276 ('Request for an Advisory Opinion from the International Court of Justice on the Obligations of States in respect of Climate Change')

5 International Law Commission

'Draft Articles on Prevention of Transboundary Harm from Hazardous Activities', adopted by the International Law Commission at its 53rd session, UN Doc A/RES/56/10 (2001)

'Draft Articles on Responsibility of States for Internationally Wrongful Acts', adopted by the International Law Commission at its 53rd session, UN Doc A/RES/56/10 (2001)

'Draft Articles on Prevention of Transboundary Harm', adopted by the International Law Commission at its 53rd session, UN Doc A/RES/56/82 (2001)

'Fragmentation of International Law: Difficulties arising from the Diversification and Expansion of International Law', Report of the Study Group of the International Law Commission, adopted at its 58th session, UN Doc A/CN.4/L.682 (2006)

'Draft Conclusions on Identification of Customary International Law', adopted by the International Law Commission at its 70th session, UN Doc A/73/10 (2018)

'Draft Guidelines on the Protection of the Atmosphere', adopted by the International Law Commission at its 72nd session, UN Doc A/76/10 (2021)

'Immunity of State officials from foreign criminal jurisdiction – Texts and titles of the draft articles adopted by the Drafting Committee on first reading', UN Doc A/77/10 (2022)

'Draft Conclusions on General Principles of Law, together with Commentaries thereto', adopted by the International Law Commission at its 74th session, UN Doc A/78/10 (2023)

6 UNFCCC Legal Complex

'Nationally determined contributions under the Paris Agreement – Synthesis report by the Secretariat' (14 November 2023) UN Doc FCCC/PA/CMA/2023/12

'Decision 1/CP.26, Glasgow Climate Pact, in UN Climate Change Conference, Rep. of the Conference of the Parties to the Paris Agreement on Its Third Session, 2, UN Doc. FCCC/CP/2021/12/Add.1

7 Human Rights Committee

General Comment No 36, 'Article 6: Right to Life', UN Doc No CCPR/C/GC/36 (3 September 2019)

8 Committee on the Rights of the Child

General Comment No 26 (2023) on Children's Rights and the Environment, with a Special Focus on Climate Change', UN Doc No CRC/C/GC/26 (22 August 2023)

9 Regional and Sub-Regional Instruments

African Committee of Experts on the Rights and welfare of the Child (ACERWC), Africa's Agenda for Children 2040

Draft Criteria for Granting African Union Observer Status to Non-Governmental Organisations (NGOs) – Annex IV of the *Report of the PRC And Legal Experts On Various Legal Matters* EX.Cl/195 (VII), Annex IV

IACmHR, Resolution No 3/2021, Climate Emergency: Scope of the Inter-American Human Rights Obligations' (31 December 2021)

10 National Legislation

Belgium

Law No 2013/11348, of Aug 17, 2013

Cook Islands

Seabed Minerals Act (Act No 5 of 2019)

Federated States of Micronesia

Seabed Resources Act (Public Law No 20–102)

Fiji

International Seabed Mineral Management Decree (Decree No 21 of 2013)

Kiribati

Seabed Minerals Act (Act No 1 of 2017)

Nauru

International Seabed Minerals Act (Act No 26 of 2015)

Singapore

Act No 6 of 2015

Tonga

Seabed Minerals Act (Act No 10 of 2014)

Tuvalu

Seabed Minerals Act (Act No 14 of 2014)

United Kingdom

Deep Sea Mining Act of 1981, as amended by the Deep Sea Mining Act of 2014

APPENDIX 3

Table of Cases

1. International and Regional Courts and Tribunals

1.1 *International Courts and Tribunals*

1.1.1 International Court of Justice

Conditions of Admission of a State to Membership in the United Nations (*Article 4 of the Charter*) (Advisory Opinion) [1948] ICJ Rep 57

Corfu Channel Case (*UK v Albania*) (Merits) [1949] ICJ Rep 15

Reparations for Injuries Suffered in the Service of the United Nations (Advisory Opinion) [1949] ICJ Rep 174

Competence of the General Assembly for the Admission of a State to the United Nations (Advisory Opinion) [1950] ICJ Rep 4

Reservations to the Convention on Genocide (Advisory Opinion) [1951] ICJ Rep 15

Fisheries Case (*United Kingdom v Norway*) (Judgment) [1951] ICJ Rep 116

Effect of Awards of Compensation Made by the UN Administrative Tribunal (Advisory Opinion) [1954] ICJ Rep 47

Certain Expenses of the United Nations (*Article 17, paragraph 2, of the Charter*) (Advisory Opinion) [1962] ICJ Rep 151

South West Africa (*Liberia v South Africa*) (2nd Phase) (Judgment) [1966] ICJ Rep 6

Legal Consequences for States of the Continued Presence of South Africa in Namibia (*South West Africa*) *notwithstanding Security Council Resolution 276* (*1970*) (Advisory Opinion) [1971] ICJ Rep 16

Fisheries Jurisdiction (*United Kingdom v Ireland*) (Judgment) [1974] ICJ Rep 181

Western Sahara (Advisory Opinion) [1975] ICJ Rep 12

Interpretation of the Agreement of 25 March 1951 between the WHO and Egypt (Advisory Opinion) [1980] ICJ Rep 73

Application for Review of Judgment No 273 of the United Nations Administrative Tribunal (Advisory Opinion) [1982] ICJ Rep 325

Continental Shelf (*Libya v Malta*) (Judgment) [1985] ICJ Rep 13

Military and Paramilitary Activities in and against Nicaragua (*Nicaragua v United States of America*) (Merits) (Judgment) [1986] ICJ Rep 14

Application for Review of Judgment No 333 of the United Nations Administrative Tribunal (Advisory Opinion) [1987] ICJ Rep 18

Legality of the Use by a State of Nuclear Weapons in Armed Conflict (Advisory Opinion) [1996] ICJ Rep 66

Legality of the Threat or Use of Nuclear Weapons (Advisory Opinion) [1996] ICJ Rep 226

 | DOI:10.1163/9789004730618_017

Gabčikovo-Nagymaros Project (*Hungary v Slovakia*) (Merits) [1997] ICJ ICJ Rep 7

Difference Relating to Immunity from Legal Process of a Special Rapporteur of the Commission on Human Rights (Advisory Opinion, 29 April 1999) ICJ Rep 62

Arrest Warrant of April 11, 2000 (*Democratic Republic of the Congo v Belgium*) (Judgement) [2002] ICJ Rep 3

Advisory Opinion on the Legal Consequences of the Construction of a Wall in the Occupied Palestinian Territory (Advisory Opinion) [2004] ICJ Rep 136

Armed Activities in the Territory of the Congo (*New Application: 2002*) (*Democratic Republic of the Congo v Rwanda*) (Jurisdiction and Admissibility) (Judgment) [2006] ICJ Rep 6

Case Concerning Application of the Convention on the Prevention and Punishment of the Crime of Genocide (*Bosnia Herzegovina v Serbia and Montenegro*) (Merits) [2007] ICJ Rep 43

Application of the Convention on the Prevention and Punishment of the Crime of Genocide (*Croatia v Serbia*) (Preliminary Objections) [2008] ICJ Rep 412

Dispute regarding Navigational and Related Rights (*Costa Rica v Nicaragua*) [2009] ICJ Rep 213

Pulp Mills on the River Uruguay (*Argentina v Uruguay*) [2010] ICJ Rep 14

Accordance with International Law of the Unilateral Declaration of Independence in Respect of Kosovo (Advisory Opinion) [2010] (ICJ Rep 402)

Ahmadou Sadio Diallo (*Republic of Guinea v Democratic Republic of the Congo*) (Merits) [2010] ICJ Rep 639

Questions relating to the Obligation to Prosecute or Extradite (*Belgium v Senegal*) (Merits) [2012] ICJ Rep 422

Application of the Convention on the Prevention and Punishment of the Crime of Genocide (*Croatia v Serbia*) (Merits) (Judgment) [2015] ICJ Rep 3

Certain Activities Carried Out by Nicaragua in the Border Area (*Costa Rica v Nicaragua*) [2015] ICJ Rep 665

Obligations Concerning Negotiations Relating to Cessation of the Nuclear Arms Race and to Nuclear Disarmament (*Marshall Islands v India*) (Admissibility) [2016] ICJ Rep 833

Obligation to Negotiate Access to the Pacific Ocean (*Bolivia v Chile*) (Judgment) [2018] ICJ Rep 507

Legal Consequences of the Separation of the Chagos Archipelago from Mauritius in 1965 (Advisory Opinion) [2019] ICJ Rep 95

Dispute over the Status and Use of the Waters of Silala (*Chile v Bolivia*) [2022] ICJ Rep 614

Question of the Delimitation of the Continental Shelf between Nicaragua and Colombia beyond 200 Nautical Miles from the Nicaraguan Coast (*Nicaragua v Colombia*) [2023] available at <https://www.icj-cij.org/sites/default/files/case-related/154/154-20230713-jud-01-00-en.pdf>

Request for an Advisory Opinion of the International Court of Justice on the Obligations of States in respect of Climate Change, UNGA Res 77/276 (29 March 2023) UN Doc A/RES/77/276, available at <https://www.icj-cij.org/sites/default/files/case-related/187/187-20230412-app-01-00-en.pdf>

Allegations of Genocide under the Convention on the Prevention and Punishment of the Crime of Genocide (*Ukraine v Russian Federation; 32 States intervening*) (Order of 5 June 2023) ICJ Rep 354

Right to Strike under ILO Convention No 87 (*Request for Advisory Opinion*) Order 16 November 2023, General List No 191, available at <https://www.icj-cij.org/sites/default/files/case-related/191/191-20231116-ord-01-00-en.pdf>

UNGA, 'Obligations of States in Respect of Climate Change (Request for Advisory Opinion)' (1 March 2023) UN Doc. A/77/L.58

UNGA, Order of 20 April 2023, available at <https://www.icj-cij.org/sites/default/files/case-related/187/187-20230420-ORD-01-00-EN.pdf>

UNGA, Order of 4 August 2023, available at <https://www.icj-cij.org/sites/default/files/case-related/187/187-20230804-ord-01-00-en.pdf>

UNGA, Order of 15 December 2023, available at <https://www.icj-cij.org/sites/default/files/case-related/187/187-20231215-ord-01-00-en.pdf>

UNGA, Order of 30 May 2024, available at <https://www.icj-cij.org/sites/default/files/case-related/187/187-20240531-ord-01-00-en.pdf>

1.1.2 International Tribunal of the Law of the Sea

Responsibilities and Obligations of States Sponsoring Persons and Entities with Respect to Activities in the Area (*Request for Advisory Opinion Submitted to the Seabed Disputes Chamber* (Advisory Opinion, 1 February 2011) ITLOS Case No 17

Request for an Advisory Opinion submitted by the Sub-Regional Fisheries Commission (*SRFC*) (Advisory Opinion, 2 April 2015) ITLOS Case No 15

Dispute Concerning Delimitation of the Maritime Boundary Between Ghana and Côte d'Ivoire in the Atlantic Ocean (Judgment, 23 September 2017) ITLOS Case No 23

Dispute concerning Delimitation of the Maritime Boundary between Mauritius and Maldives in the Indian Ocean (*Mauritius/Maldives*) (*Preliminary Objections*) (Judgment, 28 January 2021) ITLOS Case No 28

Request for an Advisory Opinion submitted by the Commission of Small Island States on Climate Change and International Law (Advisory Opinion, 21 May 2024) ITLOS Case No 31

Request for an Advisory Opinion submitted by the Commission of Small Island States on Climate Change and International Law, Order No 2022/4 (16 December 2022), available at <https://www.itlos.org/fileadmin/itlos/documents/cases/31/C31_Order_2022-4_16.12.2022_01.pdf>

1.1.3 Permanent Court of International Justice

1.1.4 International Criminal Tribunal for the Former Yugoslavia

1.2 ***Regional Courts: Africa***

1.2.1 African Court of Human and Peoples' Rights (ACtHPR)

Peoples' Rights on the Rights of Women in Africa requested by Centre for Human Rights, University of Pretoria, Federation of Women Lawyers, Kenya, Women's Legal Centre, Women Advocates Research and Documentation Centre and Zimbabwe Women Lawyers Association

Decision on Advisory Opinion No 002/2014 (Sep 28, 2018) *On Institution of legal action before the African Commission on Human and peoples' Rights or the African Court on Human and Peoples' Rights following an unconstitutional change of government, Requested by Rencontre Africain pour la Defense des Droits de l'Homme* (RADDHO)

Advisory Opinion No 001/2018 (Dec 4, 2020) *On the compatibility of Vagrancy Laws with the African Charter on Human and Peoples' Rights and other human rights instruments applicable in Africa, requested by Pan African Lawyers Union* (PALU)

Advisory Opinion No 001/2021 (Jul 16, 2021) *On the application of the principle of regional rotation in the election of the bureau of the Pan African Parliament* (PAP), *requested by* PAP

Advisory Opinion No 001/2020 (Jul 16, 2021) *On the right to participate in the government of one's country in the context of an election held during a public health emergency or a pandemic, such as the Covid-19 crisis, requested by Pan African Lawyers Union* (PALU)

The Matter of African Commission on Human and Peoples' Rights v Republic of Kenya (Reparations) Application No 006/2012 (June 23, 2022)

SERAC v Nigeria (Decision) Comm No 155/96 (AfCHPR, Oct 27, 2001)

1.2.2 East African Community Court of Justice

Katabazi et al v Secretary General of the East African Community and Attorney General of the Republic of Uganda, Case No 1/2007

Request by the Council of Ministers of the East African Community pursuant to Articles 14 (4) and 36 of the Treaty, Advisory Opinion No 1 of 2008, available at <https://www.eacj.org/?cases=application-no-1-of-2008-advisory-opinion-of-the-court>

Request by the Council of Ministers of the East African Community pursuant to Articles 14(4) and 36 of the Treaty and Rule 75(4) of the East African Court of Justice Rules of Procedure 2013, Advisory Opinion No 1 of 2015, available at <https://www.eacj.org/?cases=request-for-an-advisory-opinion-no-1-of-2015-in-the-matter-of-a-request-by-the-council-of-ministersof-the-east-african-community-for-an-advisory-opinionmade-pursuant-to-articles-14-4-and-36-of-t>

1.2.3 African Commission of Human and Peoples' Rights (ACmHPR)

Advisory Opinion of The African Commission On Human And Peoples' Rights on The United Nations Declaration on The Rights of Indigenous Peoples, Adopted by the African Commission on Human and Peoples' Rights (Advisory Opinion) 30 May 2007

Institute for Human Rights and Development in Africa (*IHRDA*) *and Others v Democratic Republic of Congo* (Decision) Comm No 393/10 (AfCHPR, June 18, 2016)

The Matter of African Commission on Human and Peoples' Rights v Republic of Kenya (Merits) App No 006/2012 (May 26, 2017)

The Matter of African Commission on Human and Peoples' Rights v Republic of Kenya (Reparations) App No 006/2012 (June 23, 2022)

1.2.4 ECOWAS Court

Adou Kouame and others v Cote d'Ivoire, Case No ECW/CCJ/APP/08/21 (Judgment) Nov 30, 2023 (ECW/CCJ/JUD/46/23)

1.3 *Regional Courts: America*

1.3.1 Inter-American Court on Human Rights

'Other Treaties' Subject to the Consultative Jurisdiction of the Court (*art. 64 American Convention on Human Rights*), Advisory Opinion OC-1/82, Inter-American Court of Human Rights Series A No 1 (24 September 1982)

Restrictions to the Death Penalty (*Arts. 4.2 and 4.4 American Convention on Human Rights*). Advisory Opinion OC-3/83, Inter-American Court of Human Rights Series A No 3 (8 September 1983)

Proposed Amendments to the Naturalization Provisions of the Constitution of Costa Rica, Advisory Opinion OC-4/84, Inter-American Court of Human Rights Series A No 4 (19 January 1984)

Habeas Corpus in Emergency Situations, Advisory Opinion OC-8/87, Inter-American Court of Human Rights Series A No 8 (30 January 1987)

Judicial Guarantees in States of Emergency, Advisory Opinion OC-9/87, Inter-American Court of Human Rights Series A No 9 (6 October 1987)

Velásquez-Rodríguez v Honduras (Merits) Inter-American Court of Human Rights Series C No 4 (29 July 1988)

Interpretation of the American Declaration of the Rights and Duties of Man Within the Framework of Article 64 of the American Convention on Human Rights, Advisory Opinion OC-10/89, Inter-American Court of Human Rights Series A No 10 (14 July 1989)

International Responsibility for the Promulgation and Enforcement of Laws in Violation of the Convention (*Arts. 1 and 2 of the American Convention on Human Rights*), Advisory Opinion OC-14/94, Inter-American Court of Human Rights Series A No 14 (9 December 1994)

Reports of the Inter-American Commission on Human Rights (*Art. 51 American Convention on Human Rights*). Advisory Opinion OC-15/97, Inter-American Court of Human Rights Series A No 15 (14 November 1997)

The Right to Information on Consular Assistance Within the Framework of the Guarantees of Legal Due Process. Advisory Opinion OC-16/99, Inter-American Court of Human Rights Series A No 16 (1 October 1999)

Case of the 'Street Children' (Villagrán Morales et al) v Guatemala (Merits) Inter-American Court of Human Rights Series C No 63 (19 November 1999)

Mayagna (Sumo) Awas Tingni Community v Nicaragua (Merits, Reparations and Costs) Inter-American Court of Human Rights Series C No 79 (31 August 2001)

Juridical Condition and Rights of Undocumented Migrants. Advisory Opinion OC-18/03, Inter-American Court of Human Rights Series A No 18 (17 September 2003)

Case of the 'Mapiripán Massacre' v Colombia (Merits, Reparations and Costs Judgment) Inter-American Court of Human Rights Series C No 134 (15 September 2005)

Case of the Pueblo Bello Massacre v Colombia (Merits, Reparations and Costs) Inter-American Court of Human Rights Series C No 140 (31 January 2006)

Case of the Sawhoyamaxa Indigenous Community v Paraguay (Merits, Reparations and Costs) Inter-American Court of Human Rights Series C No 146 (29 March 2006)

Almonacid-Arellano et al v Chile (Preliminary Objections, Merits, Reparations and Costs Judgment) Inter-American Court of Human Rights Series C No 154 (26 September 2006)

Case of the Dismissed Congressional Employees (Aguado Alfaro et al) v Peru (Preliminary Objections, Merits, Reparations and Costs) Inter-American Court of Human Rights Series C No 158 (4 November 2006)

Case of the Saramaka People v Suriname (Merits, Reparations and Costs) Inter-American Court of Human Rights Series C No 172 (28 November 2007)

Case of Cabrera García and Montiel Flores v Mexico (Preliminary Objection, Merits, Reparations and Costs). Inter-American Court of Human Rights Series C No 220 (26 November 2010).

Case of Cabrera García and Montiel Flores v Mexico, Monitoring Compliance with Judgment. Order of the Inter-American Court of Human Rights of Mar 20, 2013

Case of Gelman v Uruguay (Merits and Reparations). Inter-American Court of Human Rights IACtHR Series C No 221 (24 February 2011)

Case of the Kichwa People of Sarayaku v Ecuador (Merits and Reparations) Inter-American Court of Human Rights Series C No 245 (27 June 2012)

Case of the Massacres of the Río Negro v Guatemala (Preliminary Objection, Merits, Reparations and Costs). Inter-American Court of Human Rights Series C No 250 (4 September 2012)

Case of Gudiel Álvarez et al ('Diario Militar') v Guatemala. Merits, Reparations and Costs. Inter-American Court of Human Rights Series C No 253 (20 November 2012)

Rights and Guarantees of Children in the Context of Migration and/or Need of International Protection. Advisory Opinion OC-21/14, Inter-American Court of Human Rights Series A No 14 (19 August 2014)

Case of the Kaliña and Lokono Peoples v Suriname (Merits, Reparations and Costs) Inter-American Court of Human Rights Series C No 309 (25 November 2015)

The Environment and Human Rights (State Obligations in Relation to the Environment in the Context of the Protection and Guarantee of the Rights to Life and to Personal Integrity – Interpretation and Scope of Articles 4(1) and 5(1) of the American Convention on Human Rights) Advisory Opinion OC-23/17, Inter-American Court of Human Rights Series A No 23 (15 November 2017)

Gender Identity, and Equality and Non-Discrimination of Same-Sex Couples, Advisory Opinion OC-24/17, Inter-American Court of Human Rights Series A No 24 (24 November 2017)

Institution of Asylum and its Recognition as a Human Right in the Inter-American System of Protection (interpretation and scope of Articles 5, 22(7) and 22(8), in relation to Article 1(1) of the American Convention on Human Rights). Advisory Opinion OC-25/18, Inter-American Court of Human Rights Series A No 25 (30 May 2018)

Case of Cuscul Pivaral et al v Guatemala (Preliminary Objection, Merits, Reparations and Costs). Inter-American Court of Human Rights, Serie C No 378 (14 May 2019)

Case of Indigenous Communities of the Lhaka Honhat (Our Land) Association v Argentina (Merits, Reparations and Costs). Inter-American Court of Human Rights Series C No 400 (6 February 2020)

Denunciation of the American Convention on Human Rights and the Charter of the Organization of American States and the Consequences for State Human Rights Obligations (Interpretation and Scope of Articles 1, 2, 27, 29, 30, 31, 32, 33 a 65 and 78 of the American Convention on Human Rights and 3(l), 17, 45, 53, 106 and 143 of the Charter of the Organization of American States). Advisory Opinion OC-26/20, Inter-American Court of Human Rights Series A No 26 (9 November 2020)

Case of Baraona Bray v Chile (Preliminary Objections, Merits, Reparations and Costs). Inter-American Court of Human Rights Series C No 481 (24 November 2022)

Case Inhabitants from La Oroya v Peru (Merits, Reparations and Costs). Inter-American Court of Human Rights Series C No 511 (27 November 2023)

Request for an advisory opinion on the Climate Emergency and Human Rights submitted to the Inter-American Court of Human Rights by the Republic of Colombia and the Republic of Chile (9 January 2023)

1.4 *Regional Courts: Europe*

1.4.1 Court of Justice of the European Union (CJEU)

Case C-104/16P *Council of the European Union v Front Polisario* [2016]

Case C-363/18 *Organisation juive européenne and Vignoble Psagot Ltd v Ministre de l'Economie et des Finances*

1.4.2 European Court of Human Rights (ECtHR)

López Ostra v Spain (Judgment) [1994] (App No 16798/90) ECtHR 9 December 1994
Kurt v Turkey (App No 24276/94) ECtHR 25 May 1998
Loizidou v Turkey (App No 15318/89) ECtHR [GC] 28 July 1998
Cyprus v Turkey (App No 25781/94) ECtHR 10 May 2001
Öneryildiz v Turkey (App No 48939/99) ECtHR [GC] 30 November 2004
Mamatkulov and Askarov v Turkey (App No 46827/99) ECtHR 4 February 2005
Fadeyeva v Russia (App No 55723/00) ECtHR 9 June 2005
Ergin v Turkey (No 6) (App No 47533/99) ECtHR 4 May 2006
Budayeva v Russia (Judgment) [2008] (Apps Nos 15339/02, 21166/02, 20058/02, 11673/02 & 15343/02) ECtHR 20 March 2008
Kononov v Latvia (App No 36376/04) ECtHR 24 July 2008
Lexa v Slovakia (App No 54334/00) ECtHR 23 September 2008
Palomo Sánchez and Others v Spain (Apps Nos 28955/06, 28957/06, 28959/06 & 28964/06) ECtHR 12 September 2011
Marguš v Croatia (App No 4455/10) ECtHR 27 May 2014
Hassan v United Kingdom (App No 29750/09) ECtHR 16 September 2014
Petropavlovskis v Latvia (App No 44230/06) ECtHR 13 January 2015
Chiragov and Others v Armenia (App No 13216/05) ECtHR 16 June 2015
Vasiliauskas v Lithuania (App No 35343/05) ECtHR 20 October 2015
Al-Dulimi and Montana Management Inc v Switzerland (App No 5809/08) ECtHR 21 June 2016
Ramadan v Malta (App No 76136/12) ECtHR 21 June 2016
Georgia v Russia (II) (App No 38263/08) ECtHR 21 January 2021
X v Poland (App No 20741/10) ECtHR 16 September 2021
Savickis and Others v Latvia (App No 49279/11) ECtHR 9 June 2022
Humpert and Others v Germany (Apps Nos 59433/18, 59477/18, 59481/18 & 59494/18) ECtHR 14 December 2023
Verein KlimaSeniorinnen Schweiz and Others v Switzerland (App No 53600/20) ECtHR [GC] 9 April 2024
Duarte Agostinho and Others v Portugal and 32 Other States (App No 39371/20) ECtHR [GC] 9 April 2024
Carême v France (App No 7189/21) ECtHR [GC] 9 April 2024
Cordella and Others v Italy (Judgment) [2019] (App No 54414/13) ECtHR 24 January 2019
Yevgeniy Dmitriyev v Russia (Judgment) [2020] (App No 17840/06) ECtHR 1 December 2020

2 Human Rights Bodies and Commissions

2.1 *International Treaty-Based Bodies*

2.1.1 UN Committee on the Rights of the Child

Chiara Sacchi et al v Argentina et al, UN Committee on the Rights of the Child 'Decision adopted under the Optional Protocol, concerning Communication No 108/2019' (23 September 2021) UN Doc CRC/C/88/D/108/2019

2.1.2 UN Human Rights Committee

Daniel Billy et al v Australia, UN Human Rights Committee 'Views adopted under article 5 (4) of the Optional Protocol, concerning Communication No 3624/2019' (18 September 2023) UN Doc CCPR/C/135/D/3624/2019

3 Arbitration

3.1 *Permanent Court of Arbitration*

In the Matter of South China Sea Arbitration (*Republic of the Philippines v The People's Republic of China*) PCA Case 2013–19 (2016)

3.2 *Non-Permanent Arbitration Tribunals*

Lac Lanoux, Award (16 November 1957) 12 RIAA 281

Award in the Arbitration regarding the Iron Rhine Railway between the Kingdom of Belgium and the Kingdom of the Netherlands (*Belgium v The Netherlands*), Award (24 May 2005) 27 RIAA 34

3.3 *Conciliation*

Timor Sea Conciliation (*Timor-Leste v Australia*), Report of the Recommendations of the Compulsory Conciliation Commission between Timor-Leste and Australia on the Timor Sea of 9 May 2018

4 Domestic Courts

4.1 *Argentina*

Supreme Court of Argentina, Judgment in *Mazzeo, Julio Lilo y otros*, Recurso de casación e inconstitucionalidad. M. 2333. XLII. (13 July 2007)

4.2 *Australia*

*Tarkine National Coalition Inc v Minister for the Environment and Others** [2015] FCAFC 89

Gloucester Resources Limited v Minister for Planning and Environment (No 2) [2018] NSWLEC 1200

Gloucester Resources Limited v Minister for Planning [2019] NSWLEC 7

Minister for the Environment v Sharma [2022] FCAFC 35

Waratah Coal Pty Ltd v Youth Verdict Ltd & Ors (No 6) [2022] QLC 21

Environment Council of Central Queensland Inc v Minister for the Environment and Water [2024] FCAFC 56 (16 May 2024)

4.3 *Belgium*

VZW Klimaatzaak v Kingdom of Belgium & Others, Brussels Court of Appeal (30 November 2023)

4.4 *Belize*

The Maya Leaders Alliance v The Attorney General of Belize [2015] CCJ 15 (AJ), CCJ Appeal No BZCV2014/ 002, BZ Civil Appeal No 27 of 2010, 30 October 2015 (Belize)

4.5 *Bolivia*

Plurinational Constitutional Court of Bolivia, 2003–06127-12-RAC, Judgment No 0491/2003-R, 15 April 2003

4.6 *Brazil*

PSB et al v Brazil (on Climate Fund), Federal Supreme Court of Brazil (1 July 2022)

4.7 *Colombia*

Constitutional Court of Colombia, Judgment No T-1319/01, 7 Dec 2001

Atrato River Decision T- 622/ 16 of November 10, 2016 (Sentencia T- 622/ 16 de Noviembre 10, 2016) (Colombia)

4.8 *Costa Rica*

Constitutional Chamber of the Supreme Court of Justice of Costa Rica, Judgment No 2313–95, 9 May 1995

Constitutional Chamber of the Supreme Court of Justice of Costa Rica, Judgment No 12782-2018, 8 August 2018

4.9 *Dominican Republic*

Supreme Court of the Dominican Republic, Resolution No 1920–2003, 13 November 2013

4.10 *Ecuador*

Constitutional Court of Ecuador, judgment 184–18-SEP-CC, 29 May 2018
Constitutional Court of Ecuador, judgment 10–18-CN/19, 12 June 2019
Constitutional Court of Ecuador, judgment 11–18-CN/19, 12 June 2019

4.11 *India*

Ranjitsinh v Union of India (2024) INSC 280

4.12 *Israel*

Alian v Prime Minister [2005] HCJ 4825/04
Beit Sourik Village Council v. Government of Israel [2004] HCJ 2056/04
Mara'abe v. Prime Minister of Israel [2009] HCJ 7957/04

4.13 *Mexico*

Supreme Court of Mexico, Contradicción de Tesis 293/2011, 03 September 2013
Supreme Court of Mexico, Tesis jurisprudencial 21/2014 (10a.), 30 April 2014
Supreme Court of Mexico, Contradicción de criterios 175/2022, 17 June 2024

4.14 *Netherlands*

Urgenda v The Netherlands, The Hague District Court (24 June 2015) ECLI:NL:RBDHA:2015:7196
The State of the Netherlands (Ministry of Infrastructure and the Environment) v Urgenda Foundation [2018] ECLI:NL:GHDHA:2018
The State of the Netherlands (Ministry of Economic Affairs and Climate Policy) v Stichting Urgenda [2019] ECLI:NL:HR:2019

4.15 *Norway*

Greenpeace Nordic v The State of Norway (represented by the Ministry of Petroleum and Energy), Case No 23–099330TVI-TOSL/05

4.16 *Papua New Guinea*

Maniwa v Malijiwi [2014] PGNC 25

4.17 *Peru*

Constitutional Court of Peru, Judgment No 5854–2005–PA/TC, 8 November 2005
Constitutional Court of Peru, Judgment No 2798–04–HC/TC, 9 December 2009

4.18 *United Kingdom*

R (Friends of the Earth Limited) v The Secretary of State for International Trade/UK Export Finance [2023] EWCA Civ 14, 40

R (Plan B Earth & Others) v The Prime Minister & Others [2021] EWHC 3469 (Admin)
R (SC) v SSWP [2021] UKSC 26, [2021] 3 WLR 428 per Lord Reed
R (on the application of Finch on behalf of the Weald Action Group) (Appellant) v Surrey County Council and others (Respondents) [2024] UKSC 20
R (Hoareau) v Secretary of State for Foreign and Commonwealth Affairs [2020] EWCA Civ 1010

4.19 *United States*

Kiobel v Royal Dutch Petroleum Co., 569 U.S. 108 (2013)
Held v Montana CDV-2020-307, Montana First Judicial District Court, WL 1997864, decision of 14 August 2023

4.20 *Venezuela*

Supreme Tribunal of Venezuela (Constitucional Chamber), 01–0415, Judgment 1942, 15 July 2003

Index

Printed in the United States
by Baker & Taylor Publisher Services